YOU WANT TO DO WHAT?

Instant answers to your parenting dilemmas

Karen Sullivan

Collins

For Cole and Luke, my teena[...]

First published in 2007 by Collins,
an imprint of HarperCollins Publish[...]
77-85 Fulham Palace Road
London
W6 8JB

www.collins.co.uk
Collins is a registered trademark of HarperCollins Publishers Ltd.

Text © Karen Sullivan 2007

8 7 6 5 4 3 2 1
11 10 09 08 07

A catalogue record for this book is available from the British Library.

ISBN 978-0-00-725437-8

Collins uses papers that are natural, renewable and recyclable products
made from wood grown in sustainable forests. The manufacturing processes
conform to the environmental regulations of the country of origin.

Designed and set by seagulls.net

Printed and bound in Great Britain by Clays Ltd, St Ives plc.

*Huge thanks to my in-house editors, Laura Kesner and Helen Brocklehurst,
who offered great encouragement throughout the process, and were more than
patient and flexible. Copy editor Marilyn Inglis was resourceful and incredibly
committed. Thanks to all the organisations who offered legal, professional and
practical advice, which made this book possible. Finally, I'm grateful to my
family, who gave me the space to finish this in record time.*

Contents

Introduction

There is no one more persuasive than a teenager with an agenda, and certainly no one more capable of making a parent feel inadequate or behind the times. Conscientious parents regularly fall victim to the supreme negotiating skills of their offspring, and have to adjust their own beliefs, values and moral codes in order either to keep the peace or fall in line with current trends. After all, times change, don't they? Perhaps the way we were brought up is outmoded, and children can and should be allowed different sorts of freedoms and liberties, different levels of independence and trust, and a different role within the family.

There can be no parent in the land who has not heard regular wails of:

▷ 'I am the *only* one not allowed...' (to stay out late, walk to school on my own, take the bus into town, have my own bank account – add your own to this).

▷ 'The *only* one who doesn't have...' (new trainers, a TV in my bedroom, a mobile phone with a camera, my own room, parties, pierced ears, a tattoo...).

▷ 'The *only* one who has to...' (clean my room, work for my pocket money, visit my grandparents, have my homework checked, do my own laundry, be accompanied to the doctor...).

The lists are seemingly endless, and from the word go, parents are put in the awkward position of trying to work out if their demands, expectations and rules are fair and realistic, or if they are, in fact, creating social lepers by denying their children the norms of today's society.

There is no central database of currently acceptable thinking and practice when it comes to parenting. Indeed, most parenting manuals stop well short of the years when parents actually need the most advice. These days many parents are isolated and have less contact with others parents, the result of increased independence, and the fact that many parents work during the day. Couple this with frustration engendered by the impossible task of trying to glean information or make conversation with an adolescent – and it becomes obvious why we're often working in the dark when it comes to parenting.

It's no good relying on age-old wisdom handed down from our parents, either. Most of us will remember the irritation of being told that rules were rules, that things were 'always done that way', because: 'that's how I was brought up, so that's how you will be too'. Many of us have chosen to forge our own path on the parenting front, and to make decisions based on our individual children and their capabilities, needs and demands, rather than create rules for the sake of them. But this too can be a minefield – one ill-chosen step off that path and a child could be in serious trouble, well out of his or her depth.

So how do we make these decisions? As parents we have a responsibility and, indeed, an innate desire to raise happy, healthy, responsible children, and to invest in them the skills, morals, values and common sense that will take them into adulthood. On one shoulder we carry the weight of this responsibility, and on the other, an overwhelming catalogue of adolescent propaganda.

Consider, too, the fact that our children change dramatically – emotionally and physically – as they grow. It takes a savvy parent to understand and stay on top of their changing needs, and the developmental milestones reached at various stages. We want to support these changes, and encourage healthy growth and development without appearing to be intrusive or controlling. Most tweenies and adolescents become less open about their emotions, their bodies and even their social lives, hopes and concerns as they grow older. It's difficult for parents to know what to expect and when, and at what stage a little input, guidance or even discouragement is required. For example, when do girls normally begin to menstruate and at what age are tampons appropriate? Does a 12-year-old boy need to wear deodorant? And is a night-time shower or bath strictly necessary? When do teens reach their adult height, and do big feet mean that a child will be tall? At what age can kids drink tea and coffee? Do teenagers need vitamin supplements? When does a boy's voice begin to change? Is a withdrawn adolescent taking drugs or suffering from depression, or is her behaviour normal? Is teen faddy eating a sign of an eating disorder or to be expected? Should we worry if a child wants a lock on his or her bedroom door?

And what about independence and moral issues? Is it normal for a teenage boy to have pornographic magazines under his bed? Should a girl be allowed to change her name or her religion? Should we turn a blind eye when they experiment with alcohol or drugs? Should we allow them to ride a bike home in the dark or make their own way home from a party? When should we stop expecting to be told exactly what they are doing, when and with whom? What is an appropriate curfew? How much pocket money is fair, and should we expect our children to earn it? Are household chores a child's responsibility, and what do we do about a perpetually messy bedroom? Should we oversee their homework, allow them to use calculators, or crib from the computer? Should they have their own computers or TVs, enter chatrooms, own mobile telephones and set their own bedtimes? If children really want to leave school, can we stop them?

The list of potential battlegrounds is staggering, and the issues surrounding almost every area of our children's lives are confusing. We are, as a whole, a more liberal and tolerant society, and today's children are treated very differently from the way we or our parents were treated as children. That's not to say that we are necessarily more permissive; indeed, studies show that due to fears about abduction, accidents, paedophiles and other potential dangers, we are much less likely to allow our children to do things on their own, and less likely to encourage independence. We drive them to school and to their activities, and we are reluctant to allow children the freedom to play outside or to travel alone.

But contrast this with the obvious 'adultification' of childhood, and the irony of the situation must be evident to all parents. How can we keep reins on children who are worldly wise beyond their years and have expectations that far exceed their age? How can we curb a growing need for independence when we are fearful for their safety? How can we uphold our own beliefs and moral values when our children are bludgeoned with alternatives via the media and their peer group? How can we encourage our children to be *children* for as long as possible in a society that promotes the opposite?

Growing up too soon

One of the side effects of our modern have-it-now, 24/7 society is that children have been drawn in on the act. No longer content to wait until the appropriate age for certain activities, clothing, possessions and levels of freedom, today's children expect to be (and often are) treated as miniature adults, complete with miniature versions of everything adult. With this comes inevitable responsibility and a need for acquisition; the majority of children are too young and immature to deal with either responsibility or acquisitiveness.

Learning the art of patience is an important part of childhood. Childhood and adolescence are marked by other rites of passage – understanding the rewards of a job well done, a lesson learned and a privilege earned – which should be experienced at appropriate stages through the years. Children find it difficult to wait for the moment when their power is increased. When they are six, they can't wait to be seven; when they are ten, they can't wait to go to 'big school'; when they are sixteen, they can't wait to get their driving licence, have some freedom and go out alone with friends. This sort of impatience is normal and even healthy, but children need to learn to wait for each of the stages, and to feel a sense of pride as they reach these milestones.

Today, everything is pushed on more quickly. Children start school at an earlier age and learn to read earlier. Sporting activities at weekends are organised with 'adult' equipment, and some sports teams even go on overseas tours. Children have CD and DVD players and all the latest games; they wear mini-Calvin Klein and Paul Smith; they have mobile telephones and their own computers. Advertising encourages them to look and be seductive and cool; young girls dress in the same style as their heroines – pop stars and celebrities – many of whom are scantily dressed and earning money by being overtly sexy. The inevitable question is, 'What next?' How can a child who has already toured Europe with his football team be satisfied with playing for his school or in the park with his brother? How can a child who is bombarded with sexual messages through the media be content to hold hands at a school dance?

The pressure on children to grow up more quickly tends also to suit our modern style of parenting. If we treat our children as if they were older, dress them as if they were older and push them on to achieve things at an increasingly early age, we can justifiably expect 'adult' behaviour.

There are several other problems with the 'adultification' of childhood. The first is the boredom factor. Many children now complain of being bored, largely because there is very little to look forward to in terms of personal goals. They have 'been there, done that'. They travel, eat out, wear designer clothes and have all the trappings that matter. They perform in ambitious school productions, take part in international sports events, surf the internet and set up e-mail accounts on their own, have their pocket money paid into their own bank accounts, make their own arrangements via mobile phone and use their considerable purchasing power to buy whatever they want.

When children are exposed to an increasing number of experiences at an early age, they become bored with routine activities. They require greater stimulation and excitement to keep them satisfied. What fun can be had in the park with your parents, when you are used to watching satellite TV in your room with your mates? How boring a day trip to the seaside will seem after a two-week holiday in Florida. Who wants to watch a U-rated film, when you've seen an adult-rated movie with your friends?

This adult lifestyle is an assault on young and impressionable bodies and minds. What's more, many children are being left to make the transition from child to adult on their own. Many children come home to an empty house and have to organise their own time structure and make their own meals. Most are allowed to choose their own entertainment and this often means that they are subjected to conflicting messages on a regular basis. A vast industry has built up around consumption by children and an ever-increasing amount of advertising is directed at them. Advertisers use the media, primarily television, to convince children that they need a whole host of possessions in order to reach the status of 'cool' and to be happy.

Television also provides children with experiences of violence, sexuality, broken relationships and inappropriate mentors. Even children who are at home with parents during the day and after school have unhealthy pressures placed upon them by the various media, including television. Children in the USA spend an average of 38 hours a week exposed to media outside of school; by the time they reach the age of eleven, the average child will have witnessed more than 100,000 acts of violence on TV. Children may be exposed to as many as five violent acts per hour during prime time and an average of 26 violent acts per hour during Saturday morning children's programmes. And that's just violence.

There is a similar problem with sexual imagery, with teenage starlets paraded regularly in the media in sexy, adult clothing. Sexual precocity is evident increasingly early and teenage pregnancy is on the increase in the Western world. If children have seen it all on screen or heard it all in the lyrics of a pop song, what's to stop them trying it out for themselves? Why should they bother waiting?

Ignoring or disregarding the vital sequential steps in a child's development can have serious consequences. Children are confronted with decision-making before they have the necessary emotional or psychological tools; they are entrusted with obligations, possessions and responsibility that make them feel more independent and adult, but which may be too much to bear.

This, of course, puts more pressure on parents. Kids want things sooner and they expect freedoms, possessions, activities and independence that are often inappropriate. Most parents have a grudging sense that the demands they face regularly are at odds with what they intrinsically believe is right, appropriate, normal and moral. This is not, of course, a new problem facing parents, as children have, for generations, always wanted a little more than parents think is appropriate; however, the wealth of external influences on our children make it far more difficult to create and maintain a family policy. In a nutshell, we are in constant battle with the unknown and the ever-changing.

Different strokes

There will be class, religious, geographical and cultural elements that will affect the way you choose to raise your children. What is appropriate for an inner-city child may not be right for someone from the deepest part of the countryside. A child who grows up on a farm may be given plenty of responsibility, but would not have the street savvy of a child from a big city. So the rural child may be mowing the lawn or driving a harvest combiner at the age of ten, but may be out of his depth on the Underground railway system or on city streets. Conversely, a city kid may cope well with independence involving travelling alone, negotiating a map and dealing with street violence, but would probably risk cutting off a toe if handed a lawnmower too soon. These are factors that every parent must take into consideration.

What children need

In order to thrive physically and emotionally, children require boundaries – guidelines that will undoubtedly be tested, often on a daily basis as they move out of childhood and towards adulthood – and they need a consistent approach to discipline. They also, however, require independence as they grow older, room to make their own mistakes and freedom to explore the world around them.

In essence, children need wings to soar out into the world, but a healthy dose of common sense and a structured environment to anchor them when required.

Research tells us that, far from spending *less* time with our children, today's parents take the job very seriously. According to a study entitled 'The Changing Face of Childhood', undertaken by the Future Foundation in the UK, children enjoy significantly more quality time with their parents than children of 30 years ago, with children's views today being taken into account in the household and parents aspiring to do a better job than their own parents did. Researchers claim that we have become a generation of super parents who devote almost all our time away from work to our offspring. Typically, parents today spend 99 minutes a day with children under sixteen, compared with just 25 minutes in 1975.

'In the 1970s, the hours at home were spent on household labour, and children were typically left to spend their time outdoors with friends in unstructured play, and to get to and from school by themselves,' said Meabh Quoirin, head of business development at the Future Foundation.

'Today's parents are making the choice to engage with their children far more, taking them on outings, helping them with their homework, joining in their activities and just playing with them more. They are willing to put considerable effort into their relationships with their children and we see an increasingly professionalised approach to bringing them up.'

There can be no doubt that this increased input in our children's lives will have a positive impact. A long-term Canadian study found that a positive relationship with parents was associated with less bullying, smoking, alcohol and drug use, and less frequent affiliation with deviant peers who engage in substance abuse. It predicted higher self-esteem and fewer internalising problems. Moreover, youths who reported positive relationships with their parents were more likely to report increased school identification and commitment to education, and were less likely to take risks (i.e. to not use a bike helmet and seat belt). It's clear, therefore, that the quality of the relationship we have with our children is a huge predictor of their overall well-being on many levels.

But that, in essence, compounds the problem. As parents we wish to be there for our children, to be welcoming, accepting, open and communicative in order to establish a healthy relationship. Yet too many parents confuse a good relationship with giving in to demands, and allowing inappropriate freedoms in order to avoid disharmony. We want our children to have high self-esteem, so we grant them privileges and praise them regardless of whether either has been earned. While it is evident that a good relationship can encourage good behaviour, it is also clear that this relationship must be based on sound parenting, reasonable discipline, realistic expectations and mutual respect.

Giving in to demands does not encourage respect, nor does it teach our children self-respect. It is not easy to lay down the law, just as it is equally pointless to lay down too many laws. Every family has to evaluate what is most important to them before setting rules and establishing a code of expected behaviour. As the phrase goes, 'don't sweat the small stuff', and nothing can be more true when dealing with tweenies and teens. If you get yourself into a regular lather about every aspect of your child's behaviour, plans, perceived needs and demands, and set out to control it all, chances are the relationship will suffer and you'll encourage rebellion. Work out what is most important to you, and be prepared to offer realistic reasons for your expectations and rules.

THE IMPACT OF PARENTING STYLES

The theory of parenting styles developed from the work of American psychologist Diana Baumrind and other researchers in child development. They studied children who had the qualities most of us would want in our own children: independence, maturity, self-reliance, self-control, curiosity, friendliness and achievement orientation. The researchers then interviewed the parents of these children to ascertain which elements of parenting fostered these qualities. They identified two important ingredients: firstly, responsiveness or warmth and supportiveness; and secondly, demandingness or behavioural control. Descriptions of four styles of parenting are based on these elements.

Authoritarian

Authoritarian or extremely strict parents are highly controlling. They dictate how their children should behave, and stress obedience to authority and discourage discussion. These parents are demanding and directive, they expect their orders to be obeyed and do not encourage give-and-take. They have low levels of sensitivity and do not expect their children to disagree with their decisions.

Authoritative

Authoritative or moderate parents set limits and rely on natural consequences to help children learn by making their own mistakes. Authoritative parents explain why rules are important and why they must be followed. They reason with their children and consider the children's point of view even though they might not agree. These parents are firm, with kindness, warmth and love. They set high standards and encourage children to be independent.

Permissive

Permissive or indulgent parents are accepting and warm but exert little control. They do not set limits and allow children to set their own rules, schedules and activities. They do not demand the high levels of behaviour required by authoritarian or authoritative parents.

Uninvolved

Uninvolved parents demand little and respond minimally to their offspring. In extreme cases, this parenting style might entail neglect and rejection.

Research has found that the most well-adjusted children, particularly in terms of social competence, had parents with an authoritative, moderate parenting style. These parents are able to balance clear high demands with emotional responsiveness and respect for their child's autonomy. Both authoritarian and authoritative parents have high expectations of their children and use control, but the overly strict parent expects the child to accept parental judgements unquestioningly and allows the child little freedom of expression. Children of overly strict parents are apt to be reliant on the voice of authority and to be lacking in spontaneity. In contrast, the authoritative parent permits the child enough freedom of expression so that he or she can develop a sense of independence. Permissive parents make few demands and their children have been found to have difficulty controlling their impulses, are immature and reluctant to accept responsibility.

Be prepared to listen to your child. While pre-teens and teens have an amazing capacity to exaggerate and to dramatise, there may be some truth or basis to their argument. If your child is, genuinely, the only one in his class not allowed to walk to school alone or to have a mobile telephone, ask yourself why. Challenge your own thinking and assess your reasons. If your daughter wants to have her ears pierced and you've said she has to wait until she is thirteen, ask yourself why. Because that was what you had to do? Is that a relevant argument? Children are not always right, but they aren't always wrong either.

However, issues and demands are not always straightforward. In many cases there are legal implications and children also have well-defined rights. For example, your 14-year-old daughter is not legally allowed to have sexual intercourse until she is sixteen, but she can have an abortion without any consultation with or permission from her parents well under that age. At sixteen she can buy cigarettes and smoke them to her heart's content; she can even leave home legally, but she can't vote and she can't have a glass of wine with her cigarette unless she's in the family home or accompanied by an adult (and a meal) in a pub or restaurant. Your 12-year-old son can have his ear pierced and open a bank account; he can make decisions regarding his own health care, but you can be charged with neglect if you leave him alone in the family home and something goes wrong.

Peer pressure

Not only are our children subject to peer pressure, which often guides their demands and expectations, but parents are also at the mercy of pressure from peers. If every parent at your 14-year-old's Catholic school has decided that it isn't necessary for their child to attend Sunday mass, how do you weigh this up with what you believe is right? If all the parents in your son's social group are allowing them to take the train up to watch the football finals at a national stadium, are you being 'precious' and overly cautious by objecting? If the majority of your children's friends are not given a curfew, does that mean that your child shouldn't have one either? If other parents do not question spending of pocket money or how children spend their leisure time, if they do not encourage any responsibility around the house, or make demands upon their children's time for family outings or gatherings, should you follow suit? Are you making a mistake by sticking to your guns and parenting by instinct or belief?

It's not just kid pressure that affects the way we make our decisions; we are guided by what other parents do and by what they allow. It's not surprising that most parents worry constantly about whether they are doing the right thing, or creating the best environment for their children, and giving them the best opportunities. There is a level of insecurity that most of us feel – and when what we believe in is challenged by the media, our children, and other parents, it's not surprising that confusion ensues, and we make allowances or concessions with which we are not always happy. We don't want our children to be left behind in any sense, and unhappily, many of us spend a lot of time looking over our shoulders to work out if we are doing and allowing the same things as everyone else.

Finding a balance

There are ways to negotiate compromises with our children – to parent according to our own beliefs, to protect our children and to ensure that they have a safe, healthy and happy childhood, while at the same time giving them room to grow and develop, and to become independent and responsible adults.

That's where this book comes in. We'll look at all the important issues and aspects of raising a child from the age of about eight through to the day they leave home. In many cases, there are legal points that will guide your decision or thinking. In others, there is clear research that shows the impact of the choices we make for our children, and the results of what we might allow. Children's charities and health and religious organisations offer advice and guidelines where legislation doesn't exist – in the case of leaving children alone, for example, or dealing with peer pressure, bullying or health problems.

We'll look at what happens to our children at various ages, both physically and emotionally, and what they are capable of doing and, indeed, mature enough to do, at each stage. Every child is different, and each matures at his or her own speed. What is right for one child may simply be inappropriate for another. One child may be sensible enough to walk to school at age seven, while his younger brother may have to wait another year or so. A shy, under-confident child may baulk at taking the train into town with his mates, while his more confident sister could negotiate the journey with ease at the same age. Knowledge of your children is probably the most important factor in making any decision regarding the way you parent.

There will be areas of your child's life and lifestyle about which you feel very strongly. You may be a stickler for working hard at school or believe that children should have a role in the household, undertaking age-appropriate chores and earning their keep. You may have a faith or religion that dictates many aspects of what your child can and can't do, and some of these things simply cannot be compromised. An important part of bringing up children is sharing our beliefs and mores, and passing on pride in and understanding of our various cultures and backgrounds. This is to be encouraged, no matter how resistant a child may be to doing things 'your way'.

You may frown on anything illegal and insist that your child does not, for example, touch alcohol until the legal age of eighteen or ride his bike on the pavement or watch a film below an age restriction. You may have fears about the safety of mobile phones or your child's security while travelling alone. You may disapprove of sexual relations outside of marriage, violence on television or abortion. This, too, is acceptable. Parents have a right and a responsibility to pass on their values to children, even if they don't always fit in with current trends.

You may be aghast at the way children are brought up today – perhaps with too much freedom, too little discipline and a dearth of respect. In this sense, you may be right. In spite of the fact that we are a 'hands-on' generation who invest a great deal of our time in our children, there is no doubt that children are involved in more street crime and violence. And the problems don't stop there: bullying is rife; the drinking culture is out of control; more than 25 per cent of children are obese; and teenage pregnancies and drug use are at a high level. Many teachers complain of a culture of disrespect and rude behaviour that disrupts classrooms and even shopping malls have been forced to ban hooded jackets in an attempt to keep trouble at bay. Perhaps the decisions we are currently making with and for our children are not always right. No doubt external influences play havoc with even the strongest and most moral household rules and policies, however, there can be no doubt that a generation of teenagers running riot have missed something along the line. These factors, too, must be taken into consideration.

The information in this book is designed to guide parents so that they can make the right decisions for their children. You may be worried, for example, about letting a child travel or play outside alone for fear of abduction or safety. In this case, you may be reassured to know that there are no more children murdered or abducted than there were 50 years ago; there are no more children victim to paedophiles (although there are probably plenty more opportunities, with internet chatrooms); and that roughly the same number of children are injured or killed on the roads and while playing outside as there ever were. To put it bluntly, your child is much more likely to die from other accidental causes than from a road traffic accident. That's not to say you shouldn't be concerned, but statistics help us to put things into perspective. The number of pedestrian fatalities in the UK peaked in 1966 with just over 3,150 deaths and has declined since then. Each year since 1990 has seen a new record low; in 2002, for instance, it was 774 (adults and children).

The secret to successful parenting is to find a balance by focusing on key areas of importance. Denying a child every element of popular culture, every opportunity to share activities with friends and every possibility of freedom will backfire. Choose your battles. There is potential for locking horns at almost every stage of your child's life, and if you are resistant to the idea of change, negotiation or at least compromise, you will render your child powerless, thereby encouraging rebellion and deception, and undermine your relationship at key stages of development. Be prepared to explain yourself and to make allowances. Balance what your child says, what the government decrees, what other children are doing and what other parents allow with what you believe, and make a judgement on that basis.

Take the time to explain your thinking. Unexplained rules set for the sake of them will do nothing but cause frustration and resistance. What's more, your child will learn nothing except how to accept defeat, and the defeat will breed resentment in the process. If you explain your reasons and your thinking, and are consistent about the way you approach the things that matter, your child will learn to respect you and what you believe in, even if there

UNHAPPY CHILDREN

Children growing up in the United Kingdom suffer greater deprivation, worse relationships with their parents and are exposed to more risks from alcohol, drugs and unsafe sex than those in any other wealthy country in the world, according to a 2007 study from the United Nations.

The UK is bottom of the league of 21 economically advanced countries according to a 'report card' put together by UNICEF on the well-being of children and adolescents, trailing the US which comes second to last. The UNICEF team assessed the treatment of children in six different areas: material well-being; health and safety; educational well-being; family and peer relationships; behaviours and risks; and young people's own perceptions of their well-being.

If nothing else, this provides parents with even more impetus to get things right, and to ensure that the choices we make for our children are in their best interests and make a positive contribution to their overall health and well-being.

are a few battles along the way. This is particularly likely if you show willingness to compromise and to accommodate their demands from time to time.

For each entry in this book, you'll find practical advice and tips for dealing with tricky situations, negotiating compromise or getting the information you need to explain why certain behaviours or activities are unacceptable. You'll also find lots of information that you can share with your children, if you find it difficult to explain your position. For example, it can be hard to know when to talk about drugs or sex with children, and how to approach it in the right way. While you want to get your own views across, there are also statistics and facts that children need to understand in order to make their own decisions. You'll find plenty of advice about how to talk to your children about various subjects, what to say, when to say it – and how to get the message across in the least threatening way.

This is a book for all parents – because all parents have questions and concerns, and all of us question the way we should be bringing up our children. Use your judgement, be willing to negotiate where necessary, be consistent in your approach to issues, discipline and beliefs, and, ultimately, base your decisions on your individual child. This book is based on facts, research, theories and plenty of practical advice, which will help to guide your decision.

WHAT CHILDREN THINK

The study 'Child Maltreatment in the UK', published in November 2000 by the National Society for the Prevention of Cruelty to Children (NSPCC), revealed a general picture of close supervision by parents. Its survey of 3,000 young people between the ages of eighteen and twenty-four years old in England and Wales found that:

▷ Between the ages of five and nine, travelling to school alone is common, usually from the age of seven upwards.

▷ Most children in the UK (88 per cent) are not left at home in the evenings without adult supervision until they are at least twelve, and they don't stay at home unsupervised overnight before they are fourteen (91 per cent).

▷ Asked when they were first allowed out overnight without parents knowing their whereabouts, more than four out of ten respondents said that this had not been permitted until they were sixteen or seventeen, and more than a third (36 per cent) said that this would still not be allowed.

Meanwhile, a 1990s survey of 4,000 parents by the children's charity Kidscape found that most parents allowed children:

▷ To cross local roads from age nine.

▷ To use local transport during daytime from age eleven.

▷ To go to the cinema with a friend from age twelve.

▷ To be out with a friend in the evening from age fifteen.

What children *can* do:

Any age

▷ Can babysit (although the NSPCC recommends sixteen as the minimum age).

▷ Can enter a bar that has a child licence if you are with an adult.

▷ Can see a U or PG category film at a cinema unaccompanied by an adult; you can see a 12A film if you are with an adult.

▷ Can ask to see your health and education records.

▷ Can give consent to surgical, medical or dental treatment provided your doctor or dentist decides you understand what is happening.

▷ Can choose your own religion.

▷ Can smoke cigarettes, but you are not allowed to buy them until you are sixteen.

Age five

▷ Can drink alcohol in private.

▷ Must go to school or be educated at home.

Age seven

▷ Can open and draw money from a National Savings Account or Trustee Savings account.

Age ten

▷ Have full criminal responsibility for actions and can be convicted of a criminal offence.

▷ Can open a bank or building society account.

Age twelve

▷ Can see a 12A film at the cinema or rent one without an adult present. Can buy a pet.

Age fourteen

▷ Can get a part-time job, subject to restrictions (*see page 164*).

Age fifteen

▷ Can apply to the Navy at fifteen years and nine months.

▷ Can see, purchase or rent a category 15 film.

Age sixteen

▷ Can buy aerosol paint.

▷ Can enter a bar on your own, but can only drink soft drinks; however, you can drink beer, cider or wine with a meal when accompanied by someone over eighteen.

▷ Can join the Army, Navy, Air Force and Marines with parental consent.

▷ Can change your name by deed poll.

▷ Can hold a licence to drive a moped.

▷ Can leave school on the last Friday of June if you are sixteen by that date or turn sixteen during the summer holidays.

▷ Can work full time if you have left school, but there are restrictions (*see page 164*).

▷ Are entitled to be paid the minimum wage for 16- and 17-year-olds.

▷ Can buy a lottery ticket or use Category D gaming machines.

▷ Can leave home without the consent of your parents.

▷ Can marry with parental consent.

▷ Can choose your own doctor and consent to medical, dental or surgical treatment.

▷ Can open an Individual Savings Account (ISA).

▷ Can consent to all sexual activity.

▷ Can buy cigarettes.

▷ Can get a National Insurance number.

▷ Can apply for your own passport, with parental consent.

Age seventeen

▷ Can donate blood without parental consent.

▷ Can hold a licence to drive a car.

Age eighteen

▷ Cannot be adopted.

▷ Can buy alcohol and drink in a bar.

▷ Can join the armed forces without parental consent.

▷ Can own land, buy a home, hold a tenancy or apply for a mortgage.

▷ Are entitled to receive the minimum wage for 18-year-olds.

▷ Can see a category 18 film at the cinema or rent or buy one.

▷ Can join the Fire Service.

▷ Can buy fireworks.

▷ Can enter or work in a betting shop.

▷ Can apply to change sex.

▷ Can leave home without parental consent.

▷ Can get married without parental consent.

▷ Can join the police.

▷ Can vote in general and local elections.

▷ Can be tattooed.

▷ Can apply for a passport without parental consent.

Age twenty-one

▷ Can adopt a child.

▷ Can become an MP, local councillor or mayor.

Abortion

Can my daughter have a termination without my consent?
In the UK (although not in Northern Ireland) any girl can have a termination without telling her parents, as long as two doctors agree that she fully understands what is involved and that it is in her best interests. In a nutshell, doctors must agree that an abortion would cause less damage to a girl's physical or mental health than continuing with the pregnancy. Most doctors feel that the distress of having to continue with an unwanted pregnancy is likely to be harmful to health.

All information, advice and services are confidential; however, if the doctors believe that she is at risk of harm in any way (as a result of sexual or emotional abuse, for example), they are obliged to involve social services – but not, interestingly, the girl's parents. This applies until a girl reaches adulthood in the eyes of the law, which is currently eighteen years of age.

The implications of the government's guidance in England mean that doctors and health practitioners are likely to be more concerned about young people under the age of thirteen who are having sex; these professionals may think it would be in the young person's best interests to have some extra help from a social worker. In Northern Ireland this applies to young people under the age of fourteen. However, despite the fact that sex under the age of sixteen is illegal, girls can still have an abortion under this age without parental consent, and in full confidence.

Is abortion legal in Northern Ireland?
Abortion is legal in Northern Ireland in exceptional circumstances, but current guidance is unclear and many women

in Northern Ireland find it difficult to obtain an abortion unless they travel to England.

Will her GP let me know if my daughter has a termination?
Your daughter has a right to full confidentiality. Even her GP may not be notified if she expresses a wish that the GP is not informed. You may, in fact, be the last person to know.

Most doctors do encourage young girls to discuss the matter with their parents – if only because the girl concerned needs to make an informed choice and may not realise that there are options within a supportive family unit. However, no one can force your daughter to tell you anything.

The most important thing any parent can do is to keep open the channels of communication with their daughters, to ensure that any problems can be successfully aired, without recrimination or blame. Your daughter will not involve you in situations where she thinks that she may be punished, or lose your love and acceptance. Termination is a traumatic, distressing intervention for many girls, and without support, their emotional health can be dramatically affected. What's more, there is a medical risk to abortion procedures, and girls need to have follow-up treatment and may also require a course of antibiotics. This will need to be supervised, particularly in younger girls.

Is the situation the same in the US?
Only two states – Connecticut and Maine – and the District of Columbia have laws that allow girls under the age of eighteen to obtain an abortion on her own. In contrast, 31 states have laws that require the involvement of at least one parent in their daughter's abortion decision; in 16 of these states, a minor must have the consent of one or both parents, and in the other 15 states, one or both parents must be notified prior to the abortion.

Almost all provide a confidential alternative to parental involvement in the form of a judicial bypass, in which a minor may obtain authorisation for an abortion from a judge without informing her parents.

Because terminating an unplanned pregnancy can have a significant long-term impact on a woman's psychological and emotional well-being, US legislators believe that parental guidance is especially important. Strangely, however, more than half of the states that require parental involvement for abortion permit a pregnant minor to make the decision to continue her pregnancy and to consent to antenatal care and delivery without consulting a parent. In addition, states appear to consider a minor who is a parent to be fully competent to make major decisions affecting the health and future of his or her child, even though many of these same states require an under-age girl to involve her parents if she decides to terminate her pregnancy!

How old does a girl need to be to have a termination?

In England, Wales and Scotland a woman of any age can have an abortion (termination). In Jersey, abortion is only legal up to twelve weeks. She has no legal obligation to consult with her family or even the father of the unborn baby.

What is the situation in Europe?

In many European countries, girls must be sixteen years old to have an abortion. What's more, the gestational age limit (the 'age' of the pregnancy) is twelve weeks, meaning that anyone under the age of sixteen and over twelve weeks' pregnant will not be granted access to the procedure. Almost all countries in the EU require parental consent and a doctor's approval.

What about Ireland?

In Ireland abortion is banned under most circumstances. However, the law does allow pregnant women to receive counselling and information about all their options. Girls then have a legal right to leave Ireland in order to have an abortion. Most women travel to England where it is legal to have an abortion up to 24 weeks into the pregnancy.

Is my daughter old enough to choose termination?

Legally, any girl in England, Wales and Scotland can have an abortion without her parents' consent or approval, providing that doctors believe she has a full understanding of the decision, and that it would be in her best interests to do so.

However, if a girl under the age of sixteen does *not* want an abortion she cannot be forced to have one. In other words, the choice is your daughter's alone, and she does not need to consult anyone apart from a doctor or clinic.

Is counselling offered beforehand?

In almost all cases, counselling is offered before abortion. This is, however, not obligatory. Counselling normally involves discussing the options open to the girl, as well as ensuring that she has all the information she needs to make an informed choice. Counselling is confidential and non-judgmental, and simply involves helping a young woman to reach a decision in a supportive environment.

While abortion is a personal choice, it is often affected by factors outside a girl's control – for example, her family set-up, her relationship with her parents, finances, her relationship with the father, her age, her schooling, her aspirations, housing and emotions. It is undoubtedly true that few girls under the age of sixteen would have the emotional maturity to balance these factors and make a sound judgement. For this reason, it's hugely important that parents are involved in the decision-making process.

Parents of girls should make it clear from early on that although pregnancy and under-aged sex is not advisable, you do wish to be involved if the situation arises.

TALKING TO GIRLS ABOUT ABORTION

The single most important thing you can do for your daughter is to listen. Abortion is not an easy decision to make at any age, and a young woman needs support. If you show displeasure or disappointment, or become upset or angry, your daughter will likely avoid confiding in you in future. The decision to have an abortion has many elements, but ultimately it is your daughter's decision, and she needs to think it through.

What does my daughter have to consider?

There are many considerations – finances, education, living arrangements, her relationship with the father are all important. Some girls are idealistic and think having a baby will be fun and games without stopping to consider the reality of being responsible for another human being for the rest of that child's life. Social life will be curtailed, and education will also be affected. Many young mothers go on to complete degrees or learn a trade, but it isn't an easy option. Having a baby puts strain on even the strongest relationships, and this is significant if your daughter wants her child to grow up with a father around.

Can I object on moral grounds?

For moral, ethical or religious reasons, you may object to abortion; however, while it is important to put your views across in a calm and rational way, and to discuss them, it is important to remember that your daughter is the primary decision-maker and she has the right to choose what is best for her.

At least one in four women will have had an abortion by the age of forty-five and it is a safe procedure in almost all cases. Far fewer women under the age of sixteen have abortions than women over the age of forty. Studies show that very few girls and women use abortion as a form of contraception.

Does having an abortion lead to psychological problems?

Several studies have shown that having an abortion does not lead to psychological problems. Although women may regret having to have an abortion the vast majority find that they have no emotional problems after it. A small number – about three per cent – have long-term feelings of guilt and some of this number feel that the abortion was a mistake. But for these women the unwanted pregnancy was usually one of many problems in their lives, and these problems continued after the abortion. There is some evidence to suggest that for most of these women not having the abortion would not have improved their situation or might have made it worse.

What should I do?

▷ Stay calm – your daughter will likely be frightened and shocked, and also worried about how you will react.

▷ Avoid lecturing. While it is important to be honest about your feelings, your daughter has the right to be honest about hers too, and listening is crucial.

▷ Chastisement is useless, the damage is done. Being supportive does not preclude being disappointed or unhappy. It's fine to express your concerns and your feelings, but it is equally important to remember that this is not about *you* but about your daughter.

▷ Don't insist that she take a particular option; explain your reasoning for it.

▷ Tell your teen what you think of each of the options available to her, and offer to go with her to look into each of the options so she can make informed decisions.

▷ Be honest about the practicalities. If you are against abortion, but have no desire to help raise a baby, you have little room in your home and your finances are already stretched, there is no point in promising something that you have no possibility of fulfilling in order to sway her decision.

What should I not do?

▷ Accuse your daughter of being stupid or promiscuous.

▷ Threaten or force her to follow your decision.

▷ Press for details of her sex life. If she's pregnant, she's obviously sexually active, and this is a private matter.

▷ Ask her to leave the family home. Being homeless will only compound the problem, and leave your daughter without resources and support when she needs it most.

▷ Lose your temper. Move on and make the best of the situation. Work together to ensure that it does not arise again.

Are there any support organisations?

Listed overleaf are several organisations that can offer support for both you and your daughter, and also provide information on the procedures available and the aftermath.

Family Planning Association
Information and advice on all aspects of sexual health.
Tel: 0845 310 1334
www.fpa.org.uk

Brook
Information, advice and guidance for young people under twenty-five
on sex, relationships and contraception.
Tel: 0800 018 5023
www.brook.org.uk

Youth Access
A national network of youth advice, information, support and
counselling agencies.
www.youthaccess.org.uk

British Pregnancy Advisory Service (BPAS)
Offers information and counselling for those considering abortion. It
provides abortions for NHS and private patients.
Tel: 08457 304030
www.bpas.org

Education For Choice
Information about pregnancy and abortion, section for parents and
online decision-making tool to help clarify thoughts and feelings about
an unintended pregnancy.
Tel: 020 7249 3535
www.efc.org.uk

My son's girlfriend is pregnant and she wants a termination. What are his rights?

Your son does not have a legal right to decide whether or not his girlfriend should continue with or end her pregnancy. She is also under no obligation to tell him that she is pregnant, nor that she has had or is planning to have a termination. This can be very distressing for many young men, who may have strong ideas about the pregnancy and what is morally right. The organisations listed above can also help him to accept her decision, and to get support if required.

Alcohol

When can my son drink alcohol legally?

In the UK, the legal drinking age is eighteen. This means your son can purchase and drink alcohol without an 'adult' being present. If he's sixteen, he can have beer, cider or wine in a restaurant or a pub with an area set aside for meals, as long as the alcohol is served with food and he is accompanied by an adult. The rules are different for consuming alcohol on private premises, in other words, your home (*see page 32*).

What happens in Europe?

European countries typically have a legal drinking ages of sixteen or eighteen. For example, in the Netherlands, Germany, Switzerland and Austria, you have to be sixteen to buy beer or wine and eighteen to buy distilled alcoholic beverages (spirits).

What happens in the US?

In the US, the legal age for purchase or possession (but not necessarily consumption) in every state has been twenty-one since the passage of the National Minimum Drinking Age Act in 1984. Many states specifically allow consumption under the age of twenty-one for religious or health reasons or with parental approval. In Canada, the legal drinking age is eighteen in the provinces of Alberta, Manitoba and Quebec, and nineteen elsewhere.

At what age is it safe for children to drink small amounts of alcohol (at a celebration, for example)?

In the UK, serving a child alcohol in your own home is legally allowed from age five, but not recommended for health reasons. For one thing, even a small quantity of alcohol impairs judgement, and very little is required to become 'drunk' at such a tender age. Moreover, many doctors recommend that children under eighteen should not drink alcohol at all, because their bodies are still developing – in particular, the liver, which breaks down alcohol, is not fully developed until the age of about twenty-one. This is also the age at which the hypothalamus, the part of the brain most affected by alcohol, matures. Drinking before this age increases the risk of addiction; in fact, studies show that countries that allow youth drinking have a much higher incidence of adult alcoholism.

Having said that, a thimbleful of wine or champagne at a family celebration is unlikely to do any long-term damage. It's worth noting, too, that parents who adopt an open policy about alcohol use, and take the time to educate their kids about the potential dangers while offering supervision, are less likely to have children who drink subversively – and over drink! After all, a child is less likely to get 'drunk' while a parent is around and if alcohol is not regarded as a forbidden fruit, it's less likely to tempt kids, particularly in periods of rebellion.

What are the recommended safe levels of consumption?

It is certainly worth bearing in mind the recommended safe levels of alcohol consumption for adults and be even more cautious where your children are concerned.

Experts advise that men drink no more than 21 units of alcohol per week and no more than four units in any one day. Women should drink no more than 14 units of alcohol per week and no more than three units in any one day. One unit of alcohol is equivalent to a small 25 ml measure of spirits, 125 ml glass of wine or half a pint of ordinary strength beer.

When can you take a child into the pub?

You can take your child to the pub from any age, but he must be supervised by someone over the age of eighteen. He will not be able to enter the 'bar' of a pub, unless it has a children's certificate, and if it does have a certificate, he can only go into parts of licenced premises where alcohol is either sold but not drunk (for example, a sales point for consumption away from the pub), or drunk but not sold (for example, a garden or family room).

Between the ages of fourteen and fifteen, your child can go anywhere in a pub, as long as he is supervised by an adult, but he may not drink alcohol. After the age of sixteen your child can buy or be bought beer, wine or cider to drink with a meal, if he's with an adult. Otherwise, it is against the law for anyone under eighteen to buy or drink alcohol in a pub.

Children cannot go to the pub alone until they are sixteen.

When can my child have a glass of wine with dinner?

Theoretically, you can serve a small amount of wine with dinner from the age of five, but for obvious reasons this is not ideal!

Having said that, many children begin to experiment with alcohol outside the home between the ages of ten and fourteen, and a 2006 survey found that nine out of ten teenagers drank alcohol by the age of fifteen. The average age for drinking a whole 'drink' is twelve and a half.

One survey, published by the Centre for Public Health at Liverpool John Moores University, suggests that parents should teach their children to be sensible with alcohol by letting them have a glass of wine over dinner – from pre- to early teens. Researchers claim that teenagers who buy their own alcohol are more likely to be binge drinkers.

Professor Mark Bellis, who led the study, feels that parents should adopt a 'Mediterranean approach', where youngsters drink in moderation. He says sensible drinking is a 'life skill' and that 'the ability to drink alcohol sensibly is not a gift people are born with but one that must be learnt', confirming that 'a Mediterranean approach to alcohol consumption, with food and with restraint, is unlikely to ever develop in the UK unless parents demonstrate such behaviours and help develop them in their children.'

My son wants alcohol served at his birthday party, because all his friends apparently serve drinks at their parties. He's only sixteen. Is he old enough?
Drinking in a private home is acceptable from the age of five; indeed, it is legal for anyone over the age of five to drink alcohol. The age restrictions apply to purchasing (under eighteen years old) and location – on licensed premises or in alcohol-exclusion zones. So, theoretically, yes, you can legally serve alcohol at your son's party.

There are, however, other factors to consider. The first is that you have a duty of care to children in your home – and if there is a problem with overdrinking or an accident caused by drinking, you may be held liable. What's more, other parents may not actually have the same approach to teen drinking as you do, and will object to having their child served alcohol under the age of eighteen or outside their home.

If you feel comfortable with a small amount of alcohol being served, and the parents of his friends are in agreement, consider the following tips:

▷ Make it clear to your child and his guests what is and is not allowed.

▷ Act as barperson yourself, or ask another responsible adult to do so. Not every teenager is responsible or mature enough to make the right decisions about intake.

▷ Limit what's on offer – allowing, say, a beer or two per guest, or one or two glasses of wine or alcopop.

▷ Don't allow guests to bring drinks to the party (even soft drinks, as they may have been spiked with alcohol).

▷ Offer plenty of non-alcoholic drinks so that kids don't feel pressured to drink, and have an option when they've drunk their fill.

▷ Make non-alcoholic drinks attractive and 'fun' if possible – a juice bar with plenty of ice, fruit, juices and fizzy drinks can make this option more appealing.

▷ Avoid punches if you can – these are easily 'spiked' and it's also harder to control who is drinking what.

▷ Offer plenty of food alongside any drinks, to soak up the alcohol.

▷ Make sure that all your young guests have a safe means of getting home.

How old does my daughter need to be in order to buy alcohol legally?
In the UK, your daughter can buy beer, wine or cider in a pub from the age of sixteen, as long as she has a meal alongside and is with an adult. She can purchase any type of alcohol from the age of eighteen, from any premises.

What is the law in Europe?

In Europe, legislation is much more relaxed. Most children will be served alcohol with meals in restaurants if they are accompanied by an adult; most parents serve alcohol at home with meals and at celebrations. The legal drinking age for purchasing alcohol and consuming it on licensed premises ranges from sixteen to twenty, with eighteen being the most common age limit.

What happens in the US?

Don't expect to have a sniff of alcohol until you are at least twenty-one. Not only is it almost impossible to buy without an ID card stating your age, but there is a strong anti-alcohol ethos that encourages abstention until twenty-one.

How do I know if my son is drinking too much?

Unfortunately, binge-drinking is a part of today's youth culture. It's not social drinking as we know it, but more like an 'extreme sport' – where you drink until you pass out or vomit. Chances are that if your son is drinking, he may well be drinking too much. A few drinks a week may be acceptable for an older teenager or a little alcohol with meals, but his health (in particular his liver and brain) can be affected if he is drinking large quantities regularly. It is important that he learns moderation, and that you keep tabs on what is going on. Remember that most kids don't worry about alcohol and its dangers, because it's part of their culture, they see deaths or alcohol poisoning as freak accidents, and they think they are immortal.

If your child is drinking too much, it's important that you talk to him (*see page 105*), to explain the risks and find out why he feels the need to drink excessively.

OBVIOUS SIGNS OF OVERDRINKING

▷ Bloodshot eyes

▷ Slurred speech, giddiness, dizziness

▷ Unusual fatigue

▷ Repeated health complaints

▷ Personality change

▷ Sudden mood changes

▷ Irresponsible behaviour

▷ Irritability

▷ Poor judgement

▷ Depression

▷ General torpor or lack of interest

▷ Argumentative

▷ Withdrawing from the family

▷ Secretiveness

▷ Drop in grades

▷ Absence at school

▷ Truancy

▷ Discipline problems

▷ Changes to less conventional styles in dress and music

▷ Sudden increase or decrease in appetite

▷ Not coming home on time – or calling at the last minute to say they are staying elsewhere (they don't want to be caught)

▷ Not telling you where they are going

▷ Constant excuses for behaviour

▷ Spending a lot of time in their rooms

▷ Lying about activities

▷ Reduced memory and attention span

TIPS FOR KIDS

If your child has begun drinking, it's worth giving him or her some advice about how to approach it in a sensible fashion. For example:

▷ Don't start drinking if you are angry, anxious or depressed. Alcohol can easily become a crutch.

▷ Become aware of when you need to stop drinking – when your speech becomes slurred, when your memory is affected, when you find yourself being a little too open or brave, when you become dizzy or giddy.

▷ If you drink too quickly it is impossible to monitor how intoxicated you are getting. Slow down and let the effects spread over a long enough period of time.

▷ Eat when you drink whenever possible – it slows down the absorption of alcohol into the bloodstream.

▷ Remember that a true friend will never let a friend drink and drive or to drink dangerously. In other words, good friends look out for each other.

▷ Remember the dangers of alcohol – drinking a small bottle of spirits (or the equivalent in wine or beer) over an hour or two gives you a one in two chance of dying, according to the Emergency Services.

▷ Don't allow anyone to bully or intimidate you into drinking too much – or binge-drinking. No one who really cares about you will do this.

Should I allow alcohol in my home if my kids are under age?

This is a similar question to allowing drinks for celebrations and a little wine with dinner. There is clear evidence that children who grow up accustomed to moderate, restrained drinking with meals are less likely to binge-drink or to develop alcohol problems in later life. Therefore, there is something to be said for giving them a regular taste of the 'forbidden fruit', in order to dispel its potential power. You must, however, ensure that your children are supervised at all times, and that the amount drunk is strictly regulated. One small glass of wine or beer with a meal is adequate until the age of fifteen.

Your children may have friends who bring alcohol to parties or get-togethers. Whether you choose to allow this is up to you and your personal family policy on under-aged drinking.

What are the legal implications?

If your child or anyone in your care is under the age of sixteen, you are responsible for their health and safety. A houseful of drunk teenagers can not only lead to tragedy, but to criminal prosecution. You are well within your rights, therefore, on a legal basis, to deny drinking in your home. If you do consent, it would be sensible to ask permission from the parents of any child who will be present.

When should I educate my children about alcohol?

Young people who have access to alcohol – drinking at parties, friends' houses, in the park – quite often drink to get drunk. The number of teenagers trying drink in their early teens is growing, often influenced by peer pressure and the media. The worry for parents is that it can also be linked to risky teenage behaviour such as unprotected and early sex. Several studies indicate that kids regularly drink from about age twelve, so it's worth discussing the dangers of alcohol with them well before that time. In reality, discussions about alcohol can be a part of family conversation from a very early age.

What is safe drinking?

When kids get older, you can give them tips on safe drinking (*see page 38*), and also explain the effects of alcohol. Kids like facts because they can spout them when they feel cornered by peers.

Top tips

▷ Talk openly about the potential dangers – from health to safety – in a practical way so they don't tune out.

▷ Remember your own behaviour will influence them. Be honest about the reasons why you or people in general like drinking as well as the negatives of alcohol.

▷ Talk about how they may feel or what they may do under pressure – whether it is deciding what they do if they are offered a drink, or if a friend offers them a lift home after drinking.

▷ Encourage your child to stick to lower-strength brands and not to drink too quickly.

▷ Agree rules on parties and be around if your child has a party at home.

▷ Make sure your child has a way of getting home safely at night.

▷ Be wary of late-night changes of plan (staying at a friend's at the last minute) – chances are your child is hiding something. Try to avoid this type of secretiveness.

▷ Make them aware of the danger of drink-spiking and not putting themselves in vulnerable situations. Encourage your children and their friends to look out for each other.

▷ Explore how alcohol affects people in different ways, and how it can make some people aggressive and up for a fight. Talk through ways of keeping safe and walking away from trouble.

▷ Encourage your teenager to make sensible choices, by stressing the health risks involved rather than laying down the law or giving ultimatums.

Armed forces

When can my son join the Army?

The UK's armed forces (the Army, Royal Navy, Royal Air Force and
Royal Marines) recruit school leavers from the age of sixteen, and
they can be used on operations from the age of seventeen, the limit
under current international conventions. You can apply to join the
Royal Navy at fifteen years and nine months. Entry age and
qualifications differ according to the branch of the service your child
wishes to join. For example, your child can join any of the armed
forces at sixteen, but if he or she wishes to join as an officer, they
usually have to wait another year or so – seventeen and six months
for the Air Force, and seventeen and nine months for the Army.

The armed forces can offer a multitude of career opportunities
for young people, and not all of it involves work on the front lines.
Nevertheless, it does entail a commitment, and your child must be
prepared for some fairly hard graft and to show respect for
authority if he or she wishes to join. All of the armed forces have a
minimum period of service before you are allowed to leave. For
example, if your son or daughter joins the army and doesn't like it,
they can't leave within the first 28 days. After this, they can leave
on 28 days' notice at any time during the first six months (or if over
the age of eighteen, during the first three months). Thereafter, your
son or daughter must serve four years.

What is the Territorial Army?

A good way to experience the Army without making a full
commitment is to join the Territorial Army (TA), which is a reserve
force of civilians who undertake soldier training and fulfil
operational support on a part-time basis.

For more information on what's involved and the various careers available, visit www.armyjobs.mod.uk or ring 0845 7300 111.

WHAT IS THE ARMY CADET FORCE (ACF)?

The ACF is a 40,000 strong organisation designed to give young people of both sexes (between the ages of thirteen and eighteen), a taste of what the Army can offer. It has bases all over the UK and, a little like the Scout and Guide Associations, is run by volunteer instructors.

Can my son join the Army without my permission?

Your son will need permission to join any part of the armed forces, including those that are part-time and/or volunteer, until he is eighteen. At this age, he can join anything without parental consent.

Babysitting

How old should a child be to babysit other children?

According to the Royal Society for the Prevention of Accidents, no one under the age of sixteen should be left to care for an infant or young child. However, there's no current legislation that gives a minimum age for babysitters.

Your babysitter should be someone you trust to handle any emergency or who will at least know whom to call and what procedures to follow. Parents should assess carefully a babysitter under the age of sixteen. In some circumstances, parents can be prosecuted if any harm comes to their child while a babysitter under sixteen years old is supervising; no child under sixteen years old can be held responsible for children in their care. This changes dramatically over the age of sixteen, however, when there is a full legal duty of care.

The British Red Cross runs babysitting courses for teenagers. Children must be over the age of fourteen in order to attend. You can find out more about these courses from its website at www.redcross.org.uk. If you use a babysitter regularly, it might be worth paying for this training.

WHAT SHOULD I DO IF MY BABYSITTER IS UNDER SIXTEEN YEARS OLD?

The Royal Society for the Prevention of Accidents (RoSPA) offers the following advice for parents who plan to leave a child with someone under the age of sixteen.

▷ You must be prepared to take some responsibility for anything that should go wrong in your absence. You must also be prepared to take responsibility for the care and safety of your babysitter, including making arrangements for the sitter's safe return home. Never let a young babysitter travel home alone late at night.

▷ You need to know that your babysitter is a competent person.

▷ Define the qualities you are looking for in a good babysitter: for example, responsible, mature, reliable, honest, capable, tolerant, patient, kind but firm, has experience with young children, has first aid experience, etc.

▷ Make sure the babysitter knows how and when to call the Emergency Services if it should become necessary.

▷ Encourage your babysitter to visit your home and get to know the child or children who will be left in his or her care. It will also help the babysitter understand the particular household and the children's day-time and night-time routines.

▷ Give an honest opinion when your babysitter asks to have friends to sit with them (same sex or opposite sex). Use common sense and remember that babysitting can be a lonely business.

▷ Make adequate preparations for your babysitter not only in terms of refreshments but also by giving him or her enough information to cover all eventualities. Make sure your sitter knows where everything is.

▷ Never take advantage of a babysitter by leaving him or her to cope with an already sick or upset child who you know will not settle.

▷ Never leave a babysitter alone with several children for long periods of time.

▷ Always return home as close to the time you agreed with your babysitter as you can. If you are going to be late, inform the babysitter, if possible.

▷ Talk to your babysitter about the child's progress and give him or her up-to-date information; this is especially important if the sitter does not see your child regularly.

▷ If you feel unhappy about any aspect of the care of your child, talk it over with the babysitter.

Are the guidelines different if the babysitter is minding his or her own siblings?

At present, there are no guidelines for babysitting whatsoever, although most children's charities, including the National Society for the Prevention of Cruelty to Children (NSPCC), do not recommend that anyone under the age of sixteen be left in sole charge of other children, including siblings. So, in a nutshell, there is nothing to stop you from asking older children to babysit younger siblings, no matter what their age.

On a personal note, my two oldest children watched their baby/toddler brother from the age of fourteen; however, they usually did it together, we were never more than 20 minutes away, and our maximum time away from the home was no more than four hours. All enjoyed the experience, particularly when the older ones were given a little extra money for their efforts. I looked after my younger siblings and neighbours' children from the age of twelve and took the responsibility seriously.

What must a babysitter be prepared for?

However, no matter what the age of the older siblings, they must be prepared for any eventuality, and this applies to all babysitters.

▷ They must be reminded of the responsibility and the importance of diligence. A toddler can stick a finger in a socket, get his hands on a sharp object or ingest a poisonous substance in a few seconds' flat. Babysitters must keep an eye on them at all times.

▷ Babysitters should be able to lock and unlock doors and windows, and operate the alarm system.

▷ Babysitters should not answer the door unless they know the person well, and should never tell anyone on the telephone that they are home alone.

▷ They need to know how to contact the Emergency Services, and there should be a list of important numbers by the telephone, including the doctor, your mobile, the poison control centre, and a neighbour or two.

▷ They should know what to do if there is a power cut (torches are probably safer than candles in the hands of children; make sure they know where they are), a flood or a fire.

▷ Babysitters should know how to administer basic first aid, if a child chokes, for example, or cuts himself. Leave a first-aid kit in an agreed place.

▷ Discuss what is acceptable. Can your child have a friend round? Are there any forbidden activities (cooking, lighting the fire, drinking alcohol, for example)? Can they visit the park or the shops? Can they bathe a younger sibling?

▷ Make sure there is always someone who can act as a back-up in your absence. Sometimes children just need a little reassurance that they are doing the right thing or that fears are unjustified. Making an agreement with nearby parents who have children of similar age to act as advisor when the other is out might be useful.

My 14-year-old daughter is keen to earn money babysitting and I'm nervous about the responsibility she is taking on. Is she old enough? How can I prepare her?

If your daughter is mature and practical, it could be an ideal job. She needs to be aware that it isn't just a 'fun' or 'easy' money-making opportunity, and that looking after children can be hard work, tiring and difficult (even for seasoned adults). She must also know that it is often lonely work and a big responsibility. Although she cannot be held legally liable for accidents that occur while she is caring for other children (this remains a parent's responsibility until their sitter is sixteen years old), it can be distressing and potentially damaging to feel responsible when something goes wrong.

Are there any courses?

It's worth arranging for your child to take a babysitting course, such as that offered by the Red Cross (*see page 43*), so that she feels confident enough to deal with eventualities. Young children can become ill and are liable to accidents and mishaps, and your daughter will need to know how to cope with emergencies. Take the time, too, to talk through basic safety in the home, and help her to identify potential risks.

For the first few occasions, you may wish to be available to answer questions or to provide back-up if your daughter is uncertain.

IS YOUR CHILD MATURE ENOUGH TO BE LEFT ALONE TO BABYSIT?

If you are trying to assess your child's readiness to be at home alone, discuss the possibility with him or her and listen to your child's reactions. Do they look forward to the idea or are they hesitant about it? It is also helpful if you observe reactions to daily situations: do they rely on you to plan their every minute or do they enjoy planning their own time? Do they panic when the unexpected happens? Do they relish a little freedom and like responsibility? Are they familiar with emergency procedures, for example, in the event of a break-in, fire, flood or even a power failure?

What's the maximum length of time a child should be allowed to babysit?

While there are clear guidelines for children in paid employment (such as not working after 7 pm on a school night, or for more than two hours during term-time; *see page 164*), this does not extend to babysitting. Common sense, therefore, must prevail.

A young teenager babysitting very young children will need a break – so three or four hours should really be the maximum for any babysitter under the age of fourteen or fifteen. After the age of sixteen, longer hours are acceptable, but consider the fact that looking after children (particularly if they are not your own) can be tiring and frustrating. If you can arrange for a little cover so that your sitter can take a break, or if you know your child will have a nap or relax in front of a DVD or television programme for an hour or so, giving the sitter some breathing space, then longer periods are acceptable. However, be realistic about what is achievable and the limits to endurance. If a child goes to bed early, a longer evening stint is acceptable, and if a child regularly sleeps through the night, your sitter is over sixteen years old and comfortable with the idea, then overnight babysitting may be OK too.

Can siblings babysit younger siblings overnight?

The NSPCC does not recommend that any child under the age of sixteen babysit (which is certainly open to personal circumstances and discretion), but it also suggest that no child be left alone overnight until he or she is sixteen. On this basis, if your elder child is over sixteen, is comfortable with the idea of being left alone overnight with his or her sibling, and is aware of how to deal with emergencies, it's certainly acceptable. One recent study found that 91 per cent of those polled thought that fourteen was old enough to be left alone overnight (although not for an extended number of nights), so clearly many parents believe their children are mature and/or capable enough to manage. It may, therefore, be that your 14-year-old is deemed mature enough to watch a sibling overnight, particularly if the child or children in question are good sleepers and will get through the night without being distressed or requiring intervention. But babysitting is not the same as staying alone, and your child needs to be aware that he is being given a big responsibility for long-term care.

Should I expect my children to babysit their younger siblings on the weekends?

In a well-balanced household, it is acceptable for the weight of responsibility to be shared between all family members. Childcare certainly falls into this category. So yes, theoretically, your children should be encouraged to do their part and babysit.

If your older child is under sixteen years of age, you must be prepared to take responsibility for anything that should go wrong in your absence. You are also responsible for the care and safety of your older child.

Bedrooms

When should my child be allowed to decorate his own room?

Personal taste doesn't have an age limit, and you may have a child with very clear ideas about what he likes and doesn't like. There is no reason why a child cannot decorate or choose the décor of his own room from an early age – within limits, of course (*see below*). A bedroom is a child's personal sanctuary and as long as it is functional and the colour scheme or décor is not going to affect sleep or study patterns, it should be acceptable for him to explore his individuality and personal taste within these confines. A shared bedroom, however, might require a little more negotiation (*see page 51*).

My daughter has posters on her walls that I consider to be offensive. How can I encourage her to remove them?

A child's room is her sanctuary and she should be given some space to decorate it as she sees fit. Strictly speaking, most parents don't spend much time in their teens' rooms, so it's unlikely that they will be in contact with the offensive posters for much time. There are, however, certain cases where parents can step in and lay down the law. For example, you may wish to agree with your child that anything of an overtly sexual nature (pornography, for example) is unacceptable, as is anything 'pro-drugs'. Parents are well within their rights to set and enforce house rules regarding choice of images. This is particularly relevant if there are younger members of the family who may be affected by the nature of the posters. But try to be reasonable – what we consider offensive may actually be a normal emblem of popular culture – band posters, for example, can appear very explicit when, in fact, they are splashed across record shops and kids' magazines everywhere.

At what age can my daughter deny me access to her room?
Parents often struggle with the boundaries of their child's privacy. What is acceptable given the responsibility for your child's health and welfare? Most parents still clear up their child's room well into the teens, or enter to put away clothing or change sheets, and there is a clear temptation to investigate piles of school work, an unlocked diary or something that looks suspiciously like birth control or cigarette papers, particularly if there is any cause for concern.

Your daughter is right, on the one hand, to make her room a no-go area, because chances are you will come across something that she deems private, or which she does not wish you to see. But there are other issues. Teens retreat from the family circle. That is normal. They want special space, usually their bedrooms, that will reflect their moods, interests and search for a sense of identity. Parents need to set some guidelines up front. Tell your child her privacy will be respected unless her behaviour strongly suggests there is a serious problem that she is denying. Open communication is always the priority. But if there are strong signs that all is not well, then the rules change.

If your daughter wants no access, she must, however, agree to keep her room clean to a reasonable standard (*see page 52*) and put away her own clothes, replace her bedding (*see page 53*), and agree to some limitations – for example, no drugs, drinking alcohol, smoking, entertaining the opposite sex without permission, using the computer or her mobile inappropriately, or even lighting candles or incense if you are worried about fire hazards.

How do I know what is going on if the door is closed?
You may want to agree some terms about access – certainly you
need to know what is going on behind closed doors to some extent
as it is an element of parental responsibility.

**My son insists he needs his own bedroom – at what age is
this strictly necessary?**
Most children will demand their own rooms at some point in order
to facilitate their growing need for privacy, independence and
freedom. Sharing a room can have several advantages, including
maximising space, teaching children to share, encouraging a close
relationship between siblings (given their close proximity), and also
giving children the tools they need when sharing a room later at
university or when living with a room-mate in private
accommodation. Obvious drawbacks are the fights over space and
property, disagreements over decorating, bickering that is the
natural result of having to share a small space, and the feeling that
there are no private spaces or possessions in the household.

There is no legal precedent for room-sharing, but most councils
in the UK work on the following guidelines. Two children of the
same sex can share until the oldest child is sixteen; two children of
opposite sexes can share until the eldest is ten. A straw poll of
parents seems to back this up – opposite-gender siblings tend to be
separated at puberty, and most older teens (given space) are
allowed their own rooms by fifteen or sixteen.

When can my child have a lock on his bedroom door?
Strictly speaking, there is no reason why your child can't have
a lock on his door (except for safety reasons), but it's worth
assessing why he feels he needs one. Perhaps he has siblings who
regularly borrow his things, or perhaps he doesn't feel he can

trust you not to 'snoop'. Before resorting to locks you might try other options.

The first is that you can establish family rules where no one enters anyone else's room without knocking nor borrows property without asking first. There are safety issues with door locks. The first is that if your child has a TV in his bedroom, he may be watching inappropriate programmes without your knowledge. Secondly, if there is a computer, he may be downloading unsuitable material or involving himself in chatrooms or websites that he really shouldn't. There are many stories of parents who are stunned to discover that their angelic child had drugs in their room or night-time guests.

What are the safety implications?

Consider, too, the impact of a fire. If your child is locked inside a room to which you can't gain access, he may lose his life. It is also worth noting that if you do agree to the lock, and your child takes a long time to open the door, you may wish to investigate!

When should I begin knocking on my daughter's bedroom door before entering?

If a child's door is shut, she wants privacy. Therefore, from any age, it is respectful to knock. This can, actually, be a household rule. After all, if your door is shut, you'd appreciate a knock before entering as well. Respect is taught – if you employ it, you can expect your children to behave in the same way.

When should my child take responsibility for cleaning her own room?

Children from the age of six can certainly take on board some general tidying duties (*see page 277*), including putting away their own books and toys, and making their beds. From the age of ten they can undertake simple cleaning duties, such as dusting, a little vacuuming, and sorting their clothes for washing. Teenagers can wash their own clothes and put them away. In terms of taking full responsibility, you will need to consider a few things. The first is that no child will know what to do unless you show them, so a few instructive, cleaning-together jobs will work well to establish your expectations and to teach the required skills.

As kids move into adolescence, they often become sloppy and less hygienic, so your pristine pre-teen cleaner and organiser might suffer a few blips. In this case, set out a time each week when you expect cleaning to be undertaken – and don't be afraid to check. Obviously it makes sense to be fairly complimentary, no matter what the result, as negative feedback usually puts paid to future efforts; however, if your child is not living up to standards, you may wish to agree that you will share certain tasks or that you will help from time to time. Be draconian if required – a week with no clean clothes or a couple of weeks living in dust and debris will usually shock teenagers into action, particularly if they use their rooms for entertaining friends.

How often do I need to change bedding in the teenage years?
For health reasons, sheets should be changed every two weeks; ideally, pillowcases should be changed weekly. The reason for this is that bacteria and dust mites (among other things) can proliferate without regular laundering. It is important to implement certain standards of hygiene and to endorse them! Some teens (boys in particular) may be embarrassed by what appears on their sheets (nocturnal emissions, for example) or want to keep their rooms private from parents and the rest of the household. In this case, it's worth teaching your teen how to use the washing machine,

or setting a day where he or she bundles up their own sheets and put them in the washing machine, ready for washing by a parent. Keep a spare set of sheets within easy reach, so that they can change their own sheets when required (a word of warning, however; many teens, particularly boys, seem perfectly happy to sleep on a bed without a sheet, pillowcase or duvet cover – so make sure that the clean sheets actually make it on to the bed).

Bedtime

What is an appropriate bedtime for a teenager?
While sleep requirements fall fairly consistently between the ages of two and twelve, with the average 12-year-old getting about nine or ten hours of sleep a night, sleep needs for teenagers do not continue to fall – and, indeed, in some cases they require *more* sleep than a pre-teen. Studies show that most teenagers get somewhere between six and eight hours of sleep a night by the age of eighteen, which is, apparently, not enough.

As kids enter the teenage years, physiological changes in the brain that regulate sleep and waking cause them to stay up longer and sleep later. Unfortunately, that's precisely the time they must be at school. Add homework, sports activities, music lessons, TV and chatting with friends online, and most kids have little time to catch up on sleep. Not getting enough sleep can have serious consequences for learning, long-term memory and safety. REM (rapid eye movement) sleep is when the mind repairs itself, grows new connections, and 'puts it all together'; this type of sleep occurs about every 90 minutes and gets longer as the night progresses. Between the seventh and eighth hour, we get almost an hour of REM sleep, so it's critical that kids are getting at least this amount.

How many hours of sleep does a teenager need?

Research at the National Center on Sleep Disorders at the National Institutes of Health (NIH) in the US, shows that children who regularly sleep nine hours perform better in school, are happier, suffer fewer accidents, and are less likely to develop weight or emotional problems later on than those who try to function on less.

So count back. If your child has to be up at seven every morning, then aim for a 10 pm bedtime. It can be difficult to get some teens into bed; *see page 58* for a little advice.

When can children set their own bedtime?

Left to their own devices, many older children and teenagers would resist bedtime for as long as possible, which makes the concept of allowing them to set their own bedtimes potentially dangerous. We've established that teenagers need as much sleep, if not more, than a 12-year-old (*see page 54*). The importance of sleep needs to be made clear before any responsibility for setting bedtimes can be handed over to kids. If they understand their requirements, and are willing to act responsibly, then it is acceptable for them to choose when they go to sleep. In reality, it's hard to enforce a bedtime after the age of about fifteen, so that's probably a good point at which kids can be given the freedom to decide.

It's worth, however, laying down some ground rules, the first being that you expect your child to get an average of eight or nine hours of sleep a night. Short-term sleep deficit can normally be made up; however, research has consistently supported the proposition that ongoing sleep deprivation results in decreased academic achievement. For instance, studies have demonstrated that children with later school-night bedtimes, more irregular bedtimes and shorter total sleep time on school nights, have lower academic achievement than children with earlier, more regular bedtimes and longer total sleep time. A large study involving thousands of students whose school systems delayed start-times demonstrated that students in such systems who have longer sleep times have better attendance records, increased continuous enrolment and a slight increase in grades.

Kids do need to learn how to manage their own time and energy, so you might like to institute 'bedroom time', which means that you expect them to be in their bedrooms by, say, 10 pm every evening. Reading, listening to music or other quiet pursuits can take place after this time, but TV, computers, phones and loud music – all of which disturb sleep patterns – are out. This is a compromise of sorts, with your child effectively setting his own sleep time, while you enforce the wind-down time.

Can bedtimes be later on the weekend and, if so, by how much?
As long as your child is getting the sleep he needs, there is no reason why a later bedtime on weekends isn't possible. If he can make up the hours by sleeping in, he'll get the sleep he needs. But beware! Many families find it irritating to have a teen sleeping till noon on weekends, after spending half the night watching TV or banging around the house. If your child has homework, household chores, a part-time job or activities on the weekend to fit in, midday wakenings are not conducive to a productive schedule. Once again, set a bedroom time (*see above*) of, say, 11 pm or midnight with the same limitations on activities in place. If your child has a TV in her room, make sure it's not on all hours, and that a certain cut-off point is agreed (*see page 455*). Sleepovers, later evenings out and even one-off programmes on TV might call for the occasional later bedtime, and if you are flexible on these occasions, you are more likely to convince a teen that a reasonable bedtime on ordinary weekend nights is acceptable.

Should my child be allowed to listen to music while he falls asleep?

Many older children and teenagers find it difficult to settle (the result of a circadian of rhythms that goes awry with adolescent hormones), and tend to potter about doing the same things they enjoy throughout the day. Listening to music is often one of these. And while studies show that soft, soothing music has the ability to reduce stress hormones and encourage restful sleep, loud music does quite the opposite. Not only will it keep your child alert and awake for longer, but sleep itself will be disrupted by the impact on hormones and adrenaline. It's a good idea to set some guidelines for when loud music is appropriate (stopping, say, an hour or so before lights out). Do, however, encourage soft music – if you can agree on what is genuinely 'soft and soothing' or simply your teen's interpretation!

My son often falls asleep in front of the TV in his bedroom – will this affect his sleep?

Unfortunately, yes. Many experts frown upon TVs in bedrooms, and this is one of the main reasons why. In a recent US study, researchers found that some TV viewing habits were particularly strongly associated with sleep problems. These included: the presence of a television in a child's bedroom; the child's use of the TV as a sleep aid; and the amount of TV viewed daily. In fact, a television in the child's room was the most powerful predictor of overall sleep disturbance and bedtime resistance in the analysis the researchers performed. The study also found that television viewing at bedtime and overall heavy television viewing caused children to resist going to bed, to have trouble falling asleep and to sleep less than the recommended eight or nine hours. TV viewing habits, such as falling asleep in front of the television, seemed to cause sleep disturbances in 25 per cent of children.

ADOLESCENTS AND SLEEP

Adolescent sleep has become a topic of great concern, spawning a number of world-wide conferences to address the problem. As a group, adolescents appear to be among the most sleep-deprived in our society. Why does it matter? Sleep deprivation can impair memory and inhibit creativity, making it difficult for sleep deprived students to learn. Teens struggle to learn to deal with stress and control emotion – sleep deprivation makes it even more difficult. Irritability, lack of self-confidence and mood swings are often common in teens, but sleep deprivation makes it worse. Depression can result from chronic sleep deprivation. Not enough sleep can endanger their immune system and make them more susceptible to serious illnesses, and interestingly, it is a precursor to obesity. Judgement can also be impaired, and given that many teens are for the first time making their own decisions, and driving cars and bikes on the roads, this can pose a serious safety risk. Adolescents are involved in some 55 per cent of all traffic accidents, and most appear to happen when they are on their own, at night. Experts believe that drowsiness and inadequate sleep are at the root of the problem.

What can you do?

▷ Keep an eye on your child's activity levels. If he's playing sports every day after school, practising an instrument, has a part-time job or takes part in too many clubs, you may need to encourage him to drop something. Stick to a reasonable schedule that allows time for homework, fun and adequate rest.

▷ Make sure your adolescent is part of the family routine – eating regularly, enjoying some free time and going to bed at an appropriate time. If his bedtime is running later and later, strike up a deal and let him choose a more appropriate bedtime.

▷ Keep an eye on his diet. If he's drinking coffee or a lot of cola in the evenings, his sleep will be disrupted and he'll find it difficult to get to sleep.

▷ Intense studying or computer games before bed can be stimulating.

▷ Avoid arguing with your adolescent just before bedtime, which can make him feel stressed, under pressure and less able to sleep.

▷ Keep the television and the lights off when sleeping, and open the blinds as soon as the morning alarm goes. This can help to create a more acceptable sleep/wake cycle.

▷ Don't discourage weekend lie-ins, but limit them to no more than two or three hours later than the usual wakening time, or the body clock will be disrupted.

When should we agree to stop the pre-bed bathing?

Let's face it, most adolescents are too tired or behind schedule to jump into the shower in the morning, so a night-time bath isn't just a luxury but a necessity. Moreover, kids who are highly pressured by school work and various activities will do well to bathe at the end of the day. Various studies into stress show that night-time bathing encourages restful sleep and relaxes the body (a too-hot bath or shower has the opposite effect), and has the psychological effect of 'washing away' the day's problems. Kids who have always had an evening bath before bed will probably continue this as part of their normal routine; encourage it where you can and implement it if not. If you have a reluctant bather, give your child choices in their personal care products to get them interested.

When should I stop reading a bedtime story?

Once kids can read on their own, the bedtime story is resoundingly dropped. So, by around eight or nine years old, kids no longer enjoy a bedtime read with parents. Is this too young? Several experts believe so. Reading together, whether you take turns reading a chapter, letting your child read to you, or giving them a treat by reading to them, should ideally continue until age twelve or even later. In fact, one study found that children who are read to into their teens not only develop a greater love of books and solo reading habits, but they do better at A-level. Obviously an older teen will think you are mad if you suggest a bedtime story, but there's no reason why you can't spend time reading together, perhaps reading aloud an interesting snippet from a magazine or newspaper, or commenting on a nice use of words. One study found that some 92 per cent of children enjoy reading books for fun, but their reading time takes a steep dive after age eight. It can be no surprise to find that this is the average age at which kids stop being read to.

Interestingly, too, if you make a bedtime story part of your child's sleep-time routine, he is more likely to continue reading to himself at bedtime.

Bicycles

When can a child ride his bike to school?
There is plenty of research and many statistics relating to this question, and all seem to advise caution. One Norwegian study found that bicycle-related injuries occurring during travel to or from school are a significant contributor to the total incidence of bicycle-related injuries. Boys tend to be affected more than girls, but this is understandable given that more boys than girls choose to ride bicycles to school or elsewhere. This study concentrated on

ten- to fifteen-year-olds, and, in fact, several parenting surveys indicate that parents would not consider their children old enough to bicycle to school before this age. And the statistics appear worse as kids get older. According to the AA, one in five fatal or serious injury among thirteen- and fourteen-year-olds happens to teenage boys on bikes. It claims that teenagers are safer on foot than younger children, but not on wheels.

So what do you do?

Getting children interested in cycling at an early age is a great way to encourage exercise. Many children receive cycle training around age ten or eleven, and it is recommended that they do not cycle on roads before they are trained. Children between the ages of eleven and fifteen are most vulnerable on the roads, yet only one-third of children receive cycle training, usually at an earlier age. It is important that all young people, whatever their age, know the basics of road safety and have some proper training before cycling on the roads.

Are there any training programmes?

The Department for Transport and Cycling England are currently investing about £5 million a year on encouraging children to cycle to school. The aim is that within three years, 50 per cent of all school children will be able to receive cycle training. The funding is being spent on cycle training in schools, cycle trainers, off-road routes to school and cycle-training schemes run by the Cycle Touring Club (CTC) with its 'Bike It' programme and by British Cycling with its 'Go Ride' scheme.

The National Standard for Cycle Training three-level programme provides the skills required to cycle safely on and off-road:

▷ Level 1 for ages seven to eight: Beginners and basic cycling skills are held off-road and teach children how to control, balance and manoeuvre.

▷ Level 2 for ages nine to ten: Introduction to on-road cycling is held on quieter roads in groups. Children learn where to position themselves when riding on the road, how to observe traffic, signal, turn and manoeuvre safely and a basic understanding of the highway code.

▷ Level 3 for ages eleven to twelve: Advanced cycling is held on busier roads to teach skills required for making longer journeys and to develop strategies to deal with all types of road conditions, such as roundabouts, traffic lights and multi-lane roads.

This sounds like a sensible plan. Before your child embarks on a bicycle trip to school, you would be well advised to ensure that he has some cycling training under his belt. And make sure he has a lock for his bike!

For more information, ring the National Cycle Training Helpline on 0870 607 0415 or visit www.ctc.org.uk.

When does a child no longer require a bicycle helmet?
In a nutshell, never. Many countries, including Canada and the US, require a cycling helmet regardless of age, which indicates its crucial importance in preventing injuries. There is no such legal requirement in the UK which is, frankly, a pity. Studies show that bicycle injuries account for ten per cent of all paediatric traumatic deaths and that helmets have been proven to decrease both deaths and injuries significantly. Although it's obvious that a helmet reduces the risk of death and injury substantially, studies also show that parental perception of their children's use of a bike helmet does not actually reflect its actually use. In other words, parents

supply the helmet and assume it's being used when it is not!
Bicycle helmets are not particularly cool or fashionable, but if your
child rides a bike, he should wear one, whatever his age. Ask him
to apply stickers to make it look more interesting if necessary, but
make it a household rule. It could save his life.

Until what age can my child ride on the pavement rather than the road?

No one, children included, is allowed to cycle on the pavement unless
there is a sign to say that cycling is permitted. Similarly, no one is
allowed to cycle on a footpath that is not next to the road. This is the
legal situation. I can, however, think of no parent who does not advise
their child to ride on the pavement, where cars cannot cause injury.
If your child is inexperienced and he needs to ride his bike, you may
wish to bend the law for the sake of safety. Invest in a cycling course
by all means, but ensure that he is aware of the dangers of the road
and protect him in whatever way you feel is necessary.

Should I allow my child to ride her bike at night?

The CTC (*see above*) offers courses in night-time cycling for kids
over the age of twelve, therefore this is probably an appropriate
age at which they can begin. Having said that, unless they are
experienced in night-time cycling, you may wish to wait a little
longer. Your child must use lights to cycle between sunset and
sunrise. This is a legal requirement. They don't have to wear
fluorescent or reflective clothing, but they will significantly increase
their safety if they do so. It is an offence to cycle at night without a
white front light, a red back light and a red reflector at the back.

Remember that between eleven and twelve, the age they start
secondary school, is the peak risk period, and this new
independence increases the risks.

Birth control

Can my daughter be offered birth control without my consent?
Guidance from the British Medical Association (BMA) and others
state that 'the duty of confidentiality owed to a person under
sixteen is as great as that owed to any other person'. Guidance also
states that 'any competent young person, regardless of age, can
independently seek medical advice and give valid consent to
treatment'. Following the Gillick case in 1985 which set a legal
precedent (*see page 253*), the Department of Health issued the
following guidance on providing contraceptive advice and treatment
to young people under the age of sixteen:

A doctor needs to be satisfied that:
▷ The young person understands his advice and has sufficient
  maturity to understand what is involved in terms of the moral,
  social and emotional implications.
▷ He can neither persuade the young person to inform his or her
  parents, nor to allow the doctor to inform them that
  contraceptive advice is being sought.
▷ The young person is very likely to begin or to continue having
  sexual intercourse with or without contraceptive treatment.
▷ Without contraceptive advice or treatment, the young person''s
  physical or mental health or both is likely to suffer.
▷ The young person's best interests require the doctor to give
  contraceptive advice or treatment or both without parental
  consent.
If your child fits the bill, she can get birth control without your
consent from a very early age. Some children of eleven or twelve
have done so in the past in the UK. It's worth being aware that it
might happen.

When should I speak to my child about birth control?

Many parents feel that talking with their teens about birth control will either give the teens ideas or communicate parental permission to have sex. However, teens do have ideas about sex, and some actually have sex without either birth control information or our knowledge or permission. There's no doubt that the subject is covered in some detail in most school curriculae. However, kids are often embarrassed and don't listen; and what's more, there is undoubtedly a culture of 'it could never happen to me'. Kids need to know as early as they understand the concept that sex has consequences. Most parents do the 'birds-and-the-bees talk' when their children are around ten years old. There is certainly no harm in talking at that point about things like waiting to have a baby until you are in a long-term, happy relationship, or until you are married, and that there are ways to prevent babies from coming too soon. We all like to think that our children will wait to have sex, but the early use of alcohol, peer pressure and the encouragement of promiscuity through the media may put paid to our plans.

How shall I go about it?

▷ Engage your child whenever the moment seems right. Try not to force the issue or sit them down for 'a talk' – they'll only feel edgy and under pressure.

▷ Discuss various methods of birth control – perhaps using a book to help the discussion along.

▷ Don't hesitate to explain that you think your child is too young to even consider sex.

▷ Your values should be made clear. Explain what you believe and why. This may not sway them in the short-term, but your messages will always filter through to some degree. If you don't believe in sex before marriage, or before a certain age, or without a suitable emotion involvement, then explain why. Kids are naive and often feel pressurised by their peers; they may need some excuses of their own. Give lots.

▷ Learn about contraception, including emergency contraception, and about condoms. Learn also about STDs – gonorrhoea, syphilis, herpes, genital warts and HIV – including the ways they are transmitted, symptoms, risks and treatment options. Facts never hurt.

▷ Listen carefully. When you understand your teen's values, you can ask questions that help the teen clarify how to act consistently with those values.

▷ Avoid assumptions. Do not assume that your teen knows everything he or she needs to know about contraception and condoms.

▷ Make sure your teen know about emergency contraception, which can be taken to prevent pregnancy up to 120 hours (5 days) after unprotected intercourse or when a contraceptive method fails.

▷ Discuss being 'swept away'. Many teens say they did not use condoms or contraception because they 'just got swept away'. Be clear that this is not OK. Anyone who is mature enough to have sexual intercourse is mature enough to use protection.

Should I purchase condoms for my son so that he is prepared?
If you are worried that he may be having sex and not using them, then why not? If you son seems to embarrassed to talk about it, put a packet in his wash bag or in his bathroom cupboard (away from the prying eyes of siblings). But don't get into the habit of supplying them. Birth control is a personal responsibility and your son should learn that he needs to shoulder it. Having said that, an emergency supply may make a difference.

How should I approach the subject of birth control?

Wait for an opportune moment – a story in the paper about teenage pregnancies, a chat about a boy or girlfriend, a story about sexually transmitted diseases (STDs), for example. When you first broach the subject of sex with your child, it's worth offering the basics about birth control. Ask opinions, give some facts and insight from your point of view, and use the opportunity to express your values. Clearly, there is some sense in first discussing this when you have the birds-and-bees chat – which could happen when your child is eight or nine (for girls, it should be well before menstruation). Many kids are shocked or disgusted by the whole idea, so it's worth taking it gradually. Ask your child to come back to you if he or she has any questions, or just casually bring it up in informal conversations – adding more as you go on. Don't go in with all guns blazing, and do treat disgust with gentle reassurance – many children become phobic of sexual encounters well into adult life because they've been educated by a heavy hand and made to feel guilty or wrong before they've even started. Ultimately, you don't want a child who feels uncomfortable about birth control; better that your child is used to the idea, knows what to do and feels confident enough to purchase what he or she needs as a part of normal life. Kids have sex – that's a given. If you lecture too much about what your child should or shouldn't be doing, he or she may be distracted from the important things, which are to protect themselves from pregnancy or STDs, and also to wait until the time is right. Be casual.

When should I ask my child about his or her birth control plans?

If you have any reason to believe your child is having sex, then you must ask – gently and reassuringly. When you give 'the talk' you must also express support about using birth control and make it clear that you would like to be involved in the decision. There are many sorts of birth control available – some more effective than others, and some with health risks. Disapproving parents can alienate kids, which leaves them open to making decisions without any guidance. As much as you may disapprove, it's important to support when things do happen. In a nutshell, you should ask your children about their birth control plans as soon as they mention anyone else having sex, or discuss it themselves, have a boyfriend or girlfriend, or spend a lot of time in mixed company. Use your judgement.

Is emergency contraception safe for my daughter?

It's as safe as long-term methods such as the pill, although there can be side effects such as nausea, vomiting, headaches, breast tenderness, dizziness, fluid retention and irregular bleeding. These side effects usually disappear after a couple of days. Emergency contraception works by giving the body a short, high dose of synthetic hormones. This disrupts hormone patterns needed for pregnancy. It also disturbs the ovaries and the development of the uterine lining, making pregnancy less likely. Emergency contraception is used within 120 hours (five days) after intercourse. It is most effective within the first 24 hours. Emergency contraception reduces the risk of pregnancy by 75 per cent. It does not, however, protect against STDs, including HIV/AIDS.

Books

Should my child be allowed to read an adult book?

It does, of course, depend on the book. Some books written for adults do not touch on subject areas that may concern you, and may have little sex, violence or inappropriate language. So the first thing you need to do when your child shows interest in an adult book is to check out the publisher's website and read the reviews. You'll soon get a taste of the subject matter and style of writing – in some cases, the recommended age group (13+ for example). If you think the book is inappropriate, it *is* OK to dissuade your child from reading it. Advanced readers are not necessarily more mature than their less-able counterparts, and they could be introduced to things that will frighten or confuse them, or teach them things that they are simply not ready to learn. While every parent is pleased to have an avid reader on their hands, kids often need guidance to get their reading matter right.

Pat Scales, author of *Teaching Banned Books*, offers the following advice:

▷ Accentuate the positive. Never say 'no' exactly, as it can turn the book into forbidden treasure. Try 'that's a good book, but knowing you, you'd like this other one better'.
▷ Zero in on what he likes.
▷ Know the authors. Once your child finds a favourite author, she'll probably want to read every volume that writer ever penned.
▷ Offer to share. When your child insists on reading something that concerns you, consider this sneaky, but often effective tactic. Tell your child that you've been wanting to read that book, and so why don't you read it together. Most often, that will be a turn-off, and she'll move on to something else.

If all of this fails, you can simply say 'I'm sorry, I don't want you to read that book at your age,' and use the opportunity to discuss values and issues that the book covers. It may be that your child is readier than you think for this type of reading matter, and that the subjects covered are sensitively dealt with – more sensitively, perhaps, than the average soap or teen magazine.

For a good list of books appropriate for each age group, and details of research into literacy and reading, visit www.literacytrust.org.uk.

When should I stop choosing books for my children?

Earlier we discussed research showing that reading rates fall dramatically once children begin to read independently, hitting a low in the twelve to seventeen age group (*see page 59*). Interestingly, only 64 per cent of parents think it is 'very important' for fifteen- to seventeen-year-old children to read, compared with 87 per cent who say the same for five- to eight-year-olds. This thinking is reflected in the fact that parents stop purchasing, choosing or suggesting books for older children, and expect them to find things that interest them on their own.

Lisa Holton, president of Scholastic Book Fairs and Trade Publishing, who led recent research, says, 'We found that not only do parents need to be reading role models, but that they must play a key role in helping their older children select books that capture their imagination and interest.'

How can I encourage my children to read more appropriate books?

First of all, question your use of the word 'appropriate'. They may not be the type of books that interested you as a child, and they may address modern issues that can be distressing or challenging, but this is not necessarily 'inappropriate'. Consider what you *don't* want your child coming up against just yet – explicit sex, violence, swearing, whatever – and discuss your reasons why these are important to you. Pre-teens and teens often make sense of their world by reading about the same things that puzzle or concern them in daily life – girls may, for example, be toying with the idea of having their first sexual encounter and develop a voracious appetite for books about teenage pregnancy, young love and sex. This is not wrong or inappropriate, and if the book is reasonably well written, she can sort through her feelings as she reads. Similarly, you aren't necessarily producing a mass-murderer if your son shows an interest in books about terrorism or extremist thought – he may just be putting recent threats into context. Autobiographies of stars and athletes are often popular with boys, and tend to be 'no-holds barred' – frankly, your child will be reading nothing worse than what he reads in the papers or sees on television. If the subject interests him, gets him reading and encourages him to read more, then it may not be inappropriate after all.

In terms of encouraging wider choice, get to know their interests and tastes; buy books by authors they previously enjoyed, and on subjects you know will hook them. Go through the bestseller lists together or read the reviews, and pick out things that sound fun. Some of your old favourites might hit the right note, but don't count on it!

How can I encourage my child to read more?

Try some of the following tips:

▷ Learn more about your child's interests and suggest books, magazines and articles that relate to those topics. Clip things out of the paper that might interest him, including reviews or discussions of books that may appeal.

▷ Sometimes films are a good starting point for pleasure reading – after seeing the film, he or she may be motivated to read the book. Next time, your child may wish to read a book *before* seeing a film.

▷ Travel can spark reading – finding books that relate to a place you visit on a family holiday or that provide background information to historical places of interest can be a good starting point. For example, if you've recently visited a war museum or a battle site, a war history book, such as *Private Peaceful* by Michael Morpurgo, might catch their fancy.

▷ Keep plenty of books and other reading materials at home. If the TV isn't a constant feature, your child is more likely to pick up a book or magazine. Check to see what disappears for a clue as to what interests your teenager.

▷ Read books with your children! Children of any age can appreciate being read to (*see page 59*).

▷ Be a good role model – let your children see you reading.

▷ Give them an opportunity to choose their own books. When you and your children are out together, browse in a bookshop or library. Go your separate ways and make your own selections. Book tokens may encourage them to make their own choices, too.

▷ Build on your child's interests. Look for books and articles that feature their favourite sports teams, rock stars, hobbies or TV shows. Give a subscription to a special interest magazine.

▷ Don't sniff at reading only the sports section, Teletext, internet sites or comics – anything that gets them reading is good news, and provides a springboard for further reading.

▷ Acknowledge your child's maturing interests and tastes. Look for ways to recognise the emerging adult by suggesting some adult reading you think he or she can handle.

What is an appropriate reading level for each age?

All children read at different stages and ages, and although there is a template for how reading develops, the ages at which kids reach each level can differ wildly. Children with learning difficulties may never appear to match the levels achieved by other children in their class, while avid readers may fly ahead, leaving their classmates far behind.

In a nutshell, your child's teacher can and should tell you if your child is not reading to an appropriate standard. The Department for Education and Skills has produced lists of words that children should be able to read, depending on what school year they are in. These are part of the framework for literacy teaching, and can be found at www.standards.dfes.gov.uk. If you are concerned, try these out.

The Reading Foundation provides information on the stages of language and reading development, and offers tips for improvement at each stage. If you are worried that your child isn't reading to an appropriate level, this can be invaluable information. Visit www.thereadingfoundation.com/stages.

Finally, purchase a few books targeted at your child's age – books that will interest him, of course – and test them out. If he's eleven years old, books that fall within the nine to thirteen years banding may be a little challenging, but he should get through them without too much effort. If he's fourteen and struggling with 'young adult titles' move him back to an earlier age group and see how he fares. A year or two out of the reading age target is of no real concern, but if that same 14-year-old is more confident with the books in the ages six to eight year grouping, you might want to get him some extra help.

Bras

At what age should my daughter start to wear a bra?
Breasts can begin growing as early as eight years of age, and they don't normally stop until the early twenties. Many girls are

resistant to wearing bras for a variety of reasons, including fearing the transition to adulthood, being self-conscious (particularly if they develop earlier than their peers) and even feeling dismayed about the changes to their body. Many girls want a bra when nipples become more noticeable, as it can provide extra coverage. It's probably best to leave the decision to your daughter; when her friends start wearing bras, she will too. No damage will be done by having unsupported breasts in her early teens. You may want to suggest a sports bra with a less traditional back and straps, or a tank top with a 'breast shelf' or 'invisible support' in the interim.

If, however, your daughter's breasts are very well developed, and she is still resistant well into the teenaged years, you may wish to have a relaxing day out together and hit the lingerie department en route. Let her choose what she wants and play down the fact that you think it's time.

If my daughter is resistant to wearing a bra, when should I ensure she does?

Once a girl has developed breasts (that is, not only the nipple has emerged), a bra is a good idea, especially when the girl is exercising and playing sports. Bras can protect breast tissue and keep the breasts supported. Some girls may also like bras that smooth out their silhouettes and make them feel more comfortable. A bra can make a girl feel less exposed when she's wearing a light shirt.

Some girls look forward to getting their first bras, but others dread that event. Like anything new, wearing a bra can be tough to adjust to. As most women know, they can be tricky to undo and adjust, and they can be very uncomfortable if they are incorrectly fitted. They are also clear evidence that puberty has arrived – some girls actually wear several layers of undergarments or clothing to disguise this fact rather than protect their 'assets' with a bra.

The secret is to get the right size so that your child feels comfortable and supported. A sports bra is less obvious than some types and can be played down as a type of tank top or sportswear. Indeed, many cropped tops now come with supportive layers, so this may suffice until she feels ready for the real thing.

Take your daughter shopping, but without pressure. Find some attractive matching sets in a style she likes, and give her some freedom to choose. Choose a few things yourself to make the visit to the lingerie department a little less obvious. You can use the opportunity to discuss how you felt about your first bra, and why wearing one is a good idea. She may confess her own feelings and concerns – in which case, leave it for a little while longer. If she's particularly self-conscious, leave a catalogue around and ask her to choose what she might like to order. This way she can test out a few things in the privacy of her bedroom, and perhaps feel less pressured.

If all else fails, pick up a few types of bra yourself and pop them in to her underwear drawer. Chances are they'll get an airing at some point.

Does my daughter need to wear a bra to bed?

A number of scare stories have suggested that bras (particularly when worn at night) can lead to breast cancer by obstructing the lymphatic system. Under-wired bras have been singled out as the main culprits, and these ill informed sources claim that bras squash the fine tubes of the lymphatic system. The idea is that this stops the normal drainage of the breast tissues, causing toxins to gather in the breast and resulting in cancer. Cancer researchers have resoundingly rejected this theory. However, one 1993 study did show that women who wore bras to bed were 125 times more likely to get breast cancer than non-bra-wearers, and 113 times more likely than women who wear a bra for less than twelve hours a day.

Ask your daughter why she wants to wear a bra to bed; she may be self-conscious and wish to cover up or may believe she needs to be 'supported' even while sleeping. Although the health risks are inconclusive, it is probably a good idea to avoid wearing a bra at night. Explain why.

At what age is it appropriate for my daughter to choose and wear a bra that I consider overly sexy?

You may wish to evaluate what you consider to be 'overly sexy'. Frankly, girls go out on the streets wearing what appears to be little more than a pair of knickers and a skimpy bra-top, and this is clearly an acceptable fashion at the moment. If your daughter shows interest in sexy bras at a young age, it may well be that she is trying to emulate older peers or role models such as models or singers (many of whom model or have their own lines of lingerie). If it's covered by clothing, there is probably no real need to worry. However, if your daughter shows an interest in sexy undergarments when she has a boyfriend, chances are she wants to show them off. This may be a good time for a talk about sex and relationships. Remember that even in a loving, healthy relationship, women (even young ones) like to *feel* sexy. It doesn't mean they have become part-time prostitutes or are on course to becoming a lap dancer. Talk about what you think is appropriate and why – but give yourself a crash course on what other kids are wearing before you do so. If you put her in white cotton knickers and a practical bra while the other girls in the changing room are in hot pink and lace, she may feel left out. This is not to say that peer pressure should dictate your choices, but it's easy to lose touch with genuine fashion trends as opposed to the whims of young girls. Times change and sexy doesn't necessarily mean promiscuous any longer.

Bullying

How do I know if my child is being bullied?

Many children are reluctant to confide in their families when they have been the victim of bullies for various reasons: perhaps they don't want to disappoint parents; they are embarrassed and ashamed; they don't want their parents barging in, potentially making matters worse; or perhaps they haven't actually accepted the situation themselves. It is crucial that parents look out for signs that bullying may be taking place. Different types of bullying have different key signs (for example, if your daughter is suddenly phobic of or obsessed by her mobile telephone, cyber-bullying could be at the root of the problem). Generally, however, look out for the following:

▷ Reluctant to go to school.
▷ Complains of feeling sick; frequently visits the infirmary or nurse at school.
▷ Sudden drop in grades.
▷ Comes home hungry (because bullies have stolen lunch or lunch money).
▷ Frequently arrives home with clothing or possessions destroyed or missing.
▷ Experiences nightmares, bedwetting, sleeping difficulties.
▷ Acts afraid of meeting new people, trying new things or exploring new places.
▷ Refuses to leave the house.
▷ Waits to get home to use the toilet.
▷ Acts nervous when another child approaches.
▷ Shows increased anger or resentment with no obvious cause.
▷ Makes remarks about feeling lonely.

▷ Has difficulty making friends.

▷ Reluctant to defend himself when teased or criticised by others.

▷ Shows a dramatic change in style of dress.

▷ Has physical marks – bruises or cuts – which may have been inflicted by others or by himself.

What are the early warning signs for each age?

Primary school

▷ Regressive behaviour, such as thumb-sucking, talking in a baby voice, clinginess, temper tantrums or bedwetting.

▷ Leaves school with torn or disordered clothing and/or damaged books.

▷ Has bruises, injuries, cuts and scratches that are not easily explained.

▷ Says they 'hate' a particular person, but won't elaborate on why.

▷ Fewer play-dates or invitations.

▷ Embarrassment about things, such as clothing, appearance or material possessions, which have never been a feature before.

▷ Uses words that are age-inappropriate, and often with intent to hurt.

▷ Becomes more violent against siblings, parents or friends, without real reason.

Secondary school

▷ Does not bring classmates or peers home after school and seldom spends time in the homes of classmates.

▷ May not have a single good friend to share free time with (play, shopping, sports and musical events, chatting on the phone).

▷ Is seldom or never invited to parties and may not be interested in arranging parties (because he or she expects that nobody wants to come).

▷ Does not participate in extracurricular activities such as school clubs.

▷ Chooses an illogical route for going to and from school.

▷ Loses interest in school work.

▷ Appears unhappy, sad, depressed or shows unexpected mood shifts with irritability and sudden outbursts of temper.

▷ Requests or steals extra money from family (to accommodate the demands of bullies).

▷ Becomes obsessed with a mobile phone and reluctant to explain persistent calls or texts.

▷ Becomes increasingly sensitive about or obsessed with physical features, weight, clothing, etc.

▷ Begins to bully other family members for no obvious reason.

▷ Becomes highly critical of activities and people she used to enjoy.

How do I know if my child is bullying others?

Most parents are horrified to discover that their child is bullying others, and can actively avoid acknowledging the signs. It's important to be honest with yourself. Any of the following may suggest that your child is involved in bullying behaviour:

▷ Your child is accused of bullying at school or elsewhere.

▷ Has been in trouble for fighting (physical or emotional/verbal fighting is equally relevant).

▷ Has an excuse or 'reason' for any reports of bullying such as: denial, playing it down – 'I was just messing around'; blame – 'he started it'; or defence – 'he was looking for trouble'; or 'he went completely mad on us'.

▷ Turns the tables and says that someone else has been bullying her, when there is clear evidence to the contrary.

▷ Relies on the evidence of his friends or other witnesses to defend him. In other words, could it be that his henchmen are doing their job.

▷ Seems to have more money than he should.

▷ Comes home with items that do not belong to her.

▷ Claims she doesn't need a lunch because she'll 'get something at school'.

▷ Is quick to anger and bullies younger siblings.

▷ Is secretive about mobile phone and computer use.

At what age do children grow out of bullying?

The good news is that bullying does appear to decline as children get older; however, some experts are concerned that it merely changes shape rather than disappears entirely. And many of these changed forms of bullying are unreported – the older the child, the more embarrassing the problem and hence it is less likely to be reported. Bullies have average social popularity up to about fourteen or fifteen years old. In fact, some children even look up to bullies in some ways because they are powerful and do what they want to, or have to, to get their way with peers. However, by late adolescence, the bully's popularity begins to wane. By secondary school, if a bully is still attending school, his or her peer group includes other bullies, or more seriously, he or she has developed or is developing gang alliances.

Studies show that victimisation decreases across year levels: 26 per cent of children in the early primary years report bullying compared to 15 per cent of children in the later years of primary school. At ages eleven to twelve about 12 per cent of children appear to be bullied. Children in lower years are more likely to be victims of older bullies, whereas children in higher years are more likely to be victims of same-age bullies. Younger students experience more direct bullying (name-calling, violence), whereas older students experience more indirect bullying (social exclusion, for example).

By late secondary school, regular bullying incidents are often a thing of the past, but all victims know who the bullies are, and avoid them. By around sixteen or seventeen, bullies and victims are usually moving in different directions in terms of curricular interests in school, therefore their paths rarely cross. Social groupings are clearly defined by this time in a student's life and invisible boundaries have been drawn.

Not surprisingly, in secondary school, bullying behaviour most frequently involves teasing and social exclusion, but may also include physical violence, threats, theft, sexual and racial harassment, public humiliation and destruction of the targeted student's property. Bullying behaviour in primary years is more likely to involve physical aggression, but is also characterised by teasing, intimidation and social exclusion.

Can I go over my child's head to address the problem with her school?

It's always a good idea to involve your child – firstly because if she has been victimised in the past, she may already be feeling powerless. If you step in and 'take over' you are compounding this feeling. In reality, she needs to learn to stand up for herself and to deal with the problems she is experiencing. It's a good idea to speak frankly with your child, showing support for how she is feeling, and asking her to keep a log of incidents, including times and witnesses, in order to support her case. Make sure she understands that 'telling' isn't 'snitching' or being cowardly, and that it can help to protect other children from bullies. Offer to help her to report the incidents, and to become involved at whatever level she feels comfortable. All schools must have an anti-bullying policy and a procedure for reporting. Your daughter should have a first port of call, and she should be aware of what this is. If she gets nowhere, you can then help her to take the problem to the school head, supporting her efforts. If she refuses to do anything and you fear for her health, safety or well-being, then you have a duty of care to go above her head, but tell her that you are doing so and why.

Can I condone violence as retribution for bullying or in self-defence?

No, encouraging violence only feeds violent behaviour, which is exactly what you are trying to protect your child from in the first place. All children need to deal with problems in a non-violent way – they can't, for example, lash out at their boss or a neighbour in later life when they feel bullied or threatened. They must learn to problem-solve effectively, and violence has no part in this. Having said that, children who are regularly bullied may find some confidence in the belief that they can protect themselves through self-defence training. The idea is not that it will be used in a violent way – and certainly not without provocation – but knowing that he can protect himself will make a child less likely to take on victim status, that is, appear to be a good target.

What can I do about my child being bullied?

One of the greatest preventative measures that you can undertake is to give your child the tools and skills to deal with bullying situations when they arise. You may have a child who has never been bullied, and has only been affected as a witness. But regardless of their status, all children need to know how to deal with bullies, as the problem is so pervasive, everyone is bound to be affected at some stage of their lives. So apart from working on self-respect, resilience and your home life, as well as encouraging social skills, problem-solving and friendships, your child will need to know how to deal with bullies *practically*.

What can I teach my child to help with bullying?

▷ Learn to control your anger. No child will fail to become upset and angry when they are victimised, but responding is exactly what a bully wants and expects. If you become cool and calm, failing to rise to the bait, the bully has effectively lost, because he cannot 'control' you or your emotions.

▷ Never use physical force, no matter how often or directly it has been used against you. A bully is a dangerous commodity and you may end up in serious trouble or physical threat. What's more, violence is an 'anger' response, and once again, it's important never to show anger.

▷ Stand up tall, act brave even when you don't feel it and walk away. Ignoring a bully is a difficult feat, particularly when they push all the buttons to upset you; it may also anger a bully to the point of fury, because they fail to get a response. But if you walk away with your head held high, you are sending the message that you won't be intimidated.

▷ It sounds crazy, but try to make the bully your friend. This technique will obviously work better for younger kids (and parents take note: if your child is being bullied by one person, invite him round to play, but keep close supervision).

▷ If you want to talk back, keep your voice level and calm and look the bully right in the eye when you speak. Use 'I' statements, which are indisputable: 'I want you to stop that right now.' Or 'I do not like being treated that way.' Don't wait for a response. Walk away and ignore further efforts to hurt you.

▷ Employ some humour. Sometimes the best way to diffuse an upsetting or dangerous situation is to be funny. Not only will it be something the bully isn't expecting, but it will help you to look clever and in control and unconcerned. So make a joke about something irrelevant.

▷ Always tell an adult. Many victims are terrified of confiding for fear of being ignored, belittled or even blamed. There is a certain loss of face and pride that accompanies being bullied. But no child should have to deal with bullies on his own, and keeping quiet will not ease the situation. In fact, if the bully finds he can get away with it, he'll likely continue the behaviour. The message, again, is, tell an adult, someone you trust, whether it is a parent, a teacher or someone on lunchroom duty. It's not telling tales to protect yourself (and possibly others) from dangerous children.

▷ Don't keep quiet. Dealing with bullying alone can be soul-destroying and undermine all of your confidence. Choose a teacher, a friend, a sibling or counsellor, anyone who can give you the support you need. There is no shame in being bullied. It is never your fault.

▷ Always support your peers against bullying. You may be relieved that it's not you who has been targeted and simply want to keep your head down, but if children support one another, bullying will be eradicated. No doubt about it. A bully wants to feel recognised and powerful, particularly in front of his peers. If those peers stand up to him and say: 'Hey, that's not fair' or 'I don't like what you are doing.' or even just leave him alone, he loses his audience and his adulation.

▷ Create a buddy system, which involves choosing one or more friends to accompany you in areas where bullying is likely to occur – on the way to school, in the lunchroom or the washrooms, in the playground or even at the bus-stop, and offer the same in return. Bullies are less likely to target kids who are in a group.

▷ Consider some self-defence training or taking up a martial art. Though you will not ever want to respond with violence, knowing

that you can protect yourself will make you more confident.
And a confident child is less likely to become a bully's target.

▷ Avoid isolated places whenever possible.

▷ Don't automatically comply with a bully's requests (for money
or anything else). If you give in, you'll set yourself up for the
situation to recur. Better to walk (or even run) away.

▷ Keep a detailed record or diary of any bullying that occurs. If a
time comes when you need to report the incidents, you will have
all of the key facts to hand.

▷ Try not to cry. Although many types of bullying can be
enormously painful, including name-calling and social
exclusion, all bullies want a reaction, and if you give them one
they will continue. Stay calm and ignore them while maintaining
a confident body language. Anxiety or distress will feed the
bully's need for power.

▷ Remember that choosing a different route to school or avoiding
bullies in the halls or the playground is only a short-term
measure. If they want to get you, they will. What you need to do
is to work on being more confident, making supportive friends
and finding ways to deal with the bullies themselves.

What should I do if my child is a bully?

If you have reason to believe that your child has been bullying
others, going in with the sledge-hammer approach will only raise
his hackles and encourage further and even more elaborate
defences and lies. Many children feel guilty about bullying; others
have a defence facility that allows them to either justify it or
subconsciously deny it. Some children know instinctively that you
will not react well to hearing the truth about their actions and will
use every ploy imaginable to ensure that you never find out; still
others will be as subversive as they are at school and play the

innocent because they genuinely believe that they are blameless. Whatever the case, tread lightly. If you show immediate anger or disapproval, you will never get anywhere and will lose the opportunity both to right the wrong and to prevent the behaviour from recurring. Moreover, you will lose the opportunity to teach a lesson presenting the empathetic and moral standpoint, explaining and reassuring, and, most importantly, of working out the factors that have caused your child to behave the way he has.

Are there strategies for dealing with bullying?

▷ Experts recommend that parents and teachers take a hard-line approach to childhood aggression. Adults must make it clear that aggressive behaviour in school, in the neighbourhood or at home is not acceptable and will not be tolerated. Children should be encouraged to report aggression and threats. Parents and school staff must deal with these incidents seriously. When aggression is tolerated, everyone loses – the bullies, the victims and the bystanders. They are all learning that violence is acceptable and this is not the lesson we want to teach our children.

▷ Be sure to express strong disapproval of bullying when it occurs or comes up in conversation. Be sure students know that you don't condone any kind of harassment or mistreatment of others, whether it be teasing, social exclusion or physical violence. Teachers should, as much as possible, reassure students that the classroom is a safe and supportive place.

▷ Avoid physical forms of discipline. Hitting children when they misbehave simply reinforces the belief that 'might makes right' and that violence and intimidation are appropriate ways to get what you want. Whenever possible, model non-violent means of resolving conflicts (*see page 83*).

▷ Parents AND teachers would benefit by keeping a log of bullying incidents, including who was involved, when it occurred, how often it occurred, how often and what strategies were used to address it. Over time, this log will help to identify any patterns in bullying behaviour, as well as what kind of interventions worked best to stop it. Teachers may discover that more bullying takes place around exam time, when the students are stressed or when they haven't had any physical outlet for a week; they may discover the same culprit stirring things up over and over again. Parents will have to rely on the honesty of a child as well as the support of the school in order to complete a log with any success, but it can help you to keep tabs on your child's behaviour, work out when he's most difficult, what the catalysts might be and which methods of dealing with the problem at home are actually having some effect.

▷ Make sure your discipline system in the home is consistent, with praise and reinforcement for good behaviour, and fair penalties (never violent) for violation.

▷ Build on your child's talents and help him or her develop less aggressive and more appropriate reaction behaviours.

▷ Maintain contact with your child's school. Support the school's efforts to modify your child's behaviour. Enlist help from the school to try and modify your child's behaviour.

▷ Although certainly not all bullying stems from family problems, it's a good idea to examine the behaviour and personal interactions your child witnesses at home. If your child lives with taunting or name-calling from a sibling or from you or another parent, it could be prompting aggressive or hurtful behaviour outside the home. What may seem like innocent teasing at home may actually model bullying behaviours. Children who are on the receiving end of it learn that bullying can translate into control over children they perceive as weak.

▷ Constant teasing – whether it's at home or at school – can also affect a child's self-esteem. Children with low self-esteem can grow to feel emotionally insecure. They can also end up blaming others for their own shortcomings. Making others feel bad (bullying) can give them a sense of power.

▷ Emphasise that bullying is a serious problem. Make sure your child understands you will not tolerate bullying and that bullying others will have consequences at home. For example, if your child is cyber-bullying, take away the technologies he or she is using to torment others (computer, mobile phone). Or instruct your child to use the internet to research bullying and note strategies to reduce the behaviour. Other examples of disciplinary action include restricting your child's curfew if the bullying and/or teasing occur outside of the home; taking away privileges, but allowing the opportunity to earn them back; and requiring your child to do volunteer work to help those less fortunate.

▷ Teach your child to treat people who are different with respect and kindness. Teach your child to celebrate and *understand* differences such as race, religion, appearance, special needs, class, sexuality. Every child needs to learn that all people have rights and feelings. Teach a little history – show how oppression has affected countries around the world (parts of Africa, for example) and how intolerance has led to wars and horrific crimes against humanity (the Holocaust, for example). Sometimes children need to learn that intolerance and disrespect have very serious consequences.

▷ Find out if your child's friends are also bullying. If so, seek a group intervention through your child's school.

▷ Observe your child interacting with others and praise appropriate behaviour. Positive reinforcement is more powerful than negative discipline.

▷ Be prepared to talk to your child's school about how it can help your child to modify his behaviour. The school may have some excellent ideas that are in line with its anti-bullying policy, which will be backed up by other pupils and staff members.

▷ It can be very upsetting to have to admit that your child is a bully, but if you show humility and a willingness to set things right – perhaps by explaining problems your child may have experienced outside the school gates that may have contributed to his attitude and behaviour – you are likely to receive the support you need. Keep in touch with the school so that you can monitor and report, and it can do the same.

▷ Bullying expert Tim Field thinks that, 'School environments tend to be one of "exclusion" rather than "inclusion". Children are left to form their own groups, or gangs, and you are either "in" or "out". I believe children should be taught at the outset to show dignity and respect to other children regardless of whether they are "in" or "out", and to be proactive in their relationships to other children, especially those who "do not fit in", for whatever reason.'

▷ Remember to keep your cool. If you become angry, you will get nowhere, either with your child or the school. Your child will not confide in you and you'll never come to terms with the causative factors without appropriate communication. Show patience and unconditional love at all times; make it clear that you still love your child, even though his behaviour is *not* loveable.

▷ Bear in mind that your child is very likely to deny any wrong doing, and/or minimise his involvement. It's a natural reaction and you will need to be patient and persistent to get past this.

▷ If your child has been involved in extortion, ask yourself some questions about his material status – if he doesn't have *anything* that his peers have, he may be stealing to keep up with the crowd; if he doesn't have a lunch made for him or any lunch money offered, he may be hungry and angry about his position and take it out on others. If he doesn't have an appropriate amount of pocket money for his age and is therefore unable to keep up with normal social requirements, he may resort to stealing. Be realistic, and ask some questions of your child and the parents of your child's peers.

▷ Increase your supervision of your child's activities and whereabouts, and with whom they are associating. Spend time with your child and set reasonable rules for their activities and curfews.

▷ If your child is viewing violent television shows, including cartoons, and is playing violent video games, this will increase violent and aggressive behaviour. Change the family and child's viewing and play patterns to non-violent ones.

▷ Make sure that your child is not seeing violence between members of his or her family. Modelling of aggressive behaviour at home can lead to violence by the child against others at school and in later life.

▷ About one per cent of all bullies have a serious sadistic nature, in that they enjoy the pain of others. Such children tend to be rather unfeeling when they bully and are not anxious nor is their self-esteem low. Such children often have serious problems with criminal behaviour later and can become quite abusive. If you think your child may have sociopathic tendencies, ask your GP to refer you for counselling. He may genuinely need help.

▷ Parents may inadvertently support bullying by accepting it as just a normal part of growing up and leaving children to solve their own problems. Don't make that mistake. Bullying is wrong; this message needs to be repeated and reinforced in your home, and guidance needs to be offered at all stages and ages.

▷ Find out exactly what it is that your child has been doing. What has your child been accused of doing? What does he admit to doing?

▷ Ensure appropriate adult supervision at all times. Be aware of your child's involvement in activities inside and outside of school. Make certain that adequate adult supervision is present in every situation.

▷ Report any incidents of bullying behaviours to school officials, even if your child is the one engaging in those behaviours. This will teach your child that he or she is accountable for his or her behaviour. Engage school officials' help in monitoring and addressing these behaviours. This will show your child that you will not tolerate such behaviour and that you want to help your child avoid it.

▷ You need to give them some feedback, make them accountable for their behaviour and help them accept responsibility for it. You will need to raise their understanding of how they made it happen and enable them to look at the impact of their behaviour. Help them plan not to do it again, identify the situations to avoid and suggest alternatives to bullying.

▷ Try to avoid threats and warnings which will shut your child up. You need to get cooperation without building resentment. Concentrate on passing on responsibility not blame, focus on the behaviour not the child, solutions rather than problems. Don't bully your child.

▷ Make it very clear that it is OK to stick up for yourself, but that bullying is not acceptable.

▷ Assess what your child does and what he gets from it; what need is the bullying fulfilling in his life?

▷ Try very hard to see your child's point of view. It may be a complete anathema to side with a bully, but you need to understand in order to get anywhere. There may be genuine reasons for his behaviour.

▷ Encourage your child to see the victim's point of view, and to try to make up for his behaviour in some way. Ask him to think of a way he can make amends to the victim, perhaps by apologising. Perhaps if the victim is timid and shy he can befriend that child and be protective towards him or her.

▷ Look at yourself, too. Make sure that you never, ever blame a bullied child or show any type of bullying behaviour yourself (such as using sarcasm, joining in with teasing or name-calling as a joke). Avoid having favourites within your family unit, and do not embarrass or humiliate your child in front of others. Most importantly, perhaps, have a reasonable and rational approach to the problem – don't ever tell your kids not to tell tales or not to get involved. All kids face bullying today, whether as bully, victim or bystander, and they need to know that they have rights and the ability to get some help.

▷ Offer to talk to the victim's parents and to school staff, if the bullying has been happening at school. But do not defend him. Even if he was not the ringleader, the fault is still his. If you do determine that your child is using controlling, aggressive behaviour, experts agree that the responsibility lies first with you to teach your child non-coercive ways to negotiate.

▷ Maintaining a set family communication time – usually dinner time – is critical, Marsh says. Deliberately pose a question to the aggressive child or all the children in the family, and then give each one an opportunity to respond without interruption and without judgement. 'This is much better than dealing with this problem by jumping on the kid and saying, "What did you do today? That was terrible! You should know better! We've taught you for years".'

▷ If your child is very young, read aloud books about bullies. Let him or her take care of a pet. Invite other children over to your house and monitor them. Let them play in a non-competitive way.

▷ Enrol an older child into groups that encourage cooperation and friendship, such as social groups or Scouts. Have him or her volunteer to learn the joy of helping others.

▷ Remember: you are not alone. Other parents have had this problem and fixed it. One parent said the best thing that ever happened in their son's life was when he changed from being a bully into a compassionate human being.

Calculators

Should my child be encouraged to use a calculator for maths homework?

Many parents are unsure of what is acceptable practice and what is encouraged by the school. Your child may be completing homework in record time by using a calculator for what was intended to be mental maths homework, or he may genuinely be following instructions. Calculators form a part of most maths teaching these days (*see below*), and their use is often condoned and indeed encouraged. If in doubt, ask your child's teacher for clarification of policy regarding their use.

At what age should children use calculators instead of mental or written arithmetic?

This is a good question and one that is at the centre of much controversy. In Britain, a report commissioned by the government discourages the use of calculators in mathematics instruction for children through to the age of eleven. In fact, the final report, in response to widespread criticism, does ameliorate this advice, but still espouses little or no use of calculators until the later years of primary school.

Educators, apart from those teaching maths, appear very reluctant to encourage young children to use calculators, supporting a 'back to basics' approach. Strangely, though, computer use is encouraged, which seems rather contradictory. Calculators are always used in professional settings, just as computers are, and there is unlikely to be any assertion that the users are somehow less able because they are not working out figures with a pencil and paper. A strong body of research suggests that using pencil-and-paper methods alongside teaching the appropriate use of a calculator, is the most effective way to teach maths to children of all ages. After all, a child must know *how* to work out a problem or a function before it can be undertaken on a calculator, which means that the calculator is just a tool to gain a result rather than a replacement for knowledge. It's also a good tool for checking mental arithmetic or pencil-and-paper work for accuracy.

If calculators are used by your child's school as part of maths study, you are within your rights to question the theory behind their use, and when they should be used. But rest assured that most research points to the idea that calculators can enhance an understanding of maths rather than undermine it. There is an excellent (if long) article in defence of calculators at www.doc.ic.ac.uk/~ar9/abolpub.

Cars

When can my son learn to drive?

Your son can learn to drive when he is seventeen and in possession of a provisional driving licence. He will have to be accompanied by a licenced driver over the age of eighteen until he passes his driving test, after which he can drive alone legally.

Driving ages vary around the world, ranging from seventeen to eighteen in most European countries (sixteen on the Isle of Man), to sixteen in Canada, fifteen in New Zealand and South Africa, and even fourteen for learners in some states in the US (although you normally have to be sixteen to pass a driving test and get a full licence).

Your child can use an electrically assisted pedal cycle at fourteen, and drive a moped, a small agricultural tractor or a small mowing machine at sixteen. Disabled teenagers can often be allowed to drive at age sixteen, rather than waiting until seventeen.

My daughter falls below the height restrictions for doing without a car booster seat. Does she need to use one?

You are referring to a new UK law, which applies to children over the age of three and up to either 1.35 m (4 ft 6 in) in height or the age of twelve. So if your daughter is eleven and small for her age (under the requisite height), she will need to use a car booster seat. Not surprisingly, this may be a huge source of embarrassment to her. You may help to ease the blow by covering a regulation booster seat with a trendy fabric, applying stickers or even hiding it beneath a car blanket. Explain the reasons for the law (safety, obviously), and that you are powerless to do much about it. Encourage her to say that she feels more comfortable being higher up and that the seat belt fits better. In other words, give her lots of comeback if she feels that she might be teased.

When should I allow my son to drive on his own after getting his licence?

Legally, he can start the moment he gets his licence, whether you approve or not. You can, however, help to make sure that he develops safe and responsible driving skills. First of all, don't palm off all the driving lessons on to a professional. Get involved as much as you can, even if it causes your hair to turn white! What's more, when your child is a passenger in your car, drive safely and carefully, and point out why you do things a certain way.

▷ Children often copy parental driving habits. If you don't obey traffic laws, wear your seat belt, keep your cool in traffic, drive within speed limits or stay off your mobile phone when behind the wheel, they won't either.

▷ Teach your child about driving and the technology behind it. Show him the proper sitting distance from a steering wheel or an airbag. Point out what to look for – traffic signs, bad drivers, emergencies and more, as you drive with him.

▷ Give your teen as much supervised practice as possible on different types of roads, in all weather conditions and in all kinds of driving conditions, even after your teen receives a licence. The more supervised practice he gets, the less likely he is to be involved in an accident.

▷ If your child is using the family car, you can certainly set some limitations (no motorway or night-time driving for a few months; *see page 97*), and no giving lifts to scores of friends, who can be a great distraction to a new driver. Say, perhaps, that you are happy for him to have some freedom in the car, but on condition that he drives with you occasionally to hone his skills. One study found that teens with lenient parental driving restrictions are likely to have more traffic violations and crashes. Make clear, too, your expectations – driving within the speed limit, within certain geographical distances, with no more than, say, two friends, at certain times of day, and never after drinking or taking drugs. Even one drink can blur the reactions of an inexperienced driver. They must be aware of this.

▷ Don't rush it. Many new drivers are nervous and require a bit more practice, even if they sailed through their tests. Parents often rush the licencing process for their teens to free up their own time and to encourage their teens to run errands for them. However, driver education alone does not give a young driver the necessary experience behind the wheel. Remember, inexperience is the number one contributing factor to unsafe and potentially hazardous driving situations.

When should I allow my son to drive on the motorway?

When your son passes his driving test and gets his full licence, he can drive on the motorway legally. There have been calls to make motorway driving and night driving (*see below*) a part of the examination process, as many new drivers have never experienced motorway driving before their first solo trip. In fact, learner drivers are not permitted to drive on the motorway, which seems rather self-defeating and dangerous.

It would be wise to have a few 'motorway' lessons with your new driver, with a little advance advice about speed, lane-changing, overtaking, using exits and slip roads, and then some practice time together. Agree on, say, four hours of supervised motorway driving before he does it on his own.

In Northern Ireland, once you have passed your driving test, you must display 'R' plates at the front and back of the vehicle for one year. You must not exceed the speed of 45 mph, which effectively rules out motorway driving. This seems abundantly sensible, and could be implemented on an informal basis in your own household.

Should I let my daughter drive alone at night when she's just got her licence?

Many novice drivers' accidents happen at night and it is possible to pass the driving test without ever having driven in the dark. New drivers should practise driving in the dark with parents in much the same way that they learn motorway driving (*see above*). Encourage your child's instructor to offer a few lessons at night, too, on a variety of different roads with different lighting. The more practice, the safer she'll be.

Can my child drive abroad?

If he has a full Great Britain (GB) or Northern Ireland driving licence, he can drive in any Economic European Area (EEA) country on this licence. An International Driving Permit is not required if he has a driving licence. If he wants to drive in a country outside the EEA, he may need to apply for an International Driving Permit (IDP). This will be issued if he has a full driving licence, and can be purchased from major post offices or through motoring organisations such as the AA or RAC.

How often should I let my child borrow my car?

This is an individual choice and must be negotiated on the basis of demand for the family car. While it may make sense for your child to get himself to and from various activities, thereby freeing up your time, if you find yourself stranded without transportation, it's bound to breed resentment. Sensible ground rules for driving the family car include paying for their own petrol, contributing to the insurance (which is bound to increase with a new driver) and always asking permission.

At what age can children sit in the front passenger seat?

Over the age of three and with the appropriate child restraints, any child can sit in the front passenger seat. New car seat regulations may mean that your child will need a booster seat if he's under twelve and/or small for his age. Anyone who sits in the front seat must wear a seat belt by law. It's worth remembering that airbags can cause injuries to younger children, so if there is room in the back seat, make that your first choice. Drivers are legally responsible for making sure that children under fourteen years use seat belts or child restraints.

Clothes

When should children be responsible for buying their own clothes?

It's a good idea to start young in terms of clothing purchases and to up the expectations slowly. First of all, if your child has trouble (like most children) sorting out the difference between 'wants' and 'needs', you can, early on, suggest that you will purchase the necessities (underwear, one or two serviceable pairs of shoes and basic required clothing for school and/or sports). If he claims he 'needs' something above and beyond the obvious necessities, you can suggest either that he saves or works to pay for it himself, or that you will go half-and-half. This soon sorts out what is important, as he's not going to pay up for something whimsical.

What about a clothing allowance?

In terms of having full control over clothing purchases, many parents give a clothing allowance from the age of about fourteen or fifteen. Parents still may purchase agreed necessities for school or sports, but everything else remains the child's responsibility. This teaches a number of lessons, such as budgeting and shopping for value. If your child blows her entire allowance on one item, she'll learn the hard way that she won't have money for other things she needs, including necessities. She will also have to learn to weigh up what she really needs – whether she wants three pairs of bargain jeans (lots of clothes) or one quite nice pair. Furthermore, if your child knows there is only so much to spend on clothes, she'll learn to hunt out bargains and become a more effective shopper.

That doesn't mean you have to leave your child floundering in the dark about shopping once he or she has been given this responsibility. Offer guidance wherever possible, without being overly critical. You may not particularly like what your child has purchased with his or her money, but as long as it falls within the boundaries of decency, you may just have to accept it as a means of self-expression. Talk to your child about his or her purchases – is it good quality? Did he or she spend too much? Is it good value for money? Offer guidance without criticism.

How should I help my child learn to shop effectively?

Encourage your child to try on clothing in his wardrobe before hitting the shops. Many kids forget about clothes buried at the back and replace them with almost identical items. Help him to make a list, so that he is aware of how far his money needs to stretch.

▷ Consider giving a clothing allowance on a seasonal basis, rather than monthly, so that he is encouraged to assess what he needs for different temperatures and activities.

▷ Try to be patient with mistakes – we've all bought something unsuitable and it's the only way to learn.

▷ Consider paying for, or at least splitting the cost of, larger items, such as coats or shoes, as these expensive purchases can wipe out a budget in one fell swoop.

What is a reasonable clothing allowance to give my child?

There is only one way to work this out. Sit down with your child and discuss what he or she needs for school, social activities, sports and anything else. Your interpretation of needs will undoubtedly vary considerably from your child's, so bear this in mind! Work out what you think you should pay for as a matter of course. The most important consideration, however, is your family budget. You can only give what you can afford. If you bargain-hunt for your children's clothing and purchase things in lower-priced venues, a clothing allowance should not be seen as a free ticket to designer ranges. Like you, your child will need to work within a budget, regardless of what his friends are given or get. Work out what you would normally spend, and use that as the basis for an agreement. You might want to add in a little extra so that he or she can afford the odd 'treat'. Ultimately, however, if your child wants more expensive clothing, outside your budget, he or she will have to find the means by which to earn some money.

The good news is that it is perfectly possible to get good-quality clothing at reasonable prices, if your child is prepared to invest the time in shopping sensibly. If he blows it all on a shirt from Prada, he can wear his old trainers and jeans for the rest of the season.

'You're not going out wearing that!' What if I don't think my child is suitably dressed?

It is not advisable to engage in clothing style wars. Children use clothing to present themselves to the world, to express their tastes and interests, to show their individuality. While you may not approve of various elements of the way he or she dresses, if it isn't completely unsuitable, it is better if you stay mum. Kids make fashion mistakes just like adults do, and we need to allow them the freedom to do so. If you come down hard on your child's personal

style, he'll be more likely to dig in his heels, and perhaps wear
something even more outlandish next time, just to test the
boundaries and your shock threshold.

Are there any boundaries?

That is not to say that you can't establish certain boundaries.
For example, clothing worn to school must follow the school dress
code, as should uniforms or kit required for various activities.
On weekends and in free time, your child can have the freedom to
choose what he or she likes, but make it clear when you think
something goes beyond the boundaries of good taste – revealing
breasts, for example, is not ideal for a young girl, nor is wearing
something that you think is derogatory towards other cultures,
too sexual in nature or promotes illegal activity such as drug-taking
(slogans on printed T-shirts, for example).

But make sure you are up on the trends. Flick through teen
magazines to see what kids are wearing and visit some shops to
see what's on sale. More importantly, look around. If 90 per cent
of the kids are wearing the same gear, chances are it's the current
trend, and therefore part of kid/street culture. There is absolutely
no point in denying your child clothing that is deemed acceptable
by the vast majority, but if it's rude, offensive or too revealing, you
are well within your rights to defend your position – on safety
grounds, of course!

All my child's friends wear designer clothes and we can't afford it. How can we get the message across?

This is a common battle in many households and it needs to be
addressed sooner rather than later. A discussion about family
finances and limited budgets is a good starting point. Furthermore,
explain your value system – that you may have chosen, for

example, to pay off your mortgage, have nice family holidays or pay for education rather than spend money on expensive clothing. In this way you can teach your child some important lessons about budgeting, and prioritising spending.

But if you can help it, don't say 'no' outright. A clothing allowance is always a good idea at around fourteen or fifteen (*see page 99*), and this will give your child the freedom to spend what he has on what he thinks he needs. He may feel that one expensive designer jacket is enough to keep up his street cred, and that he'd rather do without anything else in order to get it. That's his choice. As long as you stick to your guns about clothing purchases and what you are prepared to subsidise, he'll have to make choices and possibly learn the hard way.

What if I can't afford what he wants?

Kids who want things outside the family budget must be prepared to pay for them. So if his heart is set on a Ralph Lauren jumper, then suggest he earns the money to pay for it. He could help out a lot more around the house or do some of the niggling jobs that you never get round to (painting the windowsills outside the house, raking leaves, washing windows, even steam-cleaning the carpets). If he wants something enough he should be willing to work for it.

You may agree to pay for *one* item of designer clothing each season, within an agreed budget. Again, this teaches your child to prioritise and to make choices, while for your part shows willing and an understanding of his needs.

Be prepared for the 'it's not fair' argument. Kids are always resentful when others have more than they have, but it's one of life's hard lessons. We can't always get what we want and life is easier for some people. Point out what your child *does* have, such as loving parents, nice holidays, a comfortable home, whatever it takes. It's not an easy lesson to learn, but teaching these things early on is a good way to avoid your child becoming debt-ridden later on, and it also encourages an appreciation for what he does have.

What about sports equipment? The list of required items is longer than my arm and if he doesn't have what he needs, he won't be able to play.

Second-hand is always a good bet – talk to other parents with older children who may have equipment sitting at home. Read the papers or put an ad in one of the free papers to see if anyone has anything going. Look on the internet – sports manufacturers often go out of business or change their lines; you may be able to get good-quality merchandise at much lower prices. Ask your child to contribute. Spell out how much you can afford. If he's really keen, he can do some work in the neighbourhood, perhaps, even babysitting, to contribute to funds. Suggest setting up a swap shop at the sports facility where outgrown items are placed in a bank, and anyone can use them as long as they contribute something of equal value themselves. There are always options.

If nothing works and your child can't play because you cannot afford the equipment, some explaining will be necessary. This isn't easy or enjoyable, but it's undoubtedly true that one of life's lessons is learning that we can't always undertake activities outside our budget, and that money only goes so far. It's tough, but it's the way of the world.

Should I allow my child to borrow my clothes?

The line between adult and children's clothes has been substantially blurred over the past decade, and many parents wear the same types of clothing as their children (although in the latter case, it might be the more expensive version). If the clothing is age-appropriate, then by all means do so. This is, however, one situation where you can set down some clear rules (which may also encourage your child to take some responsibility for belongings). For example, if it's a dry-clean only garment, and it becomes dirty or marked, your child is responsible for the cleaning bill. If she loses or damages it, she is responsible for its replacement (within reason). One loan does not mean open access to your wardrobe, and it should be stressed that permission must be requested for any and everything that is borrowed. You would like it returned after use, on a hanger (or in the drawer) and any spots or stains pointed out. Obviously, you can expect some reasonable wear and tear after a night, so be realistic, but if there is damage, you are within your rights to request costs.

Communication

How can I establish a good rapport with my teenager?
The most crucial element is making time. With hectic schedules in a busy household, many parents and teenagers are like ships in the night – a few words about where they are going and when they will be home and they vanish. Then there is the routine nagging about hygiene, schoolwork, bedtime, tidying, household chores – and for some parents that is the sum total of the parent-child relationship.

It is, however, important that you set aside time for your teenager and that she understands the importance of setting aside time for you. I find it disheartening when children are not taught to respect the family unit or relationship and are allowed to make plans that prohibit regular and healthy communication. If you haven't established this now, it's not too late. Here's the best way to go about it:

▷ Set up a time chart for the whole family where everyone fills in their appointments, social activities, special events and obligations (jobs, babysitting, etc.). Ask everyone to keep one day or evening a week free for family.

▷ This is not to say that once a week is enough to time to talk, but it's a beginning. In this time, plan something for the whole family occasionally, but most importantly, plan some one-on-one time with your teen – a shopping trip, a meal out, a walk in the park, a visit to a gallery – anything that allows time for some communication.

▷ When you have time together, keep things informal. Don't save up all of your concerns or 'big talks' for this day. If you do, it will never happen again! Chat as you would with a friend and avoid being judgmental or authoritarian.

▷ Everyone deserves respect, children and adults alike, and you will encourage the best possible relationship if you understand this premise and employ it. Show the same respect you would give a friend, even if you have differences.

▷ Actively pay attention to what your child says. Many of us get into the habit of saying 'mmm, yes, great, oh good ...' without thinking or taking on board what is being said. Make eye contact. Show you are interested by focusing on what your child is saying. Ask some relevant questions and avoid making judgements or showing disdain or shock.

▷ When you want to chat, look for a good moment. We all have moments when we are more receptive, and your teenager is the same. If she's stressed, on the phone, in the middle of homework, tired or clearly not interested, wait for a more appropriate time. If you force conversation or take the role of interrogator (firing off a series of questions), her back will go up and you'll get one-word answers, if any.

▷ Remember your sense of humour. If you can laugh together, this will dispel a great deal of tension.

▷ Try to keep up daily communication, even if it's only a few minutes of chat. Don't begin by asking a series of questions; instead comment on a relevant news story or even the football scores. If you are in the habit of chatting daily, it becomes easier to open up.

▷ If you are struggling, write a note and slip it under the door. Don't be heavy – in fact, you might want to simply make a joke or apologise. Or say: 'can we talk?' Sometimes kids have trouble sharing their thoughts in person (particularly if you have not always been receptive in the past), so ask her to write down what's on her mind and you can think it over. Make a date to talk later or respond in writing yourself. It's not ideal, but it's a start.

▷ Don't forget to encourage your teenager and offer praise. We are often very diligent about the praise routine with youngsters, but get stuck in a rut with our older kids – perhaps because they are often in our bad books or because we disagree with most of what they are doing or saying.

▷ Finally, don't give up! Persist with the lighthearted comments, praise, jokes and fun. Try not to nag. Choose your battles carefully and let your child be an individual, with her own rights and voice.

We've had a good relationship in the past, but I'm struggling to communicate with my daughter. What can I do?

In recent years, psychologists have revised their idea of healthy parent-teen relationships. They have found that most teens have warm, close relationships with their parents. They care about their parents' opinion of them and hold their parents' opinions in high regard. Many teens who do not have good rapport with their parents have had difficulties with them for years. If your relationship with your child has always been strained, there are ways to relate more positively (see page 201).

Parents of children in their early teens can expect an increase in the number of arguments with their children. At this time your teen is trying to establish him or herself as an independent person in the household. Once you and your family begin to acknowledge this change, the number of arguments between parents and teens usually declines.

Parents fear loss of control over the adolescent and fear for their child's safety because of this increased independence. Adolescents face stress when pushing for more freedom than parents are willing to grant. When they fail to adhere to parental advice they may engage in deviant behaviour such as alcohol and drug abuse, shoplifting and truancy. Understanding teenage developmental stages can help parents support their teens as they develop into independent, responsible adults.

Why does it feel like a rollercoaster ride living with my teenager?

During adolescence teens experience rapid physical, social, emotional and intellectual development. The most important thing to accept is that you and your parenting styles need to change in line with this, too. If you treat your child as you always have – without any respect for independence, new interests and activities, the need for freedom and privacy, the importance of popularity and the peer group, and, of course, the need to make their own mistakes and judgements – you will find yourself facing conflict.

Instead of laying down the rules, involve your child in a discussion. Explain your views and expectations, and choose a few things that really matter to you. Trying to control every element of a teenager's life is going to fail, and you'll end up having no idea what they are up to at an important stage of development. *Discuss* the rules you have in mind, and be open to a little compromise and negotiation on the things that simply don't matter that much. Remember, too, that hormones and stress can make teenagers moody. It's not necessarily directed at you, but it can hurt. Kids often take out their concerns, frustrations, moods and anger on parents, simply because they are the safest people to 'dump on'.

ARE YOU IN THE DARK ABOUT WHAT YOUR KIDS DO? YOU'RE NOT ALONE

According to a *Guardian*/ICM poll, British teenagers drink, smoke, take more drugs and lose their virginity earlier than many of their parents believe. Researchers questioned more than 500 young people between the ages of eleven and sixteen about their lives, asking them to fill in confidential questionnaires about issues such as alcohol, drug use, sex and the internet. Their parents, who gave permission for the research, answered separate questionnaires about what they believed their children had experienced.

The gap between what teenagers have done and what their parents think they have done is striking. Of children who have tried drugs, 65 per cent of parents either think they have not or do not know. Of children who smoke, 52 per cent of parents are unaware. Of children who say they have looked at pornography online, 60 per cent of their parents think they have not done so or did not know either way.

The poll shows that 15 per cent of children say they have talked about sex online. Only three per cent have gone on to meet a stranger they encountered on the internet, but of those, only one per cent of parents are aware of the meeting.

For more information on the findings, visit www.guardian.co.uk.

Secure children feel unconditional love and know that you aren't going to stop loving them if they express themselves in negative ways. They can't do it with friends and they won't do it at school, so it's often a way of letting off steam. In some sense, we can be flattered when our kids trust us enough to let it out at home.

How often should I be having regular chats with my child?

The simple answer is every day. This is not always easy, but it must be encouraged. This doesn't mean a long heart-to-heart on a daily basis, it means touching base – talking about plans, news, current events, anything of interest to your child. Sharing at least one meal a day is a good step towards this goal, and perhaps always having a chat before bedtime, where you exchange details of your day, is another one. Don't wait for a bad report card, a problem or a 'big chat' to communicate.

We argue constantly and then lock horns; what can I do?

There is one simple answer to this: refuse to argue back. Locking horns indicates a power struggle, and that means that you are both standing your ground without conceding or being willing to compromise or negotiate. For there to be any communication, one, but preferably both of you need to back down. The key is not to argue, but to encourage discussion. 'Ok, you feel this way, and I respect your views, but I feel this way (and thus expect respect as well). How can we find a middle ground?' Listen to the arguments and consider them carefully. Present your own in a calm, rational way, and take the time to *explain* them, and why they are important to you. Then actively search for a compromise.

Your child is a unique individual with her own beliefs, theories, thought patterns and experiences, just as you are, and it is important that mutual respect exists, as it is the basis for every healthy relationship. Ultimately, we need to learn to let go as our children become older – to let them make them own mistakes and explore their own individuality and dreams.

Finally, remember the most important rule in parenting: don't sweat the small stuff. Some issues are not worth fighting about. Drugs, yes. Clothing (unless it is seriously worrying) no. Truancy, yes. Pierced ears, no. Think about it carefully.

I think my daughter is lying to me regularly; what should I do?
(*See* Lying, *page* oo)

Community service

How can my children help in the community?

Children learn invaluable lessons by working in the community and it also teaches them a little humility and social responsibility. There are some legal constrictions. Many voluntary organisations give children volunteer work, provided they are covered by the organisation's insurance; however, in order to avoid child exploitation, the law limits what children under school-leaving age can do (children are under school-leaving age until the last Friday in June of the school year in which they turn sixteen). For example, under the age of fourteen, a child cannot work for a profit-making organisation – whether they are paid or not. For details of what children are legally allowed to do at various ages, *see page 164*.

What can my child do?

Your child could do some of the following:
▷ Offer to help at an old-people's home, whether helping to serve meals or just chatting to the residents, this can be enormously useful and provide a good learning curve.

▷ Help a local sports organisation, particularly with younger kids' training.

▷ Homeless shelters.

▷ Animal refuges.

▷ Hospitals.

▷ Parks.

▷ Handing out leaflets or manning stalls for charities.

▷ Literacy project in adult education or schools (when they have time off studies) where English may not be the first language.

▷ Libraries.

▷ Red Cross or Salvation Army.

▷ Environmental organisations.

▷ Helplines for children – many have opportunities for older children to offer guidance and support.

But it doesn't necessarily need to be formal. There may be an elderly man or woman on your street who could use some help with grocery-shopping, hanging out laundry, carrying things or even just a chat. Someone may need a dog walked regularly or help with little ones for an hour or two a week. The idea is that the work is not paid and that they are 'giving something back' to the community. And there are plenty of reasons for this! Even encouraging school drives to help others is worthwhile – raising funds for local charities, or organising gift drives for deprived children. Anything your child gives will be rewarded in many ways – even if he doesn't see it at the beginning!

Some ideas for volunteer work can be found at www.volunteering.org.uk.

At what age should I encourage my children to become more socially responsible?

Although there are laws about when children can begin to work and what they can take on, it's legal to work for most charitable organisations from a young age, as long as the organisation's insurance covers it. Most children will benefit from doing something, even if it's only for a few hours a week, from the early teen years. As long as it fits in with their schoolwork and other commitments, consider it possible. Many kids will resist the idea and say that they are 'too busy', but teaching children social responsibility from an early age and ensuring that they find time for others in a busy schedule is likely to prepare them well for later life – and helps create responsible, caring citizens.

But even younger children can be encouraged to do their part, whether they come along with you while you take on some community work, or are encouraged to start their own initiatives (with your help) at their school or other neighbourhood venue. For example, they could help with planting flowers at a local refuge or senior's home; they can offer peer mentoring/tutoring/support for their school anti-bullying initiative; collect toys for sick or underprivileged children; make get-well and birthday cards for nursing home residents; collect clothing for charities or needy children; organise a book drive for homeless children, make up food baskets for the elderly or homeless – anything goes. It may take a little research to discover what is required, but once you get involved, you'll find plenty of ways to help.

Try to choose something that might reflect your child's interests (gardening, sports, shopping, younger children, reading), as this will make the job much more enjoyable (and easier to sell) at the outset. However, most children ultimately find community work rewarding – and their horizons broadened.

Computers

Should my child be left unsupervised on the computer?

This is an age- and privacy-related question, and also a question of trust. Young children should not be left unattended, as they can unwittingly access unsuitable information and images, or find themselves chatting to inappropriate members of the internet community. But it's also equally true that with suitable parental controls in place (offered by most internet service providers (ISPs), or purchased separately), and a good chat about internet safety, they can be left to their own devices to some extent. It is physically impossible for most parents to oversee all computer use. If games are monitored, time limited and the computer is in a prominent place within the household, chances are, your child will be OK.

What are the risks?

One of the biggest dangers is children naively disclosing personal information about themselves. Rebellious pre-teens are especially at risk, because they may not take parental warnings seriously. Your first concern when you allow your children to use the internet should be educating them to keep personal information private. Under no circumstances should your children ever give out full names, phone numbers or addresses on the internet. Make sure your kids know that this applies equally to their online friends; kids who have access to social networking sites, like MySpace or Bebo, will make online friends you don't know about. The same goes for kids who have unsupervised access to online chatrooms, especially obscure, unmoderated chatrooms.

Older children and teens will undoubtedly have homework to do on the computer, and a full cyber-social life through MSN

Messenger or other services. They won't thank you for looking over their shoulders while they 'chat' – it's the equivalent of reading a child's diary or listening to a phone call. What's more, they'll need some experience of the internet and dealing with cyber issues on their own as they grow older – you don't want them leaving home or heading off to university having been monitored completely. The older your child is, the more important it becomes to educate him or her about responsible use of the internet rather than relying purely on technical fixes. In the end, your child must learn to choose responsibly on his or her own.

Once you've explained the safety issues, and set down some ground rules (*see page 123*), you will need to employ a little trust.

Should I do a little snooping?
One way to check what is going on is to keep tabs on your child's browsing history. It's one way to see what they are looking at, and you are perfectly justified in doing this, particularly if it is a household computer. If you see something you don't like, ask what they are up to and why. Savvy older children might erase their histories, but there are programs available to save the material. What's more, you can also make it clear that erasing the history is not acceptable; make it a household rule, if you like. It's not exactly spying – more like a measure to protect your child's safety.

There is a voluntary website rating system, called the Internet Content Rating Association (ICRA, formerly RSACi). Support for it is built into Microsoft Internet Explorer. Turning on this feature in Internet Explorer allows you to block access to websites that voluntarily identify themselves as adult-oriented. This system has the big advantage of never accidently or deliberately filtering out age-appropriate sites.

WHAT IS SAFE INTERNET USE

▷ Use a filter with some sort of parental control for younger children and pre-teens. You can set the password and decide what types of activities you will allow them to do.

▷ This type of filter is not appropriate for teens who require the internet for homework research, and who will require a little more freedom, but they can learn internet safety rules and stick to the household ground rules regarding access.

▷ Discuss with your child what they can and cannot do online. If he or she sets up a profile, do it with him or her to make sure that the information is not revealing. They should never include details of school, real name, phone number, bank account, address or include pictures.

▷ Making new 'friends' online should be discouraged. They should communicate with people they know until they are of an age (let's say sixteen) to become involved in specialist websites where they share experiences or ideas.

▷ Remind children that 'new contacts' often claim to be friends of friends. Ask them to check it out first with the friend in question and to be wary. Many predators watch interaction between children and use the information to gain access.

▷ Never allow your child to meet someone they've met online without consulting you. Make this a clear and non-negotiable rule.

▷ If your child sets up a web page, ask to see it regularly and ensure that it is not password-protected.

▷ Regularly check out the history on the computers used by your child. See if there are any new patterns or websites that are being visited a lot.

▷ Google your child's name, screen name or city. It's likely that nothing will turn up, but it's worth checking to see if something has been written about him or her, or if he or she has become involved in something inappropriate.

When can my child have his own computer?

This is a question dictated by family finances, space and practicalities. If you have several children and adults sharing the same computer, there are bound to be issues regarding access. In my household I find it hard to get near the computer between the hours of of 5 and 10 pm, because my teens are busy doing homework or chatting with friends. It may be necessary to invest in a second computer or even a third. However, if your child does have a computer, keep it out of the bedroom if at all possible (*see below*) and place it in a family room where everyone spends some time. One survey found the most children get their 'first' computer at age thirteen, although children as young as five or six have also been given their own. As long as it is supervised and in the case of older children, checked from time to time (a stipulation before purchase) to ensure that it conforms with your ideas about safety and appropriate use, it doesn't really matter *whose* computer it is that they are using.

Should my child be allowed a computer in her bedroom?

Space dictates that some children must use computers in their bedrooms. If you have only one computer, I would suggest that it be kept within a family room where activities can be supervised. The real threat is, of course, the internet. If your child has her own computer, it's a good idea to prevent internet access in the bedroom and to encourage using the family computer for downloads and research, all of which can be transferred by disk or wire. If your child has a laptop, suggest that internet activity be confined to well-travelled areas of the house. Of course they will run the risk of having siblings view any internet messaging, and will lack a certain degree of privacy, but this is something worth negotiating until your child is old enough to be trusted to follow safety and household rules (perhaps fifteen or sixteen).

According to the Kaiser Family Foundation in the US, twice as many kids have computers in their bedrooms today than five years ago. Not only do many kids forgo reading or listening to music in favour of computer time, but they often do it well into the night, disrupting sleep patterns and mood. A UK researcher found that 20 per cent of children sleep at least two hours less each night than their parents, and she laid the blame firmly on computers, games and televisions in the bedroom.

How do I monitor computer use?

Of course, wireless connections make it difficult to monitor where in the house a computer is used the internet, so it is all the more important that your children understand why you are concerned about solo use of the computer, the risks, the safety measure that should be undertaken, and, of course, agree to show you what they have been up to. Once again, this is not snooping as such – merely checking that your child is OK. You don't need to access private files, e-mails or messages; you simply need to know that what your child chooses to access via the internet is appropriate and safe.

Should I stop my child from spending too much time on the computer?

Computers, like games consoles and anything else that appeals to kids, are potentially addictive. There are no hard and fast rules about what is and is not excessive. It will vary from child to child and on the circumstances from week to week. If a child has a lot of research to do for some homework, he or she might need to make more use of the computer and the internet on some days than others. Each family needs to have its own understanding and approach.

Although there is little evidence to suggest that the moderate use of computers to play games has a negative impact on children's friendships and family relationships, recent survey data show that increased use of the internet may be linked to increases in loneliness and depression, and may be a risk factor for obesity. Of most concern are the findings that playing violent computer games may increase aggressiveness and desensitise a child to suffering, and that the use of computers may blur a child's ability to distinguish real life from simulation.

Since computers can be used for so many different things it is quite easy for a child to switch rapidly from one activity to another, making it hard for parents to know if their child is really doing homework or just playing games. As a rule of thumb, an hour or two of 'screen time', which includes leisure time on the computer and in front of the TV is sufficient for most kids – and falls within the boundaries of 'moderate' use. Two or three sessions across an evening or day may make it easier to monitor.

Are there any signs to indicate that my child is being abused online?

According to NCH, the Children's Charity, it's worth looking out for the following. Most children are not being abused online and some of these activities may be innocent, but it pays to be alert to potential dangers:

▷ If your child becomes secretive about his or her time online, maybe not using their regular computer but instead using libraries, internet cafes or friends' homes to go online, you ought to establish the reasons. It may seem like typical adolescent behaviour but you should take it seriously, particularly if it involves a sudden change in behaviour.

▷ If your child starts to download files on to floppy discs or CDs, not storing them on the hard drive where it would be easier for someone else to see them, you should seek to establish the reasons why.

▷ If your child begins to use encryption software that allows the user to convert any computer file into an unreadable jumble of symbols, numbers and letters which can only be read by the person possessing the correct decryption key, you should be concerned. If you find such files on your child's computer and you establish that encryption is being used, it is important to find out why a child is going to such lengths to conceal things.

▷ If you detect changes in behaviour, be alert; children and young people can be sexually abused online by being shown images and words. We know that victims of online child abuse can and do display similar symptoms to children who are sexually abused in real life.

CYBER-BULLYING

Experts on bullying believe that many bullies lack good communication skills and therefore the impersonal nature of e-mail makes it an ideal tool to victimise others. Unfortunately, it is not immediately possible to check where an e-mail has come from – you have to trust that the named writer is genuine. But it is not always wise to make this assumption. Take these sensible precautions:

▷ If a name is not familiar, it may be safer not to open the e-mail.

▷ If the sender is a known bully or if he has sent unpleasant or annoying messages before, then ignore it and delete it immediately.

▷ If the bullying happens through a personal e-mail account, report it to the sender's e-mail account provider – you can find this address after the @ sign.

▷ If it is not obvious who the sender is and there is continual bullying using e-mail, then there are tools to trace senders. To find out more about this e-mail tracking, go to one of the search engines (Google,

Yahoo, for example), and type in 'e-mail tracking software'; you can then download the appropriate software. Once you know the identity of the bully, get in touch with your Internet Service Provider (ISP) which can then block the sender from your e-mail.

▷ Most ISPs allow you to block any given e-mail address from your account or have it redirected to a separate file or account as 'spam'. This can be your 'clearing house' for evidence, should it be required.

▷ If the e-mail bullying is occurring in school, then this should be dealt with through the school's anti-bullying policy (*see page 81*).

▷ Keep a record of all bullying incidents either by saving or printing e-mails.

▷ If an e-mail message is disturbing or breaks the law, do not hesitate to contact the police.

▷ You may be aware of recent episodes where people have been victimised via websites – one incident involved pupils setting up an offensive website about their teachers. Of course, the victim may not always be aware that these sites exist. However, if your child realises that he or she is being bullied in this way, then the first course of action is to contact your ISP. It can find out who runs the site and can request that it be removed. If the person responsible is at school with your child, then let the headteacher know. Any false accusations or anything on the website that you feel is breaking the law should be reported to the police.

Should I put a child-safe filter on my computer or set up an intranet?

Setting up an intranet can be complicated and expensive if you don't know what you are doing; a child-safety filter is a much better idea. These are appropriate for children under the age of thirteen or so; older teens will likely require more access to complete homework projects and pursue interests. You can, however, set many filters with just one or two settings – for example, even older children and teenagers who are given full access on the computer don't need to be viewing pornography. This word, therefore, could be used to deny access to anything adult or pornographic. Be careful of the words you choose, however; preventing any sites with 'sex' from being accessed means that your child may not be able to complete a biology assignment or to look up various methods of birth control, for instance. Many children ask questions and find solutions to their own problems and concerns via the internet, which can be an excellent source of information and advice. They also share concerns with other like-minded adolescents, and this can be a valuable resource.

At what age should a child be allowed to visit a chatroom?
This is a difficult question, as there are now chatrooms on a huge range of websites, many of them aimed at young children. For example, it's possible to join a chatroom to talk about your favourite cartoon or TV programme, within safe parameters. These will normally be 'permitted' by most safety filters. Having said that, all chatroom activity should be supervised by parents of young children; before twelve or thirteen years old, most kids do not have the maturity to discern the difference between genuine chat and a potentially dangerous predator. If your child shows an interest in entering a chatroom, sit with him or her for the first few times and offer some guidance and advice – for example, make sure your child never gives out his or her real name and address and never sends a photo. If someone says something nasty, encourage your child not to respond, but to tell you so that you can report it to the chatroom hosts.

Teenagers often take part in chatrooms as part of their social life

- and many friends enter the same ones together to 'talk'. Furthermore, children can share their interests with other like-minded kids through chatrooms; a chess buff might not get the same level of enthusiasm from his classmates as he will from members of a chess chatroom. So chatrooms are not necessarily to be discouraged. The crucial thing is that your child exercise caution, are aware of the risks and that you know what your child is doing (*see page 115*).

WHAT DO TEENS DO ONLINE?

According to Microsoft, teens download music, use instant messaging (IM), e-mail and play online games. They also actively use search engines to find information on the internet. Most teens have visited chatrooms, and many have participated in adult or private chats. Boys in this age group are more likely to push the boundaries by looking for gross humour, gore, gambling or explicit adult sites. Girls may be more likely to chat online and therefore may be more susceptible to being sexually solicited online. Microsoft offers the following safety tips for this age group:

▷ Create a list of internet house rules with your teens. You should include the kinds of sites that are off limits, internet hours and guidelines for communicating with others online, including in chatrooms.

▷ Keep internet-connected computers in an open area and out of your teens' bedrooms.

▷ Talk to your kids about their online friends and activities just as you would about their other friends and activities. This includes talking to your teens about their instant messaging list and making sure they're not talking to strangers.

▷ Know which chatrooms or message boards your teens visit, and with whom they talk. Encourage them to use monitored chatrooms, and insist they stay in public chatroom areas.

▷ Insist that they never agree to meet an online friend.

▷ Teach your teens never to give out personal information without your permission when using e-mail, chatrooms or instant messaging, filling out registration forms and personal profiles, and entering online contests.

▷ Teach your kids not to download programs, music or files without your permission. File-sharing and taking text, images, or artwork from the web may infringe copyright laws and can be illegal.

▷ Encourage your teens to tell you if something or someone online makes them feel uncomfortable or threatened. Stay calm and remind your kids they are not in trouble for bringing something to your attention. (It is important that your teen does not think that their computer privileges could be taken away.)

▷ Talk to your teenagers about online adult content and pornography, and direct them to positive sites about health and sexuality.

▷ Help protect them from spam. Tell your teens not to give out their e-mail address online, not to respond to junk mail and to use e-mail filters.

▷ Be aware of the websites that your teens frequent. Make sure your kids are not visiting sites with offensive content or posting personal information or photos of themselves.

▷ Teach your kids responsible, ethical, online behaviour. They should not be using the internet to spread gossip, bully or threaten others.

▷ Make sure your teens check with you before making financial transactions online, including ordering, buying or selling items.

▷ Discuss online gambling and its potential risks with your teens. Remind them that it is illegal for them to gamble online.

For more information, visit
www.microsoft.com/athome/security/children

Is my son old enough to have his own internet account?

In the UK it is very easy to obtain CDs which will automatically and immediately establish a new internet account. This could mean that any parental control software previously installed may not work with the new account. There are no age limits on most internet accounts, particularly those that are free, such as hotmail, and children can easily type in false details (which are never checked) if they wish to open an account. It's harder to open an e-mail account if payment is required, as no one under the age of 18 can be held responsible for making payments. Having said that, many kids do have bank cards and manage a way round the system.

If he is old enough to send e-mails on his own, he is probably old enough to have an internet account. If you are concerned, give him a screen name on your family account, and ask him to set his own password to give him some privacy. You can also agree certain filters on material that you do not wish him to access. Do, however, ask to see what he's up to from time to time, to ensure that he is using both the internet and e-mail appropriately and safely.

How old must my child be to have his own e-mail address?

Once again, there is no legal age limit and any child can set up an e-mail account or a screen name on the family account, which will give him his own e-mail address. For safety reasons, and to ensure that any child filters you have in place are operational, it's best to go for the latter until your child is mature enough to deal with the responsibility. The average age at which children in the UK get their own e-mail addresses is twelve or thirteen.

At what age should I stop checking what my child is doing?

When child filters are relaxed, your child will have unlimited access to everything on the internet. Most people allow this type of freedom in the mid-teens – as one of the first steps towards independence. Frankly, teenagers can use a friend's computer or visit an internet cafe if they are hell-bent on searching out certain information, so setting tight guidelines at home will only drive him out of the house.

This does not, however, mean that spot-checks are not a good idea. From time to time, check the browser history or peek over a shoulder to see what they are up to. Ask questions, and ask them to show you what they like to do. You are unlikely to get the full story, but it provides an opportunity for conversation/communication – and, of course, guidance and warnings. Protecting your child is not snooping, by the way; it's merely one form of supervision that should, ideally, be continued into the late teens.

At what age should I relax the child filters?
Most people relax the filters at around fifteen or sixteen; sooner, perhaps, if the child has been using the computer for a long time and has earned your trust, or if complicated homework projects require wider access. You can, however, still set the odd protective filter (*see page 121*), if you wish to shield your child a little bit longer.

Cooking

When should my child start making his own meals?
From a young age (as young as six or seven) children can get their own cold breakfast (*see page 130*) or lunch, within agreed parameters. Larger, hot meals need more supervision, but the sooner you get your children involved in the preparation and planning, the better prepared they will be to take on the task themselves at the appropriate age. Preparing his own food helps a child to develop an awareness of the importance of meals and

snacks, and promotes healthy eating habits – particularly if they are taught early on which foods are full of vitamins and minerals, and which foods should be eaten only in moderation.

By early adolescence, kids should have enough experience to make simple meals for themselves, although they may need to be supervised in the use of the hob or oven (*see page 129*). If you have a late starter, get him involved in a few meals – ask him to choose a menu, perhaps, and help you to prepare it.

Are there any dangers?

There are safety issues that need to be addressed before handing an entire meal over to an adolescent, and you must be confident that they will exercise caution, produce a well-balanced meal (not just a packet of crisps and a peanut butter sandwich or the ubiquitous teenage bowl of cereal) and clear up after themselves.

Remind kids of basic hygiene regularly – for example, washing hands with hot soapy water before preparing food, making sure utensils and work surfaces are clean before beginning, washing hands, utensils and work surfaces after handling raw meat, poultry or fish, ensuring that perishable foods don't stay at room temperature for longer than two hours, and washing up carefully afterwards. Cold water and a quick wipe are not conducive to hygienic dishes, pans or work surfaces!

At what age should I try to get my child interested in helping me in the kitchen?

From toddlerhood! My 18-month-old was given a butter knife (very blunt) and a cucumber to 'cut' (a bit of a misnomer, as it was more like 'chunked'), lettuce to tear and cheese to break into small pieces for a salad. He soon moved on to stirring cold dishes, washing vegetables, peeling bananas, pouring a little liquid into bowls, measuring items such as sultanas or nuts, and removing cans or packets from lower cupboards. Four-year-olds can help with opening packets, peeling carrots or potatoes, setting the table, putting toppings on a pizza, kneading bread or placing fish fingers on a tray ready for cooking. Even 6- to 8-year-olds can help to plan some meals, find ingredients in cupboards or the refrigerator, garnish food, measure ingredients and set food on the table.

What should the average teen be able to do?

By the time your child reaches adolescence, he should be a dab hand in the kitchen – accustomed to washing up, emptying the dishwasher, setting the table, preparing simple meals, or parts of meals, such as salad, vegetables, prepared fruits, desserts, easy oven-cooked meals, and foods that require roasting, grilling or even light frying.

The key is to encourage children to help from an early age so that they learn the different elements of meals, how each is prepared and how they go together. Teens should also be aware of the importance of clearing up! Setting out a list of expectations can be useful as part of a child or teenager's contribution to the household. A rota for chores such as emptying the dishwasher, making the salad, preparing the vegetables can provide invaluable experience and help children learn how a household 'ticks'. What's more, if you are going to be late, there is no reason why a mature young adolescent can't put the basics in the oven or turn it off.

When can I allow my son to cook or prepare food unsupervised?

Each child develops at his own pace. Letting yours take on new responsibilities or try challenging tasks is a matter of knowing his individual abilities and personality. If your child is the type who doesn't 'hear' instructions, cuts corners wherever possible, is forgetful (crucial when there is an oven on or a hob flame alight) or generally unreliable, you'll need to supervise until you feel confident that the basics have been mastered, and the importance of various guidelines (hygiene, hob/oven/microwave safety) have been taken on board.

For most kids, this day comes at around fourteen or fifteen; however, use your judgement and supervise at least four or five attempts before you decide that he's ready and reliable.

When does the hob or oven become safe for children to use?
Mid-adolescence is the simple answer. If you are in the house, they may be able to undertake cooking on one or either on their own. However, unsupervised, fourteen or fifteen is about the right age. Kids over the age of ten can, according to the Royal Society for the Prevention of Accidents (RoSPA) use a microwave, toaster or toaster oven, provided they have been given clear instructions and know what to do in an emergency (turn off the power at the power point or mains if there is a problem such as burning). They'll need to learn some basics, such as never using metal in a microwave or (as my 12-year-old son once did), turn it on with nothing in it (he was using it as a timer for a cake he was baking!). Teens also need to learn that they need to be physically present when food is actually 'cooking', as diligence is the only way to prevent accidents.

The hob or the oven also need some explanation and experience – using oven gloves to remove hot food, how to deal with pots boiling over, turning off oven/hob when finished, clearing up spillages, setting the correct temperature (the celcius/farenheit difference must always be explained if they plan to use a recipe), keeping the hob flame (on a gas-fuelled hob) to a suitable level if they are using a smaller pot and knowing the signs of burning.

They will need reminders about dealing with hot food, draining pasta, rice or vegetables in a safe way, checking that a ready meal is cooked appropriately (checking the centre to make sure it is piping hot), carefully following instructions on packets or in recipe books and, of course, how to deal with a fire, should something go wrong.

Once they have successfully mastered these skills in your presence, they can and *must* be trusted to do it on their own. They will undoubtedly make mistakes, but they need to be prepared for life outside the home, and some independence within the home, as soon as possible.

When should I stop making breakfast?

During the week most children get by with a cold breakfast, which can be just as nutritious and, in some cases, even healthier than cooked breakfasts. Yoghurt, cereal, toast, fruit and muffins can all be prepared easily by children as young as six or seven – and this should be encouraged. Some parents find it easier to put out a selection of foods and ask their children to choose (thereby ensuring that they have a healthy choice). Once children are old enough to use the microwave, hob or oven (*see page 129*), they are capable of cooking some eggs, oatmeal or bacon, if that's what they are used to. Certainly, it's a nice idea for families to sit down together at breakfast, but that does not preclude children preparing it themselves.

What should my child be capable of cooking by the time he is sixteen?

By the age of sixteen, children can and should be able to cook from a simple recipe book, and produce hot and cold meals to a reasonable standard. Get them started with easy dishes like pasta or grilled/roasted meats, and then move on. A supervised 14-year-old is, for example, capable of preparing a chicken and roasting it. If he has helped in the kitchen from a young age, he'll have an idea of how food goes together – and should be encouraged to seek out different dishes in recipe books, or to experiment with various ingredients.

Crime

At what age could my child go to prison?
The age of criminal responsibility in England is ten years old, and children under this age are immune from prosecution. In Scotland, the age of criminal responsibility is eight. If the young person is aged over fourteen years then he or she is considered to be responsible for his or her acts.

Juries are not involved in youth courts. The terminology is also different where young persons are concerned. There is a 'finding of guilt' instead of a 'conviction', and there is an 'order made upon a finding of guilt' instead of a 'sentence'. The youth court is presided over by a magistrate, and there must be at least one male and one female magistrate on the bench. Serious offences, such as murder, will be heard in a Crown Court.

What kinds of punishments can be handed out?
There are a variety of different 'orders', which include supervision orders, community service, curfews, rehabilitation, fines and more. However, young people who represent a high level of risk to the public, have a significant offending history or are persistent offenders and where no other sentence will manage their risks effectively, are given a custodial sentence, called a Detention and Training Order (DTO).

A DTO can be given to children between the ages of twelve and seventeen and sentences can be between four months and two years. The first half of the sentence is spent in custody, while the second half is spent in the community under the supervision of a youth offending team. The court can require the young person to be on an Intensive Supervision and Surveillance Programme as a condition of the community period of the sentence.

If a young person is convicted of an offence for which an adult could receive at least fourteen years in custody, he or she may be sentenced under Sections 90 or 91. This sentence can only be given in the Crown Court. If the conviction is for murder, the sentence falls under Section 90, otherwise the sentence will be under Section 91. The length of the sentence can be anywhere up to the adult maximum for the same offence, which for certain offences may be life. A young person given a Section 90 or 91 sentence will be placed in custody.

If the young person is sentenced to less then four years, he or she will leave custody at the half-way point of the sentence and be supervised on licence by their supervising officer until the three-quarters point. If certain conditions apply, the young person may be released on a tag up to 134 days earlier under the Home Detention Curfew scheme. For young people sentenced to four years or more, if they are successful at their parole hearing, they will leave custody at the half-way point. If they are unsuccessful, they will leave at the two-thirds point. In both cases, they will be supervised by their supervising officer until the three-quarters point.

In what kinds of secure accommodation might a young person be placed?

▷ Secure training centres (STCs).
▷ Secure children's homes.
▷ Young offender institutions (YOIs).

When a child reaches the age of eighteen, he will be tried as an adult, in an adult court, and can receive a custodial sentence in prison.

For more information, visit the Youth Justice Board at www.yjb.gov.uk

WHAT IS THE AGE OF CRIMINAL RESPONSIBILITY?

In the UK, the age at which children have to take responsibility for their crimes and at which they can be prosecuted is ten (eight in Scotland). Some experts feel this is very young. Compare this with other countries:

Canada	12	France	13
Germany	14	Japan	14
Russia	14	Italy	15
Norway	15	Spain	16
USA	16 or 18	Belgium	18
Luxembourg	18		

How can I tell if my child is shoplifting?

There is no 'typical' shoplifter - in fact, all ages, sexes, races and backgrounds are represented. However, teenagers do make up a large percentage of shoplifters and according to the National Crime Prevention Council, about a quarter of all people caught shoplifting are between the ages of thirteen and seventeen. Some teens steal things they don't really want or need, for the thrill of it, for attention, to gain kudos with peers or perhaps as a dare. Others steal items that they want but can't afford or aren't allowed to buy, such as cigarettes, clothing, CDs and cosmetics. Still others steal in order to fund drug or alcohol habits.

Consider the fact that adolescents have poor impulse control, particularly in the pre-teen years. They have a new sense of their own autonomy and want to prove to themselves that they can do bad or 'naughty' things, which gives them a sense of power and excitement. They may be showing off – younger teens are the most influenced by their peer group, for example.

Why do people shoplift?

Most shoplifters know that it's wrong and expect to be punished if they're caught. Shoplifting experts believe that these people are 'acting out' – using shoplifting to relieve painful emotions, such as stress. Teens whose parents are going through a divorce, for example, may turn to shoplifting because of the feelings of loss they're going through. Others may use stealing as a way of getting back at someone, like a parent or a friend who has hurt them. Shoplifters are frequently bored or depressed. Experts at the National Association for Shoplifting Prevention in the US say that teens also shoplift because they:

▷ Think the stores can afford the losses.
▷ Think they won't get caught.
▷ Don't know how to handle temptation when faced with things they want.
▷ Feel peer pressure to shoplift.
▷ Don't know how to work through feelings of anger, frustration, depression, unattractiveness or lack of acceptance.

Unfortunately, it's easy for shoplifting to become an addiction. Some shoplifters report that they feel a 'high' when they get away with it – a surge of adrenaline that temporarily relieves any underlying emotional problems that may have prompted them to shoplift. Shoplifting becomes a habit that's hard to break.

How can I tell if my child is shoplifting?

Signs that a child is shoplifting include coming home with new clothes, make-up, CDs, jewellery, sweets, magazines – things that are outside her budget, and slipped into the house, perhaps, rather than paraded. Look out for goods that may have had security tags cut off rather than removed properly – or hidden goods in cupboards or under beds. Reluctance to enter certain shops is also a sign (she may have shoplifted there), as is vagueness about where things have come from.

The older the child, the more worrying the experience, as maturity does bring with it an understanding of cause and effect, and the fact that actions have consequences. Morality is better established in older teens – and they are better able to resist temptation, and to weigh the downside against the benefits.

If your child is caught shoplifting, there is no point in blithely accepting it as 'normal' behaviour, regardless of how many others have done or are doing it. Take your child back to the shop and meet with the security department to explain and apologise. In most cases, charges won't be pressed, but some shops have a strong policy of prosecuting all shoplifters as a deterrant. A child's embarrassment at facing up to what he or she did by having to return a stolen item makes for an everlasting lesson on why stealing is wrong.

What can I do to prevent my child from shoplifting?
Explain to your child that shoplifting is stealing – many kids believe that because it involves a shop, it isn't theft as such. While most kids wouldn't dream of taking something from a friend, their morality dims when it comes to businesses. It needs to be explained that shoplifting is effectively stealing money from the people who run the businesses. Stealing is a crime and can lead to a court hearing, and even a custodial sentence (*see page 131*), particularly for repeat offenders. And this can have a dramatic impact on your child's later life (*see page 136*).

One-third of juveniles who've been caught shoplifting say it's difficult to quit. So it's important to help kids and teens understand why stealing is wrong and that they may face serious consequences if they continue to steal.

How might juvenile crimes affect my child in later life?

Many youths are completely unaware that the 'petty' crimes they commit as a teen can have a dramatic effect on the rest of their lives. Anyone who is convicted of a crime, regardless of his or her age, receives a criminal record, which is a list of any reprimands, orders, final warnings or sentences received.

When your child applies for a job, she may be asked if she has a criminal record. Crimes that are committed far enough in the past do not always have to be revealed, but there are exceptions to this, and they can impact on your child's future career choices. A crime is considered to be 'spent' after a period of time. Most sentences a youth receives in a magistrate's court will be spent after 2½ years; however, sentences over six months can take much longer to be spent. Sentences for serious crimes such as murder, rape and child abuse can never be spent. A teenager who was convicted of shoplifting at fourteen and applies for his first part-time job at sixteen will likely have to reveal the crime to potential employers as it may not have been spent.

Will a criminal record affect my child in later life?

Regardless of whether it is 'spent' or not, a criminal record must be disclosed by law in certain applications, including:

▷ Any post providing access to people under eighteen years old. Such posts include teachers, school caretakers, youth and social workers and child minders.

▷ Employment involving social services to elderly people, mentally

or physically disabled people, alcohol or drug misusers or the
chronically sick.

▷ Any employment involving the administration of justice,
including police officers, probation officers, traffic wardens,
certain professions that have legal protection (including lawyers,
doctors, dentists, nurses, chemists and accountants).

▷ Jobs where national security may be at risk (for example, certain
posts in the civil service or defence contractors).

What's more, UK laws don't apply to US visa law, so if your child
wishes to travel to the US, he is required to declare the arrest and/or
conviction. In a nutshell, some juvenile crimes may be dismissed by
some employers, particularly if they took place a long time ago, but
a criminal record could limit your child's choices in life.

For more information and advice on young people and
crime/law, visit Rizer: www.rizer.co.uk.

What are the most common juvenile crimes? How can I prevent them?

More than four out of ten males and one in ten females are likely to
be found guilty of or cautioned for an indictable offence at some
point during their lives. Official records and 'self-report' studies
also show that individuals more often break the law when they are
young. The peak ages at which they are most likely to be found
guilty or cautioned are between fifteen and nineteen. Criminal
involvement typically starts before the age of fifteen, but declines
markedly once young people reach their twenties. However, young
people who become involved in crime at the earliest ages – before
the age of fourteen – tend to become the most persistent offenders
with longer criminal careers.

Surveys show that offending of some kind is common among

young people. In the UK Youth Lifestyles Survey of young people between the ages of twelve and twenty, almost half (57 per cent of males and 37 per cent of females) admitted committing at least 1 of 27 offences at some point in their lives. These included arson, theft, shoplifting, violent offences and fraud.

The Peterborough Youth Study (an Economic and Social Research Council-funded project) showed that 38 per cent of its 1,957 sample of fourteen- to fifteen-year-olds had committed offences such as arson, vandalism, theft and burglary.

Almost eight in ten of the incidents self-reported in a 2004 survey were not of a serious nature. The most common offences were non-injury assaults (28 per cent); the selling of non-Class A substances (19 per cent) and thefts from the workplace or from school (16 per cent). When violent incidents do occur, many don't involve injury and are often committed on the 'spur of the moment' against someone the young person knows. This often means a fight (maybe between friends) and usually takes place near home in the afternoon.

Consider these findings. Arson can be something as simple as larking about and setting fire to a pile of sticks in a park, which may cause unexpected damage or harm someone. Fraud can include providing false details to open a store account, perhaps, or making 'fake ID' (which many teens commonly undertake in order to drink or enter over-aged films). Vandalism can be graffiti. A crime doesn't have to be sinister in intent to be subject to prosecution.

How do we know who will offend and who won't?
A child's routines and lifestyle are strong predictors of offending. Adolescents who spend a high percentage of their time with their peers and a low percentage of their time with family tend to be more involved in offending than others. Education is also crucial.

If your child does not realise that he can be charged for doing some of the above, it won't protect him. All children need to know what constitutes crime and the ramifications of getting a criminal record (*see page 136*). Find out as much as you can about the law. Visit Rizer in the UK for good advice and information (*see page 137*) and pass on the information.

How do we recognise crimes?

It's not always easy to recognise crimes. Shoplifting may be obvious in some cases (*see page 134*), but what your child gets up to when he is on the street with his friends may be well hidden from you. For this reason, it is extremely important that you have a relatively clear idea of where your child is at all times, and that you discourage hanging around. Know who his peers are and talk regularly to your child about crime and the law – ask if he knows anyone who has committed a crime, shoplifted or done graffiti. If he comes home with paint-covered clothing it could be a clue that graffiti is being done. Watch his post; catalogues or offers for expensive goods may be a sign that he has faked ID or provided false details. The smell of burning on his clothing or hair could indicate arson. Unexplained injuries, cuts, bruises, etc. could be evidence that he is involved in violence of some description. For drug-taking, *see page 148*.

What else you can do?

▷ Build positive self-esteem. Kids who have a good self-image don't need to rely so heavily on peers and risky or illegal behaviours for recognition or status.

▷ Discuss the dangers of crime and the impact it has on communities and people.

▷ Take an active interest in your children's activities. Get them involved in organised after-school sports or activities. Busy kids won't have time to hang out on the street and cause trouble.

▷ Monitor and control their behaviour. Be firm but fair when it comes to discipline and enforcing the rules. If you find out he's committed a crime, make sure that there are serious consequences.

▷ Be a good role model. You must set the standards for acceptable behaviour. Kids who are exposed to dishonesty, drug/alcohol abuse, violence, and a lack of respect for people, property and authority are more likely to exhibit similar behaviour.

WHAT KEY RISK FACTORS HAVE BEEN IDENTIFIED FOR YOUTH OFFENDING?

▷ Being male.
▷ Having a parent or parents who are offenders.
▷ Not living with parents/being in care.
▷ Suffering bereavement or family breakdown.
▷ Drug or alcohol misuse.
▷ Experiencing neglect, physical, sexual or emotional abuse.
▷ Witnessing violence against a family member.
▷ Playing truant or being excluded from school.
▷ Associating with delinquent friends.
▷ Having siblings or other family members who offend.

What are the implications for my child if he gets an Anti-social Behaviour Order (Asbo)?

An Asbo is a civil order against behaviour which causes 'alarm, harassment or distress'. This vague definition covers things such as graffiti, truancy from school, shoplifting or even playing loud music. Although the government claims that the use of Asbos is not aimed at young people, they bring many children into the criminal justice system who haven't actually committed any crimes.

The government has been exploring the possibility of widening the scope of Asbos. It has even floated the idea of introducing 'on-the-spot Asbos', which could be issued by police officers on the street and 'baby Asbos' (so-called 'Basbos') for children under the age of ten.

Police forces (including the British Transport Police), local authorities, housing action trusts and registered social landlords have the power to apply for an Asbo to be imposed on anyone over ten years of age who is behaving 'anti-socially'. Anti-social behaviour is defined very broadly in law as any activity that 'causes or is likely to have caused harassment or alarm or distress' to someone else who is not of your household. Significantly, the authority applying for an Asbo does not have to show that the behaviour has actually caused anyone to be harassed, alarmed or distressed. Nor do they have to show that the accused intended to cause harassment, alarm or distress through their actions.

Because Asbos are imposed under civil law there are fewer restrictions on the sort of evidence that is admissible in court. Hearsay evidence given by 'professional witnesses', such as housing association or council staff, may be heard. This means that the person accused of anti-social behaviour does not have the opportunity to properly challenge the evidence against him or her by having a solicitor cross-examine the accuser, as he or she would in a normal criminal case.

How do Asbos work?
Asbos are simple banning orders which place restrictions – known as conditions – on an individual's behaviour and actions. An Asbo

cannot compel someone to do anything. Often, an Asbo will ban someone from entering specific geographical areas such as a particular street, estate or local authority area. However, conditions can apply throughout the whole of England and Wales. Asbos are also used to restrict a person's rights to associate with others or are used to impose a curfew.

In the past, people have been banned from:

▷ Riding a bike.
▷ Playing football.
▷ Being sarcastic.
▷ Swearing at people.
▷ Feeding the birds.
▷ Being seen in the garden or at windows wearing underwear.
▷ Begging 'in an earnest and humble way'.
▷ Congregating with more than two people in a public space.

Asbos last for a minimum of two years, but significantly there is no maximum time limit. This means that people can be banned from certain activities for life.

Although Asbos are imposed under civil law, breach of any of the conditions of an Asbo is a serious criminal offence. This means that your child can face a five-year prison sentence for behaviour such as that listed above which is normally not illegal – the maximum penalty for under 17s is a two-year detention and training order (see DTO, page 131).

Anyone who has been given an Asbo can be 'named and shamed'. This means that your child's name, address and photograph can be publicised in the local and national media and through leaflets and posters distributed in their community – even though he or she may have not breached their Asbo nor been convicted of any crime.

The government changed the law so that children as young as ten years old could be named and shamed in this way. Some have faced threats of violence from vigilantes, as a result. Other children regard naming and shaming as a perverse 'badge of honour', making it very unlikely to change their behaviour for the better.

How can I help prevent my daughter recommitting an offence?
If your daughter committed a crime that led to a custodial sentence (*see page 131*), she has a good chance of reoffending. Studies show that 73 per cent of young offenders between the ages of eighteen and twenty-one and 82 per cent of young males between the ages of fifteen and eighteen are reconvicted within two years of release from custody; another sign, perhaps, that these types of sentences do not work for young people. Older child offenders have higher reoffending rates than younger child offenders.

Many kids are shocked, distressed and humiliated when they are charged with a crime, and this experience can be enough to deter them from future offences. But don't take things for granted. You'll need to be extremely vigilant about keeping tabs on your child until she regains your trust. Explain to her that freedom is a privilege and will only be offered when she has proved that she is responsible enough to behave correctly. Keep her busy. If she's involved in plenty of activities, she'll be less likely to spend time causing trouble or undertaking illegal activities. There will always be temptation (working in a shop if your child has a history of shoplifting, for example), but she needs guidance and advice to overcome unhealthy urges.

If your child was stealing because she doesn't have enough money, or any of the things she perceives that she needs, you may have to negotiate a compromise on pocket money, for example, or offer her ways to increase her income. If she was stealing to fund a drug or alcohol habit, or even smoking, you'll need to address the addiction before you can expect the behaviour to change.

If your child is in with an unhealthy peer group, it's important that you explain why you are worried, and you encourage friendships and activities with other friends. In essence, you can't do anything about offending until you work out the cause. It may well have been a spur-of-the-moment event – shoplifting for a dare, getting into a fight with girls from a rival school or causing damage to property because 'everyone' was doing it, but there are issues that can be addressed. Your child may need help with how to deal with peer pressure (*see page 374*) for example, how to cope with feelings of violence or how to resist temptation. Once you've ascertained *why* your daughter behaved like she did, you can work on ensuring that it doesn't occur again.

Curfews

What curfews are appropriate for what ages?

Curfews are set for various reasons and are a fairly standard part of family life. They are set in order to protect your children (many accidents happen late at night), to ensure that they get sufficient sleep, to ensure that *you* get enough sleep and don't spend half the night waiting up, and, of course, curfews are a way of keeping tabs on your children's whereabouts – it's one time when they *have* to be where they say they are: at home.

The best way to set a curfew is to discuss it with your child so that she doesn't feel powerless. Explain the reasons why you set the curfew when you do, but give her a little scope for negotiation. Do a little research. While you don't want her to be the first to leave every party or outing she attends (unless she's with a risky crowd), you also don't want her to be the last either – in both cases, she could end up travelling home alone. Ideally, most parents will set a curfew at approximately the same time. Research indicates that most kids under the age of sixteen are home by 11 pm at the latest; and a quick scan of parent chatrooms and websites indicates that this seems appropriate. Kids under this age tend to have curfews that extend as they get older: the curfew for 11-year-olds (when they are first 'let out' on their own) is about 9.30 pm while 15-year-olds might be expected home between 10.30 and 11 pm.

In general, children under the ages of twelve or thirteen tend to be collected from activities, events or parties, so it's easier to monitor their curfew situation.

How can I negotiate a curfew?

▷ If your child thinks his curfew is too early, then offer some incentive. Offer to add another 15 to 30 minutes every four to six months, provided the curfew has not been broken in any way.

▷ Make clear your expectations. A curfew means being at home, inside the front door at the agreed time. Many parents ask that their child comes to say good night on arrival – this prevents the inevitable 'oh, I've been home for hours ....' and is also a good way to ensure that your child is *compos mentis*!

▷ Sometimes plans change, lifts are late, a taxi doesn't turn up or there is an unexpected delay in getting back. While you can be flexible once in a while, repeated incidents show a lack of respect for the agreed curfew and leave some doubt about the truth as well.

▷ A curfew doesn't give a child freedom to go out and do whatever he pleases until the agreed hour. You still need to know where he is going, and with whom, and you can expect him to ring if he is gong to be late or his plans change.

▷ Allow some leeway for special events – New Year's Eve, a big party or school function.

▷ Specifically discourage him from ringing 20 minutes or so before curfew to say he is 'sleeping over at a friend's house'. This generally means that something is up. If he wants to stay overnight, this should be agreed in advance and usually checked with the parents of the proposed host.

▷ Remember that kids don't always hate curfews. In tricky situations they can be a welcome excuse to get away from something or someone that is proving problematic.

When setting a curfew consider your child's sleep needs (*see page 55*), as well as the activities he has planned for the following day, his school workload and anything else of relevance. Agreeing an 11 pm curfew for a child who has to be up at 6.30 am the following morning may be acceptable occasionally, but in general, it will be detrimental to health.

▷ No matter how much you love your child, make sure you do set and uphold a penalty for violations. Keep it reasonable, but be firm and consistent. He will break it over and over again if he thinks he can get away with it. Some parents recommend moving the curfew earlier by an hour for every hour he is late, for the next two evenings out. This sounds a reasonable plan!

Should there be different curfews for weekdays and weekends?

Most definitely! During the week, the curfew reflects the need to balance homework, family time, sleep and friends within a short period of time. Children of *all* ages require plenty of sleep and time with their parents (*see page 54*). It is virtually impossible to fit this into weeknight evenings and still go out. An hour or so revising with a friend or seeing the odd film from time to time during the week is acceptable, along with perhaps a bit of time after school to congregate on bikes or in the local coffee shop. Most kids, these days, have precious little time during the week and reserve going out for the weekend – and then, often just one of two nights. Don't be afraid to set a firm, early curfew during the week (9 pm for everyone under sixteen or seventeen, an hour later if they are older and still at school). Weekends can be time for play, just as they are for most adults.

Should my child's curfew be the same as her friends?

Ideally, it should be similar. You don't want your child to be embarrassed about having to be collected or make her way home well before everyone else – and before the fun has begun. While we have suggested some possible and sensible curfews, they may be wildly at odds with what your children's friends are allowed. Once again, don't change your theories or beliefs because of parent peer pressure, but use the information to work out if you are setting a time that is realistic and fair. Speak to several parents – kids are notoriously untrustworthy when it comes to passing on facts about what is *really* allowed, and then adjust the curfew if you think it is reasonable to do so, given your individual child's schedule, sleep needs and everything else. If you have concerns, try speaking to the parents of your child's friends – they might offer some insight into how they worked out their own curfews, and it might be worth taking into consideration – or not! Either way, be consistent and explain your thinking to your child when you have made your decision.

Under what circumstances should I allow a curfew to be broken?

Holidays, special occasions, a birthday, a friend's big party, dances or proms – anything that is bound to run late and is important to your child. Dragging her back before the party is over is only going to spark rebellion and/or breed resentment. Be fair. There are times when you are out much later than planned because the occasion demanded it, and the same will go for your children. That is not, however, licence to stay out all night. Look at the agenda and the timings, and set a curfew that is reasonable and realistic, then stick with it.

How do I know what is appropriate?

You won't know what is appropriate until you do your homework. Sometimes schools help out a bit by suggesting reasonable 'bedtimes', or how much work should be done at a given age, per night, or the number of hours that should be leisure time. This makes it easier to work out free time and when it should take place. Talk to other parents – work out your children's individual needs, but, above all, use your common sense. There is no way, for example, that an 11-year-old should be out until 11 pm and make his own way home. There is no way that a 15-year-old should be out until midnight on a school night without very good reason. Don't just consider what your own curfews were; these are bound to have changed, and be based on tradition rather than a realistic appraisal of circumstances.

Debt

See Money, *page 337.*

Drugs

When should I start talking about drugs?

Studies show that parents are the principle influence in their children's attitude towards drug use. Educating teens about drugs and the problems that accompany drug abuse will help them to develop a healthy stance on drugs and will provide them with the knowledge to make good decisions in the future. Ideally, discussions should begin in early childhood – well before your child has his first official contact, or is under any pressure to experiment. The idea is that you will communicate your beliefs and values about drugs (and alcohol) early on, so that they build up a set of guidelines and limits to help them make healthy decisions in the future. Adolescence is the worst time to begin talking to kids about drugs, as teens are most likely to reject their parents' advice and follow the crowd – or be influenced by their peers. It is, however, never too late to begin talking about drugs, even if you've avoided the issue until you believed they were ready.

When do kids first start to experiment with drugs?

The average age at which children experiment with drugs for the first time is around twelve or thirteen (and, in many cases, a couple of years later), but the dialogue should begin much sooner. You can begin by explaining what is meant by the word 'drugs', what drugs

DRUG FACTS

It has been estimated also that in more than one in four children or adolescents will experiment with drugs at some point. A study of a group between the ages of eleven and thirty-five found that 45 per cent had used illegal drugs at least once. Overall, about 18 per cent of the UK population admitted to having taken an illegal drug at least once in their life – this works out to be approximately nine million people. There has been a threefold increase in drug misuse notifications in the last ten years alone.

do to people, how they make people feel and why they are dangerous. Kids hear and see a lot about drugs before drugs actually affect them personally – via the media, older or riskier peers, siblings or parents, and, of course, from games and the internet. There are very few 7-year-olds, for example, who don't know the word 'drugs', even if they aren't entirely clear of its meaning. Your stance on drugs should be made apparent early on, even if you haven't had a serious chat.

Studies show that many parents neglect to discuss drugs with their children, feeling perhaps that if they don't mention it, it won't happen – or feeling uncomfortable about laying down the law. The reality is that many kids experiment with drugs and they need to know the facts.

What can I do?

▷ Don't say 'we need to have a talk' and sit your child down in a formal manner. You'll probably worry him and he'll clam up. Relax and talk about it over supper or when you're in the car. If you are casual, it will help your children to be more honest and willing to talk, particularly if it is a regular discussion you've had over the years.

▷ Look out for opportunities to engage your child in discussion – for example, a newspaper article, a poster, a pro-drugs T-shirt or music, a book or a TV programme. Ask your child's opinion and approach.

▷ Make sure you know what you are talking about! Check the internet, the library, schools and even your doctor's surgery for sources of information. If your child asks questions, you will be in a position to offer an answer; if not, go together to look things up and use this as a basis for further discussion.

However, the more informed you are, the easier it will be to discuss the issues.

Your child isn't going to take you seriously if you get the facts wrong or use scare stories to deter him. Kids are savvy – many know much more than we think and won't be fobbed off with false information. Most kids will know someone who experiments with drugs and hasn't died or been hospitalised. Add this to the fact that kids are confident of their immortality and invincibility, and they are bound to be dismissive of dramatic cautions.

▷ Be accessible and open-minded – the idea is to open a dialogue. Listen to what your teens have to say. Ask questions and do not judge.

▷ But be clear. While we are all aware that experimentation is a part of growing up, and that many of our teenagers will try drugs, being taciturn about the subject, sitting on the fence about your views, or being overly permissive will confuse your child and fail to give him the guidance he needs. 'Drugs are bad news' should be the core theme of your discussions, and you can then go on to state the reasons why.

▷ 'Just say no' is not reasonable advice when it comes to drugs, as it simplifies a complex issue. The fact is that good kids do try drugs, and good kids find themselves in situations that they can't control; getting snared in drugs through peer pressure does not make your child weak or bad; it makes him normal, and in need of more guidance than ever. Your biggest concern is your child's safety and the prevention of chronic use and addiction.

▷ Drugs can be alluring and their use can promote status and acceptance in the peer group – something that may always take precedence over parental approval. Be realistic and open-minded. Make it clear, for example, that if he is in trouble, has taken too much or is in a tricky situation, you will come and get him, no questions asked. That doesn't mean you are condoning drug use – it means that you are being realistic and offering support should your child need it.

▷ If you do hear things you don't like, try not to panic or judge. Keep the dialogue going, avoid lecturing, but take the opportunity to give your opinion and explain the reasons behind your thinking. The whole point of discussing drugs with your teen is to give him a foundation for making wise decisions about drugs on his own.

▷ Peer pressure will always be an issue when it comes to drugs. Talk about how to say no, how to deal with pressures to conform and give your child facts and information to use to back up his stance.

▷ Don't try to share your own experiences. First of all, most kids will use this as a green light to experiment themselves, whether you are trying to send a negative warning message or not. Secondly, things have changed in the drug world. Cannabis as you may have known it doesn't just make you giggly and high any more; there are much stronger varieties out there now, which carry much bigger health risks. You can empathise with your teenager without needing to say you did the same thing.

▷ Many teens do not feel comfortable talking to their parents about drugs, but they will talk to others. Make sure your child has someone else to turn to; put him in touch with some of the helplines that offer invaluable, confidential advice and information. Don't feel rejected. It's normal.

▷ Remember: while you may not be able to prevent your teenager from experimenting with legal or illegal drugs completely, you can educate him as to the risks, effects and possible consequences, and ways of staying safe. This can be equally important and may even save his life.

Should I allow my child the freedom to experiment?

The simple answer is that your child may choose to experiment whether you condone it or not. Today, most kids try alcohol, cigarettes, inhalants or other drugs once or twice. Just as they experiment with music, clothing and other aspects of life as they become independent, they will undoubtedly push the boundaries when it comes to illegal substances. The key word in this question is 'allow'. You don't need to 'allow' anything. Be aware that it may happen, advise your child of the risks and how to keep himself safe, and be there if he needs help or guidance. But don't condone it; by doing so, you will simply encourage further use. It's not quite the same as alcohol, where allowing it to become a part of daily life removes the 'forbidden fruit' element. Although alcohol can, when it is abused, be as dangerous as many drugs, the fact is that it is legal and a big part of today's acceptable social culture. So what you are doing is teaching your children how to use rather than abuse. Drugs are, whatever your views, illegal, and potentially addictive. Most kids will not go further than a little experimentation, and usually do not have problems as a result of substance abuse, but it makes sense to be aware of when experimentation becomes regular or frequent use (abuse).

How do I know if my daughter is abusing drugs?

It's not easy to spot when your teenager is developing a drug habit. Most kids are adept at hiding what they don't want you to see (but also good at leaving clues if they consciously or subconsciously need your help). Don't be tempted to raid your child's room, check e-mails or read her diary, which will only undermine trust at an all-important time. Instead, look out for the following signs:

▷ Changes in sleeping pattern.

▷ Fatigue and lethargy.

▷ Mood swings.

▷ Changes in appetite.

▷ Unexpected aggression.

▷ Loss of interest in normal social life.

▷ Lack of interest in personal hygiene.

▷ Disappearance or shortage of money.

▷ Changes in appearance.

▷ Change in friends.

▷ Taking too long to come to her bedroom door when you knock.

▷ Telltale physical signs – pallor, red eyes, persistent coughing, sore, red nose, persistently runny nose, puffy face, drawn appearance.

▷ Drop in grades.

▷ Truancy.

Remember that all teens can be moody creatures and can be difficult to deal with on some occasions. This doesn't necessarily mean they are abusing drugs – just watch out for *changes* in behaviour, particularly those that are fairly sudden.

What should I do if I discover my child is abusing drugs?

First of all, stay calm. If you over-react and go into panic or punishment mode, you will lose the opportunity to help your child and he will back off immediately. It's a good idea to talk to someone on one of the parent helplines (*see below*) before you decide how to tackle your child. Not only can these give you plenty of advice, facts and information, they are very experienced in dealing with drug abuse and can offer solutions that may not have occurred to you.

When you do speak to your child, explain that you know or suspect that drug use is taking place. Explain that you are worried because you love her, and because you want to help. Explain that you are worried about her safety and that her life is precious to you.

Ask her to be honest about use – and don't over-react. Find out what substances she has tried, what effects the substances had, and how she feels about substance use. You may not get the absolute truth (this will depend on how must your child trusts you not to punish and how close your relationship is), but you'll be getting somewhere. And this is invaluable information. If your child feels confident, popular, happy or relaxed when she takes drugs, then maybe these are feelings she needs to have more regularly *without* them. Take the time to work out what may be missing in your child's life.

Be honest in return. Discuss your concerns about safety, but also about the impact on health, relationships, schoolwork, finances and future. Don't berate your child for having gone down this route; it's done. Talk about what you can do together to stop a downward spiral that might lead to addiction and serious problems.

It is often very difficult to know if there is a bit of relatively harmless experimentation going on, which will hopefully go no further, or if your child is already beginning to show signs of addiction. If you have a family history of substance abuse or dependence, you need to make this clear to him or her, and explain that 'harmless' fun can, in fact, be the first step on the road to nowhere.

Don't be afraid to *ask* (not order) your child to stop. Put forward your beliefs again, without judging, but say that he or she needs to stop for their own health and safety. Offer to help.

Ask for reasons why it might be hard to give up (all his friends do it, for example, or he really needs the release, high or elation that it brings), and see if you can find ways round this. A risk-taking adolescent who wants to push the limits might actually need some more challenges in his life – of the healthy kind. Maybe becoming involved in a challenging sport, such as snowboarding, skydiving or BMX biking will give him a 'high' without the substance. Investigate all the options.

Persuade him to contact a confidential help or support line or visit the family doctor.

Where else can we get help?

For further information and help contact:

> National Drugs Helpline
> Tel: 0800 776600
> www.ndh.org.uk.

> Re-Solv
> A charity dedicated to tackling solvent misuse.
> Tel: 0808 800 2345

If I suspect my child is experimenting with drugs, when should I intervene?

This is a difficult question because every child is different. Some can get away with a little experimentation, keep their grades, activities and friendships up, and give it all up without a murmur. Other kids have more addictive personalities and enjoy the experience to the extent that they become dependent, either physically or psychologically, in a short space of time. Once this happens, it is a chronic, on-going and possibly fatal disease.

Basically, if your child shows absolutely no signs of drug dependence (*see page 153*), but you've smelled a little cannabis, or suspect that he seems a little more elated than usual after being out with friends, you may wish to watch carefully and wait. It may have been a one-off occasion, and won't be repeated. If it happens again, or if there are signs that it is affecting his health or well-being on *any* level, then talk to him about his drug use (*see page 154*). Do not wait.

Even if you suspect it is a short-term experimentation, it never hurts to let your child know that you are aware of the activity, and that you are concerned for many reasons (*see above*). If you have a 'no drugs' household policy, you probably already have a pre-arranged penalty or 'consequences' for breaking the rules, and these can be implemented, whether they involve being 'grounded' or having freedom restricted. There is nothing wrong with expressing your disapproval of drugs throughout childhood and into adolescence, and making it clear that if he does break the rules and damages your trust, there will be consequences. But going in with all guns blazing is never going to be conducive to a healthy relationship, nor will it encourage your child to confide in you if he has problems or worries about drug use himself.

Does it matter that my husband smokes a little pot? Is he a bad role model?

Observing role models is one of the most important ways that our children learn what is acceptable and what is not; their values are defined by what they see and experience at home, long before peer pressure ever comes into the equation, and long before they are tempted by illegal substances themselves. As they grow older, all children are aware of parental shortcomings – mum drinks too much occasionally, dad still smokes and pops a prescription tablet when he can't sleep or feels stressed. All of these are legal and possibly acceptable in today's society, but it's important to remember that parental behaviour provides children with their values and morals, and what they perceive as being the norm. So they can justify getting drunk one evening (after all, mum does) or having a cigarette (dad does), or trying a few pills (they relax dad and make him more companionable, so maybe they're OK). Maybe not ideal, but perhaps not dangerous either.

However, if your husband actually takes an illegal substance and your children are aware of it, you have lost some significant moral ground, and you've also lost any possibility of having a credible argument against drug-taking. Suggesting that your husband is an 'adult' and 'not addicted' won't work, because his behaviour supports the idea that drug use and breaking the law are acceptable come a certain age (18?).

Children can and will always use your husband's drug use to their own devices – and in defence. What's more, if your husband is genuinely reliant on an evening spliff or whatever, there may be a familial predilection for substance abuse. Just because your husband has it under control doesn't mean your children will be able to exercise the same self-restraint, or fail to get caught up in more serious drug use as a result.

So the simple answer is that your responsibility is to provide the best role model you can for your children and to curb your own behaviour accordingly. This may sound sanctimonious, but it is important that your children's first experiences and influences are positive and reflect the values you want them to take with them through adolescence and into adulthood.

Ears

When is it safe for my daughter to have her ears pierced?
Many parents wait until their child is able to make the decision for herself (or himself) before piercing ears, although some parents choose to pierce even tiny infants. There is no legislation regarding legal age limits, but there are health and safety issues. For one

thing, young children and babies will not understand the risk of infection, and are notorious for pulling, prodding and fiddling with body parts. All types of bacteria can cause problems, but the most worrying is tetanus. Even though tetanus is not very common (thanks to immunisation), tetanus bacteria is everywhere, and it usually enters the body through puncture wounds. For this reason, it is better for a baby to have at least one (better two) tetanus shots before her big day. Two shots would put the event at three to five months old for most kids. Also, once babies are three months old, they are better able to handle the more common minor skin infections they might get. There is also a risk of acquiring hepatitis B, which is extremely contagious, incurable and passed from person to person through infected blood or other body fluids. This makes your choice of a reputable ear-piercing salon even more important.

What's more, anything other than safety studs can be dangerous, as the ear lobe can be easily torn if longer earrings or hoops catch.

When you do go for piercing, ensure that a hypoallergenic metal earring is used, and that the ear-piercing gun is a self-contained, pre-sterilised and disposable unit. This will help to cut down the risk of infection. Some experts recommend having both ears pierced simultaneously, with two technicians, to avoid distressing your child. Clean the area twice a day with isopropyl alcohol, particularly after playing.

What if I don't approve of pierced ears?
Lots of parents think that pierced ears look cheap and nasty in children, and make a decision early on that their children will have to wait until their tenth or even thirteenth birthday or later before they can have it done. In many cases, parental decisions reflect the views that their own parents had on the subject.

While safety is clearly an issue (particularly for girls who are too young to take care of the necessary hygiene, or not responsible enough to wear appropriate earrings when required), it's fair to say that it is not a moral or ethical issue. In our multicultural society, pierced ears are unlikely to be considered a sign of poor values, bad parenting or taste. I suggest that you be prepared to enter into negotiations with your son or daughter, and to challenge your own conceptions or preconceptions. Why does it bother you? Are you holding on to a family tradition or belief? Is it relevant? If every girl in your daughter's class has her ears pierced and they spend weekend shopping trips perusing jewellery, is there not a chance that you might be holding on to antiquated views and that you might be forbidding your child something that is now a social and completely acceptable norm?

There is nothing wrong with encouraging children to wait for significant, age-related milestones, as it teaches them about delayed gratification and patience! However, you may find you need to adjust your age limit downwards.

A straw and completely unscientific poll of 38 parents of daughters in our neighbourhood (many of whom attend a good girls' independent school) found that age ten is the norm these days. But be prepared to listen if this age is completely out of touch with your own child's peers and culture.

When can my child get his or her ears pierced without my permission?

There is no statutory age limit to getting ears or other body parts pierced (*see page 163*), though individual practitioners may refuse to pierce younger children without adult consent.

Be savvy, though. If your local beauty salon or ear-piercing venue refuses to pierce your child's ears without your permission, there is nothing to stop your child from doing it herself (we've all seen it done – a sterilised needle and a block of ice held behind the ear), having friends do it or finding an outlet that will. Determined children always find a way.

These are all good reasons why it pays to have an open relationship with your child, and to consider giving in on something that really matters to him or her. Choose your battles wisely, and don't get carried away with the small stuff. You can ground or punish till the cows come home after the fact, but if the ears are pierced, in whatever way, the battle is lost. Much better, really, to ensure that she goes to a reputable, hygienic salon and has your help in taking care of her newly pierced ears.

Should my son be allowed pierced ears?

Just when you've come to terms with allowing your daughter to have her ears pierced before the magic age of thirteen, your 10-year-old son is demanding the same.

Is it right? The fact is that many male icons who influence our children have pierced ears – from football heroes, to pop stars, film stars, models, you name it. Our kids want to dress like them, listen to the same music and model their behaviour. While the latter is not to be recommended, it's worth considering that ear-piercing is not a particularly serious issue. It's not permanent (some good advice here – many parents will allow experimentation as long as it is not *permanent* like a tattoo), and the piercing can grow over relatively easily.

What about body piercing?

Body piercing is common and increasingly popular. In the end, it is a body decoration and nothing more sinister. Many parents worry about infection, worry that it indicates a sexual preference, which does not appear to be the case any longer, or feel that their parenting will be called into question.

Once again, consider your son's argument, and work out if your own reluctance is due to personal and possibly preconceived ideas about boys and earrings. Don't hesitate to set an age limit for safety reasons (*see page 158*); after all, the hygiene of most teenaged boys is questionable and if he's off playing rugby or football every weekend, it could be a recipe for disaster. Consider, too, whether it is just a whim that will fade with time (agreeing to a piercing six months or a year down the road might nip the issue in the bud, before an argument is even necessary), or if it's the current social must-have for boys of your son's age.

Whatever the consideration, make an agreement that the ears can be pierced, once or even twice, but that the other bits remain earring-free until your son reaches the age of consent! If you've got a piercing phobia, this just might work!

When is it appropriate for girls to wear dangling earrings?
Many parents give in to an earlier piercing age on the understanding that small studs will be worn until a particular age (in many cases, it is the earrings that parents object to, rather than the piercing) say, thirteen. But if you have a younger child who is keen on pretty dangling earrings, why not accompany her and choose something together that fits her agenda, and which you find acceptable and/or tasteful. Certainly pre-teens should wear earrings that are less likely to be caught in play equipment or in rough and tumble games with friends, saving longer ones for dignified evenings out! Remember, though, that even brushing hair and catching them on a long earring can cause serious damage to the earlobe. Your child will need to be mature enough to handle the responsibility of potential accidents.

They should absolutely not wear dangling earrings while playing sports. The earrings can get caught on clothing or in hair very easily and can tear the earlobe. Many schools have restrictions on wearing jewellery and dangling earrings probably fall into that category; check your daughter's school rules to see if this is the case.

What about other body piercings?

Anyone under eighteen can receive a body piercing provided he or she has written permission from a parent or guardian or the treatment is performed in the presence of that parent or guardian. In some councils and counties, anyone over the age of fourteen can do so without parental consent. In Scotland you must be sixteen. Check the requirements in your area. In view of the somewhat inconsistent legal position, many practitioners will not hesitate to pierce your children's ears or other body part if he or she looks old enough and has the money to pay! Nipple and genital piercing is prohibited on minors, regardless of parental consent.

But beware! Headstrong, determined kids can often supply their own letter of permission, and even back it up with a friend answering from an appropriate number to verify. It happens!

Kids who want piercings often just want to express their

SAFETY NOTE

All piercings produce a white discharge during the healing period. Symptoms of infection may include pain, swelling, inflammation (area feels warm or hot to the touch), excessive redness and a discharge of yellow pus. If you suspect an infection contact your doctor, but do not remove the jewellery. The openings will close and trap the infection, which can create an abscess.

distinctiveness (or, alternatively, to follow their peers). It's possible to suggest other ways that they can fit in or be different, whatever the case: unique jewellery, unusual clothes, interesting fingernails or make-up, or even washable tattoos. Encourage your child to explore her individuality through a variety of different means.

If you disagree with body piercings (and there are certainly health grounds for this, as the risk of infection is high), you will need to establish this early on and supply some good, solid reasons. If you do agree or if your child comes home with an unauthorised piercing, it is extremely important that the site is diligently cleaned and disinfected regularly.

Where can I get more information?

For more information on dealing with various body piercings, visit the UK Health and Safety Executive at: www.hse.gov.uk/lau/lacs/76-2.

Employment

When can my daughter get a part-time job?

The legal age for a young person to start paid work is currently fourteen years old. However, some areas of the UK allow the minimum age to be thirteen years old to cover certain types of work such as delivering newspapers or working in shops, salons, offices or cafes.

What are the rules?

There are, however, very stringent rules regarding the employment of young teens (although note, this does not apply to babysitting or charity work):

▷ No work is to be carried out during school hours or during school lunch breaks.

▷ No work is to be carried before 7 am or after 7 pm.

▷ Only two hours of work can be carried out on a school weekday, of which no more than one hour of this can be carried out before the start of school hours.

▷ Work should last no longer than two hours on a Sunday.

▷ Work should last no longer than eight hours during a Saturday or during a school holiday. This is reduced to five hours for those fifteen and under.

▷ Work should last no longer than 35 hours per week during school holidays. This is reduced to 25 hours for those fifteen and under.

▷ Work should last no longer than 12 hours per week when the child is attending school.

▷ Young children should have at least a two-week break during the school holidays or at any point during the school year.

Should my 14-year-old son receive the minimum wage for his paper route?

Unfortunately not. The current law relates to workers aged sixteen and over (there are two bands: over sixteen and over eighteen). If you feel that your child is being unfairly paid, however, you do have some options (*see page 175*); however, if he accepted the job knowing the terms, it is quite likely that his wage will not increase.

Any employer who wishes to employ a child before the school-leaving age (*see page 403*), must obtain an application form from the Education Welfare Service, and this must be signed by a parent and the employer – and in many cases the headteacher of his school. A copy should be sent to the school before he begins employment. This should give you ample opportunity to question terms.

When does my son need to pay tax on his earnings?

Unfortunately, there is no minimum age for the payment of tax. Anyone who earns more than the government's set personal allowance, and is under the age of 65, has to pay tax. At the time of writing (2007), this is set at just over £5,000. So if your child earns even a penny above the set figure, he must pay tax. Chances are he won't – particularly if he's working in the summer. In this instance, it is possible to have earnings paid without the deduction of tax. Employers can give him a tax form P38, which is a declaration for students working during summer vacation only. If he works part-time and has an income below the personal allowance, he can also either request that no tax is paid or request a refund. Many kids are paid in cash, particularly in jobs such as paper delivery. If your child's income is low and well below his personal allowance, don't give it a second thought.

What jobs are appropriate for kids and at what ages?

There are certain jobs that are appropriate and/or legal at certain ages. Children under compulsory school age (which is set in the UK at sixteen) can undertake:

▷ Agricultural and horticultural work (plants and crops).
▷ Delivery of newspapers, journals and printed materials.
▷ Shop work, including stacking shelves.
▷ Office work.
▷ Hairdressing salon work.
▷ Car washing by hand in a private residential setting.
▷ Café or restaurant, but not in the kitchen and may not serve alcohol.
▷ In a riding establishment.
▷ Domestic work in hotels and other establishments offering accommodation, but not in the kitchen.

Is some work prohibited to kids under school age?

▷ Street trading (although a local authority can allow 14-year-olds to work for their parents).

▷ Industrial work (unless they are working with a member of their family). This includes mines, quarries, construction, transport work, either of goods or passengers by road, rail or waterway.

▷ Performing abroad.

▷ Scrap metal.

▷ Betting shops (a child must be eighteen to work in a betting shop).

▷ Petrol stations – no one under the age of sixteen should be permitted to serve petrol; however, this is a recommendation from the UK Home Office and not a law.

▷ Charity collections.

Are there any other prohibited occupations?

The following occupations and jobs are often banned as well, but there may be local bylaws allowing some or all. Please check with your local authority. Otherwise, your child should not:

▷ Work in a cinema, theatre, disco, dance hall or night club, except in connection with a performance given entirely by children.

▷ Sell or deliver alcohol, except in sealed containers.

▷ Deliver milk.

▷ Deliver fuel oils.

▷ Work in a commercial kitchen.

▷ Collect or sort refuse.

▷ Any work that is more than 3 m (10 ft) above ground or floor level.

▷ Work involving exposure to chemicals.

▷ Collect money, sell or canvas door-to-door, except under the supervision of an adult.

▷ Telephone sales.

▷ Any work involving exposure to adult material or in situations that are for this reason otherwise unsuitable for children.

▷ Work in a slaughter house or any part of a butcher's shop or premises connected with the killing of livestock, butchery or the preparation of meat for sale.

▷ Work as an attendant or assistant in a fairground or amusement arcade, or in any premises used for the purposes of public amusement by means of automatic machines, games of chance or similar.

After the age of sixteen, your child can do virtually anything apart from work in a gambling establishment or a bar.

As for what is suitable, there are many options available, and if they are allowable under stringent government guidelines, then they can be deemed appropriate. What you need to consider is the time required to fulfil the job, the timing of the job in relation to schoolwork, family time, homework, activities and social requirements, and whether the employer is reliable and fulfilling his legal obligations (*see below*).

Does my 16-year-old son have any legal rights when it comes to employment?

He does. He is entitled to:

▷ A minimum of four weeks paid holiday a year.

▷ A break of thirty minutes for every four hours he works (this decreases to twenty minutes for every six hours he works from the age of sixteen).

▷ Work a maximum of forty-eight hours a week, unless your child agrees to work longer hours; he has the right to ask for overtime if he does agree.

Should I pay my children for work they do around the house?

There are two different schools of thought on this one and you may need to choose! The first is that household duties are the responsibility of all members of the household and are, therefore, an expected contribution to said household. If you consider the not-so-distant past when children were expected to fulfil clear-cut chores – feeding chickens, collecting firewood, mending fences, washing dishes and preparing meals, helping on laundry day – things seem rather easier for our lot! On this basis, you may decide that no one gets paid for everyday jobs around the house, and that everyone is expected to contribute and pull his or her weight.

Taking this one step further, you should therefore offer pocket money that is independent of chores – in other words, not related to taking out the rubbish, for example – so that children learn that these jobs are part of life and have to be done by everyone. Given that children who are busy with household responsibilities have less opportunity to make money (perhaps you expect them to babysit a younger sibling frequently or do various jobs after school and on weekends), they will need an independent and fair source of income from parents (*see* Pocket money, *page 382*).

Most parents will find that children today are reluctant to take on household responsibility and instantly ask 'how much will you pay me' when you suggest a job. So you can go the other way completely, and make it clear that you will only pay for jobs that are done, with a fixed figure for every job done properly. This provides incentive for children to get things done you'll find that if they want some money, they'll soon produce the goods. Having said that, there is no doubt that kids need to learn to do some things as part of growing up and as part of being a family, such as setting the table, clearing away dishes or helping with dinner. No one needs to be paid for these things, as they are expected and fall under the category of 'family duties'. But other jobs, such as babysitting, helping in the garden, vacuuming or cleaning, doing some ironing or dusting, could be 'paid' employment within the house. Attach a value to each household chore and post a list. Then let your kids select the ones they want to do. If they want money, you can be sure they'll choose something; what's more, they have the freedom to choose as much or as little as they please, according to how much cash they are after. This is, of course, an early taste of the free enterprise system and definitely teaches a work ethic of sorts – if you want money, you have to work for it.

How do I get my child to lend a hand?

The trick to instilling a domestic work ethic in your child is two-fold: lead by example and start early. From the earliest age, your kids look to you for clues on how to act. If they see that you don't put your things away, hang up your clothes, clear your dishes from the table and so on, they'll get the message that they can leave stuff around for someone else to pick up.

On the other hand, if you start by making your toddler put away his toys when he's finished playing with them and have him straighten up his room once a day, you'll help him develop the habit of chipping in when there's work to be done. As kids get older, their duties around the house should expand to fit their abilities.

Of course, no one wants to turn their children into domestic slaves, but having a clearly defined list of chores (posting a written list is often helpful), along with who is responsible for doing each one, is an important facet of family life.

Finally, build some flexibility into your system. If one of the kids needs to spend a lot of time on a big project, make some allowances. You might offer to do the child's chores for him in exchange for an equal amount of time spent on other household chores later on.

Should my child be responsible for paying his way by taking a part-time job?

This really depends on your child's schedule, your expectations of your child, his time management skills and, of course, the family budget. It may be that you require an influx of cash once your child reaches the age of employment, in order to keep things ticking. It may be that you have a child who covets goods and activities outside your budget, such as expensive clothing, music or sports. In this case, there is nothing wrong with suggesting that if your child wants something outside the budget, he'll have to earn the money himself to pay for it. You can decide between you which items you are happy to pay for, and which fall outside 'essential goods' (*see page 99*).

But be realistic. If you expect your child to play a couple of instruments, keep up his sporting activities in his free time, become involved in the school play or orchestra, join the debating team, do Scouts, Guides or other clubs after school, and have extra tutoring in those subjects that he struggles with, then you can't possibly expect him to fit in a job as well. You'll have to balance what is important to you and to him, and what is reasonable for a child to achieve in any 24-hour period. If you have high expectations, you will need to either lower them or pay the price!

Furthermore, if you have an older child facing crucial exams or a younger child who is struggling, it is likely that a part-time job will add more pressure than is acceptable. While extremely organised children can fit in a job and revision or extra work with ease, most children are not great on time management and will end up being overloaded. Of course, a busy child is forced to learn time management early on, which is a valuable skill, but it is something that tends to develop over time in most children.

If your child has time on his hands, there is nothing wrong with a part-time job. However, unless you need the money (which he will undoubtedly be aware of), he probably does not need to contribute to the household to any great extent until he has finished his schooling. He can certainly pay for things outside the family budget, and perhaps his own fares to and from work, and meals while he's out, but there won't be much incentive to work if he doesn't come away with something for himself.

Should he save any money?

Financial advisors suggest that kids pay a portion of their earnings from part-time jobs into a savings account, which they can use for a gap year, further education or even a car at the appropriate time. Kids need to understand what it takes to get the 'big things' in life, and they should have a stake in it.

Do holidays need to be pure relaxation or should I expect my child to do something productive and lucrative, and at what age?

Given the stressful environment of school today and the number of examinations taken throughout a child's school career, it is not surprising that most children simply want to 'chill' on the holidays, and are reluctant to do anything productive. For younger children, who are usually supervised during holidays, this is certainly acceptable. Furthermore, holiday periods tend to be the times when families undertake activities together and have a more relaxed approach to daily life, which can be a very positive influence on family dynamics.

However, long holidays can be more problematic for older kids who spend most of their free time on their own or with their friends. First of all, when kids don't have anything structured to do, they often become 'bored' and bored kids get into trouble. Secondly, the temptation to spend hours in front of a computer, TV or games console can be overwhelming, and this can have a dramatic effect on mood, social skills, immunity and propensity to violence and more (*see page 112*). Thirdly, studies show that literacy, numeracy and information retention regress enormously during long holidays, with the average school spending almost a whole term covering old ground to get students back to where they were before they went on holiday.

There is also the issue of teaching children personal and social responsibility, and setting them on the path to 'real life'. Few jobs come with ten or twelve weeks of holiday per year, and older children do need to get used to this idea. There is no reason why an able child of working age should not get at least a part-time job in the summer holidays, to teach financial responsibility and time-keeping/planning, and to instil a work ethic. Most kids object to giving up their 'holiday' time, but undoubtedly change their tune when they get their first pay cheque. If money isn't important to your child, or you don't mind covering expenses until they leave home, this can be a good opportunity to offer something to the community on a volunteer basis (*see page 105*).

Many parents like the idea of their children experimenting with a little freedom – working away from home at a summer camp in the US or Canada, for example, or a children's activity centre where they can live in – before they head off to university. They earn money, meet new friends, get a taste of independent living, some pride in their achievement, and, of course, a set of new skills.

The simple answer is most children from age sixteen or so will probably benefit from some regular work or activity in the holidays, getting them on course for adult life and keeping boredom at bay.

At what age should I allow my teenager to take a paying job abroad in his summer holiday?

It depends on how mature your teenager is! Some 16-year-olds are fully capable of looking after themselves and behaving responsibly. Others will treat a break from parents' supervision as a big party, and probably get into some trouble.

For most kids, their first taste of working in another country comes during a gap year (*see page 238*), when they are eighteen, nineteen or twenty. In this case they are considered young adults and should have taken on board most of the lessons, morals and guidance you have showered on them since they were born. They require the freedom to experiment a bit, and to find their own feet in the world.

Older children who are still at school may not be ready for this kind of independence and may not have the maturity to make appropriate decisions regarding their own safety and upkeep. There are many 16-year-old boys who still find it an anathema to wash or change their boxers regularly, let alone wash a dish, change a set of sheets or eat properly. But these kids have to learn *somehow*, and often a little taste of freedom is all it takes to kick-start them into action.

I wouldn't recommend sending a 16-year-old abroad to work unless there is some element of supervision and someone they can turn to for help. Working as an au pair or in a French or North American summer camp is probably a safe option – particularly if you have friends in the host country – and most usually have living accommodation on-site, with fairly stringent expectations and codes of behaviour. If your child is keen and you feel confident that the place of work is safe and supervised, then sixteen is a suitable age for most kids. Most employers would be reluctant to take on anyone much younger anyhow, because of the responsibility and the insurance required.

What can I do if I feel my child is being exploited by his employer?

There are a series of laws protecting children from exploitation (for example, limiting what children under school-leaving age can do) and it's well worth being familiar with these (*see page 164*). Your child's employer can be prosecuted if it fails to adhere to the strict regulations, and you are well within your rights to draw these to the employer's attention.

Where can we go for advice?

The best way to go about this is to contact the Advisory, Conciliation and Arbitration Service (Acas), which offers free, confidential and impartial advice on employment rights issues and can tell you what types of claim can be taken to an Employment Tribunal. You can call the Acas helpline on 08457 47 47 47 from 8 am to 6 pm Monday to Friday.

Similarly, your local Citizens Advice Bureau (CAB) can provide free and impartial advice. You can find your local CAB office in the phone book or online.

But first consider encouraging your child to deal with the problem. There are bullies and exploitative people in all jobs in all walks of life, and all children need to learn how to stand up for themselves and to deal with difficulties when they arise. Although it can be stressful, you can help him behind the scenes by advising your child of his rights, practising how to speak (or write) to his employer, and how to make his case. If he gets no where, then you can certainly step in and make your child's case for him; but be advised that this can sometimes backfire, with your child being labelled a troublemaker or difficult.

In some cases, it might be best to bow out quietly from a job that is not appropriate and to look for something more suitable for your child. He'll get his reference if he leaves on good terms, and you can pass on details of any ill treatment to your local authorities in confidence, so that other children won't face the same problems. Chalk it up to one of life's bad experiences, work out what you and your child learned from it, what he'd do differently next time, and move on.

Entertainment

When can she go to a pop concert or gig?

Not so very long ago, music represented the ultimate symbol of the generation gap! Few parents shared the same taste in music as their kids, so there was certainly little question of younger kids accompanying their parents to concerts or gigs (although the reverse was common, with dad or mum sitting with arms crossed and earplugs in place, in a supervisory role).

So if you are happy with the music (the lyrics, the general culture of the band in question and the fans), there is little reason why your children can't accompany you from about the age of ten. Some kids are seasoned concert-goers at an even younger age, as fans of Britney, the Spice Girls, most boy bands, and Justin Timberlake will confirm. These do, however, tend to be a known quantity, and provide a relatively safe and expletive- and violence-free experience.

If you aren't sure about whether a band is suitable, listen to the lyrics of its music, and ask some questions of the concert organisers. Visit the band's website and work out their fan base. If your 12-year-old is going to be surrounded by a bunch of swearing teens on Ecstasy, you might want to give it a miss.

Top tips

▷ Prepare your child for the experience. Explain that it's going to be very loud and very crowded, and that there will likely be a lot of waiting around (for the toilets, a drink or a snack, or the band itself).

▷ Know your child. If your child hates loud noises and feels panicky in a crowd, she's probably not ready for a concert in a large venue, but a gig at a child-friendly pub might be up her street.

▷ Use foul language or behaviour as a tool for learning, pointing out, perhaps, that what a pop star does as part of her show is not acceptable in real life, and is just an act. Also, perhaps, explain that some stars are rude to draw attention to themselves, or have a problem with alcohol or drugs that makes them act inappropriately. Younger children can be frightened by crude comments, expletives and violence and this can ruin the experience for them – in some cases with a long-term impact. Ultimately, you want your children to enjoy music and live shows, so choose carefully. Furthermore, you don't want you child to mimic inappropriate behaviour because it has been portrayed as being acceptable. Draw the line and explain what is wrong and why.

▷ Use the experience as a way of communicating values, too. For example, say you liked the music but not the swearing. This is not a judgement, but an opinion. Ask your children what they thought and if they think anyone should or would really behave like that in real life.

▷ Most importantly, protect young ears. Amplified music can damage hearing after only 30 minutes, and the effects can last a long time. If you have to shout to be heard, your child needs earplugs.

▷ Have an action plan in the event that your child gets separated from you.

▷ If your child is clearly not enjoying the experience, don't push it. Go home and try something different when she's a little older.

Should she be allowed to go unaccompanied to concerts, the theatre, cinema or other outings during the week?

There are two questions here, really, and the key words are 'unaccompanied' and 'during the week'. All children need to learn to do things on their own, and the safety of a confined environment, such as a youth-friendly music venue, a theatre or a cinema, seeing an age-appropriate show, provides an ideal way to begin the voyage to independence. You may feel more comfortable ferrying to and fro for the first couple of solo trips out, and then choosing venues that are on a direct line of transportation. From the age of ten, most children are capable of sitting through some form of entertainment with their friends, provided you've done your homework first, you are happy that the venue is safe, the music/film/show is suitable for your child's age group, and your child knows what to do if she is separated from friends, doesn't feel well, loses her money or phone, needs the loo or whatever. If you want to get legal, it's worth noting that in the UK, children under five outside London and under seven in London are not allowed in a cinema unless accompanied by an adult.

The 'during the week' question is a little more difficult. Given the intense nature of today's schooling, and the sleep requirements of children and adolescents, late nights at films, concerts, gigs or theatre outings are unlikely to be fitted in easily, nor are they a particularly good idea. Many parents struggle with imposing a work ethic on school-age kids. Kids who are out late on school nights, and exhilarated and wound up after entertainment (or getting ready to go to said entertainment) are unlikely to be concentrating on their schoolwork, and unlikely to be getting enough sleep. So most parents opt for weekend-only trips out (unless something very special comes along, or it's a birthday or other special occasion), on the premise that weekdays are for school and schoolwork, and weekends are for fun. This should, ideally, hold true until a youth finishes secondary school, as it is important to impress on him the importance of schoolwork and sleep.

What's more, family time is curtailed when kids are out at all hours and throughout the week and weekend. It's nice to know that there are some days when family time is deemed more important than the next new thing.

It's possible to ease up on this ruling during holidays, which gives kids a taste of independence, and teaches them to budget their time and money appropriately. And towards the end of the final year of secondary school, when exams are pretty much under the belt, there can also be a relaxation of rules, so that teens get used to juggling social life with schoolwork – a fact of life at university or other further education institution, where they often live away from home and are left to their own devices.

But until that time, our job as parents is to ensure their well-being and give them the optimum environment in which to grow, develop and learn. Tired kids do not respond well in an academic environment (*see page 54*) and their health, weight, concentration, immunity and mood can all suffer if they don't get enough sleep. Allow them to let their hair down on weekends, but keep their noses to the books and their heads on the pillows during the week. If they are desperately keen to do more with friends who are given more freedom, you may wish to consider a weekday curfew *provided* all homework and any household chores are done in advance. Make the curfew reasonable to ensure sleep needs are met.

If my daughter can get into a pub to see a band, should I let her? Even if she is under age?

Your daughter can get into a pub with supervision at age fourteen and alone at age sixteen. She cannot drink until she is eighteen, but if the pub owners are aware of her age and happy for her to enter (which will be reliant on whether or not they have a children's certificate), there is no reason why she shouldn't. So, basically, a 14-year-old can go with another adult and it's all perfectly legal. Under this age, she can probably get away with going into a part of the pub where no alcohol is served (*see page 31*), providing she is accompanied, but this is unlikely to be where the band is playing, which rather defeats the purpose. My advice would be to stick to the letter of the law on this one. But check the band first – it may not be appropriate music for a young girl (*see page 177*). If she's desperate to go, offer to accompany her and perhaps some of her friends. You can always remove them if things look dodgy.

Should I allow her to see a film that has a restriction above her age?

Age restrictions are there for a reason – to protect children from inappropriate language, violence and sexuality. There is some rationale behind this. For example, studies show that many adult films and music videos can have a significant behavioural impact by desensitising kids to violence, and making kids more likely to approve of premarital sex, swearing and drugs. And let's face it, you'd rather your child learned about sex from you, than from a dodgy teen flick where drunken antics lead to bedroom romps.

The problem is solved simply in a cinema setting, because few venues will risk their licences by letting in underage kids. Things are slightly different in the confines of your home. The best thing to do in this case is to watch it first. If there is anything you *really* object to, then veto the film. If you think your child is unlikely to see anything he hasn't seen before, and you are generally happy with the contents, then by all means allow it. You may wish to watch it a second time *with* your child to point out a few things that don't impress you much, but use it as a talking point rather than as the basis for a lecture.

At what age should he be unsupervised in his choice of television or films?

In the UK, things are supposedly made fairly easy with the watershed hour – presently 9 pm, before which all programming is ostensibly suitable for children. However, with the advent of pay-on-demand TV and recordable DVDs, kids can often watch what they want, when they want, regardless of the hour. And the watershed hour is a bit of a misnomer anyhow, as many of the soaps, with inappropriate themes, are completely unsuitable for young children and even impressionable pre-teens.

Why is it important to supervise?

▷ Supervision helps you to keep tabs on your child's screen time. We know that children who spend too much time in front of the screen fare worse academically and tend to become obese.

▷ Violence is a real problem, as many kids become desensitised at an age when they do not understand the difference between 'real' and 'entertainment' violence. Unsupervised, the average child will watch several thousand murders on TV before they finish primary school, and then there are the muggings, robberies, bullying, etc., that form the basis of many shows. Even TV wrestling presents the wrong idea to younger children. Children who watch many hours of this type of television tend to be more violent as adults.

▷ Children are also exposed to adult sexual behaviour on

television. But on TV sexual activity is shown as normal, fun, exciting and with no risks. It does not usually show the risks of early sexual activity – or, indeed, teach kids much about responsibility and relationships.

▷ Advertising, in many forms, also has a negative impact.

You can't supervise everything, but it can be a good idea to sit down and work out their viewing with them (asking them to choose in advance how they wish to spend their 'allowed' one or two hours of screen time, for example), and get some information about the programme from a guide or the internet if you aren't sure of the content. Periodically, spend time with your children watching their shows so that you are able to monitor content and openly discuss issues and values that may be contrary to your own. The amount of time spent watching television may be less important than the quality of the shows and their suitability to your family's lifestyle and values.

From the age of about fourteen, most children will have learned about drugs, alcohol, sexuality and the dangers of violence, so you can dip in and out periodically to watch shows with them and discuss. You are within your rights to ban anything that is blatantly inappropriate – disrespectful to women, homophobic, encouraging the use of drugs, alcohol, or extolling the virtues of early sexual activity, and, of course, anything that is violent. In today's society, the latter is extremely important.

You are unlikely to convince any 16-year-old that he shouldn't watch a particular programme, but you can stick to your guns if it has a rating of 'adult' or 'eighteen'. Remember, however, that if he can't watch it at home, he'll likely find a way to watch it elsewhere. You might be better off having him under your roof so that you can discuss elements with which you disagree.

Full supervision is probably necessary until your child hits his teenage years; after that, guidance and spot-supervision are appropriate, dropping off at about sixteen.

A national telephone survey of 1,762 adolescents aged twelve to seventeen years, resulted in a study entitled *Sexual Readiness, Household Policies and other Predictors of Adolescents' Exposure to Sexual Content in Mainstream Entertainment Television*. This study found that kids who believed that their friends approved of sex, and those who had more sexual experience, were more likely to watch shows with sexual content; it also found that restrictions set by parents were equally effective at preventing this. Having a TV in the bedroom and spending more time unsupervised was associated with heavier sexual content viewing. Still more research shows that kids who watch shows of a sexual nature on TV are more likely to become involved in early sexual experiences.

When is he old enough to go to a disco or clubbing?

Do your homework first. If he's old enough according to the venue's age of entry policy, the music and the venue are safe and youth friendly, it is licenced for children of your child's age, and there is little risk of being offered drugs or alcohol, or being mugged, then it can be considered. But on these terms!

Your child should be fully aware of the dangers of overdrinking and drugs, and of things like date-rape drugs (the advice, for the record, is to choose drinks in a bottle rather than a glass or a can, and to keep your thumb firmly over the top at all times). He'll need to know what to do in an emergency, and how to get help if there is a problem. Children need to know how to respond to bullying or sexual advances, and how to avoid dealers.

In reality, most clubs are not open to anyone under the age of 18, although increasingly events geared towards younger children are being organised – in the UK, called 'under-age clubs'. These feature bands or DJs and strictly prohibit alcohol, although undoubtedly some makes its way in. They normally begin about 4 pm and end before midnight.

If you do decide to allow your teenager (or pre-teen) to attend one of these events, check first to ensure that the only adults *over* eighteen allowed are the organisers, supervisors and/or parents. Predatory adults should have no opportunity to gain entrance. Check, too, on the level of supervision and the anti-alcohol and drugs regulations and how they are enforced, as well as what emergency plans are in place in the event of fire, for example. Consider the type of music being played, and how your child will get to and from the event. If you are happy with everything, and your child is being accompanied by suitable friends with similar curfews, you may wish to allow your child to attend. Increasingly, these events form the basis of extracurricular activities, and are a part of youth culture, whether we like it or not.

Is my daughter old enough to spend the weekend at a music festival?

Increasingly, music festivals cater for younger crowds and many of the ticketholders are, in fact, in their mid-teens. The main worries are sex, drugs and alcohol. If you are confident that your child understands the risks, is able to resist peer pressure, understands the difference between gentle experimentation and risky behaviour, and is responsible enough to look after herself across a weekend (bathing, washing, getting some sleep, and acting responsibly in terms of alcohol intake, etc.), then sixteen or seventeen is probably an appropriate age.

This may seem young to some readers, but there is plenty of evidence supporting the fact that many, many nice kids do attend at this age. In some ways it is a fairly safe environment, and if your daughter is with a group of friends who have also been read the riot act, and if she is prepared to stay in regular contact via her mobile telephone, then it is a good opportunity to experiment with a little independence. She will probably have a fantastic time and live up to your expectations.

Giving children unexpected little freedoms throughout their teens often has the effect of making them feel proud and respected, and they will usually live up to your expectations. Be firm, however, about the things you don't want happening, and have a good, honest talk about the dangers of drugs. Don't lay down the law too hard, or you'll encourage rebellion, but spell out your concerns. Unprotected and early sex is often linked to alcohol and drugs, especially if it's for the first time. Most who have sex under the influence regret what happened – and a recent statistic showed that 40 per cent of sexually active 13- to 14-year-olds were drunk or stoned when they first had sex.

Try to keep talking about responsibility and choice. Let your daughter know you understand that drinking, trying drugs or having sex may be a part of teenage life but that she must be responsible and avoid taking undue risks. She should understand the importance of staying with her friends or at least one friend at all times, and arranging regular meeting points.

Exams

See School, *page 403.*

Exercise

When should he be left in charge of his own exercise regime?
An important part of parental responsibility is ensuring the health
and well-being of our children, and exercise fits firmly into both
categories. According to current UK guidelines, school-age kids
need at least 60 minutes per day, although a 2006 study published
in the *Lancet Medical Journal* recommend 90 minutes. Presently,
only one in ten children achieves the lower limit, which is a major
reason why obesity and other related problems are on the increase.

If your child is *not* getting the recommended number of hours
of exercise, you can do a great deal to ensure that he does.
Establish what is happening at school and on what days. As soon
as he's old enough suggest that he cycles or walks to school, or
takes public transport that involves at least some walking.

Many kids have very busy schedules after school, but many of
these activities are sedentary (art and computer clubs, music
lessons, etc.) so you'll have to ensure that your son balances his
leisure load between exercise and other activities. Not all kids are
naturally sporty nor indeed, enjoy it, but there will be one or two
sports that will catch their fancy. Do some homework and find out
what is available locally and give your son several options to choose
from, one or two days a week.

If he has friends round, throw them out in the garden or the park
for an hour or so before letting them settle down in front of the TV
or games console. Take your kids swimming on the weekends or in
the evenings – just 30 minutes can make a big difference to overall
fitness, even if they are only splashing about. Try to make your
family activities more active – walks in the park, swimming, cycling,
a game of frisbee, football, rounders, tennis, basketball – and
encourage your children to walk the family dog (or a neighbour's),

mow the lawn, wash the car, help rake leaves or wash windows. Send them on errands by foot or on a bicycle to get the newspaper or run errands, and avoid driving them to all of their activities. While not strictly aerobic exercises, these all contribute to fitness.

When do you stop? When your child has established a regular, healthy lifestyle that includes good levels of exercise. Until then, nag as required. Kids need to learn the importance of exercise for health, and it is a habit they will take with them into adulthood.

Should I persist in encouraging exercise when he's in his late teens and not interested?

The simple answer is yes. It is in his best interest for you to carry on encouraging exercise for as long as he is under your roof, because the alternative can damage his health, perhaps irreparably. Exercise really does matter, as does getting outside to boost vitamin D stores for healthy bones. Make it one of your household rules that every member must be active for at *least* 60 minutes per day. He can certainly choose what he wants to do, but it has to happen. Set limits on screen time, and if he's not a great organiser, help him with some time management so that he can fit in all of his homework, jobs, leisure time with friends and still find time for exercise.

When should I stop paying for his exercise activities?

Exercise is crucial, but if the activities that your child chooses are well outside the family budget, you'll have to negotiate. There are plenty of activities that are free or fairly cheap, such as walking, swimming, cycling, park games with friends, and tennis or basketball in local parks. Classes and organised sports clubs tend to be more expensive, but they may well be worth the money if your child is reluctant to do much else. What's more, organised activities provide good opportunities for children to meet friends, learn good sportsmanship, play as a team member and, of course, because you pay for the privilege, they do require a regular commitment.

If the activity your child chooses is too expensive, ask him to contribute half the cost by taking on some extra jobs (around the house or for neighbours, or working part-time after school), or by foregoing something else. If you want your child to exercise, you may well have to pay for it until he has the means to do so himself.

Should I pay for my child to go to the local gym?

If it's good value for money and your child is committed to going frequently, why not? But check first that there is plenty to do and that there are lots of options included. Like most adults, children often view gym memberships as an alluring prospect, but soon lose interest and motivation. If you agree to pay (all or a proportion, depending on your family budget and whether your child wants to go enough to contribute some of his own money), you must make a deal with your child that he will attend on a certain number of days for a certain number of hours. Frankly, if your child is busy at the gym he's not going to be out on the street causing trouble!

Is my son too young to use weights at the gym?

The optimal time to begin strength training is between the ages of eleven and thirteen for girls and the ages of thirteen and fifteen for boys, although the use of high resistance should be avoided until well into adolescence. Even then this needs to be monitored very carefully, because the adolescent growth spurt causes limbs to grow at different rates, leaving teens uncoordinated, clumsy and even weak. The clumsiness likely stems from the body's nervous system trying to adjust to the rapid growth of limbs, muscles and nerve lengths.

During adolescence, lengthening of the bones occurs before growth in the connective tissues. As a result, there may be a relative decrease in flexibility during this period. Girls tend to be more flexible than boys and peak in their flexibility around age fifteen years compared to boys who develop increased flexibility later in adolescence.

During and immediately after growth spurts, teenagers should avoid training on hard surfaces and should monitor the intensity and duration of their workouts. It is also important to stretch regularly and perform low-level strengthening exercises. Heavy weights should be avoided throughout adolescence for this reason.

One study found that weights can be useful for building bone mass in youths, an important deterrent to osteoporosis and even fractures in general, but it is important that your child waits until later adolescence to do anything with heavy weights. A good fitness instructor can advise on gentle weight training for overall health (including bone health) and fitness.

What about injuries?
It's worth noting that most injuries occur when free weights as opposed to machine-held weights are used, largely because the movements are less controlled. But other research shows that weight machines can also cause injuries, including severe injuries of the back, pelvis and neck.

Experts recommend that when your child does begin a programme of weight-training (also called strength training), he limits it to two or three times a week, and undertakes other aerobic forms of physical activity, has good warm-up and cool-down phases, with particular attention given to the development of abdominal, spinal and scapulo-thoracic muscles that are essential to posture. They also recommend that youngsters avoid power-lifting and body-building until their musculature is fully developed in the twenties.

At what age should my child be allowed unsupervised visits to the gym?

The good news is that now there are many gyms and programmes designed specifically for children which are well supervised by expert staff who understand the physiological needs of children, as well as the need for close guidance. Many parents are worried that their children can be the victims of predatory adults. For this reason it is a good idea to check out the gym first; ensure that there are periods of 'kids-only' activities in various rooms, or at least be sure that there is a responsible adult overseeing the proceedings. Until your child understands the potential dangers (inappropriate adult behaviour, using equipment without care or supervision, staying too long in the sauna or hot tub – ten minutes is appropriate for children – failing to warm up and cool down, dehydration and over-exercise), it's best that he or she attends a gym designed for children or that you supervise. Most children can take some responsibility by the age of thirteen. If they've been regular attendees with you, and know the ropes, you can knock a couple of years off this.

When is regular gym exercise appropriate?

Classes such as spinning, aerobics, yoga, Pilates and T'ai chi are all appropriate for children, but they *must* be supervised by someone with experience of children, who knows the risks of over-exercise, and is prepared to adapt the exercise for adolescent needs. The flexibility of children is vastly different from that of adults, so even gentle yoga poses (*asanas*) can cause problems if they are undertaken incorrectly or by a youth who has entered his growth spurt. Rowing machines, step machines, stationary bikes and treadmills are all safe and good forms of aerobic exercise, and swimming is also a great overall strengthener and toner. Gentle weight or strength training can be undertaken in older adolescents (*see above*), but only under close supervision. All exercise must be preceded and ended by stretching.

At what age can my child accompany me to the gym and not visit the crèche?

Talk to the experts at your gym first. If they have a kids programme, it will be adapted and suited to certain ages and your child should fall within the appropriate ages before commencing any of the exercise. Having a tall child or one who appears physically more mature than his peers is not grounds for an early start, as children who are in their growth spurt periods (*see page 188*), are at even greater risk of injury. Otherwise, if you are prepared to supervise your child, most of the basic machines (rowing, stepping, cycling and the treadmill) are fine for kids from about the age of nine or ten, as long as your child is not pushed too hard and stops whenever he or she feels at all uncomfortable. Swimming is great exercise, too. Avoid weights until your child is older (*see page 188*).

How much exercise should my child be doing at school?

In the UK, the government has set a target of two hours of physical education per week at school – but this target isn't expected to be reached until 2010. This is a very sorry state of affairs, given the pledge to combat childhood obesity in this country. Not only is exercise essential for weight control, but it also aids concentration, improves mood and immunity, prevents a multitude of health problems, helps encourage good sleep patterns, and is a great stress reliever. Given the fact that many of our children are considered to be 'unhappy' (UNICEF report 2007) and under pressure, we could be doing a great deal to encourage more exercise within school hours. At present most children get about an hour a week.

As a parent you have a right to campaign for more exercise in schools, even if it takes the form of after-school teams, clubs and events that allow kids to become fitter.

When should children stop doing extra-curricular exercise at school?

Many kids stop the before- and after-school clubs and activities in their teens, when it is perceived to be not 'cool' (unless you are the star of the football or netball team, perhaps), and also because they have other plans that do not involve exercise *or* school. And to be fair, if none of their friends is doing anything at school, it might be pushing things too far to insist that your child sticks his neck out and gets involved.

Having said that, all children require exercise and if he's not getting it anywhere else, or is reluctant to become involved in sport at other venues, you can certainly suggest that school sport is required until he replaces it with something else. This might spark him to set up a regular game of tennis with friends, do some swimming on weekends, cycle to school and back, or whatever strikes his fancy. Not all parents will see the value of exercise or encourage it, so he might have trouble convincing sedentary friends that exercise should be a priority. You may wish to invest in a gym membership, an aerobics or tennis class, or something like yoga or Pilates, which appear to be more grown up.

If you feel that the activities your school offers are not suitable for teenagers – or likely to interest or motivate them – ask for different options to be made available. Schools have a responsibility to provide exercise for children under government guidelines.

When should I allow my child to opt out of regular family exercise?

There comes a time when many children think they are old enough to opt out of all family activities (*see below*) because they have their 'own lives'. There are two ways to view this: firstly, is she spending any family time with you on a regular basis; and secondly, is she getting enough exercise. If the answer is 'no' to both, you are certainly within your rights to encourage (or insist) that she takes part as a family member. Make an effort to choose an activity she enjoys (a walk in the countryside, a family tennis tournament, a cycle ride, perhaps) and ask her to bring along a friend if she thinks she'll be 'bored'. But stick to your guns. Exercise is important and so is family time.

If she's getting plenty of exercise outside the family unit, let her choose to spend time with you doing other things – shopping, seeing a match, film or play, or perhaps having a meal. As long as both happen, it doesn't matter how or when. As long as she's under your roof, you can encourage the idea of family and the importance of exercise – till whatever age.

Eyes

At what age should I get my daughter's eyes checked?
Children should have their eyes checked several times in the pre-school years, with a full check at five. This is usually undertaken by a trained professional as part of a developmental check. You may, however, want to watch out for some of the following, which can indicate vision problems:

▷ Squinting, frowning, excessive blinking or excessive eye rubbing.
▷ Shutting or covering one eye with a hand.
▷ Holding objects too close to the eye.
▷ Tilting or thrusting the head forward.

▷ Extreme sensitivity to light.

▷ Crossed or misaligned eyes, or abnormal movement of the eyes.

▷ Inflamed, watery, crusted or red-rimmed eyes.

▷ A white pupil (centre part of the eye) instead of black.

In addition to these behavioural and physical symptoms, a child also may indicate difficulty seeing, complain of sore, burning or itching eyes, blurred or double vision, or suffer from dizziness, nausea and headaches. If you notice any of these symptoms or other eye or vision abnormalities, you should discuss them with your GP who will refer your daughter for a professional eye examination.

If left uncorrected for too long some sight defects cannot be put right, but establishing a routine of regular eye examinations can minimise the chances of a sight defect being carried into adulthood. At certain stages children's eyes may need to be examined at intervals of months rather than years, and your optometrist is the person to advise you on the frequency of visits. Most optometrists recommend yearly visits, just as you would take your child to see the dentist. Tests for children under sixteen (under nineteen, if they are in full-time education) are free of charge in the UK.

My son refuses to wear his glasses. Will this cause damage? How can I encourage him to wear them?

Sometimes it can be as simple as encouraging your child to choose his own frames. You may have to pay slightly over the odds (more than free prescription glasses) in order to satisfy his sense of style, but it's worth it if he will then wear them! Research shows that kids do not decide to wear their glasses until they are convinced, themselves, that they need them. When they can't read what others are reading, see a film, do their homework properly, or get on with what normal kids do, they will eventually see the light (literally!)

and begin to wear them. It's best not to make a fuss – studies show that unless there is a serious problem with vision, academic work and progress will not suffer if your child refuses to wear his glasses. While some corrective work on the eyes will obviously not take place, failing to wear glasses will also not make his eyes weaker. Show understanding (many kids with glasses are teased as a matter of course), and tolerance. You can, however, insist that he wears glasses while driving or cycling, and perhaps for doing homework under your own roof. A few opportunities to see properly will encourage him to wear them more regularly – particularly if they are 'cool'. You can help, too, by showing pictures of celebrities or sports stars (whatever interests him) in glasses, and move on to contact lenses at the appropriate time (*see below*).

Is my daughter old enough for contact lenses?

There is some research indicating that a responsible child, who is aware of the necessity for hygiene, changing contacts, and taking care, can wear them from age eight. Other studies show that there is a perceived improvement in quality of life in kids who make the change from glasses to contacts, including increased confidence in their ability to participate in activities. If your daughter is over eight, it's well worth considering.

Family

At what age can my children stop visiting family members?

The importance of family cannot be overemphasised. Families provide a sense of support and identity – who we are and what is unique about us. And extended family is important to this as well, as intergenerational and extended family relationships are a valuable resource. Studies show that close extended family relationships can have educational, economic and professional implications; people with extended family contacts tend to be more literate and reach out to get more education and better jobs. People who cultivate extended family relationships are also at an advantage emotionally and are often more successful in their personal lives. Both children and adults benefit from these relationships during times of great stress, such as tragedy, death or divorce. They also reap the rewards when joyous events enter their lives, whether it is a new job, a new child or a milestone birthday. Some research shows, too, that interaction with extended family can have a positive effect on lifespan and physical health.

Quite apart from this, the family provides the optimum environment to learn – everything from values, religious beliefs, our past, good table manners, respect and etiquette, social skills through to responsibility, work ethic, negotiation, relationships, finances and budgeting and ethics. And there is more. In a nutshell, we all want our children to have a positive experience of family life, and a respect for family members of all ages, as this teaches the importance of relationships in general, and how we function within them. We are genetically wired to bond with family members, and, indeed, our memories of family life form much of the foundation of our lives.

Friends are undoubtedly important, but in most cases it is to our families that we turn when we need help and advice, and it is our families that guide our values and choices.

A healthy family unit is important to almost every aspect of a child's emotional life, no matter what his or her age. While relationships can falter at various points of growth and development, there is normally a fairly firm understanding that family equals sanctuary and unconditional love.

So every parent should encourage the importance of family

time. It doesn't have to be hours and hours spent talking on a daily basis, but there does need to be a regular commitment to spending time together as a unit, individually, and with extended family members. Sadly, it often takes the death of a family member to kick-start kids into understanding what they've lost. It is of the utmost importance to initiate, cultivate, maintain and prioritise family relationships from toddlerhood through to adulthood.

It's regrettable that we often feel we have to 'force' our kids to take part in family visits and gatherings, but it's worth pointing out that as long as you live together, you are expected to do some mildly boring chores, participate in activities that are not always first choice for entertainment, and even visit 'boring' relatives on occasion. Having to spend time with the family is part of the deal of having a family.

So what age?
For as long as they wish to be a family member! This doesn't mean forcing them to spend hours every weekend; let them have a little choice. If there are three gatherings coming up, suggest that they bring a friend to one, and choose one other. Occasionally missing a family event isn't crucial, but in general family time must take priority. Be respectful of your child's time by asking what she's got on before making arrangements – a little negotiation and compromise can make it much easier to organise.

The idea is that kids will get used to being unselfish from time to time (visits matter a great deal to grandparents, for example, even if they bore kids to death), and also will become accustomed to incorporating family time into their lives, a skill that will stand them in good stead in later life, when they start their own families.

At what age can my children opt out of family gatherings?

If you've played your cards right, your children will grow up valuing and understanding the importance of family, even if it sometimes requires 'boring' interaction and takes the place of something much more 'pressing' in their social calendar. Children don't need to attend every family gathering, but if it's important to another family member, if their support is required, if an extended family member has specifically asked them to be there, or it's a family milestone, then it should be considered carefully.

When do my children have a right to give up family time – weekend outings, holidays, etc.?

As long as your child is living in the family home and intends to be part of the family, then family time is essential – for all family members. As your children get older, you'll have to make some allowances. First of all, they have the right to some freedom to make their own plans, so you may have to get your diaries out to agree on timings for holidays, get-togethers and other activities. If your child can't make it every weekend, don't worry. Show some respect for their other commitments and reschedule. As long as they are spending some time with the family on a regular basis, you can be flexible. Secondly, you'll have to adapt activities to appeal to kids as they become older. Holidays might need to include age-appropriate fun, and the opportunity to mix with other kids of the same age. Some kids enjoy going on family holidays well into their twenties, and later bringing their own families too. Others like to strike out alone and show some independence, which is also good, as long as they do make time for family.

Should my children show responsibility for the care of their grandparents?

If your parents need care and you are shouldering the responsibility yourself, then yes, just as older kids should help with younger siblings, they should also be expected to help with the other end of the family unit. Families do require responsibility, and a lot can be learned from caring for others.

It's easy to underestimate the importance of a connection between children and elder family members, but studies show that the relationship between grandparent and grandchild is second only to that of parent and child. For the elder person, grandparenting is an opportunity to satisfy a natural wish to continue in a family role. It allows him to pass on feelings and attitudes to another generation – to share what is important in his life with someone whose life is important to him.

What can my teen do to help with grandparents?

Keep it simple. Don't expect a child or even a teenager to change incontinence pads, bathe an elderly person or lift them. Instead, focus on things like chatting, playing cards or board games, listening to some music (grandpa's favourite maybe), looking at photographs, reminiscing, preparing simple meals such as sandwiches, or maybe helping with a little tidying up or cleaning if a grandparent isn't coping very well. Running errands can be hugely useful, as can reading to a grandparent whose eyesight isn't so good. Anything that would be useful – watering the plants, helping in the garden, washing some windows, but most of all, spending a little time.

If your teen is reluctant, explain that it falls under the heading of 'family duties', which are shared. But go a little further and point out that everyone gets old and some day he will be in the same position, and hopefully have a little help and company when he most needs it.

Should my children show responsibility for the care of their younger siblings?

Yes, of course. Childcare is a crucial element of family life and provides your child with valuable experience. Kids aren't always easy, but your children will undoubtedly see what you do, and how you relate to their younger siblings and what is required in terms of care. Encourage them from a young age to help out, fetching nappies, helping with the bath, helping to tidy the toys and simple feeding. When they are older and can be of real use, they will know the ropes and what is expected. And unlike many babysitters and childcarers, they will know your child intimately and be confident about routines and methods of dealing with issues that may crop up.

Do try to remember, however, that older siblings are live-in babysitters on an occasional basis, but they should never be given too much responsibility or be relied upon too much. If you expect them to babysit every weekend night (*see page 42*), you are bound to breed resentment; and if you turn over too much of the care, they'll simply resist or feel overly burdened.

How long should children spend with their family/parents and to what age?

There are two elements to this question, so two different answers. Children should spend as much time as possible with their parents. Age, social life, other interests and, ultimately, relationships will begin to encroach on what is normally seen as 'family time' from about the age of thirteen and sometimes earlier, depending on how precocious your child is; however, every member of the family should commit to spending at least three or four hours a week (an evening, for example, or some time on the weekend) together. Activities can be decided by mutual consent.

Younger children will require much more input and time; and indeed, the only thing we can give our children of any real value is our time. Until children have their own schedules and social lives, they can expect to spend the better part of a weekend with their families, and as much time as possible every night.

Most of a child's basic learning takes place in the many informal situations that occur in the daily life of the family. These include all of the times that family members are together doing ordinary events, such as getting dressed, taking baths, preparing to leave for school or work, eating, cooking, shopping, preparing food, reading or whatever. The goal of parenting is to help your child become a responsible adult. To achieve this goal, parents help children learn about life and living in today's society. The time spent with your child is important.

Children learn about families from the time they spend in their own families. They learn about birth and caring for another person when a new baby comes home from the hospital. They learn about loss when a family member dies. They learn about marriage and relationships by watching their mothers and fathers interact. By living in a family, children learn to share, how to stand up for their own rights and how to love another person.

How do I keep the lines of communication open once he gets older?

It's a myth that older children don't require as much parental attention or communication; if anything, they require more guidance, feedback, reassurance and confirmation of their boundaries and, of course, your unconditional love. Make a point to spend at least 30 minutes with your teenager each day (*see* Communication, *page 105*), and longer periods on the weekend. Or go for bust and go away for the weekend together, or spend a whole day shopping or doing whatever interests your child. Quality time is nonsense in many senses, because it appears to mean that full-on, intense time is more important than the lazy, spur-of-the-moment or as-required communication that takes place when your child needs it.

Kids who are around their parents a lot don't have to store up things to tell them (or forget them or find other ways to deal with them); they don't have to wait their turn; they don't have to wait for the prime 30-minute allocated slot, either. They communicate easily and naturally as part of family life – when and as things happen. While it is a good idea to leave some time every night to say goodnight and have a chat about the day (something a child can relish as part of a routine, and also look forward to as an opportunity to discuss things), it's equally important just to be there for them when required.

This may sound idealistic for busy parents, but the key is to include your child in what you are doing (cooking, tidying up, picking up some shopping, bathing a younger sibling, or just reading the newspaper together or watching TV) so that your child feels that your time is his or hers too.

At what age will my children stop fighting?

The simple fact is that some kids never stop fighting or arguing, well into adulthood. Fighting or arguing is commonplace in many families, and it can be driven by sibling rivalry (*see page 206*) or simply frustration and anger. They may feel a sense of injustice and believe that their only recourse is to fight. They may also feel hurt and want to hurt someone back. Remember, however, that it takes two people to have an argument, and if one of you fails to rise to the bait, it simply won't take place. Arguing can be enormously satisfying for a child because he can express his emotions and get things off his chest, and usually, in the heat of the moment, tell you or another family member exactly what he thinks. The end result is rarely pleasant, and children can feel insecure (as if they may have tested you beyond the radius of your love), guilty, frightened by their own rage, and equally frightened by yours.

What can I do?

▷ Make it a family policy to avoid arguments and fights. They are bound to happen, but if everyone aims towards a positive goal, it shows willing.

▷ Model appropriate behaviour. If you have a tempestuous relationship with your partner and your child hears or sees you fighting or arguing regularly, he is more likely to see it as a way of dealing with problems.

▷ Don't be drawn into a slanging match. It's all too easy to join in. After all, pride is at stake, as is our authority. But children need reassurance, not angry words. They need to know that you love them, despite their angry feelings, and that you are prepared to help them find alternative methods of expressing their anger (*see page 83*).

▷ Help your child to verbalise his feelings. Arguments often occur when a child (or adult) feels that things have built up to bursting point, and he needs to air his views. Listen carefully to his perceived grievances. Respect his feelings and help him to see that it's easier to talk small problems through than it is to wait until they have built up and grown into something over-significant.

▷ Diffuse the situation with humour. When faced with an irate, shouting child, you can do a lot by saying something silly, to make her laugh. Then you can sit down and talk rationally.

▷ Above all, encourage your children not to hold grudges. When a fight or argument is over, it's over. There's no point in harking back to past grievances. Far better to look forward to better ways of doing things.

Encouraging a good relationship between your kids is important. When they reach those crucial teenage years, they'll welcome the support and guidance as well as the friendship of their siblings, particularly in situations when they aren't sure about talking to you. Siblings who get on will cover for each other and show support when required. Don't take this as a ganging-up mechanism; instead, be proud that they have a good relationship and care about each other.

Am I to blame for the rivalry between my kids?

Unlike the ties between parents and children, the connection between siblings is a horizontal one. That is, siblings exist on the same plane – as peers, more or less equals. Although one may be stronger or more dominant than others, brothers and sisters rarely exert the kind of power and authority over one another that parents hold over their children. Nor are there rules, codes of behaviour for different stages of life, or biblical commandments mandating siblings to respect and honour one another as they must respect and honour parents. As a result, they are freer, more open and generally more honest with one another than they are with parents, and less fearful of punishment or rejection. As children, they say what is on their minds, without censoring their words or concerning themselves about the long-term effects of their emotions on one another. Even as adults, many siblings speak more bluntly to each other than they dare to friends or colleagues.

How can I treat them the same when they are so different?
It is perfectly normal, natural and appropriate for parents to have
different feelings toward each of their children, and to treat those
children differently. The challenge parents always face is to
appreciate what is unique about each child, and to show that
appreciation in a balanced way so that over the course of years,
all children feel equally loved and valued. Parents fail in that
challenge when the line between different treatment and
preferential treatment become muddied, and without even
realising it, they begin to slip from one to the other.

Unintentionally, the most achieving child, the most affectionate
one, the first born or the last, the one most like or unlike a parent
or relative can move from a position of equality with the other
children to one of receiving or seeming to receive special attention.
Parents may not be aware of slipping from a normal course of
treating children differently to giving one preferential treatment,
but siblings – whether children, adolescents or adults – are highly
sensitive to such slips. And the more so because they pick up
signals of favouritism not only from the way parents behave toward
them but also from parental behaviour toward their brothers and
sisters. Young children monitor their parents' treatment of their
siblings, just as they monitor their own treatment, and that
relationship of parent to siblings becomes as important as the
relationship of parent to self. It is certainly true that what young
children label favouritism may be far from the real thing.

But herein lies the crux of the problem. It's perception rather
than reality that colours a sibling relationship. If a child perceives
that he is being treated less fairly or not getting enough attention,
even if parents are scrupulously fair, they will feel disempowered
and more likely to initiate rivalry.

Sibling rivalry is exhausting for everyone involved, and often siblings are the only outlet that stressed children have to exert control, to lash out, to scrap, fight, bicker, taunt, tease and harass. You will often see your children exhibiting horrendous behaviour towards each other, and it can be a sign that things are just too much.

WHAT CAN I DO ABOUT SIBLING RIVALRY?

Although advice books admonish parents not to compare their children, and to view each only as an individual, most parents find it almost impossible not to make some comparisons. It is when the comparisons turn into labels used to define and pigeon-hole children that this becomes problematic. Labels, stuck on in early childhood, become part of the internal image children have of themselves, later to be incorporated into the roles they assume with each other and in the world outside the family.

Remember the following:

▷ Sensitive parenting can restore the balance and, in many cases, often prevent serious rivalry from taking hold.

▷ Make each child feels special. Older or younger, every child needs to feel that she is as important as any one else in the family. If one child thinks that her sibling is held in higher esteem by her parents, then jealousy will arise.

▷ Show enthusiasm for all your children's achievements. You may find that you are less excited about your younger child's milestones (such as her first step, her first word) than you were with your older child.

▷ Give each of your children responsibility. Resist the trap of giving your oldest child all the household chores. There is no reason why she has to do everything, just because of her age. Her younger siblings can also help, for example, by tidying toys. And the oldest child does not need to take her younger siblings with her whenever she goes out to play.

▷ Respect all your children. Every child has the same psychological need to be loved and accepted by her parents, no matter what position she has in the family. She has feelings and ideas that she wants to express, and she has a right to receive respect, and to be taken seriously, whether she is the youngest, middle or oldest child.

▷ Unless rivalry declines into violence or regular bickering, it's usually best to ignore it. Children need to learn to sort out their problems, negotiate and find a happy middle ground. If you constantly intervene, they will always expect you to act as referee.

▷ Make kindness to siblings a family policy and reward all efforts towards this goal. Children will soon see that it's easier to get along than it is to waste energy fighting a useless cause.

▷ Remember that children will lash out at each other from time to time, and it's completely normal. Try to teach them other ways of relieving frustration and anger (*see page 83*), and make it clear that it is not acceptable to treat others in ways that they would not like to be treated themselves.

▷ Above all, show understanding and patience. Sibling rivalry occurs in almost every family and you need to look for ways to shift the balance of power or attention, and be alert to occasions when one or more of your children need some extra love and time.

Should my children's friends be included in our family events?

When your children reach an age where they have their own interests and social life, and are also expected to attend family gatherings or events that they consider 'boring', you can help to make things more positive by including friends from time to time.

This also goes for holidays. While intimate and exclusive family time is essential to harmony and a healthy family dynamic, it is also important that each family member feels happy about the occasion. So continue to stress the importance of family as one of your policies, but lighten the load a bit by allowing your children to share that time with friends as well. They'll undoubtedly feel happier about giving up precious social time if they can combine the two elements.

But do make it clear that your child is expected to interact with other family members and not just hide away with a friend. If you are on holiday, ensure, perhaps, that you all meet up for meals and a drink in the evening, or a swim in the afternoon. If it's a shorter affair, ask that they do not stand in a corner together, but take part as other family members do. It's reasonable for them to vanish for short periods, but the point of being there is, of course, to be there! And remember: ask any host in advance if an extra guest is OK. Some family members might want to stick with family only.

Fizzy drinks

Is nine too young to have fizzy drinks?

Fizzy drinks are bad news for children of any age, in fact, well into adulthood. Studies show that 60 per cent of all kids in the UK now drink one can of fizzy drink a day, and one in five drinks ten a week. The intake of fizzy drinks and sweetened non- or low-fruit juices has increased by more than 900 per cent over the last 40 years, which is a worrying trend. There are a multitude of health risks, including increasing the risk of obesity, and damage to bones and teeth (*see below*). At a time when children are laying down all-important bone mass, and growing and developing both physically and emotionally, nutrition is crucial. Fizzy drinks not only take the place of milk and other calcium-rich drinks, such as fortified orange juice, they also fill children up with empty calories, which means they are often not hungry enough to eat nourishing, healthy foods necessary for strong bones and teeth.

The majority of fizzy drinks contain nothing but artificial sweeteners, flavourings, sugar, caffeine and water. Some fizzy drinks contain a little fruit juice (watch for the percentage), but not enough to make these drinks worthwhile. Even fizzy mineral water, with a 'hint' of a fruit juice tends to be artificially sweetened and flavoured. Most fizzy drinks are full of 'anti-nutrients', the types of chemicals that actually prevent the good elements of your child's diet from being absorbed. If meals are accompanied by fizzy drinks, many of the nutrients in the food will be negated, and still others will not be processed properly by the body.

The best advice is to avoid them at any age.

What is the maximum number of fizzy drinks that a child can have each day?

For health reasons, it is best to avoid them altogether (*see above*). If your child has a craving for something sparkling, add fresh juice to fizzy mineral water, which contains some nutrients, including calcium. There are some fizzy juice drinks made with spring water that at least offer some nutrition, rather than depleting the body, but make sure that there is no added sugar, and that the juice percentage is relatively high (over ten per cent, if possible).

How can fizzy drinks cause health problems?

First of all, fizzy drinks either contain sugar or sugar substitutes, and both are linked to poor health. Sugar-containing drinks are high in calories; research shows that drinking just one can of sweetened soft drink per day increases a child's risk of obesity by 60 per cent. Just one can contains 150 calories and about ten teaspoons of sugar, which affects mood, concentration, immunity and weight (*see page 456*). The sugar also causes tooth decay, and the acid causes erosion of the tooth enamel. The other option, 'diet' drinks, use sugar substitutes, usually aspartame.

Aspartame (Nutrasweet) has been linked with dizziness, headaches, epileptic-like seizures and menstrual problems, as well as low brain serotonin levels, depression and other emotional disorders, numbness, muscle spasms, weight gain, rashes, fatigue, irritability, tachycardia, insomnia, vision problems, hearing loss, heart palpitations, breathing difficulties, anxiety attacks, slurred speech, loss of taste, tinnitus, vertigo, memory loss and joint pain. According to researchers and physicians studying the adverse effects of aspartame, the following chronic illnesses can be triggered or worsened by ingesting aspartame: brain tumours, multiple sclerosis, epilepsy, chronic fatigue syndrome, Parkinson's disease, Alzheimer's, mental retardation, lymphoma, birth defects, fibromyalgia and diabetes.

A good idea for kids? Not a chance.
There are several other concerns about fizzy drinks. Many contain caffeine (which has its own health risks, *see page 213*). Substituting caffeine-containing soft drinks for water and other beverages may lead to dehydration because caffeine acts as a diuretic. This is particularly dangerous when youngsters rely on colas as fluid replacers during sports or active play. High quantities of fizzy drinks can also affect the health of your digestive system. In some parts of the UK, children suffer from the oral equivalent of Crohn's disease, with mouth ulcers, bleeding and pain.

Not only do caffeinated beverages contain empty calories but kids who fill up on them don't get the vitamins and minerals they need from healthy sources, putting them at risk of developing nutritional deficiencies.

What other evils lurk in fizzy drinks?

Fizzy drinks also contain phosphoric acid, which actually leaches calcium from the bones and prevents healing when there is a fracture. A study entitled 'Teenaged Girls, Carbonated Beverage consumption and Bone Fractures', published in 2000, found that physically active adolescent girls who regularly consumed soft drinks were more likely to suffer bone fractures than their milk-drinking peers. During puberty, children with normal levels of calcium increase their bone mass by almost 40 per cent. But kids who are deficient in calcium do not develop nearly as much bone mass. Normally, adult bone loss begins later in life (usually sooner in women than in men), and that's when problems such as osteoporosis can occur. If kids today do not have enough bone mass, osteoporosis can occur much, much earlier. In fact, in the US, many teenage girls are now showing signs of the disease.

Are fizzy drinks appropriate with meals or between?

Neither. Drunk with meals fizzy drinks often interfere with the absorption of nutrients; between meals, they can fill your child up with empty calories and damage teeth. Eating something with a fizzy drink can neutralise the effect of sugar on teeth, but this does nothing to prevent erosion caused by the phosphoric acid.

Obviously there will be times in a child's life where fizzy drinks are on offer and she'll want to take part, but these should be kept to an absolute minimum, and other options considered instead.

How can I stop my kids from purchasing their own fizzy drinks?

The simple answer is to educate them about the dangers – the very real health impact. Show them a couple of pictures of what osteoporosis does to the body, and explain how normal sporting activities could be out of the question because of the risk of fractures. A good exercise is to pop one of your children's milk teeth (does the Tooth Fairy keep them in your family?) into a glass of fizzy drink overnight. Look in the morning at the damage caused. That should help make your case. There are many healthy options, such as smoothies, fruit juices, water, good-quality fruit drinks, yoghurt drinks, milk and very diluted squashes, and even some 'fizzy' drinks made with mineral water and fruit juice rather than chemicals and phosphoric acid. Encourage these instead. In a party situation set up a juice bar or even invest in a juicer, so that your kids can make their own concoctions.

Food and drink

Should I let my children make their own packed lunches?

All kids need to learn to eat properly, to take responsibility for the preparation of meals and to know what foods constitute a healthy lunch. From an early age (*see page 126*), they can be encouraged to make their lunches – first with your supervision (ensuring that it doesn't comprise a jam sandwich and a packet of crisps), and then with the aid of a list of healthy options. For example, write down six or seven possible sandwich combinations, a few good ideas for 'snacks' and drinks, such as yoghurt, raisins, plain popcorn, good-quality muesli bars, nuts and seeds, cheese or breadsticks, and some fruit suggestions. Encourage your children to make their lunch by choosing one or two from each category. Avoid buying things you don't want them to eat; if you don't want your kids eating crisps and chocolate, it's a lot easier if there aren't any in the house! Teach them good lunchbox hygiene: keeping it in the fridge to prevent food spoilage; maybe freezing some drinks to keep the contents cold the next day; washing it carefully before use; and covering all food.

When is my child old enough to drink tea and coffee?

The biggest problem with tea and coffee is the caffeine content, and this is an issue with caffeinated soft drinks as well. A stimulant that affects children and adults alike, caffeine is a drug that is naturally produced in the leaves and seeds of many plants. Caffeine is also made artificially and added to certain foods. Caffeine is defined as a drug because it stimulates the central nervous system. At lower levels, caffeine can make people feel more alert and feel as if they have more energy; however, too much can cause:

▷ Jitteriness and nervousness.
▷ Upset stomach.
▷ Headaches.
▷ Difficulty concentrating.
▷ Difficulty sleeping.
▷ Increased heart rate.
▷ Increased blood pressure.

It doesn't take much caffeine to produce this effect in young children. If your teen has acquired a coffee-drinking habit, one cup a day can easily turn into several (as most adults know), especially if he is using coffee to stay awake during late-night study sessions.

Anything else wrong with caffeine for kids?

Caffeine also acts as a diuretic, causing the body to eliminate water (through urination), which may contribute to dehydration. Caffeine is an especially poor choice in hot weather, when children need to replace water lost through perspiration. It can aggravate heart problems or nervous disorders, and some children may not be aware that they are at risk.

One thing that caffeine doesn't do is stunt growth, but there are other issues. Tea and coffee contain compounds called polyphenols which bind with iron making it harder for our bodies to absorb it. So everyone should avoid drinking tea and coffee with meals or within 30 minutes after a meal. This is important particularly for young women, pregnant women and toddlers, who are most at risk of iron deficiency anaemia.

Young women are particularly vulnerable during the teenage years and early twenties to iron deficiency because of the onset of menstruation and continuing periods, and their growth spurts. Not having enough iron in your diet can lead to serious health problems from iron deficiency or anaemia. Symptoms include tiredness and lethargy, difficulty in concentrating and a shortened attention span, and growth and development can be affected.

Are there any benefits?

There are some health benefits to tea, but few to coffee – which is one of the most heavily sprayed crops in the world, and contains numerous chemicals. Postpone tea and coffee consumption for as long as possible – well into teenage years, if possible, and discourage drinking it with meals. Watch out for the calories in added milk and sugar too, and for the effect of sugar on teeth. Encourage green or herbal teas instead, or dandelion root coffee, which is great for the liver.

How often should I allow sweets?

Prohibiting sweets will normally have the effect of making them forbidden fruit and therefore that much more attractive. There is no doubt that some people are born with a sweet tooth; in fact, studies show that soon after birth many babies show a preference for sweet solutions. In moderation, there is nothing wrong with the occasional sweet. Some families allow children to choose a few from the sweet jar after dinner one night a week; others allow them once a day, but limit this to one or two small sweets rather than a bag or box.

The main problem with sweets is, of course, sugar. Refined sugar has no nutrients and although it is undoubtedly a source of 'energy', it enters the bloodstream so quickly that it produces the classic 'high' as blood-sugar levels soar and then plummet, causing fatigue, headaches, irritability, poor concentration and tearfulness. Sugar causes tooth decay, which is one reason for offering them after a meal, when the enzymes in saliva will break it down more quickly, rather than between meals. Too much sugar can lead to obesity, as quantities not used by the body for energy are laid down as fat. Sugar also stimulates the appetite, causing overeating, and it lowers immunity significantly.

Sweets or chocolate?

Most children get plenty of sugar in their diets – both healthy, such as that found in fruit, and unhealthy – so they don't need sweets. While they can certainly be offered as a regular treat, once or twice a week is ample. But bear this in mind. Good-quality chocolate is rich in iron, so would make a better choice for a sweet treat. Chocolate-covered nuts or raisins are equally good, as they contain important essential fats and minerals. Sticky sweets are more likely to damage teeth, as are those that are sucked. Try to avoid offering sweets as a reward for good behaviour, or as a comfort if your child is distressed; these associations can lead to overeating later in life. Avoid offering sweets before meals or as a dessert, and stick to small quantities – one or two is quite enough. Throw a few healthier options into the sweet jar, such as small bags of dried fruits and nuts, raisins (even chocolate-covered), seeds, fruit bars or fruit flakes.

When can sweets be introduced?

Sweets are not appropriate under the age of eighteen months, as they can discourage kids from trying new foods, and negatively affect their palate. After that one or two can be offered as a regular treat.

Is it really a problem for my child to eat a lot of salt?

High salt intake is linked to high blood pressure, which increases the risk of heart disease. People with high blood pressure are three times more likely to develop heart disease and stroke, and twice as

Recently, recommendations for target levels of salt intake have been set for children according to age. Based on these levels, the Food Standards Agency in the UK has issued advice for parents on the amount of salt that children and babies should consume.

Age	Grams salt
0–12 months	less than 1 g
7–12 months	1 g
1–3 years	2 g
4–6 years	3 g
7–10 years	5 g
11 years and over	6 g

likely to die from these diseases than people with normal levels. A 2006 study carried out by Dr Feng He at St George's University of London Blood Pressure Unit, found that reducing children's salt intake by half results in an immediate fall in blood pressure, which in turn could lead to major reductions in the risk of developing stroke, heart attacks and heart failure later in life

But beware, it can be very easy to reach and surpass recommended levels (*see box*). Processed foods and snack foods aimed at kids are often very high in salt (about 75 per cent of our salt intake is from processed foods), but it's also found in healthy foods, such as breads, cheese, cereals, soups and even tinned vegetables. You'll have to read labels carefully, and discourage the eating of salty snacks on a regular basis. It's also a very good idea to discourage your children from adding salt to meals. There are some good herb and spice blends that can be sprinkled on for extra flavour if required, but better still to let kids get used to and appreciate the natural flavours of foods. So many kids are brought up on junk and processed foods, that they find anything home-made to be terribly bland; however, a few weeks on a salt-reduced diet can alter taste perceptions.

At what age should my child be encouraged to choose her own diet?
As they enter their teens, many kids experiment with different diets – perhaps choosing vegetarian or vegan diets, weight-loss programmes, detoxes and the newest trend outlined in magazines. None of these may sit particularly well with your family meal plans, and quite rightly most parents baulk at preparing separate meals for individual family members. But there are two issues here. First, everyone has different tastes and as long as your child's diet is healthy and balanced, she does have the right to experiment a little

and adapt her diet for ethical reasons, perhaps, or because she
genuinely wants to eat differently. In this case, you can encourage
your child to prepare some part of her own meals, and eat the
appropriate bits of the meals that you have prepared for the family.
It's obviously not healthy to provide a vegetarian teenager with a
plate full of vegetables only, minus the chicken or fish you are
serving the rest of the family, because she'll end up woefully short
of key nutrients. Do a little investigation and see if you can find
ways of changing the family diet so that everyone eats well and
most tastes are catered for. For example, consider using quinoa
instead of rice from time to time. It's rich in omega oils, and
contains all of the amino acids (building blocks of protein). Perhaps
as a family you could eat a little more fish or salads, if your child
wants to lose some weight.

Having said that, your first responsibility is to ensure that your
child is eating healthily. No growing child should ever be put on a
weight-loss diet or adopt one (*see page 464*). The idea is, even for
very obese children, that adopting a healthy diet and exercise
regime will allow them to grow into their weight. Faddy diets can
be dangerous for growing kids – particularly during the teenage
years. About 95 per cent of the maximum strength of the body is
laid down by the late teens, and the adolescent growth spurt
requires great quantities of every vitamin and mineral. Even fat is
important. The onset of menstruation means that girls' iron
requirements almost double. And given that many teens skip
meals, eat on the run and experiment with food fads, it can be hard
enough work to ensure they are getting what they need without
them throwing a spanner in the works and demanding a completely
different meal plan. Oversee any dietary changes your child
suggests, and bone up on what might be missing and how it can be
obtained. Try to include at least some of these elements in your

family diet, so that everyone does eat much the same thing. By sixteen many kids will be making their own food choices but, as mentioned on *page 217*, as long as they are a member of a family unit that values and promotes healthy eating, they can be expected to have their diets supervised.

At what age should I allow my child to make decisions about school meals?

Fortunately, schools have upped the ante in the UK, so your child will probably be unable to choose burgers and chips for lunch every day. Most kids, given freedom, will choose what they please, regardless of what you say or decree, and many will go for the junky, kid-friendly fare because that is, quite simply, what they like. It's worth, however, making a pact. Chips once a week, burgers once a week, at least three fruits and/or vegetables eaten alongside the meal and potatoes don't count! Try to impress upon them the importance of variety (eating pasta with cheese every day is not balanced, for example), and encourage them to eat healthy foods whenever they can by explaining that they won't do well at school (this does actually matter to some kids) or at sports without the right 'fuel'. If you can't or don't trust them to make the right decisions, send a packed lunch three or four days a week, and let them go for broke on the other days. By thirteen, most children should be able to make the right decisions, if they've been given the facts and encouraged to eat healthily at home.

At what age should my child be allowed to spend her pocket money on junk food?

Unfortunately, most kids will spend their pocket money on the foods their friends eat, and also on the foods that they aren't normally allowed at home. A very big percentage (two-thirds) of pocket-money spending goes on food in the UK – in fact, the total spending power of children between the ages of five and sixteen is over 60 million pounds per year. The poll found, for example, that 84 per cent of those between the ages of eleven and sixteen bought crisps, sweets and chocolates, making these the top purchases for this age group, and only 45 per cent of this age group saved anything.

Encourage your child to eat regular, healthy meals at home, and supply him with good-quality snacks when he goes out. It may mean that he's not actually hungry enough to bother purchasing food, or having a full meal with friends. Take the time to explain why junk food is *called* junk food, and what the high levels of fat, salt and chemicals do to his body. It's not likely to have a dramatic impact, but it can be food for thought. And teach a little financial sense – four or five burger meals with mates on the run equals the cost of the designer T-shirt he's been coveting. Explain that spending money on food when you have a fridge groaning with healthy fare at home is really just a waste of money. But then leave it to him. The whole point of pocket money is that it is money of his own and eventually a little sense will sink in.

You can encourage savings by paying his pocket money directly in to his bank account (*see page 338*), so that it doesn't burn a hole in his pocket. You can also make a deal, suggesting that 10 per cent of pocket money and 30 per cent of gift money should be put into a savings account. This can be used to offset a key purchase or pay for a holiday when your child is a little older.

At what age should my child stop drinking milk with meals?
Some children don't drink milk at all, because of allergies (on the increase) or because they dislike the taste. The benefits of milk are well recognised – it's a good source of protein, an excellent source of the calcium needed for a child's growth, development and

functioning, and in particular for strong teeth and bones, and a source of fairly healthy fat. However, if your child has milk on his cereal in the morning, eats plenty of cheese and/or yoghurt, as well as leafy green vegetables, salmon and some seeds, he should be getting what he needs, so milk is not essential at mealtimes.

If, however, your child is a faddy eater, it's an easy way to get key nutrients into his diet. Children who can't or won't drink milk will have to get calcium from other sources, such as those above, or from soya or fortified rice or oat milks. There are now a number of juices with added calcium. Children require the nutrients in milk well into adulthood.

What is the recommended amount of milk for a child to drink at various ages?

A study undertaken by the US Department of Agriculture has found that nine out of ten teenage girls and seven out of ten teenage boys do not get enough calcium. During the peak bone-building years between nine and eighteen, a daily calcium intake of 1,300 mg is recommended. Doctors and dietitians agree that dairy foods – those containing milk or milk products – are the best source of calcium, and research indicates that adolescents who eat dairy foods have stronger bones and better overall nutrient profiles.

Researchers confirm that children between the ages of four and eight should have three 240 ml (8 oz) glasses of milk per day (or the equivalent in yoghurt, cheese, yoghurt drinks) and from eight years old through adolescence, this should be increased to four 300 ml (10 oz) glasses. Note that 240 ml (8 oz) of yoghurt or 25 g (1 oz) cheese, will provide the same amount of calcium as a glass of milk.

But don't go overboard. For one thing, milk is filling and, although nutritious, can take the place of other, varied foods in your child's diet. From the age of five, parents should change from full-fat milk to semi-skimmed or skimmed, which contains equal if not more calcium, and helps to prevent overweight. Avoid offering flavoured milks, which can be high in sugar, calories and fat. And remember that butter, milk on cereal, added to hot drinks and used in cooking, good-quality ice cream and yoghurt in smoothies, all go towards your child's daily requirements.

Bone growth peaks in the late teens and early twenties, when bones are at their very strongest. It levels out until the early thirties, when bones start losing mass and density. So milk or other good-quality sources of calcium and protein are a daily necessity until this time, at the very least.

Does my teenager always need breakfast?

Breakfast skippers are less productive and less efficient than those who eat breakfast, and doing without this vital meal impairs memory and mental performance. Children who eat breakfast regularly think faster and clearer, solve problems more easily and are less likely to be fidgety and irritable during the day. So the message is, very simply, yes, your teenager needs his or her breakfast, every day.

Several US studies undertaken between 1992 and 2005 show that children who skip breakfast are not as adept at selecting the information they need to solve problems. Ability to recall and use new information, verbal fluency and attentiveness are hurt by hunger. Teachers in Scotland reported that concentration in class improved as a result of introducing breakfast clubs, while the children said that it helped them enjoy school more. Earlier studies showed similar effects of skipping breakfast among teenagers and adults. Over all, breakfast skippers were less productive and handled tasks less efficiently than those who ate breakfast. Among both young and elderly adults, skipping breakfast impaired memory and mental performance.

A continental breakfast?

A sweet roll and a cup of coffee or a breakfast bar is not enough, either. These may suppress hunger but do little to enhance brain function and mood, not to mention their lack of nutritional value and contribution to overall health. What's more, studies show that children who eat no breakfast are at a higher risk of obesity because they tend to snack later on, and their bodies enter 'famine' mode after so many hours without food, and their metabolism slows down.

Studies of teenagers show that those who skip breakfast have an intake of calcium and vitamin C that is 40 per cent lower than those who eat breakfast.

What does a good breakfast supply?

A good breakfast should supply about 25 per cent of the day's protein, plus fibre, complex carbohydrates and some fat. In order to meet daily targets of five to seven servings of fruit and vegetables per day, a fruit or vegetable is also suggested. Good breakfast ideas include: boiled eggs on toast with fruit juice; fruit and yoghurt with porridge or cereal; wholemeal toast with cheese or baked beans; grilled tomatoes and cheese on toast; good-quality cereal with milk and fruit; good-quality bacon in a wholemeal roll with some tomatoes or avocados; wholemeal toast with nut butter – you get the idea.

If my child won't eat fruit or vegetables, how can I encourage her to do so?

In general, intake of fruit and vegetables among children in the UK is pathetically low. These foods are crucial to good health, supplying your child with the key vitamins and minerals she needs to grow and develop properly, to balance hormones and moods, sleep well, do well at school, concentrate, have good immunity, and strong teeth and bones – among many other things. There can be absolutely no question about eating fruit and vegetables. They have to be eaten; it's just a question of how.

Don't hesitate to be sneaky. Purée vegetables into soups, casseroles, sauces and stews whenever possible. Give your children some choice – there are usually a few vegetables that kids will eat, so give them some options. Get them involved in food preparation. Few children will refuse to eat something they have prepared. Similarly, encourage your kids to experiment with recipes that contain vegetables and fruits they might not have tried or which they claim to dislike. Catch them when they are hungry – leave out a platter of fruit or veggies and dip (such as houmous) when they return from school. Hungry kids will normally eat whatever is easy and to hand. Make big healthy salads to go with most meals – give them some bacon bits, croutons, nice dressings or cheese and olives to dress it up if they aren't keen on the taste.

Offer fruit as a pudding instead of unhealthy desserts. Offer fresh fruit and vegetable juices, smoothies – any more palatable form you can find. Put dried and fresh fruit on cereal; in fact, you can create a breakfast bar or a dessert bar with fresh and dried fruit, yoghurt, cereal, coconut, seeds, nuts and even a handful of chocolate-covered raisins. Keep a variety of fruits and vegetables (fresh, frozen, dried and canned) in plain view. Keep a bowl of fresh fruit on the kitchen table. Cut up favourite raw vegetables and store them for easy access.

Most importantly, impress upon them the importance of meeting their daily target of five to seven servings and why it's necessary. Eventually the message will sink in.

When should I stop preparing my children's' meals for them?
Family meals are important both for communication and to ensure healthy eating for all family members. One or more family members should, therefore, undertake to produce a good, healthy meal for the whole family at least once a day. Children can certainly help with the preparation (*see page 126*). If you don't have time to cook for your kids, then make sure there are plenty of ingredients available for them to produce a healthy meal on their own. If they are busy, working at a part-time job or have an active social life that precludes being around when you normally eat, do supervise what they are eating. Supervision of a child's eating habits should continue until you are confident that he or she will make the right decisions about good health, and have a healthy balance in his or her diet. There is no reason why kids can't put together meals for themselves from the age of twelve or thirteen (*see page 128*), but it does, ultimately remain your responsibility as a parent to ensure that your children are eating properly. And it's a pretty sorry state of affairs if kids are always eating on their own.

When should I allow money for meals instead of sending a packed lunch?
Once again, if you are confident that your child will make healthy choices and can be relied upon to eat a decent, balanced meal instead of the ubiquitous junk food, you can give money instead of preparing a packed lunch or dinner from about thirteen or fourteen – when most kids are familiar with healthy eating patterns and have the maturity to make good choices. If you have a junk food

addict on your hands, continue to supervise packed meal preparation or make it yourself to ensure overall health.

When do children start and stop being faddy eaters?

Many children go through a phase of not eating well. In fact, a recent study of 10,000 children reported that as many as one third were 'difficult to feed' at times. Some refuse to eat a particular group of foods such as vegetables or meat, while others will happily eat a small range of foods over and over again.

There are two prime ages for faddy eating. The first is toddlerhood, when children first exert their independence. In some cases, they cotton on to the fact that parents are obviously concerned about what they eat, and know they'll get a good bit of attention by refusing foods. Refusing to eat, eating slowly and rejecting certain foods or textures are all common 'assertive' behaviours among toddlers. The key at this age is not to show that you mind. Simply offer the same foods over and over again and remove them if they aren't eaten. Don't make a fuss and don't offer an alternative. Eventually hunger gets the better of even the most strong-willed child and no child will starve himself to death.

A second period of faddy eating tends to begin at around eleven or twelve, just as hormones start to circulate in advance of puberty. Children of this age tend to jostle for more freedom and use an emotive issue such as food to rile parents or assert themselves and their independence. What's more, kids of this age start to think about their weight and what 'looks good', even if they are sophisticated enough to know exactly what healthy eating entails. They want to do the pop star diet, or whatever their magazines are pushing at the moment. They may toy with vegetarianism or veganism; they may try to lose weight or eat more protein to build muscles. And, of course, the average adolescent tends to be very resistant to parental interference, the most prominent of which is obviously supervision and preparation of healthy meals!

Teenage eating habits can often be peculiar and erratic although the problem is less common than faddy toddlers since by their teens most kids have tried more food flavours and enjoy the variety of food available. The best advice is to ensure that you have only the foods you want your child to eat in your household. If the choices are limited, he'll end up having to eat what is on offer. But it is important for both age groups to have *some* choice in order to avoid a locked-horns situation. Get in a few of the new faddy elements that you know your teenager will eat; give your toddler a choice (before cooking) of pasta or rice, or peas or courgettes, for example. Show some willing to respect their food choices, but only within the confines of a healthy diet.

If your child is growing and developing well, and seems in good health, short-term faddiness is not a problem. If you are concerned, however, that a limited diet is having an impact on health, see your doctor for some advice. Watch out, too, for eating disorders (*see page 465*), which can be characterised by erratic eating patterns and unusual food choices.

Is it normal for my child to live on snacks?

Many older children and teens appear to be constantly hungry, and can't seem to get from one meal to the next without another small meal or series of snacks in between. Given the big growth spurt that takes place around puberty (*see page 392*), this is very normal and should be encouraged. There are two reasons why snacking may not be ideal – the first is if your child is overweight. Eating little and often is a sensible way to eat for overweight kids, because it keeps blood-sugar levels steady and prevents bingeing and cravings; however, if your child is eating large snacks *and* full meals, he's probably eating too much. Snacking may also start to take the place of regular healthy meals if they are too frequent and eaten too close to meal times. In this case, keeping a snack-free zone of at least 90 minutes before meals will help.

Finally, and perhaps most importantly, however, snacks should be healthy whether they are irregular treats or form a big part of your child's diet. Overweight caused by snacking has much more to do with the quality of the snacks than the quantity, so choose good-quality, healthy foods that add to your child's overall nutritional picture. Snacks should be viewed as mini meals in terms of quality rather than something to fill up your child.

If your son is eating only snacks and missing out main meals, it's possible that he isn't getting the nutrients he needs. He's also missing out on the opportunity to spend family time (*see page 198*) by sitting down to a meal. If he's got a busy schedule, slot in a few

GOOD IDEAS FOR SNACKS

▷ Unlimited fruit and raw vegetables.
▷ Wholegrain cereals with milk, or soya or rice milk.
▷ Unsalted popcorn or pretzels.
▷ Salsa, houmous and yoghurt dips.
▷ Wholemeal toast with nut butters or fruit spreads.
▷ Dried fruits (unsulphured if possible) and fruit bars.
▷ Yoghurts, yoghurt drinks and smoothies.
▷ Breadsticks.
▷ Raw nuts and seeds.
▷ Rice cakes.
▷ Oatcakes.
▷ Cheese.

meals a week (at least once a day if possible) when he can agree to be there.

Friends

I'm concerned about my child's friends. What can I do?

It is a seriously bad idea to forbid your children from spending time with friends, even if you disapprove. Unless there is a serious problem, such as stealing, drugs or truancy, for example, you are probably best to take a step back, grin and bear it. Many kids adopt friendships because it makes them feel cool; because they feel they might be targeted or bullied if they aren't in with a certain crowd; because they feel insecure and hanging out with risk-takers or cool kids makes them feel accepted and more important. One thing is for certain, if you forbid a friendship, you will encourage your child to become subversive, rebellious and perhaps even lie.

It's worth working out why you aren't happy about the friendship. Do you just 'instinctively' dislike the friend/s? Or do you have real cause for concern. Have an innocent conversation with your child and ascertain more about the children in question – what they are like, what he likes about them, what he likes most about their friendship. You may find, in fact, that they have common interests and that your child isn't being steered off track at all.

Putting down your daughter's friends indirectly criticises her and shows your disapproval of her choices. Ask open-ended questions about your daughter's friend. If you've observed this girl engaging in behaviour that you disapprove of, you can ask your daughter, 'How do you feel when your friend teases other kids?' or 'I've noticed that your friend is quite rude to other kids. Does that bother you?' or 'Do you think it's cool that she smokes at her age?'

Throughout our lives we all choose friends who prove not to be friends at all; they let us down in some way, or encourage us to do things we weren't happy about doing. For our children, choosing inappropriate friends is part of peer pressure (*see page 369*) and a longing to fit in and feel part of the crowd. Most of the time, children will come to their own conclusions; they might be hurt one time too many, or feel out of control, frightened, bullied or cornered. They might realise that being part of a cool crowd isn't all it's cracked up to be, and that finding like-minded friends is more fun and more relaxing. Kids do see negative behaviours and bad habits, even if they don't admit it straightaway. But intervening by forbidding or criticising is only likely to make your child dig in his heels and stick with the friendship out of stubbornness. Much better to give him space to come to his own conclusions.

However, if your child is being bullied and seems to be struggling to hold his or her own, or if her self-esteem is being dented, and she is being encouraged to undertake risky behaviours, it's well worth having a chat. Let her come to her own conclusions – maybe suggesting that the friend or group in question might be making them feel less good about themselves; or under pressure to do things they aren't sure about, or ready for? Let your child talk to you about it – encourage her to ask for help if she needs it. If there is a bullying situation, for example, you can get some help from organisations or your child's school (*see page 81*). Don't leave your child defenceless or resourceless, but give her space to make her own decisions.

How do I get to know her friends?

A good first step is to simply get to know your child's friends better. You can then invite the kids you feel good about to family get-togethers and outings and find other ways to encourage your child to spend time with those kids. In time you may see what your child finds attractive about certain friends you didn't take to. Either way, show support, keep the lines of communication open, particularly in regard to issues that might affect your child. Also, talk directly with your child about the qualities in a friend that really count, such as trustworthiness and kindness, rather than popularity or a 'cool' style. Sometimes it takes a few mistakes and a lot of experience to recognise the value of true friendship.

What can I do if my child doesn't seem to have any friends?
Peer rejection in childhood often brings with it serious emotional difficulties. Rejected children are frequently discontent with themselves and with their relationships with other children. Many of these children experience strong feelings of loneliness and social dissatisfaction. Rejected children also report lower self-esteem and may be more depressed than other children. Peer rejection is also predictive of later life problems, such as dropping out of school, juvenile delinquency and mental health problems.

It is important that your child has friends – the support network is invaluable in academic life, in emotional development, in understanding relationships, and, of course, self-respect and self-esteem. You can do a great deal to encourage friendships.

Is my child a loner?
You may have a child who is a natural loner and is perfectly happy enjoying his own company. This is fine to some extent, but limiting in many others. Find out who he likes and encourage him to have them round, or invite them to a family gathering or outing. Sometimes kids need lots of encouragement to get themselves out and about – it is, after all, much easier to stay at home and read, bug your younger brother, watch TV or play on the computer. You may have a child whose interests are not

standard – your son might hate football and your daughter might hate shopping. So get them involved in group activities that focus on things they do like – where they are likely to meet like-minded friends. If you know some parents, ask them round with their kids for Sunday lunch – or arrange an outing on your child's behalf (with his permission, of course). He may well be grateful not to have to do the legwork himself.

Isolated children may have a serious problem with self-esteem, and may be the target of bullies. Talk to your child about the importance of friendship and see if you can work out why he finds it difficult to make or maintain friendships. Don't judge or bully him; he may just need a little encouragement and a lot of love and support to feel better about himself. It's worth remembering that not all of us will have 'cool', wildly popular children. Many parents define themselves by the popularity of their children, which adds pressure and makes things even harder for them, because they always feel that they are letting us down and failing to meet expectations. A quiet child may want only one or two good friends, and be perfectly satisfied with that.

Is my child disliked for a good reason?

But be honest with yourself. Is your child a bully? Is he critical or hard to be with, hard to get to know? Has he proved himself an untrustworthy friend at some point? It may well be that he needs to develop some key relationship skills, learn to negotiate, learn to share, learn to open up – any one of a multitude of things. The best thing you can do is to teach the value of friendship and act as a good role model by having healthy relationships yourself.

There is quite a bit of research into characteristics associated with peer acceptance. For example, acceptance is linked with a child who has a sense of humour, who is participatory, resourceful and cooperative. Kids who are rejected tend to be aggressive, disruptive, bossy, withdrawn and/or have low cognitive skills. Trustworthy, reliable and loyal children are always more popular, while aggressive, dishonest or children who betray are not. Key things that draw friends to friends and create friendships are common interests, respect for peer conventions and being of the same gender, race and/or age.

So help your child develop skills he may be lacking; help him to find friends that he will find it easier to communicate with by enrolling him in courses, classes or activities that suit him and his interests. Encourage cooperation, teach how to initiate friendship and how to maintain it; how to praise and support rather than find fault.

Kids who resist any attempts to encourage friendship or are out of their depth completely may need some emotional support, so see your GP.

Gambling

When can my child buy a lottery ticket?
In the UK, children can buy a lottery ticket at the age of sixteen. In the US and Canada, tickets cannot be purchased until the age of eighteen.

Is my child old enough to gamble on horses?
Many families choose some of the big racing (or other sporting events) to have a light-hearted 'flutter', usually with a competitive element between family members. While in theory the odd little gamble may not appear dangerous, it does create in a child's mind the idea that gambling is a bit of a buzz, that winning can provide

comparatively big incomes with little effort, and that gambling is an acceptable activity. Frankly, it's a mistake. Kids who 'win' their family pools may not go on to become gambling addicts, but they immediately correlate success, praise and money with the 'sport' and for a child who wants attention, seeks a buzz, likes 'risky' behaviour, is in need of some cash or has addictive tendencies, this can be perilous.

I would discourage all gambling in children, regardless of their age. When they hit the magic age of eighteen, when gambling is legal, they should be aware of the risks, the dangers, the potential for addiction, have an idea about 'chasing' (struggling to win back your lost money with more and more gambling), and know that it is not a healthy occupation. There are very few people who earn a lot of money from gambling and many, many whose lives are ruined by it.

There doesn't seem to be any real restriction on internet gambling – should I allow my under-age child to gamble online?

In fact, there are restrictions and a child must reach eighteen before gambling on the internet. It's easy to get round the system, though, because there appear to be few checks in place and a false birth date can easily be entered. Gambling is a minefield of potential dangers, and it is wise to discourage your child from partaking, and also to put suitable software on your computer to prevent access to gambling sites. A recent study found that children as young as eleven have been setting up gambling accounts online; many become addicted and steal from family members in order to continue.

At what age is it acceptable to allow gambling 'play'?

Gambling takes many forms. Having a bet between family members about a score or a big horse race, where a small sum of money is put into the pot by all, is probably fairly harmless, in that there are no instant, big winnings, and no encouragement to carry on. Gambling without money is probably a better idea – trading 'favours' is ideal; you wash the car if you lose, and the winner gets a day without chores or a trip to the cinema, for example.

Legally speaking, what can children do in terms of gambling and at what age?

In England and Wales, if you are under sixteen, you can go into arcades but must not play on fruit machines giving a £10 or more cash payout. If you are between the ages of fourteen and eighteen you can go into a pub, but you are not allowed to play on fruit machines with a cash payout of £10 or more. A sign stating that the machines are restricted to over-eighteens must be displayed.

There is no lower age limit for playing on fruit machines with a maximum cash or token prize of up to £8.

In Northern Ireland, there is no lower age limit for playing on fruit machines with a maximum cash prize of £8 in amusement arcades and similar premises. The maximum prize in a pub is £15 cash. There is no legal age restriction on playing fruit machines in pubs, but different premises may have different rules.

If you are under sixteen, you are not allowed to buy tickets (or scratch cards) in a registered public lottery. You are allowed to buy tickets in a private lottery.

Outlets that allow gambling to minors and British firms operating gambling websites that are used by children face unlimited fines and removal of their licences.

How do I know if my child has a gambling problem?

There are many studies showing that a small but significant minority of children and adolescents in the UK have a gambling

problem. In 2000, successive surveys were commissioned by the
National Lottery Commission as part of an ongoing tracking survey
to monitor young people's gambling behaviour. The latest round of
research found that 22 per cent had gambled weekly on fruit
machines (55 per cent in the previous year), 9 per cent had gambled
weekly on National Lottery scratch cards (36 per cent in the
previous year), and 7.6 per cent weekly on the National Lottery
draw (26 per cent in the previous year).

Even more recent research found that about 3.5 per cent of
those aged eleven to fifteen have a gambling problem, according to
the International Gaming Research Unit at Nottingham Trent
University, which has just produced guidance for schools to teach
children about gambling. In a recent study of more than 8,000
youngsters, a quarter admitted to gambling in the previous week.
The more money the child had, the more often he or she gambled.
Forty per cent of those earning £30 a week or more had gambled in
the past week, compared with 21 per cent earning £10 a week or
less. Boys were far more likely to participate than girls

Who are these adolescent gamblers?

Further research has shown that adolescent problem gamblers are
more likely to be male, have begun gambling at an early age, have
had a big win early on, and to be from a lower social class. This
research has also indicated that the most addictive gambling
activities are those in which the time gap between gambles is very
short (slot machines and internet betting), and there are short
intervals between stake and payout, near misses and a combination
of very high prizes and frequent winning of small prizes.

According to the Salvation Army, the proportion of problem
gamblers among adolescents in the UK could be more than three
times that of adults, at 1.7 per cent for those aged sixteen to

Phillip Hodson of the British Association for Counselling and Psychotherapy explains that young people are especially vulnerable during the formative stages of their life. 'Growing up is only completed at the age of twenty-five – some parts of the brain do not mature until then. So it's foolish to expose people to highly addictive behaviour at this stage in their lives. It normalises their behaviour and then they are stuck with it for life.'

twenty-four against 0.5 per cent for adults aged twenty-five and over. In fact, the UK is still the only Western country that still allows children of any age to gamble.

Online gambling is becoming increasingly popular, and there are now an estimated 1,700 gambling websites on the internet. As well as the internet, you can now gamble through interactive television and mobile phone.

The convenience of gambling at home, the ease of setting up a gambling account and the variety of forms of gambling – from traditional betting, to casino gambling, bingo and lotteries – makes online gambling very appealing.

Is there any help out there?

The links below are organisations that provide software and information to protect children from accessing gambling on the internet:

www.childnet-int.org
www.cyberpatrol.com
www.gamblock.com
www.netnanny.com

Gamcare offers a helpline for young gamblers or parents worried about their children gambling. Contact 0845 6000 133 or visit www.gamcare.org.uk.

How do I recognise a gambling addict?

Unfortunately, there are not many ways to recognise an addiction, and it's not until a child is caught that you realise the problem. Unlike drugs or alcohol, there are no obvious physical signs, but you can look out for:

▷ Erratic behaviour and a buzzy kind of countenance, perhaps alternating with depression or withdrawal.

▷ Secrecy on the computer.

▷ Betting slips in pockets or hidden away.

▷ A sudden need for more money.

▷ A knowledge of stakes or races/sporting events that your child might not normally discuss.

▷ Conflict with family members – a sign of stress.

Gap year

How old should my child be before taking a gap year?

Gap years are traditionally taken after secondary school and before university or other further education, when a child is about eighteen or nineteen. This is the perfect age – the age when children evolve into fully-fledged adults, with responsibility for their own actions and a need, desire and right to independence. It's also a good time in terms of career prospects and finances. At this age, most kids haven't yet embarked on employment with a set number of holidays, and this may be the only real opportunity they have to take a year off to see the world and live a little on their own.

Similarly, most kids don't have regular financial responsibilities at this age, and before they get laden with mortgages, student loans, rent and bills, they can experience a little freedom.

Should I oversee my daughter's gap year programme or leave her to her own devices?

Part of the pleasure of a gap year is the planning and the opportunity to show some independence by choosing a year of activities that cater to a child's own interests and goals. In theory, she should be left to her own devices to find a way of supporting herself, making money before or en route to sustain her lifestyle, planning her time within a budget, and showing some initiative. This year is all about her and offers her the opportunity to flex her muscles a little. It may be the last opportunity she has to do exactly what she wants before starting full-time further education or work, with the responsibilities that these and adulthood entail, so let her choose.

Having said that, she may enjoy your ideas and input, and you can offer valuable guidance by helping her plan sensibly, and ensuring that she has the wherewithal to undertake her plans safely. You can help her to budget and make travel plans, where required, and even help her do a little of the research. But leave the big decisions to her.

If I am against her plans, do I have a right to deny them?

If she's eighteen, you don't. In fact, if she's paying for her gap year, it becomes her own and she should be shown some respect for her choices. Consider why you are against her plans. Does it seem dangerous? If so, voice your concerns and explain them. Perhaps some alterations can be made to keep her safer. Is it too expensive? Some adjustments can make it easier to fit within a budget, or you can make some suggestions for making some money en route or in advance. You might even consider a loan to help get her on her way.

You might be worried that her plans are too frivolous and that she should be doing something more worthy on her year off, such as volunteering in less-developed countries or helping others in some way. Certainly these are valid concerns, as one thing we do want our children to achieve in a gap year is some understanding of the world around them, and their responsibilities as citizens of the world. Giving a little of their time for others or for good causes at a point in their lives when they are time-rich and fairly responsibility-free should be encouraged. Perhaps she can fit a few weeks here and there into her plans.

If you have other objections, analyse them carefully. You may find that you are simply reluctant to let your child spread her wings a little. You may worry that she is not mature enough or has inadequate financial sense. Your guidance can help to put these things right well in advance and should ease your mind.

Should I pay for my child's gap year?

In theory, children should finance their own gap years. There are several reasons. The first is that they will have to work towards something they really want – perhaps for the first time in their lives, and then work within a budget to achieve that. This teaches them the value of money and also balancing needs versus wants. Secondly, gap years are about independence from parents, and to achieve this, your kids should be prepared to *be* fully independent, and not count on the bank of mum and dad to get there. Thirdly, many kids have absolutely no understanding of the cost of things or the value of hard work and achievement. One of the roles of a gap year is to teach them to look after themselves within the confines of a limited budget and to work for what they want. This then imbues them with a sense of achievement and self-respect. If parents finance a gap year, it becomes one big holiday rather than a valuable experience.

Certainly, some parents offer loans to help their children out, particularly if they don't have much opportunity to earn money before their year. Some offer to match what their child earns, which at least provides some incentive to earn something. Others pay for one element, such as a round-the-world budget ticket (it's surprising how cheap these can be) and expect their children to cover the remainder of their expenses. Still others provide a small allowance, or an 'emergency' credit card with a low credit limit, to ensure that they have some backup if things go awry. Whatever you choose, do put the onus on your child to provide as much financing as possible, to make the experience useful.

Many kids learn that they can't do whatever they want because it's simply too expensive; this leaves them with the option of trying to raise funds through hard work before and during their break, or choosing something that fits their budgets. This is a good learning experience for any child, whatever route he or she takes. A first taste of real life and money!

Should I pay for a phone link during my child's gap year?

Some parents choose to pay a certain amount of credit on their child's phone to ensure communication while the child is away. Frankly, these days it's probably not necessary. Most hostels, hotels and cities have internet facilities and pay phones which will allow your traveller to reverse the charges if she is out of money. You can provide her with a phone or credit, but chances are it will be used up long before you get your first phone call; and because international calls require credit from the caller as well as the recipient, it may be impossible to get in touch with her. Regular texting is a good idea and much cheaper.

How often should I keep in touch?

All parents will be concerned about their children, particularly if they are away for long stretches of time or living on their own for the first time. While you don't want to inundate your child with calls and messages, you are certainly within your rights to expect regular communication. Why don't you agree a certain time every Sunday night, for example, when you'll touch base by phone, and request a midweek text or e-mail just to let you know he's safe.

What if my child wants to stay close to home and work or volunteer?

This is his year and his choice. There is nothing wrong with taking time out a little closer to home, and the benefits can be just as valuable. Although travelling is a mind-broadening experience and will help children to understand the world around them a little better, there is no doubt that a taste of the real world in any shape or form will have the effect of enhancing maturity and the ability to take on responsibility, as well as taking pride in achievements. But allow more freedom; encourage him to budget any earnings, saving some (*see page 338*), and contributing a little to the household – or at least covering the costs of his own expenses and some you might usually cover. The idea is that he will be taking the first steps to independence before he enters further education and must learn to look after himself.

Growth

How much should my child be growing at this age?

There is a wide range in what is considered normal growth, and children pass through various growth phases during adolescence

before finally reaching adult height. Some children begin early on –
girls, in particular – while others are 'late bloomers'. Most girls
reach their peak growth rate at about twelve years of age or about
two years after puberty begins (*see page 392*). Menstruation almost
always begins after the peak growth rate in height has been reached
(average age for the onset of menstruation is 12½ years). Once girls
start to menstruate, they usually grow about 2.5-5 cm (1-2 in),
reaching their final adult height by about fourteen or fifteen years
old (younger or older depending on when puberty began).

Boys tend to show the first physical changes of puberty between
the ages of ten and sixteen years, and usually grow most quickly
between the ages of twelve and fifteen. The growth spurt of boys
begins, on average, about two years later than that of girls. By age
nineteen, many boys have stopped growing, but their muscles will
continue to develop.

Growth in puberty accounts for between 20 and 25 per cent of
final adult height. In total, this works out as an average of 23-28
cm (8¾-11 in) in girls and 26-28 cm (10¼-11 in) for boys. Obviously
some kids grow more and some less. The average growth spurt
lasts between two and three years.

When will my child have her 'growth spurt'?

This differs for all children, according to when they enter puberty
(*see above, and page 392*). And even this isn't necessarily a rule of
thumb for every child – there are some children who have their
growth spurts very soon after puberty begins, rather than two years
or so into the process, and others towards the end. What you can
be sure of is that your child's main growth will take place between
the ages of nine and fifteen for girls and ten and nineteen for boys.

Within the adolescent 'growth spurt,' teens and pre-teens
experience 'mini-spurts' of intense growth. They may experience

growing pains; after all, their skeletons are being formed. During a one-year period of intense growth, boys can gain about 10 cm (4 in) and girls about 9 cm (3½ in) in height.

When will my child reach full adult height?

Once again, it's a question of when puberty begins in your child and how close to the beginning of puberty he begins his major growth spurt. Early bloomers tend to grow at a faster rate and reach their adult height before late bloomers. On average, however, girls have usually reached adult height by the age of fifteen, and boys a little later, around eighteen or nineteen, although many will have achieved their adult height a year before this.

IS THERE ANY WAY TO WORK OUT MY CHILD'S ADULT HEIGHT?

While predicting adult height is a difficult task, experts often use 'midparental height' as most individuals have an adult height that is within 5 cm (2 in) of the midparental height. This is calculated (in centimetres) using the following formulae:

For girls

$$\frac{(\text{father's height} - 13 \text{ cm}) + \text{mother's height}}{2}$$

For boys

$$\frac{(\text{father's height} + 13 \text{ cm}) + \text{mother's height}}{2}$$

What's more, it is generally true, but not always the case, that a healthy adolescent will stay on the same height percentile during most of childhood and adolescent growth and development. This makes sense since an adolescent cannot alter his or her potential height. So it's a good idea to check your child's height regularly and record it in his health record book or on a height chart that can be obtained from your GP.

Is it true that children get their height from their mother's side?
Genetics and the child's gender account for 70 per cent of what goes into deciding how tall a child will be. The other 30 per cent comes from environmental factors such as nutrition, exercise and any underlying health problems. One 2006 study found that children get their height from their father's side and their weight from their mother's, although looking around this appears to be a vast generalisation. There's no doubt that six 'height' genes are passed from parents to baby – three from dad and three from mum. If all three genes from dad are 'tall' genes and only one of three genes from mum is a 'tall' gene, his height would effectively have come from his dad. If the tall genes came from the mum's side and the dad's side (it's possible to be very tall, with six of six tall genes), then it's shared.

There does seem to be some evidence, however, that all boys are taller than their mothers, unless there has been illness affecting growth.

When does my child's diet stop affecting her growth?
As long as your child is growing, her diet will have an effect. Birth weight and nutrition both in the womb and during infancy are extremely important, and strong determinants of adult height (*see above*), but the food your child eats until she stops growing is crucial

to every element of growth and development. Extra nutrients are required to support the adolescent growth spurt – and this boils down to calories and vitamins, minerals, protein, healthy fats and carbohydrates. It has been shown, for example, that children suffering from eating disorders during adolescence, where their intake of food is neither adequate in terms of quantity and quality are shorter and suffer from other health problems, including calcium deficiency (which causes the onset of early osteoporosis) and iron deficiency, hormone problems, delayed menstruation and more.

The period between nine and twenty years of age seems to be critical for achievement of peak bone mass (so therefore the period during which calcium in particular is most important). From birth until about age sixteen, bones are in a phase of rapid growth and bone modelling. After this period, the skeleton is in a process of constant remodelling throughout life. The period of bone mass accumulation extends from puberty to the late twenties. So even if your child has stopped growing, her diet will affect the growth and mass of her bones well into her twenties. Consider, too, the fact that many boys reach adult height by age eighteen, but continue to develop muscle and other supporting structures into their twenties.

So, in a nutshell, your child's diet at this time of huge physical growth and development is crucial during adolescence, and remains very important well into her twenties.

Does sleep affect my child's growth?

Research suggests that teens actually need more sleep to allow their bodies to conduct the internal work required for such rapid growth. On average, teens need about 9¼ hours of sleep a night (*see page 55*). Even more important, perhaps, is the fact that some two-thirds of total growth hormone production occurs during deep sleep. Growth hormone is a protein that is produced by the pituitary ('master') gland and is vital for normal growth. If your child is sleep-deprived, his growth will be affected.

If my child is taller than everyone else in her class/year, will she always be taller?

This depends on a few things. The first is that if your child was tall from birth and throughout her childhood, she is likely to stick fairly closely to her 'percentile' line on growth charts. Most tall young children continue to remain tall. If, however, she becomes taller around the onset of puberty (*see page 392*), she may well be an early bloomer, which means that she will achieve her adult height earlier than other children. In this case, she may well stop growing soon and be perfectly average in height.

Hair

My daughter wants to dye her beautiful blonde hair black. Can or should I stop her?

Teenagers spend a great deal of their time searching for something called a 'comfortable identity' – trying out various looks through hairstyles, clothing, accessories, nail varnish, etc., in order to feel more comfortable with their peers or to be accepted by them. Often kids change their looks in order to fit in with a crowd – or because they have been influenced by media idols. In all honesty, there is no point in battling over things that are impermanent, such as clothes, hairstyles or hair colour, unless they are likely to cause a risk to her health (*see also page 248*). Forbidding your teenager to do something that actually has little impact on anything other than your concern about the way she is viewed, or how, perhaps, her appearance reflects on your family or represents your values, is more likely to encourage her to do it on the sly, or out of a sense of rebellion. As kids get older their freedom increases dramatically, but many of them believe that they should be more empowered than they are – and allowed far more control over their lives. If you allow the small stuff and show some tolerance of individuality, your daughter is less likely to feel that she has to battle for everything, which makes negotiating the more important issues that much easier.

HAIR DYE AND ALLERGIES

According to a group of European dermatologists, the incidence of hair dye allergies is increasing as more kids dye their hair. The culprit is a common chemical ingredient in permanent hair dyes, called para-phenylenediamine, or PPD. PPD is found in more than two-thirds of commercial dyes, the researchers say, including many of the top-selling brands. Patients with severe PPD reactions commonly develop painful rashes around the hair line or on the face, which often require treatment and can occasionally lead to hospitalisation. Facial swelling is also common. First-time users can greatly reduce their risk of allergic reactions by conducting a skin-sensitivity test 48 hours before colouring their hair. It's also worth encouraging your child to use a natural hair dye, or have it professionally done, rather than risk serious reactions. And given that allergies in general are on the increase in today's youths, this seems sound advice.

Should my son be allowed to shave his head? In my view he looks like a thug.
The crucial words here are 'in my view', because 'your view' is not his, nor that of his peers and group identity. I agree that a shaved head presents a certain image, and it may not be one that you

either identify with or condone; however, it is a short-term issue because hair *will* always grow back (and quickly in healthy kids). Once again, if you give your child the space he needs to experiment with his image, and allow him some personal power over his life, you are showing respect. And as respect is a mutual commodity, you can expect some respect for your views over the important issues in future.

Health

Does my child need a vitamin supplement?
If your child is a picky eater with a limited diet despite your best efforts, you may need to consider supplements. There is no reason why a good multivitamin and mineral supplement shouldn't be offered anyhow, as it will top up even marginal deficiencies that can cause health problems. The most important nutrients for growing kids are iron and calcium – all vitamins and minerals are crucial, of course, but a lack of these can cause more serious problems. Supplementing these nutrients can only help.

At what age should I stop giving vitamin tablets to my children?
There is, of course, an age when your child will stop *taking* them, whether you give them or not, but it's worth *offering* for as long as your child is under your roof. Leave the bottle out and encourage them to help themselves. Explain that a poor diet leaves a teenager subject to deficiencies that can affect so many aspects of his or her life, including energy levels, concentration, growth, memory, overall health and even weight. In particular, calcium and iron are extremely important as many adolescents do not get enough of

these and a deficiency can have a serious impact on health.
A child's need for these latter nutrients, in particular, continues
well into their twenties.

Which nutrients are most important to supplement?

One common deficiency in children's diets are the omega-3
essential fatty acids (EFAs). EFAs are essential for proper nervous
system and brain function. Omega-3 fatty acids are known to help
prevent heart disease and they can improve the condition of some
patients with depression and bipolar disorder. What's more,
recent studies have concluded that they also aid intelligence,
concentration and help with learning difficulties, improving 'brain
power' all round. One study found that 40 per cent of children will
experience clear improvement in things like coordination, academic
ability and progress. This essential fatty acid can be found in
pumpkin seeds, oily fish such as tuna, mackerel and salmon,
as well as in canola oil and flax (hemp) oil. Most kids don't get
enough, so this is definitely worth supplementing.

If your child is a poor fruit and vegetable eater, vitamin C will
be low. This vitamin is important for our immune system and for
the connective tissue under our skin. Vitamin C protects us from
damaging free radicals and is crucial for brain function. Older kids
who may have taken up recreational smoking will be particularly
deficit, as are kids who are under pressure (during exams) and run
down in any way.

What about probiotics?

Probiotics are also worth considering. These are 'healthy' bacteria
which provide a multitude of functions, including preventing
respiratory and gastrointestinal illness, improving digestion and
intestinal tract health, enhancing the immune system, reducing

allergies and lactose intolerance symptoms, and increasing the absorption of various nutrients. Children who are run down, under pressure, have frequent tummy bugs or have been on antibiotics in the last year will undoubtedly benefit. Live yoghurt is the best natural source, but a supplement will be useful.

When should my daughter have her first cervical smear?
Cervical cancer is the second most common cancer in women under thirty-five. The idea of a cervical smear is that precancerous changes in the cervix can be detected, allowing for prompt treatment. The UK government suggests that women between the ages of twenty and sixty-four should have a smear every three to five years as a precautionary measure. However, I suggest that if your daughter is having sex, she should be seen within a year of her first experience. Obviously, you may not be aware of when this occurs, but when you do discuss sexual relationships, it's important to point out that early sex, multiple partners, infection with certain types of human *papilloma* virus (HPV) which is usually transmitted via sex, failing to use barrier methods of contraception (such as condoms), smoking and even the contraceptive pill are all risk factors. Cervical cancer kills a significant number of women every year, and although your teen might think she's invincible, it's better to be prepared.

What immunisations are required in the teenage years and are they mandatory?
At present, in the UK diphtheria, tetanus and polio, given as a single injection, is offered between the ages of thirteen and eighteen. If your child was immunised as a baby, these are considered to be booster vaccines, with the view that they provide longer-term protection and make up for the fact that some children

do not achieve full immunity first time round. Between ten and fourteen, kids are also routinely offered the BCG vaccine, which protects against tuberculosis (TB).

If your child was not offered the MenC vaccine (which protects against a type of bacteria causing meningitis and septicaemia), it may be suggested that your child has one dose. NHS research shows that there is a greater risk for people between the ages of twenty and twenty-four than for most adults.

Unlike the situation in the US and Canada, you are not obliged to have your child immunised before she can attend school, and it is not mandatory, although immunisation is highly recommended. Many parents are wary of immunisation after the MMR vaccine scares, and I think it is worth doing a little research. Many vaccines have side effects. To get an honest appraisal of these, visit www.immunisation.org.uk. Some are more important than others. For example, TB is becoming more common in urban settings, but it still remains rare and treatment is very effective. Most children do not need boosters for diphtheria or polio because not only have these diseases been largely eradicated, but the first three shots should have been effective. Tetanus is a different story, as kids are easily injured and susceptible to germs found normally in soil or on rusty nails which enter the body via open cuts or burns. There are few cases of tetanus these days that have serious consequences as treatment is effective, but this one may be worth considering.

If your child has had a reaction in the past, ask some questions and, if possible, ask for your child to have immunity levels tested before agreeing to a vaccination that may not only be unnecessary but cause problems. Ultimately, vaccination is a personal choice, but I do think it's worth doing your homework before you agree to something that may cause damage.

Can my child decide not to undertake her school immunisation programme, even if I disagree?

The importance of consent cannot be underestimated. Parents are normally asked to sign a document giving consent, but your child can make a decision to override this. Providing your child is 'Fraser competent' (commonly known as Gillick competent), which effectively means that she understands what the treatment involves and also the impact of choosing not to undergo it, she is allowed to decline. In most cases, children are encouraged to involve their parents in the decision, but ultimately, they have the final say.

If you are worried and believe your child is at risk by not undergoing routine immunisations, you can ask your GP or health visitor to provide more information. Take the time to talk to her yourself about what worries you and how you think that the decision may impact on her health. Obviously, all parents have a responsibility to ensure that their children have the best possible healthcare and are protected from diseases through a variety of measures. You may be able to convince your child; however, she does have the right to refuse.

Until what age can I insist that my daughter has scheduled immunisations? Can I insist that she not have scheduled immunisations?

Any child who is competent enough to understand the implications of having and/or not having immunisations can make her own decisions under Fraser's Law (*see above*), regardless of her age. Some children are given licence at ages as young as six or seven, provided they are mature enough to take on board the issues. So, unfortunately, you have no legal right to insist on immunisations or to deny them to your child if she does not agree. In most cases, parents will be consulted, but it remains within your child's jurisdiction to make the final decision.

Does my child have the right to refuse to see the doctor?

In England and Wales, young people aged sixteen or over but under eighteen can give independent consent to their own treatment, without the consent of a parent or guardian. A young person in this age group can, however, be overruled by a court order if it is considered that treatment is not in your child's best interests. If your child is suffering from a disability or if they have a history of psychological or emotional problems, your consent must be obtained.

The reality is, however, that children under sixteen can give their own consent to treatment provided they are judged capable by a doctor of understanding what is involved. There is no general test for assessing this capability, and each case will be decided on its own merits.

If a child under the age of sixteen does not have sufficient understanding, parental consent (or a court order) will be required for any treatment, except in an emergency. If a child under sixteen who does have sufficient understanding refuses treatment, treatment can still be given with their parent's or guardian's consent or by a court order.

So, in a nutshell, if your child doesn't want to see a doctor or obtain treatment offered if and when he does, there is not much you can do about it, apart from fighting through NHS trusts and/or the courts.

What if my child is not capable of making the right decisions?

Frankly, if you have serious concerns about your child's ability to make the right decisions, it's worth battling to ensure that he at least seeks some sort of diagnosis, even if he resists treatment. You'll know what you are up against and may perhaps be able to help in other ways. But if there is no clear-cut reason why your child must see the doctor, it is unlikely that forcing the issue or commencing a fight that will disrupt family harmony and relationships with your child could do anything but more damage.

The situation is much the same in Scotland and Northern Ireland, although most hospitals in the latter will require parental permission to perform an operation on a young person under eighteen.

Can my child agree to test an experimental drug without my approval?

Usually not. Young people or children under the age of eighteen cannot give their own consent to experimental operations, drug experiments or blood donations, unless they have sufficient understanding of what is involved. And in most cases this will be declined.

At what age should kids be given a sexual health check?

The biggest problem with STDs (sexually transmitted diseases) is that not everyone experiences signs and/or symptoms. What's more, some of these don't appear for weeks and months, and some do not ever appear to manifest. This has a few implications. Your child may be completely unaware that he is carrying a disease or suffering from something that could seriously affect his health and fertility, but also, your child may be having sex with someone who has also unwittingly passed one on.

Children need to be educated about STDs, and to know what to look for (*see page 424*). They also need to be encouraged to use barrier forms of contraception, even if they do take the pill or use other methods. Most importantly, however, they should be encouraged to have a check within a few months of commencing sexual relations. This will mean, of course, a little honesty on their part, but they certainly don't need to tell you about it for a check to take place.

Until what age should I accompany my child to her doctor's appointments?

From a legal point of view a a child of sixteen years old is deemed competent to make decisions regarding her own health. The simple answer is that you should attend as long as your child is willing and whenever you are concerned. Your child's doctor cannot release information to you unless he/she is concerned that your child is in danger in any way, or unfit to make decisions regarding her own health.

All parents have a responsibility for their children's health and in this case, what you don't know *can* harm you or her. If you have doubts that she is attending appointments or receiving the right advice and/or care, you can, until she is eighteen, ask for dispensation to see records and options for care. After the age of eighteen, you have no rights.

Can my child make an appointment on her own without me?

Yes she can, and the details of her appointment will remain confidential if her doctor deems that she is fit to understand and make decisions on her own.

Until what age do I have a right to see my daughter's medical notes?

Those with parental responsibility also have a statutory right to apply for access to the health records of their child, although children who are mature enough to express views on the issue also need to be asked for their consent before parents see their record. If they deny permission, you will have to go through various routes to get permission.

I'm divorced and don't live with my child. Can I still access her records?

If both parents have parental responsibility in any sense, neither loses it if they divorce; responsibility also endures if your child is in care or custody. It can, however, be restricted by court order and it is lost if the child is adopted. However, once again, if your child is deemed responsible, she can ask that her notes remain private, at whatever age, something that can usually only be overturned by tribunal or a court of law.

In England, Wales and Northern Ireland, parental responsibilities may be exercised until a young person reaches eighteen years. In Scotland, children over sixteen are given more responsibility.

I don't like the idea of the treatment suggested for my child. What should I do?

In cases of serious or chronic illness, parents are often given time, respite facilities, possibly counselling, and certainly support from health professionals, but in most cases parents are considered to be best placed to judge their young child's interests and decide about serious treatment. There are limits on what parents are entitled to decide, however, and they are not entitled to allow inappropriate treatment for their children or to refuse treatment which is in the child's best interests. For example, where children need blood products to prevent death or serious deterioration, a refusal by a parent who is a Jehovah's Witness is unlikely to be binding on doctors.

Unfortunately, if your child is old enough, responsible or mature enough to override you, and your child's doctors or consultants agree, it will be very difficult to prevent treatment from taking place without legal recourse.

What happens if my ex-partner and I disagree about the treatment of my child?

Generally, the law only requires doctors to have consent from one person in order to provide treatment lawfully. In some cases, therefore, the competent child's consent is sufficient in law although it is always desirable to involve parents with the child's agreement. In practice, however, parents sometimes disagree and doctors are reluctant to override a parent's strongly held views, particularly where the benefits and burdens of the treatment are finely balanced and it is not clear what is best for the child. Disputes between parents can be difficult for everybody involved in the child's care.

Discussion aimed at reaching consensus is normally attempted, but if this fails the doctor or consultant in charge can go ahead if he has the consent of one parent and/or the consent of the child in question (who is, again, deemed responsible and fit to make decisions about health care).

If my ex-wife doesn't live with me, can she see my child's health records?

Anyone with parental responsibility has a statutory right to apply for access to their child's health records. If the child is capable of giving consent, access may only be given with his or her consent. If a child lacks the competence to understand the nature of an application but access would be in his or her best interests, it should be granted.

Parental access is never given where it conflicts with the child's best interests and any information that a child revealed in the expectation that it would not be disclosed will not be released unless it is in the child's best interests to do so. Where parents are separated and one applies for access to the medical record, doctors are under no obligation to inform the other parent, although they may consider doing so if they believe it to be in the child's best interests.

At what age can I let my daughter make her own decisions about her health?

Unfortunately, if your child understands what is involved, she can legally make decisions about her own health from that point onwards. And there is no minimum age set on this one. In reality, most parents want to ensure that communication with children remains strong, regular and genuinely helpful for as long as possible. Keeping an interest in your children's health will mean that you are always involved to some extent, and she should be encouraged from a young age to discuss things that worry her about physical or emotional health, and to ask for help whenever she feels she needs it. There may be problems that some children find embarrassing, or which they know will upset or anger you, and on these occasions they may wish to go it alone. But do ask that you be kept informed as much as possible, and explain that you are more concerned about her overall health and well-being than what she might or might not being doing wrong. You will find it hard to make decisions about your child's health if you don't know what is going on.

From the age of sixteen, most kids can be trusted to get themselves to the doctor and, in consultation with you, make a decision about treatment. But ask to be involved in as many stages as possible, so that you can provide the right guidance.

How do I know if my child has a personality disorder?

Many parents are convinced that their adolescents have personality disorders, due to the influx of hormones and their impact on behaviour. It's worth knowing what is normal and what is not.

In general, you want to look at how your child behaves and how he appears to think and feel. If his moods are more bizarre than you would expect, his personal relationships are unhealthy or non-existent, his thinking seems confused or abnormally contrary, and he is unable to control impulses, then there may well be a problem.

If his behaviour is inflexible, maladaptive and antisocial, then chances are he does suffer from a personality disorder.

Most personality disorders begin as problems in personal development and character which peak during adolescence. They are not illnesses as such, as they do not always disrupt emotional, intellectual or perceptual functioning. However, those with personality disorders suffer a life that is not positive, proactive or fulfilling. Not surprisingly, personality disorders are also associated with failures to reach potential.

It's beyond the scope of this book to go into the fine details, but it's worth noting that there are ten distinct personality disorders now identified. Things like self-centredness that manifests itself through a me-first, self-preoccupation (beyond the scope of normal teenage self-interest, of course), lack of individual accountability that results in a victim mentality and blaming others, lack of empathy, manipulative and exploitative behaviour, serious unhappiness, distorted or superficial understanding of self and others' perceptions, and self-destructive behaviours are all indications that there might be a problem. For more information, either visit your GP or www.mind.org.uk.

I think my child is dyslexic, but how can I tell?
The best thing you can do is to have him assessed by an educational psychologist, who can not only diagnose correctly and establish the severity of the problem, but also make recommendations for helping your child, which can then be employed at school and at home.

'Dyslexia' comes from a Greek word meaning 'difficulty with words'. Dyslexia affects reading, spelling, writing, memory and concentration, and sometimes maths, music, foreign languages and self-organisation. Some people call dyslexia 'a specific learning difficulty'. It tends to run in families, and can continue throughout life. If your child is dyslexic, he is not alone. At least ten per cent of the population is dyslexic, four per cent of whom are severely dyslexic. Dyslexics may have many creative, artistic and practical skills, and can be extremely bright, which makes the condition all the more frustrating for a child.

According to the British Dyslexia Association, there are many ways to diagnose dyslexia at different ages:

Pre-school signs

▷ Family history of dyslexia problems.

▷ Learning to speak clearly later than expected.

▷ Jumbles phrases – 'cobbler's club' for 'toddler's club', 'teddy dare' for 'teddy bear'.

▷ Quick 'thinker' and 'do-er'.

▷ Use of substitute words or 'near misses'.

▷ Mislabelling – 'lampshade' for 'lamp post'.

▷ A lisp – 'duckth' for 'ducks'.

▷ Inability to remember the label for known objects: colours, for instance.

▷ Confused directional words: 'up/down' or 'in/out'.

▷ Excessive tripping, bumping and falling over nothing.

▷ Enhanced creativity – often good at drawing – good sense of colour.

▷ Obvious 'good' and 'bad' days for no apparent reason.

▷ Aptitude for constructional or technical toys: bricks, puzzles, Lego, control box for TV and video, computer keyboards.

▷ Enjoys being read to but shows no interest in letters or words.

▷ Difficulty learning nursery rhymes.

▷ Finds difficulty with rhyming words: 'cat mat fat'.

▷ Finds difficulty with odd-one-out: 'cat mat pig fat'.

▷ Did not crawl; was a 'bottom shuffler'.

▷ Difficulty with 'sequencing': coloured bead sequence.

▷ Appears bright; seems an enigma.

Children nine and under

▷ Particular difficulty learning to read and write.

▷ Persistent and continued reversing of numbers and letters (15 for 51, b for d).

▷ Difficulty telling left from right.

▷ Difficulty learning the alphabet and multiplication tables, and remembering sequences such as the days of the week and months of the year.

▷ Continued difficulty with shoelaces, ball-catching and skipping.

▷ Inattention and poor concentration.

▷ Frustration, possibly leading to behavioural problems.

Children between nine and twelve

▷ Continued mistakes in reading or a lack of reading comprehension.

▷ Strange spelling, perhaps with letters missed out or in the wrong order.

▷ Taking a longer-than-average time over written work.

▷ Disorganisation at home and at school.

▷ Difficulty copying accurately from blackboard or textbook.

▷ Difficulty taking down oral instructions.

▷ Growing lack of self-confidence and increasing frustration.

Children of twelve and over

▷ Tendency to read inaccurately or without comprehension.

▷ Inconsistent spelling.

▷ Difficulty with planning and written essays.

▷ Tendency to confuse verbal instructions and telephone numbers.

▷ Severe difficulty with learning a foreign language.

▷ Low self-esteem.

▷ Difficulty with perception of language, following instructions, listening comprehension.

OVERWEIGHT

See page 458

EATING DISORDERS

See page 465

Homework

When can she plan her own study/revision schedule?

It's a good idea to encourage independence on this front as early as possible, as children have a huge number of demands made on their time these days, and the sooner they get to grips with basic time management, the better. When your child hits her first set of important exams which require revision (perhaps the 7-year-old or 11-year-old SATS in the UK), sit down with her and establish what needs to be learned and in what period of time. Work out the time she has around other activities, and the time set aside for breaks, relaxation, play and family. Then help her break down the work into manageable chunks around these other slots. Help her with this for the first or second set of exams, and then provide guidance for the first couple of times she plots her schedule herself. Even older kids could do with a look over the shoulder to ensure that they've not missed anything out, and that their schedules are practical, achievable and actually useful!

The 35-minute daily study period is an efficient way of learning. Thirty-five minutes is a period during which most people can concentrate well. If your child revises or does homework without a break for as long as an hour, the last 20 to 30 minutes are likely to be less efficient, as concentration diminishes. It's also much easier to encourage your child to get down to work knowing that it is for a 35-minute stretch. If your child has a huge workload, divide it into 35-minute segments, with breaks and fun in between.

WHAT MAKES FOR SUCCESSFUL REVISION?

▷ Create a good study environment. It is most dispiriting if the workplace fills you with gloom. Try to keep a particular space, room or part of a room for work. Make this place attractive, with an inviting table top and minimum clutter.

▷ Encourage your child to leave the workplace tidy, instead of trying to tidy up and find things at the beginning of the next session.

▷ Find your child's best time of day. He may have little choice when to study, but some people work better or more easily at particular times of the day.

▷ Encourage your child to plan beforehand what he wants to achieve. A little advance planning – writing a list of things to do and the order in which they should be done – can save a lot of time. Set specific targets that can be managed in the time available.

▷ Space study sessions: several short sessions usually result in better retention than a single, longer session. It is much better to have more modest goals and actually do the work.

▷ Encourage your child to reduce material to a manageable amount: looking at a chapter and writing out the four or five key points that summarise what it being said works well for term tests and exams. Help your child to set small, manageable tasks that will eventually lead to his dealing with the large task.

▷ Encourage 'periodic retrieval'. Instead of passively reading and rereading material, ask him to test himself periodically to see if he has actually remembered anything. Breaking the work into small chunks and quizzing your child at the end of each will help to see whether it's actually going in.

▷ Don't stop when he reaches 100 per cent accuracy. One researcher found that he could improve his retention of material by repeating it once or twice more after he had effectively learned it. Once your child is at that point, a quick review might be all he needs to remember it all.

▷ Encourage your child to finish whatever he starts.

▷ Use breaks and rewards. Humans can only function for so long at maximum efficiency before concentration begins to wane. Encourage your child to take a break every so often, and do something rewarding or have a snack in between sessions. Rewards make children more inclined to do the work again. Allow an hour at the end doing whatever your child finds relaxing. At the end of an exam period, plan a big outing or treat!

When should my children do their homework unsupervised?
The first thing you need to ascertain is what your school's policy is on homework. Many schools actively discourage any parental intervention and want the children to motivate themselves, plan their time and fulfil their obligations on their own. Having said that, there is nothing wrong with supervising the process – at any age; in fact, most kids need a nudge to begin and finish what is required, and to be encouraged to check that they have completed everything assigned.

In many cases this goes for revision too, and late teens will spend a great of time revising in advance of major exams. Most will need help with time management and planning, as well as some supervision to ensure that they are getting on with the job at hand, using their time wisely and getting through the work required. This process should be eased as they become older and move towards independence. Look at it as guidance, rather than supervision in the latter stages – be there to help, but don't overplay their schedules. Studies show that kids who have highly structured and supervised homework and study tend to panic in higher education because they've never learned to do it on their own.

If you are lucky enough to have a child who sits down and completes homework without nudging and has good grades, supervision is probably unnecessary. Many girls are better at organising themselves and can be left unsupervised from the ages of eleven or twelve; boys tend to need more supervision and for longer, but by fifteen or sixteen they should be able to tackle most homework without constant monitoring. But a word of advice: continue to spot-check. You'll never know if there is a problem if you don't keep your eye on the ball.

Is homework really necessary? My child resists and I feel he has far too little free time as it is.

There are a number of reasons why homework is set, and many of them seem valid. The idea is that while kids do their homework they will:

▷ Review and practise what they've covered in class.
▷ Prepare for the next day's work.
▷ Learn to use resources such as libraries, reference books and other materials, and the internet to enhance and expand their knowledge of a subject.
▷ Explore subjects more fully than classroom time permits and at their own pace.
▷ Use skills they've learned and apply them to different situations, and integrate that learning by taking on things like projects.

Homework helps develop good study habits and a positive attitude by encouraging kids to work independently and to encourage self-discipline and responsibility (meeting deadlines, for example). It provides parents with an opportunity to see what their children are doing and to encourage the process of learning through parental/child communication.

Having said that, homework is only valuable if the work assigned is actually meaningful, and designed to fulfil the above. Rote memory work night after night, for example, will be boring and will fail to teach students to use the skills they are learning. If homework isn't finished, kids don't achieve many of the benefits of discipline or feelings of achievement. And if the homework is not marked and returned with constructive comments, it's fairly useless.

If the homework your child gets is eating into his time to such a degree that he has no time for rest, relaxation and play or family time, then it's worth consulting the teacher. It may be that your child is slower than others, and may be permitted longer periods to complete bigger projects, or perhaps allowed to stop after a set period (let's say an hour of maths, for example). It may also be that there is too much homework set and that it is not motivating or interesting your child sufficiently, which defeats its purpose.

All assignments should have a specific purpose, come with clear instructions, be fairly well matched to a child's abilities and help to develop a child's knowledge and skills. If this isn't happening, then find out why.

How much homework should my child be assigned and at what age?

There are no strict guidelines on this, but there are plenty of studies that point to the benefits of sensible amounts. These must, however, be considered in the context of your child's day. If he has only three or four classes a day and plenty of study time in the latter years of education, or only attends school for short periods, then homework will necessarily be increased to make best use of this time. Children who have long school days, are younger and expected to take part in extracurricular activities should be given less.

From kindergarten or reception years through to year two, children should have no more than about ten to twenty minutes a day, although they may be given reading above and beyond this. From years three through to six (primary school), homework will be gradually increased to between a half hour and an hour per day. By year seven, students can expect to have at least an hour a night and perhaps more, but on a more elastic time frame, which means they can often spread their workload throughout the week and catch up on bigger projects over the weekend. Studies show that students who complete more homework score better on standardised tests and earn better grades, on average, than students who do less homework. The difference in test scores and grades between students who do more homework and those who do less increases as students move up through the grades.

ENCOURAGING CHILDREN TO LEARN

It is now well established that self-esteem, and perhaps more importantly, self-respect play a huge role in a child's long-term scholastic progress. Research shows that, in general, levels of achievement are influenced by how we see ourselves and, more specifically, that self-belief, respect, esteem and academic performance are strongly associated.

Parents are in the best position to influence the way that their children feel about themselves through their relationships with their children. When this is valuing and caring in nature, children's self-esteem will be elevated. Success and failure in themselves have no effect on a child's motivation to learn, but the reactions of parents, teachers and other significant adults to success and failure can have a devastating effect. It is important for parents to be aware that, while unrealistic demands lead to low self-esteem, no demands at all lead to the same end. In both cases, children are doomed to low academic achievement or over-achievement. The ideal is to apply optimum pressure; just enough to cause children to feel challenged and positive but not so much that they become distressed.

The following guidelines will help parents encourage learning in children:

▷ Parents should never persist in encouraging learning when a child demonstrates a lack of interest or reluctance.

▷ A child's efforts should never be criticised nor the child made aware that parents are disappointed with the progress being made.

▷ Parents should make sure that there are times when the child has their full attention.

▷ Children should share in their parents' everyday activities and be included in their daily life as much as possible.

▷ Children should be talked to, not talked at. Parents should create opportunities when they and their children can respond to one another.

▷ Parents should try to see things from the child's perspective, acting as 'guides' rather than 'teachers'.

▷ Parents should be serious about directing their child towards experiences that provide opportunities for learning and discovering.

Can my children do homework while listening to music or watching TV?

In terms of music, this will depend on your child. Some children must work in silence to take things on board and to concentrate; others find that music (at an appropriate level, of course) helps them to relax. TV, however, is a big problem as it engages children on too many levels and provides a distraction that inhibits both retention, concentration and logical thought processes. Most children watch far too much TV (*see page 455*) and can certainly give it up for the period during which they should be working. Many children complain that their homework takes all evening when, in fact, they've been only half engaged because the TV is on.

How much help should I give?

Younger children often need extra help with homework. The best thing you can do is to ensure that your child understands the instructions. You may want to get him started by doing a few questions or problems together, or planning an argument or even just helping him to refine and organise his thoughts in advance of writing. You can then encourage your child to come back if he is stuck or offer a read-through at the end, or partway to ensure he is on course. This does not mean doing your child's homework for him. Teachers need to see where your child is making mistakes, and where there are problems with learning.

Beware, too, of teaching your own 'methods' for homework. Subjects like maths are taught very differently these days, and you can end up completely confusing your child.

I end up arguing with my child over homework, and always lose my temper. How can I make homework an easier process?

First of all, don't get too involved and don't look for perfection. If your child is making mistakes, gently point out how you think things could be done differently, or suggest, perhaps, that they could take a little more time. Avoid getting frustrated with her, calling her stupid, assuming she is underachieving, doing things for her in an attempt to get it right, or insisting on rewrites or extra work because you think what she's achieved isn't good enough. Let her get on with it herself and encourage her to come to you when she has problems. If your child is not fulfilling expectations at school, or her homework isn't meeting standards, your child's teacher will undoubtedly tell you. Until then, back off and be there when required.

Is there an optimum time to do homework?

Asking kids to settle down the minute they get home will backfire. They are likely to need something to eat and drink, and a little down time. However, leave it too late and they'll inevitably find many other ways to fill their time and be up till all hours to finish their homework (or not finish it at all). Studies show that children need at least 30–60 minutes after the school day to unwind before commencing homework. There is also evidence that kids perform better in a structured environment and within a routine – which means, simply, that the same time (and preferably the same place) every day will work best. There is no point in saying that your child will do better at certain hours, because every child is different and some have much greater powers of concentration and at various times.

If there is weekend homework to be done, however, it's worth noting that most children are more alert first thing in the morning after breakfast, so slotting in work at that point might mean that it is done quicker and more efficiently.

Research shows that late-night homework is less productive and less retained than work done earlier in the evening; it seems that our brains require time to digest material, which is further disseminated and stored to memory while we sleep. So work done immediately prior to bed is unlikely to stick in your child's memory in the same way.

THE 35-MINUTE STUDY PERIOD

An efficient way of learning is the 35-minute daily study period. Thirty-five minutes is a period during which most people can concentrate well. If your child studies or does homework without a break for as long as an hour, the last 20 to 30 minutes are likely to be less efficient, as concentration diminishes. It's also much easier to encourage your child to get down to work knowing that it is for a 35-minute stretch. If your child has a huge workload, break it into 35-minute segments, with breaks and fun in between.

Should I test my child for revision purposes?

By all means. This shows interest in your child's work, and also makes clear the idea that you value homework and revision – all which can encourage learning. But hold the frustration. If your child fails to learn a subject correctly or competently, you can encourage him to go back to the drawing board, or help him find ways to remember the things that he's not retaining. However, if you become angry or demand hours more work, you'll only discourage him and he will undoubtedly lose heart and motivation. Praise whatever you can find to praise, and he is more likely to come back for more.

When should I check that he is doing what he says he is doing?

Regular spot checks will help, even with a disciplined, achieving child. It also shows an interest in what he is doing, which improves communication between you and enhances the learning process. Children who are encouraged are statistically more likely to achieve higher grades and to value their work and achievement. Offer to check rather than insist, as this may make your child feel that he isn't trusted; however, you do need to keep an eye in case he goes badly wrong somewhere or has not taken on board what is required of him. Ask what he's got for homework every day; put major deadlines on the family calendar or white board; make a point of discussing progress over meals, perhaps; and offer your own ideas for him to take on board if he's keen.

Should I ban computers, TV and games to encourage more work?

Unless a child is using the computer for schoolwork, it's a good idea to keep them turned off while she is working, as they can provide an unwelcome distraction. It's difficult to do in many cases; kids ostensibly doing 'research' on the internet or preparing work on the computer often have other things going on, such as instant messaging, whose screen can be reduced when they hear your footfall at the door. In this case, you need to make it clear that messaging is acceptable (for a given number of hours per night, perhaps), but NOT during homework time. The house should, ideally, be a quiet zone for homework purposes. If one child doesn't have enough homework to sustain him, suggest he reads a book or listens quietly to music in another room. If you have youngsters it is not always easy to keep things relatively silent, but designate a room in the house for work to take place, with all distractions firmly off.

It's not a good idea to ban computers and TV indefinitely. In fact, they can act as a carrot to get work done more quickly and efficiently. If your child has nothing to look forward to in terms of rest and play, he'll probably dawdle and feel frustrated and angry, or actively rebel. That's not to say that these should not be limited during the week (*see page 455*); however, a full ban will achieve nothing but discontent.

Should I buy revision manuals for her key stage exams?
Research indicates that these can be extremely useful and provide additional explanation where your child is unclear about theories, problems or processes, as well as an opportunity to self-test and practise learned skills. Don't overload your child, though. If she's been given regular homework or revision work that fills her time, this may well be enough. However, if your child is struggling in a particular subject or subjects, revision manuals can help clarify and refine skills. Let your child be involved; if she thinks a few would help focus her revision or make things clearer, then by all means go ahead. If she's confident that she's got it under control, and you've got evidence in the form of grades to support this, then leave her to her own devices.

Until what age should I stay in touch with my child's teacher regarding homework requirements and its completion?

Most younger children have some sort of homework diary or contact book where parents are encouraged to make comments on the length of time spent and any obvious difficulties. This practice is normally discontinued later on, and you will need to rely on your child's teacher to advise you if there is a problem. If you feel that your child is doing too much or too little homework, it's also a good idea to contact your child's teacher, or to advise of any areas that seem to frustrate or discourage your child. For older children, you can do this somewhat covertly, as you may be perceived as meddling otherwise. It is in your child's best interests that you have some idea of what is expected, that there is some feedback on both sides when you or your child's teacher feel that homework isn't being completed to an appropriate standard, or when there is a shortfall or excess.

If my child seems to be struggling, should I engage a tutor?

You'll need to discuss this carefully with your child's school before hiring a tutor. If the school feels that extra tuition outside of regular homework and school hours would benefit your child, it's worth considering. Some children need a little one-to-one attention to focus their minds, and to get across material that they might otherwise find difficult. This may be a short-term measure for kids to learn important skills such as essay-writing, perhaps, or dealing with maths problems, or understanding chemistry and physics equations, most of which underpin progress in a given subject. It may be that your child will always need a little support in one or more subjects.

But there are two things to consider. Firstly, if you are considering tutoring to move good results to 'excellent' results, stop and think. Inflating a child's grades by pushing him beyond what is healthy and normal for his intelligence level will do him no favours in the long run. It might get him into a better school or into further education, but his grades will not reflect his ability or capacity to deal with the curriculum, and he may always struggle. In a good school he might be bottom of the heap and need to rely even more heavily on extra tuition; in further education, he may be out of his depth and be unable to deal with the demands without help. In reality, you need to appreciate your child's individual strengths and weaknesses – by all means, *help* with the weaknesses, but not in an effort to make him out to be something he can never be. For example, attaining A grades in physics through regular and rigorous extra tuition does not make him a natural physicist, and he may find himself pointed in completely the wrong direction as a result of these efforts.

Secondly, if you do go the tutoring route, broach the subject carefully. You do not want your child to feel that he is a failure and that he can't do what is required without extra help. Ultimately, children perform at their own appropriate levels, and in theory the education system is designed to pick up on shortfalls and address these, while also focusing clearly on a child's innate abilities.

Finally, check your tutor carefully. There are different systems and methods of learning all subjects, and conflicting approaches can just cause confusion. You should always check with your child's teacher first, and perhaps even get a recommendation for an appropriate tutor.

Household chores

At what age is it safe for my son to mow the lawn?

A child who has been brought up around machinery and is familiar with the risks of electrical equipment (and electricity) will obviously take to this sort of job much more quickly than a child who has been at ballet classes or playing football for most of his or her life. It makes sense for a parent to teach the ropes, supervise a few times and also encourage safety. I know of three children who have had a toe cut off by a lawnmower, so don't assume knowledge and throw your child out into the garden because you think he or she is at the appropriate age.

A child should be capable of mowing the lawn from the age of twelve, but supervised for the first few attempts.

At what age should kids start helping around the house (age-related activities)?

Children should be encouraged to help around the house from toddlerhood, taking responsibility for their toys or transporting clean laundry to bedrooms and even helping with some cooking. From there, the jobs can increase and expand with age (*see page 170*). Through this adolescents learn to assume responsibility, gain autonomy and get practical life skills, including decision-making, before they reach adulthood.

At first, keep the chores relatively simple – picking up toys and emptying the rubbish. By age ten, increased cognitive development allows children to expand their work repertoire. Some begin to use equipment such as a lawn mower, washing machine or hob (the latter with supervision, *see page 129*). This is known as 'task complexity'. The older the child, the more complex the task he or she is able to accomplish.

WHAT CAN KIDS DO?

They can choose from the following chores. If you want success, go through each chore step-by-step so that he knows clearly how to do it, and then observe him doing it at least once to make sure he's got it.

School-age kids

▷ Routine household chores: set and clear table, put dishes in dishwasher, put clean ones away, vacuum, dust, sweep.

▷ Empty rubbish bins, sort rubbish and recycling.

▷ Laundry: gradually increase the repertoire until your child can do the majority alone.

▷ Meals: make lunch, help with preparation (*see page 128*), set the table, clear away dishes, put away shopping.

▷ Pet care: feeding, taking them on walks, brushing, bathing, cleaning out cage.

▷ Gardening: weeding, watering plants, raking leaves, mowing the lawn, sweeping patio.

▷ Bedrooms: their own room should slowly become their sole responsibility including dusting, making the bed and changing sheets.

▷ Laundry duties: putting dirty clothes in bin, emptying bin, folding and sorting lights and darks, hanging up clothes.

Pre-teens and teens

▷ Cooking: learning a few basic recipes to cook alone, washing up, basic grocery shopping.

▷ Replacing light bulbs.

▷ Cleaning the cooker or grill.

▷ Helping to wash the car.

▷ Bedrooms: cleaning their own rooms.
▷ Laundry: capable of doing own laundry from sixteen, ironing.
▷ Bathroom: cleaning the shower, sink, toilet, bath.

In theory, by age sixteen, teens should be handling more tasks than their younger siblings. However, studies show the amount of household chores completed by those aged sixteen to eighteen declines sharply. One reason for this is that older kids face many of the same predicaments that adults encounter in modern society, including complex schedules, complete with too much stress and too little time. Educational requirements are also tougher for kids today than those just two decades ago.

There is, however, no good reason why kids by age ten shouldn't make their beds, clear up after themselves, help with food preparation and clearaway. After this age, vacuuming, some gardening, helping to care for any family pets and emptying the dishwasher are all appropriate. By sixteen, most teens can look after their own clothing, either washing and ironing it themselves or at least getting it into the machine. They should be able to change their bedding, care for younger siblings, babysit and do some cooking; anything, really, that an adult can take on. But watch their schedules as they get older – they'll become resentful if the only thing filling their leisure time is housework. Make a list of chores (*see page 169*) and ask your kids to choose what they want to do.

When should my child be responsible for his own laundry?
From a very early age, you can start teaching the basics, from carrying and sorting laundry through to distribution to the right rooms. By the age of ten most kids can be taught how to use a

washing machine and/or tumble dryer (and the washing line), so that by their mid-teens they can handle it alone. That's not to say they always have to do it – for environmental reasons, it makes sense to wash bigger loads, and your child may not have enough to sustain this. The idea is that they are capable of doing it and should do it from time to time as part of taking personal responsibility for themselves and their belongings.

Little ones can help by shuffling clothes to and from the machines, and as soon as they know their colours they can help to sort laundry. Watching you is the first step to understanding the process, so get them involved from a young age. Teach kids how to fold things early on, too – sticking with easy things like tea towels or bath towels. They can then be given responsibility for these 'chores'. From age nine or ten, teach them how to look for and treat stains, load the washing machine, add soap and fabric softener and choose the right setting. They can learn to read basic clothing labels, so they understand that some things can't be washed in a machine, or must have a lower temperature, or shouldn't go in the dryer. At age eleven or twelve, get them used to loading the machine and/or transferring to the line, dryer or drying rack. A good idea is to provide two laundry baskets in their bedrooms – one for lights and one for darks. If your child is doing a load for himself, he can easily visit other bedrooms to gather enough for a load without having to sort through everyone else's laundry for the right colours! Encourage them to do at least some of their own laundry by age fifteen or sixteen.

At what age can I insist that my child does a share of the household chores?

Giving children chores to do around the home can boost their sense of responsibility and help them to play a productive part in family life. Younger children often love the chance to help with simple chores, although as they get older, they may be a bit more reluctant. For tips on encouraging them to help, *see page 169.* It's also worth tailoring jobs to suit your child's interests and abilities – a dreamer might be better off dusting than preparing food or sorting laundry, while a high-energy teen might be best suited to garden work, washing the windows, vacuuming or sorting and taking out rubbish. You'll also want to select chores that are appropriate for your child's age and maturity level, to ensure that it is a positive work experience. You want your kids to feel they've done a good job, or they'll give up and wander off.

Either way, you can insist that your kids help from the moment they can – even toddlers are keen to mimic mum and dad and will adore feeling important enough to have some responsibilities. Every family member should have a share of responsibility for household chores from the word go. Share it out as a family. For example, you might want to take over the cooking and keep tabs on the laundry and the outdoor work, each of your kids might choose two big chores that he likes and does well, and then you can all take responsibility for clearing up after yourselves, making your own beds, and taking turns with the family pet or toddler!

Most importantly, make time to teach. Don't assume that children know how to clean the toilet, empty or load a dishwasher or vacuum, even if it seems simple to you. Promoting teamwork can also help – it's more fun and time-effective to do things like washing dishes, washing the car or raking leaves in twos or threes!

Finally, avoid gender stereotyping! Boys need to learn to cook, wash clothes, iron, dust, vacuum and clean just as girls should be aware of how to run the lawn mower, handle tools, change a light bulb and take out the rubbish. While taking part in household chores is about sharing the load within a family, it's also about encouraging life skills and independent living.

Independence

How old must my child be in order to be left alone in the house?
There is no minimum age, unfortunately, so you need to use
common sense. A report on child welfare by the Commission of
Families and the Well-being of Children states that babies and very
young children should never be left unattended, while children
under thirteen should be left alone for no more than 'a short time',
but this is not legally enforceable. What *is* legally clear is that you
are responsible for your children until they are sixteen, whether you
are at home or not. So if something happens while you are out, it is
your responsibility.

Thirteen seems to me to be rather old. Most children are capable
of looking after themselves for a few hours by the age of ten or
eleven, provided they are aware of what to do in an emergency,
know how to contact you or another responsible adult if they are in
trouble, are mature enough to stick to the household rules (such as
not touching the oven or hob, for example) and are, most
importantly, happy and comfortable doing so.

How old must my child be to spend the night alone?
The same report suggests that children under the age of sixteen
should not be left alone overnight. This seems like a reasonable
age. You may have a child – perhaps with older siblings, who is
accustomed to being left and understands the rules and
procedures – who is mature enough to be left a year or so before
this age. Remember, though, that not all kids are happy being left
overnight, even when they are older than sixteen, so talk things
over with your teen carefully before making any decisions.
Obviously, every child needs to learn to be alone and to develop

independence at some point, but all kids are different. Some relish the freedom and responsibility; others are frightened or wary. Some are mature and will follow your instructions to the letter; others will view it as a great opportunity for a party, which may then spiral out of control. Use your judgement. It's worth noting once again that if something happens when you leave any child under the age of sixteen alone, for no matter how long, both parents can be prosecuted for wilful neglect.

When is my child old enough to get him- or herself home from a party?

There are several stages in the process towards being independent enough to come home at night. The first is that your child is accustomed to coming home from school in daylight, either by public transport, cycle or walking. The next step is to ensure that your child understands the transportation system – knows what to do if a bus or train doesn't turn up or is cancelled, if there is a diversion, if they need to transfer en route, what tickets to purchase and their validity periods, and when the last buses or trains run. Your child must have experience of travelling at night, and be fully aware that the streets look different in the dark. He or she must be streetwise enough to understand potential dangers (everything from gangs of youths, muggers, rapists and other predators, to fast-moving car drivers who might not see a child) and know what to do. Your child must have a form of communication with him or her, or access to one.

So if your child has most or all of these things under her belt, and some experience in travelling at night, she's probably ready to get herself home. There must, however, be some fairly strict conditions. First of all, it's generally wise to insist that kids travel with someone else rather than alone. If there is no one local, perhaps suggest a sleepover at your house so that she has someone to come back with. If you are worried about transportation, perhaps you could split the cost of a cab – or she could share one with friends. At least she'll be driven to your door. You are within your rights to insist that she does not attempt to make her way home if she's had too much to drink – say you'd rather be called out at the eleventh hour than risk her finding herself in trouble. It's also worth stressing that you want to be called the moment she is worried about something or in a difficult situation. Curfews (*see page 144*) are extremely important in this situation. You will undoubtedly worry if she doesn't turn up when expected, and you will have no way of knowing if she has been hurt or is in danger. The freedom and independence to do things on her own involves a certain level of personal responsibility. It's also important that you know exactly where she is going and how she plans to get back, so if problems arise, you can trace her route and help her.

What age? Kids who have been travelling to activities at night on their own from an early age can probably manage it by thirteen; otherwise fourteen or fifteen seems about right.

At what age can my child be left on her own while I go away for a few days?

According to the NSPCC, it is acceptable to leave your child for a few days (but no longer), at the age of sixteen, but only under the following conditions:

▷ She is given clear instructions about what to do if there is a problem.
▷ She has a list of people whom you trust that she can contact or go to, such as neighbours or close relatives.
▷ You put all obvious dangers out of reach before you go, such as medicines, chemicals, matches or sharp objects.

▷ Your child is happy about the arrangement and knows how to contact the emergency services if necessary.

▷ You leave a contact number where he can contact you.

▷ You lay down some ground rules with your teenager about friends coming over, and decide together what comprises acceptable behaviour and what things he can do with his friends.

As an addition to this, I would suggest that you do not leave any child with emotional, medical or behavioural problems that might affect judgement or decision-making skills. In these instances, your child will need to be supervised.

When should a child be given the freedom to plan leisure time on his own?

All children need to learn to organise their own social schedules and also to plan their time, fitting in schoolwork, family time, household chores and leisure. By the age of eleven most kids feel comfortable arranging things with friends after school and on the weekends, and they should be encouraged to do this. They should, however, as a matter of courtesy, check with you before confirming details, and ensure that they leave enough time for family (*see page 200*) and homework. This is not to say that children are, at the age of eleven, necessarily capable of getting themselves to and from social activities. This type of freedom comes with maturity and age. You should, as a matter of course, always have a clear idea of what your child is doing and when, and he should abide by an agreed curfew (*see page 144*). Your child should also be aware of the activities you think are appropriate. He may think it's a grand idea to hop on a train to the seaside for the day with his mates, but if you do not think he is mature enough to handle it, you can certainly explain why and offer some ideas for alternatives. Too much freedom can be as damaging as too little; all children need some boundaries.

When should I stop asking for details of what he is doing on his evenings out?

Studies resoundingly show that a lack of parental support and guidance is one of the primary causes for risky behaviour such as drinking, smoking, taking drugs and having unprotected sex. While there is certainly a balance to be struck, it's absolutely imperative that you keep tabs. For safety reasons and for peace of mind, you should be kept abreast of your children's plans, well into the late teenage years – including when those plans change. You don't need to know the nitty-gritty details, but you should have a clear idea of where he is going, with whom, and when he'll be back. Hopefully, in a good communicative relationship, your child will feel comfortable telling you his plans (one reason why it is important not to judge, lecture or lay down overly rigid rules when he does confide) and also enjoy telling you the details afterwards. This is the only way that you will ever know if he is experiencing problems or undertaking risky behaviours with perhaps unsuitable friends.

Is she old enough to walk to school on her own?

Children need to learn independence and part of this involves allowing some sensible risk-taking. If your child's school is a short distance away and she doesn't need to cross busy roads, she can probably make her own way there from about the age of eight or nine, although it is advisable that she travels with friends. However, there is no doubt that you need to pre-plan and set some strict guidelines. Your child must know the rules of the road, how to look both ways before crossing and how to wait for the appropriate lights. She must always cross streets at lights or pedestrian crossings, or with the help of a lollipop person. She must know that if she's given the freedom to walk to and from school, she must go directly there and directly back, sticking to an agreed route, unless something has been pre-arranged. She must know not to talk to strangers, and how to get help (from a shopkeeper, a policeman, teacher, other parents or neighbour) if she is in trouble or worried for any reason.

Walk with your child to school several times and explain as you go. Then suggest that you walk behind her and her friends for a week or so, just to reassure yourself that she is behaving sensibly and exercising appropriate caution. When you are convinced that she can manage it, by all means give freedom.

It's worth noting that the Child Development Research programme, conducted by the Department of Environment, Transport and Regions says: 'Even at nine and ten years of age the level of awareness is far below that of adults.' So you may need to reiterate over and over again what needs to be taken on board.

And there is reason to do this. The start of secondary school and reduced supervision, means that ages eleven to twelve are the most dangerous years for child pedestrians. An eleven-year-old is twice as likely as a ten-year-old to be killed or seriously injured in a road accident on the school journey. One reason may be that children are suddenly given freedoms at a certain age (and the end of primary school is often a big turning point) without enough guidance.

If your child has to walk by or cross very busy roads, you might want to wait until she is twelve. According to the Road Safety expert at the Automobile Association (AA), pedestrian casualties decline from the age of twelve as kids become more aware of the risks.

Should I allow her to walk home from school when it's dark?
According to research, children are no more likely to be killed or injured in a pedestrian accident after dark than before and, in fact, light hours and autumn appear to be peak times for pedestrian accidents. This does not, however, mean that there are not other

dangers. Robberies, assaults and muggings are more common under the cover of darkness, and children may also be frightened and behave uncharacteristically. If your child is with a group of friends, it's obviously safer, so you could encourage this until your child is at least twelve. You could offer to meet her halfway, which provides a little independence but also a measure of safety. Kids should be discouraged from walking through parks or down alleys when it is dark, and encouraged to stay firmly on the pavement. They should ideally have a reflective strap or belt, even on their schoolbags, to make them more visible to motorists.

Should I allow my children to hang around shopping malls, streets or cafes in their spare time?
It is natural behaviour for adolescents to congregate, and yet this activity is frowned upon by a population in fear of hooded youths. In reality, there are few places that kids in groups can go; many shopping malls now prohibit groups of kids who appear to be loitering or are dressed in a way that is considered inappropriate, parks are closed at dusk, activities are proportionally more expensive (swimming or bowling, for example, can cost half a month's pocket money for one evening), and there are so few leisure centres that welcome or have been set up for children, it's woeful. So what are the options?

Studies show that many kids are no longer 'getting together' in person and instead interact by internet (e-mails and instant messenger) and mobile phone, largely because there is no other way. This has serious drawbacks because adolescents require face-to-face interaction for the development of healthy social and relationship skills, not to mention some fresh air and exercise, none of which cyber relationships provide.

You could campaign your local authority to offer some facilities for youths to commune – somewhere where supervision is unobtrusive and where kids can be themselves and interact, ideally with some sort of recreational facilities available. You might agree with other parents to take turns opening your garden or sitting room for small groups on a rota basis, and contribute some drinks and snacks and just let them be. But the fact is that kids want to be out and about, and to have the freedom to explore their burgeoning independence without a parent looking over their shoulders.

The streets aren't ideal, because kids tend to draw attention to themselves and this leads to complaints by residents or shopkeepers, which in turn can lead to brushes with the law and even Asbos (*see page 140*). What's more, big groups of kids do often end up getting themselves into trouble, and the lure of risky behaviour in front of peers may be too tempting for many kids to resist.

While all kids need time to be themselves without supervision, it's a good idea to ensure that all of your child's time isn't spend 'hanging around' or on the internet. Encourage him to round up smaller groups of friends to go to the cinema or for a bite to eat, or even to watch a match or film on television at home. Try to keep him active and engaged in a few organised events, even if he organises them himself. For example, if your son loves sports, he could arrange a tennis tournament or five-a-side football team at a local park or venue, or visit the gym; if he likes music, he could 'jam' with friends at home or in someone's garage; if your daughter loves dancing, she could organise a bunch of friends to do dancing classes or make a home video (very easy these days with home equipment) ; if she's clothes-mad, perhaps suggest a 'swap party' where everyone brings along a few articles of clothing they are prepared to exchange; if she loves make-up and accessories, perhaps she could organise a girlie evening with nail polish, a few hot irons and hair dryers, and some non-permanent dyes. This may sound very trite and obvious, but the idea is to keep kids occupied in other ways, so that their entire social life isn't located at a mall or on the streets, or sat behind a computer. You cannot direct your children's social life, but you can certainly make as many constructive comments as you can! And give a big, big nudge.

That's not to say that kids can't mix. If there are no facilities in your area for your children to do anything productive within a mixed gender group, then as parents you might want to get together and help. Perhaps get a discount for a group to attend a bowling alley, film or even a restaurant. And every single idea above does not need to be strictly isolated between the sexes; there are plenty of girls who love and are good at football or other sports; plenty of girls who will 'jam'; plenty of boys who like to cook or muck around with girl stuff and even shop. If kids are supported with ideas for entertainment they are less likely to hang out on the streets, and will experience more meaningful interaction.

When can she take the bus into town alone?

Parents have many worries, ranging from predatory adults, pedestrian accidents and theft, through to children getting lost, frightened and afraid, or getting into trouble. Freedom needs to be granted when children are ready, and when they have established that they understand the various rules and the safety mechanisms; they are confident and know the routes; they know what to do in an emergency; they are capable of understanding that they should not speak to or meet with strangers; they are prepared to enlighten you about what they are doing, and return home at a certain time. This might sound strict, but it is probably the only way you will ever know what's happening with your child, and the only way you can be sure he'll get where he is going and be safe en route.

It's often a good idea to start by taking your kids into town by train or bus regularly when they are young, so they become familiar with the system, with the idea of buying tickets, making a bus or train on time, embarking and disembarking, and dealing with late, diverted or cancelled trains or buses. Some parents have even been known to 'shadow' their children in their cars, following a bus, to ensure they make the right connections. It's also a good idea to make sure your kids are accompanied by friends for the first few visits, so that they can rely on some combined brain power to get them through any situation.

What age? If they can do it, know the ropes and are capable, start thinking about it from the time your child is twelve.

Languages

What is the optimum age for children to learn a second or third language?

Many people believe that young children are more adept at learning second languages and that children find it easier when they are young. Studies show, however, that this is not the case. Experimental research in which children have been compared to adults in second language learning has consistently demonstrated that adolescents and adults perform better than young children under controlled conditions. Even when the method of teaching appears to favour learning in children, they perform less well than adolescents and adults. One exception is in the area of pronunciation, although even here some studies show better results for older learners. Similarly, research comparing children and adults learning second languages as immigrants does not support the notion that younger children are more efficient at second language learning.

At what age can my child decide to stop learning a second language?

In most cases, children are given the option to drop languages in secondary school, and many do. However, it's worth noting that children in foreign language programmes have tended to demonstrate greater cognitive development, creativity and divergent thinking than monolingual children. Several studies show that people who are competent in more than one language outscore those who are speakers of only one language on tests of verbal and non-verbal intelligence.

Studies also show that learning another language enhances the academic skills of students by increasing their abilities in reading, writing and mathematics. Studies of bilingual children made by child development scholars and linguists consistently show that these children grasp linguistic concepts such as words having several meanings, faster and earlier than their monolingual counterparts. What's more, brain research in Canada has revealed that bilinguals and individuals highly proficient in a second language showed a markedly slower decline in mental powers with age.

There is also the question of future benefits. Learning other languages offers an expanded world view, and greater intercultural appreciation and sensitivity. Studies also show that being competent in one foreign language improves your ability to learn additional languages. And it goes without saying that it offers a competitive edge in future markets and the global marketplace – in a world that is becoming increasingly small.

The simple answer is that children should be encouraged to carry on with a second or third language for as long as possible. If necessity dictates dropping languages, it's worth trying to find local clubs to keep up what's been learned, to encourage an exchange with a student from another country, perhaps working in another country for holidays and using languages through travel and pleasure reading.

Leaving home

At what age can I insist that my child leaves home?

A recent report has shown that more than 20 per cent of students now carry on living at home in the UK – with nearly half saying they do so not because they can't afford to move out, but because they prefer an easy life. Other young adults find that financial pressures such as debts, spiralling housing prices and the high cost of living, combined with low starting salaries, force them to return home after a few brief years of independence.

This is a tricky question. Many parents love having their older children around, and dread an empty nest and the prospect of losing regular contact with their kids. There can be no doubt that a helpful, respectful young adult in the house, who is prepared to take on his share of the work and perhaps bills, and spend time with family, can be a bonus. However, in many cases, parents feel pressured to provide a home for children who should have long since become independent and show no signs of taking any responsibility for themselves. They treat the family home like a hotel, coming and going when they please, and expecting laundry, cleaning and meals to be provided as part of the package.

No matter how much you love your child or enjoy his company, this is unacceptable. A big part of our job as parents is to encourage our children to become responsible adults, and to guide them towards full independence. We are actually letting them down by failing to do so. Obviously, there are times when kids need to move back home – in between moves, in a spell of further education or unemployment, to save money for a house, for example – but these should be short-term stays and be provided with the understanding that the young adult does his share of work around the house, looks after his own belongings and clothing, contributes what he can financially (even if it's just a token sum), and shows respect for his parents and the household rules.

In general, when a child has his first paying job and has a few paycheques under his belt, he should be ready for independent living.

On what grounds can I ask my child to leave home?

After the age of eighteen you have no legal obligation (parental responsibility) to your child, and you can, at this point, ask them to leave. Obviously, no loving parent is going to throw a child out on the street, but if your young adult is abusive, lazy, unmotivated, taking advantage of you, and taking no responsibility for herself whatsoever, it might be time to spur her into action. For one thing, you can insist that she pays some rent, and looks after herself and her belongings – everything from clearing up after herself, to doing her laundry and preparing her own meals. You can also insist that household rules are maintained, even if she is above the age of 'consent'. You can help her to find an appropriate job and somewhere to live within her budget. If she's completely unmotivated either to continue in further education (for which grants are normally available or which you might be happy to contribute towards) or get a job, you can lay down the law and give her a time frame within which she must be self-reliant. It may sound harsh, but it is our responsibility to move our children towards independence, and if you give her no motivation to do so, she may never take the plunge. If you are supportive and helpful, your child will be more likely to keep in touch – she will probably want and need your love, reassurance and advice for a long time. Make it clear that the door is always open for visits or even short stays, and be positive about what she is capable of achieving on her own. Encourage her to take pride in her independence, and to enjoy the freedom and responsibility that comes with adulthood.

At what age can my child decide that he wants to leave home?

Your child can decide to leave any time he wants; however, he cannot legally do so without your permission until he reaches the age of eighteen, or is married or has been adopted by someone else. From the age of sixteen, your child can leave with your permission. Under this age, he can leave under certain circumstances – for example, if living conditions are poor or dangerous, there is abuse or alcoholism, or real problems with a relationship. In this case, the police and social services will become involved, and matters are taken from there. Under the age of sixteen there is no legal way for a child to rent or purchase a property, even if he has the resources, as he is too young to sign contracts (eighteen is the minimum age for this).

My child wants to leave home, but I'm worried about her. What can I do?

It is always difficult to say goodbye to young adults who move out and onwards with their lives. From the age of eighteen, parental responsibility finishes in the eyes of the law, although this should not in any way affect a close and loving relationship. Some kids are definitely ready to spread their wings at this age, either moving on to further education in another part of the country or world, taking a job or training, travelling, say, in a gap year, or even entering a stable relationship and moving in with a partner. If this is the case, and your child is mature and capable of looking after herself, give your blessing and do everything you can to make the transition easier (*see below*). If, however, your child is genuinely ill-prepared and unreliable, you may be right to have concerns. She must be able to look after herself, keeping herself, her home, clothing and bedding clean, be able to prepare nutritious meals, pay bills and budget, behave sensibly, and adopt a reasonably healthy lifestyle.

HOW CAN I PREPARE MY CHILD FOR LEAVING HOME?

Families that have dedicated time and effort to skills-building derive a great deal of confidence through this process of readying children to enter the adult world. Parents experience the satisfaction of knowing they have done their job and done it well. Kids feel self-assured and prepared for what lies ahead. When you are confident that they are ready, you can help the process by:

▷ Discussing areas that you are still prepared to help with – maybe dad will continue to file the income tax return, help with her car or put up shelves; maybe mum won't mind preparing a few meals for the freezer for a reluctant or hopeless cook.

▷ Letting him make mistakes. Don't bail him out the minute he hits a snag; he needs to learn to problem-solve and cope with things on his own. Make it clear that you will always be there to provide advice, love and support, but that independence means being independent!

▷ Avoid the bank of mum and dad trap. Young adults will never learn how to budget or live within their means if they are constantly subsidised. Obviously, you may wish to offer a little support now and then, or to pay a proportion of a big purchase, but this should be minimal.

▷ Teach him some sensible strategies for preventing crime, such as locking doors and windows, installing a burglar alarm, perhaps, getting appropriate insurance and a timer to turn off lights and a radio. Householders in the sixteen to twenty-four age group are the most affected by crimes such as burglary, probably because they don't take adequate precautions.

▷ Trust her to stand on her own two feet. The more confidence you show in her, the more self-esteem she will have. If you ring her every day to 'check', she'll feel frustrated and undermined. Let her know that you are there for her if anything does go wrong, but leave the ball in her court.

It's important to remember that leaving home isn't an event, it's a process. The process begins from the moment children are born and continues until they leave home and assume the responsibilities of adulthood. For the child, growing up and, for the parent, letting go, is the central process of family life. Children develop more and more skills and push for more and more freedom. Parents develop more and more trust in those skills and loosen supervision. If your child hasn't picked up what he should have over the years – perhaps because he hasn't been given appropriate levels of freedom at the right stages, or learned to take care of himself while still at home – then the process of education will have to start before he will be capable of looking after himself. While you can't prevent a young adult from leaving home after eighteen, you can certainly express reservations and agree after a certain period of time, during which you can actively prepare your child for independence by guiding them through all the various things that 'keeping house' and looking after himself entails.

Leisure

When can children use a hot tub or sauna?
A Finnish study found that children over the age of two can use a hot tub or sauna, but only for a maximum of ten minutes. Children can't handle temperature changes or extremes as well as adults. Children can't dissipate heat as efficiently as adults for a number of reasons: a child's body surface area to total mass ratio is different than an adult's; they don't sweat as well and their hearts don't have the reserve capacity needed to pump the extra blood required to cool the skin and extremities. After this age, gradually longer periods are OK, but it is extremely important that kids are

supervised well into their teens because of the risk of increases in heart rate, blood pressure and body temperature.

Children should sit on the lowest bench in a sauna where the temperature is slightly lower. They should not submerge their heads in a hot tub. The maximum time that any adult should stay in a sauna is 20 to 30 minutes, and *only* if they are comfortable and feel well. Some studies show that 10 to 15 minutes is adequate even for adults. It's also important that your child has plenty to drink, as kids very easily become dehydrated.

The maximum safe temperature for hot tubs is 40 ºC (104 ºF); 15 minutes per soak is the recommended maximum time. Remind your kids that they should never use a sauna or hot tub under the influence of alcohol or drugs.

At what age should I allow my child to quit her regular activities – or until what age should I insist that she sticks with things?

Time management is an important skill for kids to learn, and we need to give them the freedom to make decisions on their own in order to fit in everything they want to do. Many parents are used to organising their children's timetables from an early age, and have a clear idea of what they think those kids should be doing in their spare time – including activities that will enhance their potential in some way. However, as kids get older and the demands on their time with schoolwork, exams, social lives, and perhaps jobs or community service, something has to go. Most kids should be able to make some of these decisions by about age eleven, but with plenty of guidance. When social lives and the lure of mobile phones and the internet mean driving out healthy activities such as organised sports, swimming lessons, regular tennis matches or dance classes, you may need to be firm. All kids need to exercise (*see page 188*) and these activities should be given equal footing with social life, down time, family time and schoolwork. Many adolescents also become languorous and seemingly unmotivated as hormones take over, and are keen to give up activities that they've always found rewarding and which they are actually very good at. It's a shame, for example, to allow a musical teen to drop his music lessons because he doesn't have 'time'. Perhaps make a compromise and suggest a term off every year, or a final 'grade' at which he can give up (in our family, I asked them to stick to piano till grade five, which ensured they were largely competent and had reached the stage where they could easily pick it up later). There's nothing like a 'you can be finished when ...' message to spur on a child to reach that goal.

Think back to your own childhood, too. How many times have you rued the fact that your parents didn't encourage you to continue with a sport or instrument at which you showed promise? Therefore, explain clearly to your children that they may never have the time or opportunity again, and that they may regret giving things up.

Watch out for natural quitters. Some kids give things a go for a few weeks or sessions, and then move on to something else – never achieving much, and therefore never gaining any of the positive benefits of accomplishment and improvement. Encourage your children to make a commitment to things they want to try for a minimum period of time.

Ultimately, when your child hits mid-teens, he'll start making his own decisions about his time. You can help him to ensure a healthy balance of activities by overseeing the process, and reiterating the importance of healthy activities such as exercise and family time.

What if I don't approve of his leisure activities?
Ask yourself why. If he's safe, busy and not hanging out on the streets with his mates for hours on end, it may be that you are

either being overprotective or disappointed because he is not doing something stimulating or improving himself or his prospects in some way. It's often hard for parents to give up the reins of organising a child's time and activities, particularly if they've put a lot of time and effort into ensuring that he is given a broad variety of options and choices, which will stand him in good stead in later life. But it is important to remember that social life becomes increasingly important during the adolescent years, as teens become less dependent upon the family unit for relationships and interaction. This is natural and to be encouraged. They still have the same needs for a healthy lifestyle and family time, but more and more of these decisions and activities will be undertaken without parental involvement as they progress towards adulthood.

If you don't like the company he is keeping (*see page 229*), or think that his free time is being wasted, you can certainly encourage him to take up some more appropriate activities, such as doing community work, regular exercise, or even a cooking class or dance lesson, but you are unlikely to be able to force him. Don't underestimate the importance of the social group. It really isn't wasted time, but you can ensure that the time he spends with friends is perhaps more productive.

Can I force my child to do activities he is reluctant to do?

Young children will always need guidance to ensure that they have a balanced lifestyle that is healthy and stimulating. Many parents have clear ideas about what they think their children should achieve in their spare time, without considering individual interests and needs. The best thing to do is to suggest a wide variety of suitable options and ask your child to make a choice.

As they become older, they will have defined likes and dislikes, and these must be respected. They form your child's individuality and reflect his personality. Once again, as long as he is getting enough exercise (whether in the form of regular, organised activities or through his own initiative) and has good, regular interaction with other like-minded children, he should be given some freedom to decide. In the case of music or dance, at which your child may show promise, or language classes or extra tuition that may be essential for his later career aspirations, you may need to compromise while encouraging him to continue for as long as possible, even on a less rigid basis.

Until what age do I have a say in who he spends his time with?
Children, especially during adolescence, begin to spend a lot more time with their friends, and less time with their family. This obviously makes them more susceptible to the influences of their peers. It is important to remember that friends can have a positive influence on your children, so it's worth encouraging them to find friends who have similar interests and views as those you are trying to develop in your children, including doing well in school, having respect for others and having a sensible approach to drinking, smoking, drugs, violence and sex. You can do this by encouraging activities that interest your kids and keep them busy and occupied with other children.

But it's important to remember that you can't choose your child's friends, and your disapproval may undermine your own relationship with your child and encourage him to be more secretive.

In reality, past the 'play dates' ages, when kids need to have their activities planned for them, you'll have little say in who your child chooses to spend his time with, and, as they get older, even less say in how they spend that time. Studies show that children start showing a preference for different people and friends from pre-school years, and by six will have clear ideas of who they want to spend time with. Allow them to do this, even if you think they are mixing with the wrong crowd.

But keep your eye on the ball. If your child seems upset, down or less confident after interactions with certain friends, you may need to intervene and find out what's going on. Sometimes kids make choices based on who they think is popular, to placate another friend, or to prevent being bullied – none of which is conducive to a healthy friendship. Keep up the communication with your child so that he can express honestly when he has problems with friends and friendships, or when he finds himself with a person or group who doesn't respect him or his beliefs.

Other ways to minimise the influences of negative peer influences is to help her to have high self-esteem, confidence, a sense of self-worth, and to feel needed and loved by her friends and family.

Lost property

At what age should I stop covering for my child and bringing into school things he's forgotten at home?

One of the things we have to teach our children is the concept of personal responsibility. If you regularly cover for their mistakes, oversights, laziness or poor organisation, they will never learn to be independent and learn the skills that independence requires. You may be a chaotic person yourself and perhaps do everything at the last minute, or rush home to retrieve forgotten items, forget to make or put out the packed lunches, or to put the washed sports kit out to dry in time. In this scenario, it's difficult for kids to learn how to be organised themselves, because they are relying on a disorganised person both to guide them and to provide them with an appropriate role model. What's more, they are reliant on you to organise them (they can't bring a lunch that isn't made or go to school with wet sports kit, for example). So first and foremost, make sure you set a good example, and have things ready when your kids need them.

Secondly, help them out. Put a list on the front door of items required for each day of the week. A quick glance before leaving will remind kids what might have been forgotten. Suggest that schoolbags and anything else required are organised and set out the night before, so that hazy morning brains have little to challenge them. You can also opt for fixing a bulletin board up in his room to create a central location for reminders or notes and a calendar. If necessary, tape a note inside your child's schoolbag to remind him which books are required for which homework on different nights, and a nice empty plastic folder into which all homework assignments, letters for parents, reminders, outings permission forms and the like can be placed. There is nothing more frustrating than a child managing to forget or lose all key documents between school and home.

It's important to remember that not all kids are the same. For some kids, forgetfulness may mean working on their memory skills rather than a problem with responsibility. For others, it is an attitude problem.

In both cases, you need to teach responsibility, and provide the help kids need to remember what has to be done and when – reinforcing responsibility with subtle reminders and clues. And, as hard as it may seem, it's also important that they learn the consequences of forgetting or losing things. Forgotten homework or sportswear can mean a detention; a forgotten letter can mean missing a fun school outing. I might draw the line at a forgotten lunch, as no parent wants their child to starve, but if it's a regular occurrence, maybe this type of draconian measure is necessary. Sometimes it only takes one experience to jog the mind in future.

At what age should my child be responsible for replacing things he's lost?

Teenagers nowadays have far more material things than we had at their age and these items come to them far easier. They do not appreciate, cherish or value their belongings because they have so much and they often do not have to pay for them. If they've paid for things themselves, it's often with the aid of generous pocket money, so they still don't feel personally responsible. What's more, there is, in our culture, a real problem with the 'disposable ethos', as I like to call it – when things are broken, dirty or slightly out of date, they aren't recycled, mended, upgraded or cleaned; they are simply thrown away and replaced. For this reason, kids never learn to value things, because ultimately they know that a replacement is on its way.

From the earliest age, children should be asked to replace things they've lost. It's a tough lesson but an extremely important one to learn, teaching the value of possessions and money, the importance of personal responsibility, and also experiencing the consequences of doing without. Very young children will not have the wherewithal to replace a pair of trainers, perhaps, but they can be given a less satisfactory replacement, or asked to do various household jobs to earn some money (say half) before they are replaced. Until then, they have to do without.

From the age of eleven, when most children have some pocket money, spending power, choices and an ability to look after their belongings, lost items should be replaced by the child. Some may require a loan (a lost musical instrument, perhaps), which they have to repay from pocket money or they may have to use savings or, indeed, save up to replace them. A few missed outings with friends because of lack of cash or fewer CDs and treats is sometimes the only way that a child will register that carelessness has consequences. Bear in mind that kids are often very frugal with their own money, and yet are pleased to spend their parents' money randomly, so putting the onus on them to replace lost or damaged goods will get the message across that they are valuable and cost real, hard-earned money.

Magazines

When should I allow magazines that give advice on sex?
This is an interesting question, largely because there are two distinct ways of approaching it. The first is that much of the sexual content of magazines aimed at teens is too explicit and may actually encourage irresponsible sexual behaviour, precocity or promiscuity by teaching kids things they are simply not ready for. For example, one magazine aimed at pre-teens and young teenage girls recently carried a piece about oral sex, including step-by-step instructions. On the other hand, however, a project headed by the Centre for the Study of Children, Youth and Media at the Institute of Education, is keen to use these magazines for kids twelve to fifteen years old in a school environment, after research found many young people preferred to gain information on sex and relationships from the media.

Pupils interviewed were 'generally very critical' of sex education lessons in school, but were also embarrassed to discuss such issues with their parents, the study concluded. 'They preferred media such as teen magazines and soap operas on the grounds that they were often more informative, less embarrassing to use and more attuned to their needs and concerns.' This programme is being widely criticised by the Association of Teachers and Lecturers who, not surprisingly, are concerned about the content, which glamorises sex and breast enhancement, relationship 'tricks' and orgasms.

These magazines are, therefore, completely inappropriate for most young teens. I would suggest that before you purchase any for your child or allow her to do so, you have a look at the contents. Obviously some sexual information can be used as a springboard for mutual discussion, if you go through the magazine together, but the overall messages may in fact be dangerous, and undermine your own stance on the subject and your values. In reality, anyone under the age of sixteen should not be reading them.

That's not, of course, to say they *won't* read them, but if you express your reservations, your reasons for believing them to be unsuitable, and suggest other reading matter, your daughter will certainly not be obvious about doing so, and probably lose interest after a while.

At what age can my son buy top-shelf magazines?

Strictly speaking, legally acceptable pornographic magazines displayed on the top shelf of a newsagent can be sold legally to anyone of any age. They are sold on the top shelf and to over eighteens only by convention, so it is down to the discretion of the newsagent.

At what age should my daughter read women's magazines?

Women's magazines are written for *women* not girls, and discuss many subjects that may be wholly inappropriate for teens. I'm not talking about gardening, cooking, knitting or lifestyle magazines, but those aimed at mature women who normally have an active sex life and an understanding of sexual relations, a defined sense of self and relationships with the same or other sex, a responsible view of body image, usually an income so therefore an ability to afford new clothing, make-up and 'must haves', and probably a better developed sense of irony and values than the average teenager.

Many women's magazines focus heavily on sex, including technique; they talk about diets (even those that are extreme) and fashions that may be largely inappropriate for growing girls; they examine real-life stories that may be beyond the breadth of the average teen's understanding. They assume their readership has a level of maturity and education or understanding, and do not therefore qualify what they write. In a nutshell, these magazines potentially result in inappropriate exposure to issues that children are not prepared for.

If your child flips through a copy of one of your women's magazines, use it as an opportunity for discussion, and explain why it's not ideal reading matter. Better still, don't bring them home. There are literally thousands of books, and probably dozens of magazines that are innocent and will appeal to your child at the appropriate age. Under sixteens should not be reading magazines for women.

Should I ignore the pornographic magazines my teenager has under his bed?

Probably not. While you can reassure yourself that it is very normal for adolescent boys to find these sorts of magazines stimulating (boys aged twelve to seventeen are among the biggest consumers of pornography), because they have raging hormones, they are naturally curious and often haven't had any personal encounters (thankfully) upon which to draw, there are issues that need to be made clear regarding pornography. We'll discuss these in more depth later on (*see page 386*), but in this instance, it's worth taking things slowly and carefully. First of all, don't overreact. Secondly, remember that the way you respond to the situation can have more of an effect than the material itself. All parents want their children to develop a healthy approach to sexuality, and magazines do not tend to reflect normal, healthy relations between the sexes. However, if you respond by shouting or making your child feel dirty, you'll only manage to create a sense of shame, which will be carried over into his later relationships. Sex is not dirty; sex is not wrong; but pictures of women being compromised is wrong. Sex should take place within a loving relationship and be an experience of fulfilment for both partners rather than one dominant male. Women who pose for the photographs are often taken advantage of, and buying these magazines feeds an industry that does not always take care of its 'stars'.

It's also important to remember that kids reading these magazines often have little or no personal experience, and therefore their approach to and understanding of sex can be skewed in an unhealthy direction. This is one reason why it is important to have a little chat. Pay a thought to your child's first girlfriend, who may find herself in a tricky position if his ideas and notions about sex are derived from pornographic magazines. Don't take the magazines away. Leave them, but also leave him with your message: 'I understand normal, healthy curiosity, and the fact that you are on the brink of becoming a sexual adult; however, pornography is not ideal for these reasons' (see page 386).

Don't ignore your child and hope that his curiosity and interest in sex will go away! If you are uncomfortable to the point that you can't have this discussion, it is your responsibility to help your child find someone he respects and with whom he feels at ease who can. This is not to suggest to your child that he has a problem, but that he should learn and understand the implications of pornography.

Make-up

Is she too young to wear make-up to go out?

Make-up is marketed to children as young as pre-schoolers who tend to mimic their parents and want their own 'set' of accessories and accoutrements. Therefore, children who become accustomed to being just like mum and apply make-up regularly, will think nothing of continuing on with the real thing well before their tenth birthday. In fact, one of the most popular parties for under tens is the 'makeover' party, where kids are encouraged to experiment with make-up, hair styles, manicures and pedicures, and different clothing. Your daughter may not have been to one of these parties, but the overall message is clear: make-up is an 'accessory' for girls of every age. If you think differently, you are fighting a losing battle. Many of us had parents who insisted that we wait until we were well into our teens (thirteen was often the magic age) before we were allowed to wear make-up, and even then it was strictly monitored.

Today's kids are far more sophisticated, something that is encouraged by their magazines (*see page 305*), celebrity role models, and indeed, their peer culture. There is make-up designed for girls of every age, and an expectation that they will use it.

This appears to be one of those 'accept the beast' situations. What you can do, however, is teach your child to use make-up appropriately. Help her define her best features subtly, and try to play down the idea that make-up will create a 'different' and 'superior' face. It's her face and it's beautiful without make-up; however, if she wants to look a little smarter when she goes out, you will allow a little lip-gloss at age ten; a little mascara at, say, age eleven or twelve, and a little blusher in the winter months at any of these ages.

Foundation should probably be avoided until your daughter is about thirteen or fourteen, because it clogs her pores (and adolescent skin can be problematic) and also provides a 'mask', which can make your daughter think that she is hiding her own face under something else. Teach her to wash her face properly (*see page 430*), to hide blemishes if she is embarrassed, to use subtle make-up to enhance her natural beauty, and to play it down. I know one mother who covered her face with make-up just to show her daughter that it was both obvious and not very attractive, and it worked.

You are probably going to have to accept it, so why not make sure she doesn't go out looking like she's heading for the red-light district!

When is it appropriate for girls to wear toe and fingernail varnish?

Once again, even young girls (and I'm talking pre-school here) wear nail varnish, largely because it is encouraged in little-girl packs. There is no point in arguing on this one. It's a part of young girl culture, and for the foreseeable future, it's here to stay. What you can do is provide guidance. Teach your daughter from a young age (say, nine or ten) how to look after their cuticles and nails, how to clean and cut their nails, and how to dress them appropriately. The best advice would be to teach a simple French manicure, which looks natural and yet gives a child the feeling that they are wearing grown-up varnish. Most girls will relish being pampered in this way, and take pride in learning a new skill.

The good thing, too, is that because there are *two* sets of nails on your daughter's body, you can negotiate. Only clear varnish on fingernails, which need to be kept relatively short for hygiene reasons and for computer/calculator use, but go wild on the toes! Obviously in the summer months toes are on show, but for the rest of the year, they are usually well hidden. But provide some guidance once again! Lovely peach or pinks look far more attractive on young girls, so perhaps buy a selection and wear them yourself. There are obvious trends towards deep primary colours, and if she's keen, limit them to her toes.

Finally, make it clear that in her spare time and on holidays nail varnish is acceptable within your limits; however, during the school day, unadorned nails must prevail!

Is it right for my son to wear make-up?

Once again, the boundaries between acceptable accessories and accoutrements for men and women is blurred. With very 'macho' sports stars like David Beckham wearing the odd bit of make-up, and many more pop stars and celebrities doing the same, it's obviously going to be a lure for some boys. What's more, the wealth of 'beauty' and 'hygiene' products now developed for men has made it clear that men can not only take care of themselves in the same way that women do, but also enhance their looks through various means.

And, of course, there are the fashion/trend issues. As I write, the 'new romantic' movement has resurfaced, and there are a lot of teenage boys around with blurred eyeliner and mascara.

It's one of those battles not worth fighting. If your son is prepared to leave the house looking like a drag queen, he will undoubtedly meet with some embarrassing comments, and realise that perhaps he's gone overboard. I wouldn't exactly say 'condone it' or offer to do his make-up for him, but you could gently point out that a little bit of eyeliner might be sexy to some woman or in some youth cultures, but that plastered make-up normally looks a bit overdone. As you would with girls, point out your child's natural beauty and features, and some sensible suggestions. But leave him to it. There are very few men who wear make-up into adulthood, and it's often just an adolescent phase. Let him explore and experiment a bit, and then let him come to his own conclusions.

Can my daughter have 'permanent' make-up applied (tattooed eyebrows, eyeliner) with or without my permission?

Tattoos (*see page 444*) must not be given to children under the age of eighteen in the UK. However, the beauty market has often circumvented this ruling because although it is 'permanent' it is unobtrusive and undertaken as a part of routine enhancement. You will find, therefore, that most salons will not request parental permission, and particularly so now that children are routinely given manicures, sun bed or spray tan treatments, and makeovers. Many parents bypass this issue by telling kids that they can experiment with anything non-permanent, but that anything permanent must be discussed well in advance or even forbidden till a certain age, say thirteen. Apart from undergoing treatment at the hands of an unregistered or unhygienic practice, there are few side-effects or potential dangers, apart from allergies and contamination. However, it's worth suggesting to your daughter that she experiments with various cosmetics and their effects before embarking on anything permanent. Fashions and trends change, and her lovely new tattooed eyeliner or eyebrows may be out of fashion in a few years' time. Better to have fun with the non-permanent stuff.

Marriage

What age does my child need to be in order to marry?

In all areas of the UK the minimum age you can legally marry is sixteen. In England, Wales, Isle of Man, Guernsey and Northern Ireland you will need written parental consent if you are under eighteen. In Jersey parental consent is required if you are under twenty. In Scotland, however, you can marry at sixteen without the consent of your parents.

Can my child get married without my permission?
From the age of eighteen (twenty in Jersey and sixteen in Scotland), your permission is not required and your child can marry at any time, as long as both parties are the ages stipulated above, and anyone between sixteen and eighteen has parental permission (this can be permission from one or both parents or a guardian or foster parent). It's worth noting that if your child does go ahead and marry between the ages of sixteen and eighteen without your permission, the marriage IS valid, but she has committed a criminal offence.

Can I refuse permission?
If your child is under eighteen (twenty in Jersey), you can refuse permission. Do note, however, that if you do refuse permission, your child can apply to the Magistrates' Court, County Court or the High Court for permission to marry (in Northern Ireland, the County Court), which have the authority to supersede your decision.

Can my daughter be forced to marry?
A forced marriage is one where people are coerced into a marriage against their will and under duress. Duress includes both physical and emotional pressure. Forced marriage is an abuse of human rights and cannot be justified on any religious or cultural basis. It is, of course, very different from arranged marriage (*see below*), where the consent of both parties is present. The tradition of arranged marriages has operated successfully within many communities and many countries for a very long time. In many cases, children under the age of consent (some as young as twelve or thirteen) are forced

into marriages abroad. Under UK laws, this is illegal for British citizens, even if the laws of the country in which they are married differ. If your child is being forced into marriage, you can telephone the Forced Marriage Unit at the government's Foreign and Commonwealth Office, confidentially, on 020 7008 0151.

Can my son refuse an arranged marriage?

This is a tricky question. In an arranged marriage, both parties must consent to be married, so there are no legal issues regarding being forced to do something unwanted. If your son does not want to marry the woman or girl arranged, he has a legal right to refuse. However, the cultural and religious issues and implications are very different. In many cases it is seen as a sign of utmost disrespect to the family to refuse an arranged marriage. Children who refuse their parents' marriage plans for them face being ostracised or even expelled from their families and community, often at a time when they are not financially or otherwise able to look after themselves. The best thing to do is for your son to speak to the party wishing to organise the marriage, to try to arrange a compromise. Some families are happy for there to be a little choice in the matter – that it is important your son likes the person he is matched with before he gets married.

Young people are gaining veto power over their parents' decisions and financially independent adults often choose their own mates despite their parents' wishes and plans. A few years ago, even Saudi Arabia declared that a man could not force his daughter into marriage.

Can my daughter marry her second cousin?

Cousin marriages are allowed in the UK, whether first, second, third, or further down the line. There is some pressure to change this ruling, as there appears to be some evidence that children born into these marriages are more likely to have genetic defects.

Masturbation

At what age do kids begin to masturbate?

Many babies and toddlers begin masturbating as a part of general body exploration and sensory pleasure. It's normal and healthy in terms of development. It is, however, a private activity and this must be explained to young children. It's OK in the bathtub or in bed, but not at playgroup!

At about eleven or twelve when the hormones of puberty kick in, many kids begin to masturbate as they begin to experiment with their sexuality, and discover that masturbation can provide a release of sexual tension. Recent surveys suggest that in the US about 55 per cent of all 13-year-olds (both boys and girls) masturbate. This figure increases to more than 80 per cent in 15-year-olds.

Despite the fact that this is an exceptionally common practice, about half the teenagers and adults who masturbate feel guilty or anxious about their behaviour, not surprisingly, given that it is still frowned upon in many cultures and societies or simply not 'discussed'. At one point, children were warned that they would go blind or their genitalia would 'fall off' if they practised masturbation, and the hangover from this era has not been completely healed.

Although there is nothing abnormal or unhealthy about masturbation from a medical point of view, some people have strong religious, cultural or moral objections to the practice. For those who hold these values, choosing not to masturbate is normal, too. There is nothing weird, odd or unhealthy about this choice.

It's worth remembering that masturbation is a very good, healthy way of relieving sexual urges felt by teenagers: there is no sexual encounter involved (so therefore no STDs or unwanted pregnancies); it encourages the release of endorphins (the feel-good chemicals in our brains), relaxes muscles, reduces stress and even relieves menstrual cramps.

How will I know if my child is masturbating? Is it any of my business?

Unless you stumble across it or see the evidence in the form of discharge (males), you are unlikely to know; and no, it isn't really any of your business. Many children feel guilty and ashamed because of parental disapproval, which can then impact on their normal sexual development and overall feelings about sex, their own bodies and relationships in general. If they feel they have to 'hide' their sexuality from you, you also lose an important element of communication. That's not to say masturbation ever needs to be discussed, but later sexual activity might be shared with parents, particularly if there is a problem. Therefore, if your child feels guilty about normal feelings and behaviour, he may well hide everything from you.

Masturbation is private and should remain private. It should not be considered a problem unless:

▷ Your child does it in public (which is an offence).
▷ It is performed excessively (normal behaviour extends from a few times a day to once a month or less).
▷ Becomes time-consuming or an obsession.
▷ Interferes with your child's daily routine or social functioning.

You may, obviously, not be aware of most of these factors, but if it's becoming an obsession, you are likely to stumble across it. If you are worried, speak to your GP in confidence.

Menstruation

When can girls wear tampons? Is it safe?

Most young girls begin wearing pads (sanitary towels) because they are easy to use. A pad should be changed every three or four hours, and possibly more often on days when the flow is heavy.

There is no right age for starting to use tampons and it will be your daughter's decision. Some girls have a small vaginal opening, which can make it difficult and uncomfortable to insert a tampon. If your daughter tries and fails, it's probably a good idea to wait until she has matured a bit more physically, and the vaginal opening naturally enlarged. There are 'junior' or 'slim' tampons available, and many do not use cumbersome applicators; this makes insertion easier.

A girl also needs to be mature enough to feel comfortable about inserting a tampon into the vagina. She also has to be responsible enough to make sure to change the tampon frequently as there is a higher risk of developing toxic shock syndrome if tampons are left in for long periods of time. Additionally, some young girls may 'forget' that it's there, and be at risk of other types of infections.

For many girls, the use of tampons makes it possible for them to comfortably continue all of their regular activities (such as swimming) and less likely to see their periods as something that restricts their lives. Thus for an active, responsible adolescent there is no reason why she can't use tampons right away.

How do I explain to my daughter how to use a tampon?

Many girls are embarrassed about the intimacy of tampon insertion and won't actually want any instruction from a parent. Furthermore, most tampons come with instructions that are fairly easy to follow. Leave it to your daughter. If she expresses an interest in using tampons, you can offer a few bits of advice and guidance. For example, suggest that she takes her time, relaxes and inserts the tampon slowly. It's better to do it with a full flow, otherwise it can be more difficult to insert. She needs to allow the muscles of the vagina to relax, which will allow the tampon to go in easily. She should be reminded that the string remains on the outside of the vagina for removal, and that to prevent infection, tampons should be changed often and not worn overnight.

She may well make the choice and just get on with it. If you notice a packet of tampons around, just reiterate the main messages to prevent infection, and say that you are happy to help if she has problems.

Should I allow my child to be excused from games or swimming when she has her period?

There is absolutely no physical reason why a girl should stop her regular activities when she has her period; in fact, if your child suffers from cramps or other discomfort, exercise can actually help. However, some girls who may not be ready to use tampons find pads embarrassing, obtrusive and obvious. There may not be facilities for her to change on her own and she may be afraid of 'leaks' – particularly in a swimming suit. If she is genuinely embarrassed, you may allow her off swimming until she is comfortable wearing a tampon; however, she can probably still manage games without a problem.

When is her period likely to start?

When girls begin puberty (usually between the ages of eight and thirteen, *see page 392*), their bodies and emotions change in many ways. The hormones in their bodies stimulate new physical development, such as growth and breast development. About two or so years after a girl's breasts begin to develop, she usually gets her first menstrual period. Most girls get their periods by age fifteen or sixteen, so it's worth checking with your child's doctor if it hasn't appeared by this time.

It's worth noting that there is often little warning before a first period, other than a bit of cramping, which your daughter may not recognise. To avoid embarrassment, ensure that she is prepared well before, perhaps carrying a pad in her school or sports bag, and providing her with a supply in a discreet part of the bathroom or in her bedroom. Explain that you just want her to be prepared and ask if she wants help or needs to be shown how to use them.

Your daughter should understand what menstruation is by about the age of nine, as some girls do get their periods this early, and she may be shocked if she doesn't understand what is happening.

My daughter has a clear vaginal discharge. Is this normal?
About six months or so before getting her first period, your daughter might notice an increased amount of clear vaginal discharge. This discharge is common. There's no need to worry about discharge unless it has a strong odour or causes itchiness.

My daughter's cycle seems irregular. What's normal?
The amount of time between a girl's periods is called her menstrual cycle (the cycle is counted from the start of one period to the start of the next). Some girls will find that their menstrual cycle lasts 28 days, whereas others might have a 24-day cycle, a 30-day cycle or even a 35-day cycle.

Irregular periods are common in girls who are just beginning to menstruate. It may take the body a while to sort out all the changes going on, so a girl may have a 28-day cycle for two months, then miss a month or have two periods with hardly any time in between them, for example. Usually, after a number of months, the menstrual cycle will become more regular. Many women continue to have irregular periods into adulthood.

When my daughter begins to menstruate, should I let her do her own laundry to save any potential embarrassment?
By all means, but leave this to her. If you suddenly decide that the onset of menstruation means that she is in charge of her own washing, she may think that there is something dirty or wrong with her underclothing, or any leaks that appear on clothing or sheets. It's important that she feels comfortable with normal body function. You may suggest that she has her own laundry basket, so that anything she finds embarrassing is not on view to the whole family. If she seems a little secretive and self-conscious about stains or leaks, you can show her how to use the machine, if she doesn't already know how, and make little other comment.

Is the Pill an appropriate means of controlling period pains?
In the past, heavy periods and period pains were sometimes dealt with by using the contraceptive pill, which has the impact of making periods regular, reducing the flow and reducing the discomfort associated with periods. However, because of the risk to health (breast cancer and fertility problems have been linked to long-term use of the contraceptive pill), this practice is no longer encouraged. What's more, girls who are put on the contraceptive pill for other reasons may begin to engage in sex earlier than they might have done, because they are 'covered'. Exercise and gentle painkillers such as paracetamol are known to reduce the pain of cramping, and some studies indicate that supplementing vitamin B1 and magnesium can help. A hot water bottle can also ease the pain.

Up to 15 per cent of girls (and women) have period pains severe enough to interfere with their daily activities. This can lead to missing days at school or work or decreased participation in social or sporting activities. Period pains are often worse in adolescence and tend to improve as girls get older. If your daughter's pain is absolutely debilitating and doesn't respond to any of the above, see your doctor, who can rule out anything more serious, such as fibroids or endometriosis.

Mental health

What are my daughter's rights under the Mental Health Act? Can she be sectioned at seventeen?

Your daughter can be 'sectioned' at any age, which means that her mental health has declined to such a degree that she is considered to be incapable of making reasonable or rational decisions regarding treatment and that treatment is required. If you believe she has a mental health problem, you can ask that she be sectioned, particularly if she refuses help. If, however, she is viewed to be mentally competent enough to make her own decisions, you cannot override these, unless you are prepared to seek a court order (*see page 254*).

How do I know if my child has mental health problems?

Like adults, children and adolescents can have mental health disorders that interfere with the way they think, feel and act. When untreated, mental health disorders can lead to school failure, family conflicts, drug and alcohol abuse, violence, problem behaviours such as theft, eating disorders and even suicide. There are many, many mental health problems that affect children, such as depression, attention-deficit hyperactivity disorder (ADHD), anxiety and personality disorders, and eating disorders. Mental health problems affect one in every five young people at any given time.

Children and adolescents with mental health issues need to get help as soon as possible. A variety of signs may point to mental health problems or serious emotional disturbances in children or adolescents. It is, therefore, very important to look for warning signs which include your child:

▷ Feeling sad or hopeless for no reason.

▷ Feeling angry, overreacting or crying most of the time.

▷ Feeling worthless or guilty.

▷ Feeling constantly anxious or worried.

▷ Unable to get over the loss or death of someone important.

▷ Being fearful for no obvious reason.

▷ Being frightened that he/she feels out of control.

▷ Showing declining performance at school.

▷ Losing interest in things once enjoyed.

▷ Unexplained changes in sleeping or eating patterns.

▷ Avoiding friends and/or family and wanting to be alone.

▷ Daydreaming and showing worrying lack of concentration.

▷ Feeling overwhelmed regularly.

▷ Experiencing suicidal thoughts.

▷ Inability to make decisions.

▷ Performing 'routines' over and over and over again, such as washing, tidying or organising.

▷ Persistent nightmares.

▷ Racing thoughts or speech that is almost impossible to follow.

▷ Using drugs or alcohol in the extreme, often to blot out problems.

▷ Bingeing and purging or using laxatives to avoid weight gain.

▷ Dieting or exercising compulsively.

▷ Constantly breaking the law without any empathy for others.
▷ Setting fires.
▷ Taking inappropriate risks (life-threatening).

In general, however, behaviour that changes dramatically for no obvious reason or behaviour/habits/demeanour that seem odd or out of sorts should be brought to the attention of your GP. If your child refuses to go, you can see his or her doctor on your own and come up with the best course of action.

ADHD

My son has been given a diagnosis of being 'hyperactive'. What does this mean?

Watch out for this diagnosis. Over the past few years it has become increasingly common to label lively and uncooperative children – some of whom do or do not have emotional or learning difficulties – as hyperactive, or suffering from ADD. The term ADD developed after several years of mislabelling for children who failed to conform to what were probably idealistic standards of learning and behaviour. Such children were considered to have minimal brain disease (MBD), which later became minimal brain dysfunction, when no 'disease' could be diagnosed. But it became clear that there was no dysfunction either, and with parents and practitioners demanding an explanation, the terms ADD and ADHD were developed.

In *The Limits of Biological Treatments for Psychological Distress* (S. Fisher, R. Greenberg, 1989) Diane McGuinness says, 'It is currently fashionable to treat approximately one-third of all elementary school boys as an abnormal population because they are fidgety, inattentive and unamenable to adult control.' She insists that two decades of research have not provided any support for the validity of ADD and concludes that there is no convincing evidence that medications help learning or attention problems. She says that while the drug Ritalin may 'reduce fidgety behaviour', it does so in ALL children, regardless of diagnosis. She says, 'The data consistently fails to support any benefits from stimulant medication', and cautions that stimulant medication is a drastic invasion of the body and nervous system. She also notes that the majority of children labelled as being ADD are, in fact, normal, healthy energetic children.

ADD is not a medically diagnosed condition; in fact, it is diagnosed when a child fits the description of eight out of fourteen items on a checklist of characteristics, and has done so for six months or more. Some of these characteristics include:

▷ Loses things necessary to complete a task.
▷ Fidgets in his seat.
▷ Can't wait his turn.
▷ Blurts out answers.
▷ Shifts from one uncompleted activity to another.
▷ Has difficulty remaining seated.
▷ Interrupts or intrudes.

It doesn't take a psychologist to assess the fact that the majority of these characteristics are common to most children, particularly those in stressful conditions.

Many experts now believe that ADD has become nothing more than a buzz word from the 1990s. The fact that children are hyperactive or have difficulty concentrating is probably due more to the fact that Western diets are so poor, children are forced at an increasingly early age to sit still in a classroom or nursery with large numbers of other children, they watch too much television, get inadequate sleep and get little or no exercise. Place these restrictions on any adult, and the same behaviours could be expected.

Alarmingly, there are numerous studies showing that teachers believe that most of their students have deficits, disorders or problems. In one study, 57 per cent of boys and 42 per cent of girls were deemed 'overactive'. In another study of boys, 30 per cent were called 'overactive', 46 per cent 'disruptive', 43 per cent had a 'short' attention span. It also appears that the vast majority of children labelled ADD are boys, which throws into question our societal expectations of children who have natural activity, aggression and independence.

The solution has been using drugs, in particular, Ritalin, which has the effect of temporarily calming children (all children). But this practice is now under review. For example, Sweden has abolished Ritalin as dangerous and too easily abused. *Clinical Psychiatry News* cites a Duke University study that concluded, 'the amount of trouble that children are causing adults, particularly teachers, appears to be the driving force determining children's referrals to mental health services'. In March 2000, the US government announced an effort to reverse the dramatic increase in prescriptions for psychotropic drugs such as Ritalin in pre-schoolers. In addition, the US Food and Drug Administration (FDA) is developing new labelling that addresses paediatric indications for Ritalin and other psychotropic medications, and the National Institutes of Health (NIH) is conducting a nation-wide study of the use of medication for attention-deficit/hyperactivity disorder in children under the age of seven.

What can I do?

▷ Make your daily routine as simple and straightforward as possible. It will help to keep your child calmer and he will have more chance of remembering what comes next. Try to avoid rushing around, or eating on the hop, which will make him feel unsettled.

▷ Be very specific when talking to your child. Explain everything, and don't expect too much.

▷ Avoid over-stimulation. Playtime should be calm and reassuring, and no more than one or two other playmates should be involved. When things get out of hand, change the room or the venue (head off to the park, for example).

▷ Remember that hyperactivity is not bad behaviour. There can be learning difficulties present, and your child may have some difficulty with coordination or controlling movement.

▷ Some studies show that children with a tendency towards hyperactivity benefit from increased parental attention – on a one-to-one basis.

What if my child simply needs to blow off steam regularly?
Some children naturally have increased energy and physical requirements, and it is important for any child with these tendencies to get plenty of exercise. This can mean a break not offered to other children in a school environment. Talk to your child's teacher about allowing more breaks for physical release of tension (running around the playground, for example), which will help children to focus more in a school environment. If your child is extremely active, you may want to consider whether early schooling is a good idea. Many children are not able to handle the confines of a school environment until they are older, and it can exacerbate a problem if you start too early. It is, of course, very difficult for parents to deal with a constantly active child, and you will need to get as much support and help as you can from friends, family and professionals.

What changes can I make to his diet?

Researchers who performed five-hour oral glucose tolerance tests on 261 hyperactive children found that 74 per cent displayed abnormal glucose tolerance curves, suggesting the connection between hyperactive behaviour and the consumption of sugar.

Behaviour, learning and health problems were compared between boys with high and low intakes of EFAs (*see page 250*). More behavioural problems were found in those with lower omega-3 intakes, and more learning and health problems were found in those with lower omega-6 intakes.

Of 76 hyperactive children treated with a low-allergen diet, 62 improved and a normal range of behaviour was achieved in 21 of these. Other symptoms such as headaches and fits also improved. Forty-eight foods were incriminated and artificial colourings and preservatives were the most common culprits.

In a study of habitual juvenile delinquents with an average age of eleven, all the children were found to be very low in zinc, and had high hyperactivity scores. Some also had manganese and chromium deficiencies.

The hyperactivity ratings of 19 out of 26 children given a diet excluding wheat, corn, yeast, soya, citrus, egg, chocolate, peanuts and artificial colours and flavours, dropped from an average of 25 (high) to an average of 8 (low).

Strict elimination diets can be dangerous for children, so it's important that you alter their diet only under the guidance of a registered nutritionist. Suspect foods include all forms of refined sugar and any products that contain it, artificial colours, flavourings or preservatives, and foods that contain salicylates (including almonds, apples, apricots, cherries, currants, all berries, peaches, plums, prunes, tomatoes, cucumbers and oranges). Include plenty of fruits and vegetables in his diet, plus breads, cereals and biscuits

that contain only rice and oats. If diet is the culprit, your child will
not have to remain on a strict regime for the rest of his life. Many
children will outgrow the problem.

Mobile phones

When can my child have a mobile phone?

There are various points of view on this one, and some families
believe that mobile phones are essential, even from pre-school
years, for communication and social interaction. In reality, mobile
phones do form an integral part of our children's social life from an
early age. Furthermore, when children start to exhibit some
independence and are allowed various freedoms, a mobile phone
provides an invaluable way of keeping in touch and ensuring that
we are aware of our children's movements.

Having said that, most children do not need a mobile phone
until they are at least ten or eleven, leaving primary school,
perhaps, and use the phone as a method of keeping in touch with
old school friends and also to plan their own social lives by text
message or calls. The jury is still out on the health impact of
mobiles, but there is some clear evidence, disputed or not, that they
can cause damage and/or tumours in children's brains. Therefore,
supervising use and leaving the purchase of a phone as late as
possible is probably recommended.

You may have to play this one by ear. If it can be proved (not
child hearsay or propaganda) that all of your children's friends and
schoolmates have a phone, it's probably worth investing in one
simply because much social interaction and arrangement will take
place by phone and your child could lose out. If he's one of a few
without them, stick to your guns. The 'too much, too soon' culture

is very pervasive, and children need to learn to wait until an appropriate age to get some things, and to be treated as children not mini-adults with the same accessories.

It is worth considering whether your child really needs a mobile phone and why. My son was desperate for one at age eleven (when I said 'wait till twelve') and gave in as a special birthday present. Two years on, the credit I originally put on the phone remains largely intact, and he usually can't find it in his room. A waste of money? Yes. I should have asked some questions.

Should my child be expected to pay her own phone bill?

This depends on what the phone is used for. If you would regularly pay your child's share of the bill on your home phone when she makes arrangements with friends and if you insist that she keeps in regular contact by mobile when she is out, there are grounds for at least making a contribution. This can take several different forms. You can provide slightly more pocket money to cover the calls, you can take out a monthly pay plan with a service provider and ask your child to pay for a percentage, or you can purchase a certain amount of credit for a pay-as-you-go phone each month, after which she is on her own.

Consider whether the monthly plan idea might be a little too easy for most kids, as they can often run up bills that are not spotted until the statement arrives, and have little means by which to pay. What's more, providing a budget within which your child has to work is a sensible idea, as she needs to learn some budgeting skills, and also to make some choices about the way she uses her phone. Some kids get involved in expensive update and download services, or use WAP constantly, seemingly unaware of the cost; they may also use texting indiscriminately. Providing some financial boundaries can help to curb these habits, particularly if they have to cough up the money themselves.

Do I have the right to read her messages if I am concerned about her behaviour?

No, not really. Telephone messages, like diaries and e-mails, are personal and should not be read. However, if you have reason to believe that she is engaging in dangerous activities (perhaps selling or arranging to buy drugs, having a relationship with someone who could endanger her well-being, or using her phone to harass or abuse others) or being bullied by phone, you may want to spot check, in the interests of protection. If you think your child is lying to you or doing things you are not happy about, it is better to have a face-to-face conversation, rather than relying on spying or skullduggery. If your child discovers a breach of trust, she'll be more inclined to be secretive and to hide things from you. It's easy to erase mobile phone messages, so once she cottons on to the fact that you are looking, she can hide her tracks. If you do find something that worries you, do not confess to having looked, as you will immediately put her on the defensive. Give her the benefit of the doubt and talk things through.

How old do children need to be to access toll numbers and use them?

Unfortunately, anyone with a mobile phone can normally access toll numbers and subscribe to services providing downloads, updates, upgrades, ring tones and more. You can contact your child's service provider and request that a bar be put on use outside of national calls and texts; however, if the phone is purchased by your child and paid for by him, you will not have the right to do this. In most cases, this service is only provided for monthly paying customers. The most important thing to do is to warn your child of the expense of these services, which are very often unclear or misleading. In some cases it takes a bad experience to make your child realise the pitfalls. Look for companies that offer an 'alert' service where you can be notified when the bill reaches a certain amount or check how much your child owes at any time.

If my daughter's phone has a camera, should I check to see how she is using it?

Once again, you will be invading her privacy if you check her phone. You can ask what she uses it for and encourage her to show you some of the images. If she seems reluctant, ask why and use this as a platform for discussing inappropriate use of camera phones (happy slapping, downloading compromising images of other children or anything of a sexual nature on to websites or texting them to others, which represents bullying and could be subject to legal action). If you have reason to believe that she has been doing dangerous, illegal or threatening things with her camera you could, once again, spot-check, but do not tell her you have done so. With the evidence, you can start an important discourse on the subject or take appropriate action.

How do I know if my daughter is being bullied by phone?

Mobile phone bullying doesn't leave bruises, scratches or torn clothes and books. The culture of secrecy that often prevents parents knowing about bullying is harder to crack when young people are reluctant to tell parents who they are texting or calling anyway. Mobile phone bullying often happens when a child or young person is alone, perhaps at night in their bedroom. It may feel even harder to work out what's happening than usual.

But parents may be able to pick up on other signs – is your child upset after particular phone calls or texts? Is she reluctant to go to school? Is she reluctant to text or phone in your presence?

What should I do if my child is being bullied by phone?

The most tempting thing is to remove a child's mobile phone, change the number or to set up a new e-mail account or supplier. But remember, children are amazingly resourceful, and new numbers and e-mail addresses can be accessed very quickly when required. There is a slick network out there, and numbers and addresses change hands quickly. If your child engages in MSN or another instant messaging service, it won't be long before a new screen name or address is identified.

The second reason not to bother with instant changes is that evidence is crucial. If you change the number, any problems associated with the old number cannot be linked. You and your child need to be scrupulous about noting down bullying phone calls, texts or e-mail messages. Keep a diary of the time of every problematic call, even if it comes up as 'number unknown'. Police and other specialists can trace calls even from 'withheld' numbers. Similarly, if your e-mail account or instant message screen name is targeted, save everything into a separate file.

There is absolutely no need for children to read texts or to listen to messages; set phones to 'divert to message' and let the messages provide the authorities with the appropriate details. Encourage your child to avoid opening texts or e-mails, and simply save them (or forward them to your computer or phone) in order to keep a record.

It's important to realise that a child's phone may be a lifeline to her, and an essential part of her social life. So tread with care when suggesting a replacement or its removal.

If your child is very distressed, you may wish to purchase a second phone – continuing to operate his or her sim card in a phone to keep an all-important record – and allowing your child to continue his or her social life on a new number. A determined bully will likely obtain this number, but there is no harm in trying. A similar ruse can be used with screen names.

A RECENT SURVEY BY NCH FOUND THAT MOBILE BULLYING INCLUDED:

▷ Anonymous texts of a generally threatening nature. These were seen as the least threatening, except when an anonymous caller or texter kept getting in touch and/or knew names and personal details. Then it became scary.

▷ Persistent personal threats by text and phone, where the caller knew the young person.

▷ Happy slapping (*see page 335*).

▷ Taking pictures of violent, embarrassing or ridiculous situations, for example, people kissing, opening car doors when cyclists are riding by or doing dangerous dares. These photos then get circulated round, sometimes to friends, sometimes as wide as year groups at school.

▷ Being part of a chain texting, with implied threats if the person doesn't pass it on.

What else can I do?

▷ Always encourage your child to talk about how she uses her mobile phone. If she seems distressed after a phone call, discuss the topic of malicious calls and messages.

▷ If your child knows and attends the same school as the sender, contact your child's class teacher or school head as soon as possible, even if the phone calls and text messages happen outside of school hours.

▷ Keep a record of the calls and text messages to show to the school.

▷ Change your child's mobile number as soon as possible, but keep the old number (sim card) in order to provide a trail of evidence if there is doubt about the perpetrators.

▷ Talk to your mobile phone service provider. They usually operate a 'malicious calls' helpdesk as part of their customer service.

Encourage your child to:

▷ Avoid giving out any information about himself, such as phone number and address, unless he knows and trusts the caller.

▷ Avoid leaving alternative contact details as part of a voicemail greeting.

▷ Avoid replying to any text messages unless he knows the caller.

▷ Show any message that is wrong, worrying, from strangers or simply malicious, to a trusted person, such as a parent, teacher or another family member.

▷ Always check the caller ID. If he doesn't know the number or it comes up as unknown or withheld, don't answer!

▷ Leave his phone near loud background noise if he does answer a malicious call. If children appear to be alone, it may prompt a further bullying incident.

▷ Divert his calls to a mailbox, where they can be used as evidence of bullying.

▷ Make a note of the sender's details at the end of the message.

▷ Be careful and selective of who has your child's mobile phone number.

▷ Ensure that friends do not pass the number on to other people that they don't know – no matter how tempting!

▷ Never reply to an abusive text – it will just encourage the bullies.

▷ Avoid replying to a missed call if he doesn't recognise the number. If it's genuine, the person can leave a message or call back.

▷ Keep abusive texts or pictures (or have them forwarded to your phone for safekeeping if they are distressing). These provide an important record in case you need to call the police.

▷ If your child is being bullied when he feels particularly vulnerable, for example, late at night, encourage your child to switch off the phone.

WHAT IS THE SCALE OF THE PROBLEM?

According to a recent survey by UK children's charity NCH, one in five kids has been bullied via digital phone or computer. Bullying by text message was the most common form of abuse reported, with 14 per cent of children interviewed saying they had received upsetting messages on their mobile phones, a figure that was echoed in a recent Australian study. The interactions run the gamut from disconcerting to downright terrifying. Insults, silent calls and threats target hapless victims, and because so many kids are the owners of mobile phones, there is a ready market for this type of bullying. In the US, 55 per cent of children between the ages of thirteen and seventeen have mobile phones; in the UK, it's even higher – 80 per cent of those between the ages of eleven and fourteen own a mobile phone.

The NCH survey, titled 'Putting U in the Picture', collated responses from 770 youngsters aged eleven to nineteen. One in ten said someone had used a camera phone to snap their picture in a way that made them feel uncomfortable, embarrassed or threatened. Of those, 17 per cent believed the images had been forwarded to others. The report cited instances of so-called 'happy-slapping,' an extreme form of techno-bullying where physical assaults are recorded on mobile phones and distributed to websites and other phones via video messaging.

Should my son be allowed to make phone calls or send texts during meals or family time?

Some families have different ideas about meal-time etiquette and allow children to take phone calls, read the paper or a book, or even listen to personal music players or watch TV. While the odd meal (Sunday mornings, perhaps, reading the papers) may be OK, in general, allowing kids (and adults) to do their own thing wastes an important opportunity for communication, interaction, teaching table manners and also for learning the boundaries of 'personal' communication in group settings. I would suggest that phones should not be answered or used during meal times, unless there is a genuine (very one-off) and important call that needs to be received. To some extent, the same goes for family time. If your child spends the entire time texting or speaking to friends, the purpose of the venture has been undermined. Why not suggest that urgent texts and calls be taken (no more than a minute in length), but that phones should be on silent or switched off when you are together as a family – out and about, at the table, in a restaurant or wherever.

Should I allow my child privacy while he makes his calls?

In a word, yes. You wouldn't like people (including your children) listening in on your calls, and the same goes for your child. It is important to show respect and to allow her some freedom to converse in private. If she chooses to make or take calls in your presence, perhaps at the dinner table, then she obviously foregoes that right.

Should I give my son a mobile phone so I can know where he is?

Many parents supply their children with phones in order to keep tabs on their activities, and there is nothing wrong with this. It gives kids the opportunity to ring if they are running late, having problems with transport, want to change their plans, want to make plans or want to ask permission or just chat. It's a good vehicle, from an appropriate age. However, don't harass your child! If you text him every few minutes and make repeated calls to find out his whereabouts, he'll simply turn off the phone or ignore your messages. Use it circumspectly and, if he's out, only in an emergency or if you are concerned about his safety.

Money

At what age is she responsible for her own debts? Am I responsible until then?

Generally speaking, you are not responsible for your children's debts; however, there are a few grey areas. For example, if your child runs up phone bills on the household phone or a phone that you have purchased for her and signed for, then you are responsible. You may also be held responsible if your child downloads music or anything else on the computer, even in his own name, if he is under sixteen. This is also extended to piracy or sharing of copyright materials on the internet; several recent cases have found parents liable for compensation and/or costs.

However, it is a criminal offence for anyone to send material inviting a child under the age of eighteen to borrow money or obtain goods or services on credit or hire purchase. If a child is over fourteen but under eighteen, they can enter into a credit or hire purchase agreement if an adult acts as a guarantor. Children can borrow money at any age, but access to loans may be limited because a lender will not usually be able to take a young person to court if he or she breaks the terms of a loan. This is because a child under the age of eighteen cannot usually be legally held to a contract.

A child or young person cannot normally be taken to court for debt because of the same ruling – no one under the age of eighteen can be held to contract. There are, however, some exceptions to this rule. Your children can be held legally responsible for any debts they run up to purchase necessities such as food, shelter or clothing.

As a parent you are not usually under any obligation to pay the debts of your child. Some parents feel morally obliged to do so, but it's worth thinking twice before doing so. Sometimes kids need to learn the importance of money and the dangers of debt the hard way.

When can he open a bank account?

According to the British Bankers' Association, children can open a savings account from the age of seven (although this varies from bank to bank) and can normally open a current account from the age of eleven or twelve. There is no legal age limit, but some banks will not allow a chequing account until the age of fifteen or sixteen, or overdraft facilities until eighteen (because children cannot be held responsible for their debts in most cases). A current account is a good option for most older children, as it provides a bank card to withdraw money or to use for purchases (debit card), and usually supplies statements by post or by the internet, so children can keep tabs on their money. A savings account should also be encouraged for all children, so that they learn the importance of putting aside money regularly.

When can he get a credit card or a store card?

Children must be eighteen to apply for a credit card or store card, although you can ask for an additional card on your own account in their name. You are, however, responsible for any expenditure on that card.

When can she get an overdraft?

Overdrafts are not normally given until the age of eighteen because they represent a form of credit; however, if your child is younger than eighteen and in full-time employment, some banks will allow a small overdraft on the basis of income. Students in full-time further education are usually offered a small interest-free overdraft on their accounts, regardless of age – although most are obviously at least seventeen or eighteen.

Should I expect my child to pay 'rent'?

If your child has an income of his own and is still living at home, it can be a good idea to ask for some contribution towards household expenses in the form of rent. This should encourage children to become used to the idea of budgeting and paying their own way before they have to take full responsibility. Many young adults become accustomed to spending their income indiscriminately when they have no financial obligations, responsibilities and commitments, and it can be a shock when they first begin to live on their own. Of course, many kids stay or return home in order to save money towards the deposit on a home, towards living expenses or towards further education, so the idea is not to hit them hard, but to encourage them to commit a token amount each month towards their upkeep. This also prevents kids from taking advantage of parents who supply everything they need free of charge. Some parents initiate the idea of a nominal rent when their children get their first real jobs (summer jobs, for example). (*See also* Pocket money, *page 382.*)

Morals

When do children begin to know what is right and wrong?
There are various stages of 'morality' that develop throughout a
child's life. These are influenced by parental interaction and
guidance, balanced discipline, the peer group and a child's own
choices. In reality, children begin to learn right from wrong through
their earliest experiences. Based on the work of Jean Piaget and
Lawrence Kohlberg, there are three levels of moral development.

▷ **Preconventional:** During this first level children are concerned
with avoiding punishment and ensuring their own needs are
met. This level and its stages fit into the framework of young
children, up to the age of ten years.

▷ **Conventional:** During this level children are more concerned
with living up to the expectations of others and want to do the
right thing because it is good for the group, family or institution.
This level and its stages fit children over the age of ten years and
on to adulthood.

▷ **Postconventional**: During this level individuals govern their
behaviour by the relative values and opinions of the groups
within which they live and interact. Right behaviour is based on
a 'social contract' with others and in the validity of universal
moral principles.

In the context of this developmental chain, children should know
right from wrong in the most basic sense from age ten, but not
really understand the principles of why until mid-teens. The
average fifteen-year-old can understand the difference between
right and wrong, but he's not able to restrain his impulses as a
mature adult can – certainly not without supervision. Therefore,
our role as guides continues well into adulthood.

What if my child shows no empathy towards others?

What is empathy? It's the ability to recognise and understand another person's perceptions and feelings, and to accurately convey that understanding through an accepting response. It's an essential trait in moral behaviour, and involves values of tolerance, cooperation and respect. Many experts believe that poor empathy or lack of empathic skills are at the root of so much violence and crime in today's society, so you are right to be concerned. Most studies show that bullies, for example, almost always lack empathy, which makes it possible for them to behave in completely unacceptable ways.

Children without empathy cannot see things from anyone's point of view but their own. Some of this may be due to the fact that they have never been taught empathy as children, and see little of it in the world around them. We live in a competitive society where the message is often 'look out for number one' at whatever cost, and this message undoubtedly filters down. The overemphasis on self-esteem may also be partly to blame, creating a generation of kids who think they are superior to their peers, have a divine belief in their own ability to do and get what they want, and the full support of parents who think they are 'wonderful' and 'the best' no matter how they behave. I also question the motivation of some parents to encourage self-esteem rather than self-respect. For many years, it was believed that creating high self-esteem in children made them 'super kids' and able to do or be anything they wanted. Given that many parents are so competitive for their children, often living their own dreams through their children, some parents have actually considered the development of self-esteem to be a tool for success, rather than something that will make their child well-rounded, happy and a positive member of society.

In his book *Empathy and Moral Development*, Dr Martin Hoffman says that the most advanced stage of empathy involves the ability to catch nonverbal and verbal messages from others, their cues in social interactions and to use these to understand lives outside your own. Some children, such as bullies, see things only from their own point of view and they care only about their own feelings. They are not good at sharing, empathy, caring about others or making friends. These are behaviours that can be taught and learned.

WHAT CAN I DO?

▷ Many experts suggest that teaching very young children to empathise is the key to discouraging aggressive behaviour, and there are several studies backing this up. Instead of showing anger or aggression when a child hurts someone, the idea is that you say things like: 'Ouch. Oh, that hurts. Oh, that's so painful', rather than losing your temper and punishing the errant or aggressive child. Even young children are able to make the connection that their actions can cause discomfort or pain in others, and it's an important lesson in cause and effect that helps to teach empathy.

▷ Again, for younger children ensure that all attention is given to the hurt party when dealing with aggression, in order to make the aggressor's bid for attention fail. You can encourage the offender to offer a soft toy for the victim to hold or to hold ice on a bump – all in all, to be attentive and affectionate. This takes the focus away from negative behaviour, helps a child to feel better about himself by being kind, but also pushes home the message that hurting others hurts.

▷ In a classroom or home scenario, much the same thing can work with older kids and teens. Don't hesitate to show your emotions when your child is rude to you or if he is violent in any way. Although this is in direct opposition to what we suggest for younger victims in a school bullying scenario, in the context of a supervised environment with adults, it is very important that bullies learn the effect and consequences of their words or actions. A cold, angry parent responding to a cold, angry child will end up in a power struggle rather than anything positive. A warm parent who shows the occasional chink of weakness and the ability to be 'human' can help to teach children compassion for others.

▷ Similarly, if your child hits another child, or bullies a sibling in your presence, ensure that he is involved in the 'mopping up'. Ask him to run a warm bath or get a cold cloth. As him to explain to you how he thinks the victim feels – and wait patiently for an answer. Focus your attention on the needs of the victim, and, once again, use emotive words: 'Ouch, that must have hurt. Poor you, that looks dreadful. You must be very upset.' Only through teaching can children learn empathy.

▷ The younger you can teach your children empathy, the better. Begin by putting a name to your child's behaviour so he can recognise emotions. Say, 'Oh, you're being so kind,' when he kisses your hurt finger. He'll learn from your reaction that his responsiveness is recognised and valued.

▷ Point out other people's behaviour. Teach your children to notice when someone else behaves kindly. For example, if someone returns your stolen purse or phone, or runs after you on the street with something you've dropped, point it out. Say 'That was so helpful. She really made me feel better.' In the classroom or in your home, create opportunities for children to work together – on assignments, household chores, anything that requires sharing and collaboration.

▷ Praise your child for acts of kindness and respect. Although this alone is unlikely to make a massive difference, it can teach your child that he is a valued and respected member of the family.

▷ As often as you can, give your child the message that there's almost always something good about other people. Choose anyone and everyone, even a crotchety neighbour, to make this point. If someone winds your child up or upsets them, be sympathetic and understanding, but when your child is feeling better, examine the other child's behaviour – is he being bossy because he's insecure? Is he a new boy and trying to find his place? Is he having trouble at home? Is someone bullying him?

▷ Finally, let your children know that they don't have to like everyone. Not everyone can be a friend. But it's not acceptable to be mean to those you don't like, and it's never right to join others who taunt unpopular kids.

How can I get across my moral values without lecturing?

The most important thing you can do is to practise them yourself. You can shout or lecture for years and you will get nowhere if you do not practise what you preach, and show your child, through example, what is right and wrong and what represents thoughtful, kind, compassionate, tolerant and understanding behaviour. The first and foremost lesson in morality and values comes from the way parents interact with their children and the world around them. Initially, a child believes behaviours are right or wrong because you tell her so or she considers the consequences. By five years of age your child begins to internalise your values: what's right for you becomes right for her. Your values, virtuous or not, become part of your child.

Between seven and ten the child enters the age of moral reasoning. Now the child begins to act correctly because it is the right thing to do. By seven years of age, most children have developed their concept of 'what's normal'. If sensitivity, caring, politeness and empathy have been standard operating procedure in the child's home, those are his norms, and he operates according to them. Later on, kids begin to develop more autonomous thinking (in line with a sense of right and wrong; *see above*) and are also subject to the influences of others. A poorly grounded child will always be more likely to shed or compromise his own values and morals than a child who is confident, is respected by parents, has high self-belief and a firm sense of self. This is just one reason why parenting is so important – not just to present a set of morals and values, but to guide a child through the murky waters of adolescence as he makes decisions based on them. A child who is consistently and lovingly parented grows up with more understanding of others and himself, and develops that all-important respect.

Take advantage of teachable moments, ordinary events in family life that offer opportunities to talk your child through the process of moral reasoning. For example, your son finds a mobile on the train. Does he return it? Talk him through how the owner must be feeling and how he would feel in the same place (missing sim card, for example). Maybe the owner saved for ages to buy it. Maybe he's got important numbers or data on it. And therefore we must return the phone – the core message is respect for other people's property and returning goods to their rightful owner.

Encourage discussions about current events: controversial sports figures, newspaper headlines, social issues. Raise your children to express their opinions. Encourage lively family debates. Respect their viewpoints even if you don't agree. Studies show that children who come from families who encourage such open discussion are more likely to think in a morally mature way. A California study of a thousand students looked at the relationship between the student's level of moral reasoning and how they were parented. Students who scored high on moral reasoning came from families who encouraged open discussion of controversial topics. Other studies have shown that highly permissive parents who did not expect obedience from their children and gave inappropriate praise produced 'me-firsters,' children whose only thought was to satisfy themselves. And the other extreme, over-controlling parents produced conformist teenagers who couldn't think for themselves. In these studies, families who gave their children a voice in decisions produced teenagers who were able to reason morally. Getting children to preach to themselves becomes the most lasting morality lesson.

What should I do if I do not approve of my child's morals

First of all, show some respect. If he has differing views based on what comprises the basic moral values of today's society, then you have grounds for discussion and guidance. You may also find that what you perceive to be a lack of morals is, in fact, merely a period of morals being comprised because of peer pressure, bullying or a problem with emotional health. Morals that are taught well form the fabric of a child's emotional make-up and cannot be 'unlearned'. If you show respect for your child's belief system, you can then go on to explain why your feelings and beliefs differ, and what comprises important values in terms of society – the way we relate to others, the reasons why having morals is important, the importance of self-belief and strength in defending what is right, and even how to discern between right and wrong. You may simply want to ask the question: 'does this feel right to you to behave in this way? Do you have any reservations about the way you are thinking or behaving?' Most kids do have a niggling sense of unease when they behave outside the moral code, and simply need a little retracking to get back to base.

Should I report my child to the police if he has broken the law?

For some children a brush with the law may be a last resort and the ultimate expression of tough love by parents. If your child has made a genuine mistake, shows remorse and appears to have a normal self-concept and understanding of moral values – knowing what he did wrong and, most importantly, why it was wrong, then calling the police may well do nothing other than humiliate him and perhaps damage his future (*see page 136*), particularly if the police take it seriously. However, if the crime is very serious and your child shows no understanding of what he has done, then you may need to resort to the law in order for the consequences of his behaviour to sink in. A child who shoplifts once or twice is not a born thief, and there may be reasons for his behaviour (*see page 134*); a child who is dealing drugs to younger children or who has committed rape or another sort of extreme violence may have flawed moral judgement. Certainly in the latter cases you have a legal responsibility to report the crimes; otherwise you can be considered an accessory and even be charged with perverting the course of justice. While family loyalty is incredibly important, a child who is capable of committing a serious crime needs help and he also needs to be dealt with appropriately by the law. I have my doubts that the youth justice system provides an effective deterrent to further crime, nor does anything to provide a child with a moral framework, but the law is the law and you must abide by it and show your child that you are doing so.

In the case of less serious crimes, you may find a child psychologist or psychiatrist can get to the root of the problem and provide more help. Either way, your child must understand the seriousness of his crime. If you feel confident enough to address this on your own, through a series of talks, appropriate penalties and careful modelling and further teaching of values, then the police may not be necessary. There may be no point in calling the police if your child has stolen from you. If he's shoplifted (*see page 133*) and has returned the item, it is up to the shop to make the decision to prosecute or not. The most important thing that you can do is to help him to right the wrong; if he has been tagging (graffiti), he should confess and offer to clean it up. If he's damaged property, he should offer to pay for the damage, even if you have to loan him the money. As parents we have a legal obligation to report crimes, but the police do not always need to be called if the action has been dealt with, and repaid or amends made.

How can I help my son to be environmentally aware?

Once again, model the behaviour you want to see. Show an interest in green issues and use the TV, newspaper and other media to discuss what's going on around us, and how our behaviour can have an impact. I was shocked to hear one of my sons say that he'd very much enjoyed a film about climate change and its effects, seen at school; however, he added that it didn't really concern him as he'd be long dead before the world fell apart. He'd never thought of the idea that his children and his grandchildren might be affected. So that film provided a platform for a discussion of why we should be aware, and led on to things we could do to help. Make it a household policy to walk or cycle instead of drive whenever possible; recycle waste, turn off lights and change to more energy-efficient lightbulbs, have showers instead of baths, turn down the heating a few degrees, wash clothes in a cooler cycle, turn off appliances not being used, and choose more environmentally friendly produce at the supermarket and in your other consumer choices. In this way, kids learn through osmosis. Other ideas are to join him up to an organisation such as Greenpeace, which will provide regular literature and also ways in which your child can help – raising money, perhaps, or becoming involved in a campaign. It's also important to get kids out into the natural world more often, so that they actually understand the implications of poor policy and behaviour, and value the world around them. Kids who are slouched in front of a TV, games console or computer are unlikely to feel much at all for the natural world, as it does not impact upon them in any way. Research shows that real-life hands-on learning effectively reaches and teaches children.

How can I encourage my child to take an interest in social issues and current affairs?

The best way to teach children and to stimulate their interest is to make it relevant to them. Like most of us, children are assaulted by media on a dramatic scale, so important news and events become meaningless, and they feel absolutely no connection. For example, unless your child has been the victim of mugging or robbery, he's unlikely to know or care much about anti-crime measures in your neighbourhood or the country; unless he has personal experience of domestic violence, poverty, global warming or, let's say, mental health problems, he is unlikely to be interested in or understand policy, initiatives and practice. For this reason, the world has to be brought to your child on his own level. If a local park is being threatened by property or commercial developers, get him involved. Explain how he and others will be affected. Read the newspaper aloud at breakfast time (perhaps on a Sunday when time is not usually so tight), and pick out stories that might interest your child. Engage him in a lively debate. Show respect for his opinions and ideas, and ask what he would do to change a situation, a policy, a problem or anything else that comes up. When children become accustomed to feeling that they have a valid opinion and the wherewithal to have their ideas and opinions heard, they develop a greater interest in what is going on around them because they feel they can make a difference. Clip things out of the newspaper. Watch the news together. Encourage discussion and debate about issues and politics. Find policies that relate to your child in the various manifestos put forward by politicians and ask if they think they are accurate or what changes could be necessary? The more your child understands about the world around him, and the more it becomes relevant to him, the more it takes hold in terms of interest and activity.

Music

At what age can my child begin to learn an instrument?
The importance of music in our children's lives cannot be underestimated. Not only does it provide an important break from the 'surround sound' of technology, exams, parental pressure, competitive sports, shopping, games and peer pressure, but it promotes relaxation and involves the mind on a completely different level to academic education. Research has shown that children who are actively involved in music (who play or sing regularly), do better in reading, learn coordination, concentration, goal-setting and cooperation; are more likely to do better in maths and sciences because music helps build reasoning skills and cognitive development; get along better with their peers and have higher self-esteem; and are more likely to go into further education.

One study demonstrated that year two students who were given keyboard training while also using maths software scored higher on proportional maths and fractions tests than students who used the software alone. And students who have been involved in public school music programmes score higher on their SATs than those who don't.

The best age to start an instrument is between the ages of five and seven, however, it is never too late. Before embarking you'll need to consider several things. First of all, does your child show any interest in music, any sense of rhythm, any inclination to learn an instrument? If not, you may end up making music a chore rather than a joy. If your child exhibits absolutely no interest or music ability, then you might be better off waiting until he does. There is no reason why singing in the car, listening to different types of music in your home, doing karaoke for fun, joining the school choir or singing in a mate's band can't be equally effective – perhaps encouraging your child towards learning an instrument when he is interested and ready.

A good starting instrument is the piano or keyboards, which provides a basic understanding of notes and music which can be easily combined and then translated to other instruments. The important thing is learning how notes on paper translate into action with hands, and through that sound. String instruments are another good place to begin. Brass or wind instruments can be more physically challenging and may not be appropriate until years four or five; however, many kids take to them and enjoy the challenge at a much younger age.

There are physical demands associated with playing an instrument, so if your child is perhaps slower on the physical development front or with his fine motor skills, he might not actually be physically ready. He will need some powers of concentration – sitting relatively still and learning for 30 or 60 minutes. He also must understand that instruments need to be practised regularly, lessons attended and a commitment made. You will need to be involved with this to some degree.

What ages are recommended for starting which instrument?

From five to seven, keyboards and string instruments are the best choices. Piano is an excellent starting point because it is easy to learn, and the association between notes on paper and the sound the keys make when struck is relatively uncomplicated. String instruments may seem a daunting prospect, but studies show that many kids adapt to them easily, as long as they have an instrument of the appropriate size and they are given good instruction. Experts recommend leaving wind instruments until a child is nine or ten, because in many cases multiple fingering and blowing techniques are required for a single note.

Here's a helpful breakdown:

▷ Violin: Can be started from as young as five and is not extremely expensive. Good opportunities later to play with other people (orchestras, even rock bands are now including them!).

▷ Viola: Also one that can be started early; and is relatively cheap.

▷ Cello: More expensive, but can be started from age five and upwards.

▷ Guitar: Many kids start quite young – around aged ten – although classical guitar is more difficult than pop or folk. It's an inexpensive instrument.

▷ Flute: Comparatively inexpensive, and can be started from age nine or ten.

▷ Oboe: More complicated and expensive; start at ten or eleven.

▷ Clarinet: Reasonably inexpensive and can be started from age ten.

▷ Bassoon: Normally started from age twelve and can be quite expensive.

▷ Saxophone: Smaller sizes can be started from age ten, but it's expensive.

▷ Trumpet or cornet: Reasonably inexpensive; can be started at age ten.

▷ French horn: Quite expensive and difficult to play. It can be started at age eleven or so, but it is not uncommon to transfer to the horn from other brass instruments at a later age.

▷ Trombone: Reasonably priced and can be started at age ten or so.

▷ Tuba: Very expensive and can be started at age eleven; many players start on another brass instrument like the tenor horn or euphonium and transfer later on. It's also very bulky!

▷ Piano: From age five, as soon as little fingers can reach the keys. Remember, though, that it is a fairly solitary instrument. Many kids use it as a starting point and move on to other instruments – or combine them.

▷ Drums: A good sense of rhythm is important. From age eight or nine, most kids can learn the basics easily.

How often should she practise?

Ideally, every day. It's difficult to fit in practice time (particularly if you have more than one child sharing an instrument and your children have busy schedules) but making a regular commitment, at a certain time of day, can help. Ten to twenty minutes per day is adequate, although some music teachers demand a half an hour. The key is to go over difficult bits and problem areas until they are solved, and to do every piece a few times through (plus scales or other set homework). If your child is feeling overwhelmed by the daily grind of practising, perhaps offer a day off on the weekend.

When does a child's singing voice appear?
There is no set date for this, but be assured that all children have the ability to sing in tune; experts say there is no such thing as being 'tone deaf'. Supposedly tone deaf children (or adults) have simply not been taught nor given the correct practice. Many children are not consistent with pitch until around aged eleven or twelve; some appear to have a natural singing voice and are in tune much earlier. If you are concerned, encourage more musical activities in your home, and general singing! Remember that if a child gets the idea that they can't sing, then they won't.

When will my son's voice break?
As a boy enters adolescence, his muscles develop, his chest gets broader and along with these and other physical changes, his voice begins to get deeper. The larynx, typically called the voice box, lengthens. As this happens, the voice 'breaks' on its way to becoming deeper. Sometimes it happens very quickly, perhaps even overnight. Amusingly to others, but embarrassingly to the boy, he may have times when his voice is higher one moment and then lower even just a minute later! The speed of the overall change relates to the speed with which the larynx grows. Voice change in the average boy begins in early puberty when a boy's testicles begin to enlarge and produce testosterone. The specific age this takes place will depend on when puberty begins, and puberty may begin any time between the ages of ten and fourteen. There is then a gradual change or deepening of voice throughout puberty. The average age for completion of voice change is between fourteen and sixteen years, but just as there is a significant variation in the timing of puberty so is there in voice change.

When should I allow my child to give up learning music?

There are two aspects to this question. The first is that kids who do not enjoy learning an instrument or playing in a band, and who do not achieve what they wanted or hoped to do, may just want to opt out completely. In this case, you may end up flogging a dead horse. Your child may not be musical; he may have no interest; he may be playing the wrong instrument for him. Try to work out the underlying situation: maybe changing instruments will do the trick (although confirm and ask him to commit to a reasonable length of time or he'll be instrument-hopping all over the place), or maybe just giving up is the answer.

However, if your child wants to drop music because his social life is more important or he feels he has too many other demands on his time, try to work out whether it is necessary. Perhaps a little time management will do the trick. It is a shame for musical children to give up instruments, not just because they may regret it later, but because it does provide a good diversion from other activities. Work out if your expectations are too high. Perhaps giving up taking a 'grade' for a year will help or switching from a structured curriculum to something more contemporary for a short period in order to encourage your child to see the fun and benefits of being able to play. Music should be fun and relaxing, not one more stress for a child. Let him go at his own pace and see what happens.

How long is music compulsory in schools?

Despite government pledges, music provision in schools is inconsistent and patchy – often taught by untrained teachers. Children are to be given free musical instrument lessons from age eleven, but this does not appear to be happening either. At the most, children appear to get about 30 minutes per week, but this varies greatly. In most secondary schools there are no compulsory music lessons. It's worth asking some questions.

Motorcycles

When can a child ride pillion on a motorbike?
At any age provided the crash helmet fits properly and both feet reach the passenger footrests.

When can my son get a licence to drive a motorcycle?
Under the law, there are three different types of motorcycles: a moped (or scooter), which has an engine up to 50cc and a maximum speed of 50km/h (31mph); a learner motorcycle, which has an engine up to 125cc; and a 'large motorcycle', which has a power output of at least 35kW. On this basis, you can work out the age at which your child can drive any or all.

▷ **Mopeds:** Your child can only hold a provisional licence if he is at least sixteen years old. It entitles him to ride a moped on the road as a learner with L-plates (D-plates in Wales). He cannot carry pillion passengers or use motorways. This provisional licence is only valid while he holds a current DL196 certificate issued by an Approved Training Body to show that he has completed a Compulsory Basic Training (CBT) course. CBT certificates are valid for two years from the date of issue.

A CBT certificate obtained on a moped is also valid for motorcycles once he has reached the age of seventeen and has the necessary provisional licence.

A full moped licence (obtained after passing a moped test) automatically gives him provisional motorcycle entitlement. However, he must be at least seventeen years old to take up the provisional entitlement.

▷ **Motorcycles:** Your child must be seventeen to get a provisional motorcycle licence. It entitles him to ride a moped or a motorcycle as a learner with L-plates. He can practise unaccompanied on a learner motorcycle after he has completed a CBT course. He cannot carry pillion passengers or use motorways.

▷ **Car licences:** A car licence allows your child to ride a moped providing he has completed his CBT (which he must do before riding on the road). A car licence will also give your child a provisional motorcycle licence, but again he must take CBT before riding on the roads. After this he may ride a learner motorcycle with L-plates, but cannot carry pillion passengers or use motorways until he gets his full licence. At this point he will have passed the practical test and can ride any motorcycle.

Should I allow my daughter to ride on a motorcycle with her boyfriend?

Per mile travelled, a motorcyclist is approximately 27 times more likely to die in a crash than someone in a car, and head injury is a leading cause of death in motorcycle crashes. Moreover, the risk of motor vehicle crashes is higher among those sixteen to nineteen years old than among any other age group. A motorcyclist without a helmet is 40 per cent more likely to suffer a fatal head injury and 15 per cent more likely to suffer a non-fatal injury than a helmeted motorcyclist involved in a crash.

On this basis, it is clear that your daughter should wear a helmet if she is considering riding with her boyfriend. In the UK it is law to do so, but there are many cases of motorcyclists and their passengers failing to wear a helmet. It would also be useful for your daughter to wear protective clothing, including gloves and suitable boots, to protect her from potential injury.

I would think twice before allowing your teenager to ride on a motorcycle. Motorcycles can be dangerous, particularly in the hands of inexperienced drivers and unwitting car drivers who often fail to see cyclists. If you are concerned, say no.

Mouth guards

From what age should children wear mouth guards for sport?
According to the American Dental Association, children should wear mouth guards from the age of seven. Between 13 and 39 per cent of all dental injuries are sports related, and the highest rate of sports-related injuries occur between the ages of ten and nineteen. Each year in the UK more than 70,000 sporting accidents injure the mouth and teeth, and more than 13,000 people end up at hospital accident and emergency units every year with injuries to the mouth and teeth suffered playing sport. The British Dental Health Foundation recommends that children wear mouth guards whenever they play sport that involves physical contact or moving objects. This includes: cricket, hockey and football – which can cause broken and damaged teeth; and American football, boxing and rugby – which can all cause broken or dislocated jaws. In the US, it is also recommended that they are worn for martial arts, snowboarding, rollerblading, weightlifting, wrestling, basketball and skateboarding.

How often do mouth guards need to be changed?
Until your children's teeth and jaws have stopped growing, they will need to be replaced fairly regularly (in some cases, when new teeth are coming through in early adolescence, for example, every three to six months). If the mouth guard feels too tight or loose, it needs to be replaced. Otherwise, once a year is the normal replacement time – largely because they suffer from wear and tear.

It's a good idea to take your child's mouth guard with you when he goes for dental appointments. The expense of replacing mouth guards constantly during adolescence can be prohibitive if they are professionally made at the dentist. The 'boil and fit' mouth guards do not provide quite as much protection, but they are much cheaper and are a suitable alternative, particularly during growth spurts.

Can I insist that he wears a mouth guard even if his school has no policy?

Absolutely. Thankfully most schools do now insist that children wear mouth guards for all contact sports, and often will not allow them to play without one. This is to be applauded. Ensure that your child always has a well-fitting mouth guard in his sports equipment bag and encourage him to use it. Obviously, if there is no policy at your child's school or sports club it will be difficult to monitor its use; however, make it very clear to your child that you expect him to wear it, and the reasons why (*see above*). Not many teens relish the thought of wearing false teeth for the rest of their lives or suffering disfiguring mouth injuries, and there is one simple way to prevent this.

Name change

Can my child change his name?

Your child can change his name at any time after the age of sixteen, without your permission. There is no legal procedure to follow in order to change a name. Your child simply starts using the new name. He can change his forename or surname, add names or rearrange his existing names.

He may need evidence of a name change, when getting a passport, for example. This can include a letter from a responsible person, a public announcement, a statutory declaration or a deed poll. He cannot change details on his birth certificate, except in limited circumstances.

Can I change my child's name without his permission (when I remarry, for example)?

A child's name can be changed at any time, provided it is not to deceive or defraud another person. There is no legal procedure which must be followed in order to change a child's name, providing all the people who need to give their consent have done so. The parent simply starts using the new name. If you require evidence of this change, you can use any of the above.

If your child is under the age of sixteen his consent does not have to be given for his name to be changed. However, if he objects, he can apply for a court order to prevent the change, provided the court is satisfied that he has sufficient understanding of what is involved.

Organisation

When should my child be responsible for organising her own school kit, etc.?

Children should start taking responsibility for their own organisation when they start school. This simply means ensuring that she has all the necessary equipment, books, sportswear, lunch or snack, and any required letters with her before she leaves the house. In the early years this will obviously have to be supervised heavily, but the sooner she gets used to organising herself, the easier it will become. Get her into the habit of laying out her school clothes or uniform the night before (including shoes and ties, which have a habit of disappearing), and putting out her book bag and anything else required. Children are often groggy or grumpy in the mornings and appear to suffer from amnesia regarding belongings, so it pays to get them used to being organised the night before. If necessary, put a checklist on your child's bulletin board in her bedroom, or on the front door or fridge outlining what is required on what days. By the age of eleven or twelve, most children can be entirely responsible for their own organisation.

Orthodontics

When do children need braces (orthodontics)?

Depending on the type of work being undertaken, children as young as seven may be referred to an orthodontist. In this case, work is done at the time that most of the baby teeth are being lost and the permanent teeth are arriving. This is classically between the ages of seven and ten. Other orthodontists prefer to wait until most of your child's adult teeth have appeared, at around eleven to thirteen years old. Most treatment is undertaken before the jaw has finished growing, which makes it easier to sort out potential problems.

If my child doesn't want braces, can he refuse them?

Yes. Consent must be given before orthodontic treatment takes place. You can consent on your child's behalf, but if he is deemed capable of understanding the proposed treatment, as well as any risks, he can decline.

For how long are braces worn?

In general, braces are worn for between one and three years. The actual treatment time depends on the severity of the problem, the growth of your child's face and jaws and her cooperation. Some problems may require less time. Some children respond faster to treatment than others. A retainer is normally given after the braces are removed in order to stabilise the teeth, and hold them in their corrected, ideal positions until the bones and gums adapt to the treatment changes. This can take a few months or several years.

Are the guidelines provided for forbidden food and drink accurate?

Foods that can damage or dislodge braces are off limits for the duration of treatment. These include hard foods such as sweets, raw carrots, hard fruit, corn on the cob, popcorn, nuts, pretzels and crushed ice. Sticky foods such as gum and sweets are also not recommended, as they can get stuck between the teeth and gums, or bend wires and knock bands or brackets loose. If the braces are damaged, treatment normally takes longer. Furthermore, fizzy drinks, sugary foods and sweets can damage the teeth because the braces can cause more plaque than usual to build up – one reason why regular, thorough cleaning is essential.

Obviously, it's a lot to ask any child to go without sweets and fizzy drinks, as well as hard fruits for up to three years, but it should be encouraged. Drinking a fizzy drink with a straw can help to prevent damage because the drink bypasses the teeth to a certain extent. Apples and carrots can be cut into small chunks, corn can be cut off the cob, and sweets can be eaten after meals rather than as snacks to reduce the damage to enamel. Eating a small piece of cheese after sweets or sugary foods can also help to prevent damage because the calcium encourages hardening of the teeth, and discourages softening, which is the first stage in the process creating cavities or tooth decay, and also because it contains antibacterial elements that prevent the growth of unhealthy bacteria in plaque.

Can I make my child attend appointments if he is reluctant to do so?

If your child agrees to treatment he is effectively making a commitment to attend appointments as and when they are required. In most cases, adjustments are made every four to seven weeks, so regular appointments are necessary. Point out to your son that failing to turn up simply means that treatment will take longer, and that it may not be as effective.

Parties

Should I allow my child to go to an unsupervised party?

Until the age of sixteen, all parties for children should be supervised by an adult. Firstly, you are legally responsible for your child until this age, and if harm comes to him when he is unsupervised, you can be liable (*see page 34*). Secondly, parties can easily run out of control if alcohol is supplied or brought in, if uninvited guests turn up, if there is trouble of some sort such as fighting or property is damaged or stolen. The average teenager does not have the ability to tell a bunch of uninvited kids to go away, nor the ability to deal with an emergency (a fire, for example, or a child who is injured or becomes ill) or out-of-control guests. Even under the best of conditions, teenagers are not generally known for their decision-making skills, but in a crisis situation the consequences can be devastating. There are some terrifying stories from the US, where unsupervised teenage parties have led to stabbings, drownings and deaths. In one case, out of 150 guests, not one managed to call for an ambulance when a fight broke out and one child was fatally stabbed and three others eventually hospitalised when a neighbour intervened. The party in question started as an unsupervised get-together for a small group of close friends. It happens. After the age of sixteen, it is still worth being around to ensure that your child has some support if things go wrong, and that you can provide some control.

When are mixed-sex parties appropriate?

There is nothing wrong with mixing the sexes at any age. Children need to learn to relate to the opposite sex in an unstructured, unpressured environment, and parties can offer a good opportunity for this. In early to middle adolescence, teen 'crowds' emerge; these are large groups of teens who cluster together because they have characteristics that identify them with a particular crowd. Crowds help a teenager to sort peers into groups of people she would like to spend time with – and those she wouldn't. Crowds and cliques serve as a basis of self-definition, especially during early adolescence. Through choices in style of dress, language or 'hangouts', she shows other people who she is (even if she hasn't completely worked it out herself). One element of the crowd mentality is, of course, parties! Social gatherings represent an opportunity to interact with others, to flirt with relationships without the pressures of one-to-one contact, and to use their peer group as support while they find their 'social feet'. They learn socially acceptable behaviour with both sexes, how to talk and hold a conversation, how to tell a story or a joke, and what comprises popularity and interesting people – much of this from their peers.

So, encourage mixed sex parties as soon as your child shows interest. The earlier they learn to relate to the opposite sex in a normal, healthy, everyday way, the better. There's nothing worse than a child heading off into the world without any experience of communicating with or spending time with the opposite sex, often the case with children who have attended single-sex schools. Some adults are still uncomfortable with members of the opposite sex because they've never had the opportunity to develop healthy friendships through regular contact, and view the opposite sex in terms of sexual relationships or mate material only.

When are sleepover parties appropriate?

Interestingly, research from the US suggests that the ideal time for a first sleepover at the house of a family member (such as a grandparent) is between the ages of three and four. It is recommended that children have a few overnight visits to family before they sleep over with a friend, to ensure that they feel comfortable and understand the concept of sleeping somewhere else. By the age of eight, most children have had a sleepover with a friend. Sleepovers often become very popular in early adolescence, when the 'crowd' mentality kicks in, and they should be encouraged for this reason; kids in their teens naturally prefer doing things in groups, and a sleepover offers an opportunity to experiment with playing 'host or hostess', planning and catering for guests, and, of course, sitting up into the wee hours talking in an intimate environment.

The newest trend is co-ed sleepovers, which begin in some cases in early teens. There are several pros and cons to these. Many parents like having their children under their own roof and under supervision. They accept that teens are likely to experiment with alcohol and even sex, and prefer it to take place at home. I'm not sure I agree with the latter, as condoning early sex is irresponsible and puts children who are not ready in a compromised position. There is no question that sexual experimentation takes place at co-ed sleepovers. In one US survey undertaken by *Teen People*,

83 per cent of respondents reported that their peers were 'fooling around' at co-ed sleepovers. A sleepover obviously provides an intimate opportunity for this to take place and many kids may feel pressured to take part.

Some parents acknowledge that teens want to stay up late with their friends, and co-ed sleepovers are an option in this case – you know where your children are, and you know they are safe. If your child is invited to a co-ed sleepover it is absolutely essential that it is supervised, as the potential for disaster is high. There should, ideally, be a small number of guests and facilities for children to change/undress in privacy, and sleep *only* with members of their own sex; in other words, no dormitory set-ups and certainly no shared sleeping bags. You should seriously limit or prohibit alcohol, which will have the effect of lowering inhibitions. Parents should be visible, entering periodically, so that children don't get carried away. Make sure that your child is aware that she should ring if she feels at all uncomfortable, compromised, frightened or unsure.

Personally, I think this trend is just more evidence of overly sophisticated children who are not prepared to wait for normal milestones and rites of passage at appropriate ages. Certainly the occasional late party or get-together should be allowed, with a view to giving kids time to settle in, chat, play games, watch films or eat together in a home environment, but equally, most kids (and certainly those of the opposite sex) should probably make their way home after that. Spending the night together seems unnecessary and puts far too much temptation in the way of kids who do not have the maturity to make the right decisions.

Is my child required to take a gift for the host when he goes to a party?
It is undoubtedly correct etiquette, even in today's more relaxed

society, to bring a small gift for the host. Adults normally bring some chocolates, flowers or a bottle of wine; children can do the same, in a kid-friendly fashion. Obviously you do not want your children to feel embarrassed turning up with a gift when everyone else slouches past the host or his parents without even a hello, and in some cases children don't even *know* the host of the party they are attending. In these cases, you can probably give it a miss. However, if the host is a friend, explain to your child that the gift is basically a 'thank-you' or appreciation for the effort his friend has gone to. It doesn't have to be expensive: a small box of chocolates or biscuits are fine for younger kids; older teens might like to bring a nice bottle of soft drink, or something unobtrusive that they can slip to the host if they feel embarrassed by their gesture. The idea is, really, that you are teaching your children some appreciation and showing them how to show it politely – something you hope they will take into adulthood.

Does anyone write to say thank you anymore?

The act of writing thank-you letters has been replaced to a large extent by technology; phone calls, e-mails and texts are now considered to be appropriate ways to thank someone for a gift or a social event. And to be honest, as long as it happens, it doesn't matter what form it takes. But your child should learn to say thank you in one form or another, regardless of the size of the gift or the type of event/party attended.

Can I refuse permission for my child to go to a party that is unsupervised or at an inappropriate venue?

Ultimately, you are responsible for your children and if you allow them to do something that is potentially dangerous, you are not fulfilling an important aspect of being a parent. While it may prove unpopular, you can and should refuse permission for your child to attend something that you have strong grounds to believe may compromise her safety or security. Unsupervised parties are an accident waiting to happen in many cases (*see page 363*), and some venues are simply not suitable for children, with inadequate supervision, inappropriate clientele, perhaps problems with drugs, or safety regulations, or under-age drinking. It's not a great idea to come in with a flat 'no' without discussing it with your child first – making it clear why you are concerned. You may find that your fears are ungrounded in some cases. It is worth speaking to other parents to work out if they are equally concerned; it's certainly easier to veto something if there are a few of you taking the same step. Other parents might feel the same as you do and not want to rock the boat; there is, however, power in numbers. Be realistic about why you are saying no; for example, if three or four girls are getting together for a sleepover and no parents will be around for most of the night, you might feel comfortable allowing this, particularly if you know the children in question. But a few ground rules should be established, such as no extra guests to be admitted, no alcohol, no 'party' and everyone stays put. If your fears are, well, just fears rather than based on facts or experience, you should think carefully and work out if they are valid. It's hard to allow new freedoms to our children, but we do need to let go in stages. If, however, there is genuine cause for concern, pull parental rank and refuse.

Passports

At what age can my child apply for his own passport?
Children aged fifteen or under should apply for a child passport, which is valid for five years. Applicants aged sixteen years or over

should apply for an adult passport, which lasts for ten years. Children can apply for their own passport at sixteen, but require their parent's signature (permission/consent). Over eighteen, children can apply for a passport without parental permission.

Can either parent give permission?
If a child's parents are married, either parent can give permission. If the parents were not married at the time of birth (or when the mother became pregnant, for those living in Scotland), only the mother can give permission, unless they have since married or the father has a parental responsibility order or agreement.

If the consent form is signed by someone acting as a guardian, then they should supply a letter explaining the circumstances. This should be supported by a letter from a head teacher or someone similar, who is aware of the facts and can confirm the circumstances.

Peers

What can I do if my daughter is spending more time with her peers than her family?
As difficult as it is for parents to accept, peers do become increasingly important throughout adolescence. Although peer groups are important at all ages, it is not until mid- or late adolescence that friendship takes the role of intimate relationships. These peer groups are characterised by trust, self-disclosure and loyalty. During adolescence, kids begin to show autonomy or a sense of being a separate person. Another factor is the cognitive changes that enables adolescents to see situations from another person's point of view. As a result of these developments, teens

experience a greater need for intimacy and an increased capacity to enter close relationships or peer groups.

Friendships often fulfil developmental needs at this stage better than relationships with parents. Thus, adolescents distance themselves from parents and focus more on peers, sometimes to the point where the influence of parents seems to be almost neutralised. It seems logical, then, that peers, at least in part, would supplant parents with regard to social support. Don't underestimate the importance of your children's peers. Research shows that the peer group plays an important role:

▷ Teaches children how to interact with others.
▷ Provides support in defining identity, interests, abilities and personality.
▷ Encourages autonomy without the control of adults and parents.
▷ Offers opportunities to witness the strategies used by others to cope with similar problems and to observe how effective they are.
▷ Gives emotional support.
▷ Encourages the creation and maintenance of friendships.

Adolescents must be prepared for social independence, for relationships with both sexes, marriage and adulthood. For these reasons, teens need the support and guidance of their peers.

This is not to say that your role is supplanted, but that adolescents are gradually moving away as they learn to make their own decisions on the road to independence, and peers take the role that parents once monopolised. Encourage healthy friendships, as peers can provide much that is positive. As long as your child is communicating with you regularly (*see page 110*), and making time for family (*see page 200*), it's acceptable to view this as a healthy and normal transition.

Until what age can I insist on supervision when she is with her peers?

All adolescents need privacy – it's part of growing up and a recognisable requirement for all human beings of whatever age. As children become older, they can be given increasing amounts and kinds of freedom, and the need for supervision declines. If your child always feels that you are charting her movements, monitoring her activities and looking over her shoulder, she will feel that she is not trusted and probably begin to hide things from you – either because she feels contrary and threatened, but also because she probably wants some parts of her life to be her own. Kids need time alone with their peers – at home and out and about – and they need to be able to undertake an increasing number of activities that are not supervised. This doesn't mean throwing your child out into the big bad world without a care as to what she is doing, but giving her some freedom and space. You'll always need to know where she is and what she is up to (*see page 145*), and there will be times where supervision is always necessary: when she has a party or sleepover, for example, or when she has a boyfriend to visit; her internet activities and television viewing. But act with respect and courtesy. Knock on the door before entering, allow your child to know that you are there when she needs help, advice or support, but gently pull back.

Remember that most adolescents believe they are old enough to take care of themselves. They often feel invulnerable, believing they can handle any situation and that nothing could possibly happen to them. Of course, that's not the real world and it is the responsibility of adults to protect children from life's very real dangers. Hence, adolescents do need some supervision. The idea is that supervision becomes non-intrusive rather than non-existent. They should have some room to 'spread their wings' but this doesn't mean that adults should stop doing their job. Studies show that children who are regularly but sensitively supervised and given appropriate freedoms at the right age, are less likely to model problem behaviours.

Can I insist that she meets more suitable peers/friends?

You can't 'insist' that she does, but you can encourage her to widen her social network by helping her to become involved in clubs, activities and sports where she'll meet like-minded kids. You can ask her to invite specific friends to family gatherings, holidays or outings, or suggest inviting key friends round to your home.

We all want our children to be with individuals who will have a positive influence and we want them to stay away from those who will encourage or engage in harmful, destructive, immoral or illegal activities. Parents can support positive peer relationships by giving their teenagers their love, time, boundaries and encouragement to think for themselves.

My child doesn't seem to fit in with her peer group and I'm worried she might be bullied. What can I do?

One of the greatest and most common reasons why children are targeted by bullies is because they don't 'fit in'. It's a sad state of affairs that being the 'same' as peers is the only way to be socially acceptable, but unfortunately it seems accurate. That's not to say that being 'different' is wrong, but a child must have the confidence and self-belief to carry it off, and many victims simply do not have the wherewithal to defend their own views and to stand up for themselves.

So, helping your child to fit in is essential. This can mean any one of a number of things, from encouraging him to find a group of like-minded friends who will support him and offer much-needed 'group' protection, as well as giving him the sense that he does 'fit in' *somewhere*, to making sure that he has at least some of the 'right' clothes and material possessions.

Under no circumstances am I encouraging materialism; indeed, this can backfire shamefully and leave a child with an even poorer self-image when he learns to equate popularity with what he has rather than what he is. Seek out kids who are popular without all the 'gear' and point out some of the reasons why this is so – confidence, sense of humour, kindness and generosity, self-belief, etc. All children need to learn that fitting into a peer group involves a lot more than having the right trainers or the newest iPod.

But having said that, there is nothing worse than feeling like a social leper. Don't be the one parent who refuses to let his child watch TV, play on the Playstation, go to the cinema on his own or have a mobile telephone. Don't be the one parent who insists that your child wears only hand-me-downs or 'sensible' shoes. If your child stands out in a negative fashion it will create scope for bullying and undermine his confidence. All kids want to feel that they are part of the social fabric of their environment, and like it or not, things like TV and mobile phones are tools with which kids bond – a point of discussion and a shared interest. If your child has nothing to 'share' with his peers and is the only one who can't make his arrangements by text, for example, he's going to feel left out. And for a victim, that can be a good proportion of the problem.

So open your eyes a little. Look at how other kids are dressing, what freedoms they are allowed, what gadgets seem to form a big part of their social life, and what seems to be an important aspect of your child's school culture. If you aren't sure, ask other parents. It doesn't have to cost a great deal to achieve this and you can t each some valuable lessons along the way. Then negotiate a compromise. Agree on one or two new things during a specific time space, which will help him to focus on what he really does want, rather than what he 'must' have. If he wants more, he'll have to earn the money to get it, perhaps with a paper round, for example, or babysitting, or helping out around the house. This will help to teach him the value of money and make his possessions more valuable because he has earned them. One or two small 'in' things will help him to feel normal and he will learn to take pride in what he has. The same goes for freedom. Find out what is the acceptable norm and try not to let your child be the only one with unreasonable rules and expectations.

You may find that you have a natural rebel, who enjoys being 'different' and actively dislikes what the majority of other kids like and do. In this case, there is nothing wrong with encouraging independent thought and actions; however, if your child is viewed negatively by his peers and bullied as a result of his beliefs or actions, there may be more to it than you think. Confident, friendly children can, as studies have shown, be very popular, even if they are less attractive or overweight or without the material possessions of their friends. But they add something to a group and are popular for a reason – they are good company, probably nice people and likely good friends. If your child's attempts to be different are simply making him feel isolated, try to work out why. And also work out why your child has a need to be very different, if it is making him unhappy and the target for bullies.

I think that my son is bullying others because he's in with the wrong crowd. How can I encourage him to resist peer pressure?
Many kids bully to seek attention from their peers or feel the need to exert power or authority over them. Some kids begin to victimise others in an attempt to join in with the crowd, to avoid being bullied themselves and as a response to peer pressure to conform.

The need for acceptance, approval and belonging is vital during the teen years. Teens who feel isolated or rejected by their peers –or in their family – are more likely to engage in risky behaviours in order to fit in with a group. In such situations, peer pressure can impair good judgement and fuel risk-taking behaviour, drawing a teen away from the family and positive influences, luring him into dangerous activities.

Several studies have shown that 85 per cent of bullying episodes occur in the context of the peer group, and although a 1997 study found that 83 per cent of students indicate that watching bullying makes them feel uncomfortable, observations indicate that peers assume many roles in the bullying episode: joining in, cheering, passively watching and occasionally intervening. In fact, peers who form the audience for bullying may be critical in starting and supporting it.

Peers tend to give positive attention to the bully, rather than the victim. Their reinforcement of the bully may serve to maintain the bully's power over the victim and within the peer group. Two studies have found that boys are more likely than girls to be drawn into bullying episodes and become actively involved in the bullying. But studies have also shown that by intervening, peers have the capacity to stop and reduce the bullying. In playground observations, one study found that peers intervened in significantly more episodes than adults did (eleven per cent of episodes versus four per cent).

What you can do

▷ You can get to know your child's peer group and work out his role within it – is he a 'henchman' or a 'leader'? Do kids follow his example or is he quick to act in response to a more popular or powerful child's leadership? Use this as a talking point and explain that although peer relationships in childhood (and often into adulthood) are always very political and there is often a defined pecking order, it is wrong to lead others into trouble, it is wrong to follow the lead of someone who is causing trouble and it is always wrong to hurt others.

▷ Raising your child's self-respect and self-image can make him more resistant to peer pressure and less willing to follow a gang mentality.

▷ Teach your child that a big part of being an individual involves making decisions based on what is best for them. It can mean we take ownership and responsibility for what we do and how we think. Being an individual can still mean that your child is a valued part of a group, but he must have the confidence to believe in himself, and the self-respect to stand up for himself. Children with self-respect ultimately gain the respect of their peers, even if they are taunted a little along the way.

▷ Encourage your child to spend time with peers who like doing the same types of things and share common interest. It isn't essential to hang out with the soccer team thugs just because you are on the team, nor is it essential to choose the most popular clique and do whatever you feel you have to do to stay on their right side to belong. This may help to avoid a situation where children feel pressured into doing things they don't want to do. Remind your child that the 'in' crowd may not be as fun as it looks.

▷ Teach your child how to say 'no', and to have the strength to do so. Teach him to explain in a calm way why he doesn't want to be part of something, and impress on him the fact that sticking to beliefs does actually earn respect. Show this in the way you deal with your child. When you believe firmly in something, say no. Explain your views, listen to counter-arguments calmly, but show fortitude.

▷ Having the strength to say 'no' may be hard. However, it may also feel good to stick with what you believe in.

▷ Encourage your child not to place judgements on other people's choices. If he is tolerant of others, peers will be more likely to respect his choices.

▷ Encourage a positive relationship with your child and keep it up into the teenage years. When parent-teen interactions are characterised by warmth, kindness, consistency, respect and love, the relationship will flourish, as will the teen's self-esteem, mental health, spirituality and social skills.

▷ Being genuinely interested in your child's activities is crucial. This allows parents to know their children's friends and to monitor behaviour, which is essential to keep kids out of trouble. When misbehaviour does occur, parents who have involved their children in setting family rules and consequences can expect less flack from their children as they calmly enforce the rules. Parents who, together with their children, set firm boundaries and high expectations may find that their children's abilities to live up to those expectations grow.

▷ Encourage independent thought and expression. In this way, children can develop a healthy sense of self and an enhanced ability to resist peer pressure.

▷ Do not attack your child's friends. Remember that criticising his choice of friends is like a personal attack.

▷ Help your child to understand the difference between image (which is an expression of youth culture) and identity (who he or she is).

▷ Encourage your child's independence by supporting decision-making based on principles and not other people.

▷ Encourage reflective thinking by helping your child think about his or her actions in advance and discussing immediate and long-term consequences of unacceptable behaviour.

Personal hygiene

When can he cut his own fingernails?

There comes a point when all children begin to take care of their own personal hygiene, but it's undertaken in steps, and usually needs to be supervised (or they need to be reminded to do various things) into the teenage years. Many adolescents have poor personal hygiene habits and don't rate brushing their teeth, bathing, washing their face or cutting and cleaning finger and toenails until they have their first serious encounters with the opposite sex. This is normal and you may need to nag and cajole to ensure that even modest standards are met. You'd feel pretty silly cutting the fingernails of a strapping adolescent, but when does this transition happen. Do you just stop the regular Sunday evening snip and leave it to them? Like everything else, children need to be shown what to do and encouraged to do it regularly – that is, until it becomes a habit. Most kids can start cutting their own nails at around age ten or eleven (girls sometimes earlier; some boys later) with scissors or clippers.

When do boys begin shaving?

Most boys begin to get facial hair between the ages of fourteen and fifteen (although there are always some who start earlier and some who start later). Hair normally develops on the upper lip first, followed by cheeks and chin. It is during the final stage of puberty (between the ages of about fourteen and nineteen) that facial hair fully develops and it is at this stage that boys start shaving. While shaving does not increase facial hair, it does make it harder and more bristly. Many boys are self-conscious about 'peach fuzz' or unevenly distributed hair and begin shaving before they have full facial hair. In the early stages, once a week is sometimes enough, depending on the colour of your child's hair, how thick it is and how quickly it grows. Some youths do not shave every day until their mid-twenties, and some can get away with shaving every other day for the whole of their lives.

At what age should my child start to wear deodorant?
The issue of when to start using deodorant depends on your child's development and age. As children grow, their endocrine glands begin to release hormones. When your child is active and perspires, an odour is emitted through these glands and deodorant suddenly becomes a necessary item. If your child doesn't see the need yet for smelling good, take heart. Once she has developed an interest in the opposite sex, he or she will be more aware of personal cleanliness. Some children have strong body odours even before puberty. If your child hasn't noticed the smell herself, you can discreetly purchase some deodorant and put it with her other personal hygiene items; if she doesn't use it, you may have to be a little less tactful. Most kids start needing deodorant right from the beginning of puberty, so say from age nine onwards in girls and age ten in boys.

Do note, however, that deodorants (which kill the bacteria-causing odour) are quite different from antiperspirants, which use aluminium salts to block the sweat glands and prevent perspiration. The safety of these products has been in question for some time now, with notable concern about long-term damage to sweat glands, discolouration of the skin and links to breast cancer and Alzheimer's disease. The risk appears to be higher when they are used over long periods of time. Given that your children are only beginning their use and are probably in contact with quite enough potentially harmful chemicals as it is, antiperspirants should be given a miss. Deodorants (preferably natural ones) are a better alternative.

Is he too young for cologne or 'aftershave'?

If it makes him feel good, then no! Showing an interest in the way he comes across, looks and smells is a good sign. Just make sure he doesn't buy something cheap and nasty that will become the source of jokes! Boys can wear cologne at any age, but most show an interest somewhere around the ages of thirteen or fourteen and later in some kids.

Is it a good idea for a pre-teen to pluck her eyebrows?

If your daughter is concerned about her appearance and perhaps self-conscious about bushy, uneven or 'unfashionable' eyebrows (and yes, according to the teenage girls I know, there are definite fashions for eyebrow shapes!), then there is no reason why she shouldn't begin plucking her eyebrows or at least tidying them up. You might want to give her a hand the first time, perhaps taking her to a salon to get them waxed or professionally shaped so that she has a model to follow when she starts on her own. While it may seem an adult thing to do, girls are very conscious about what they look like, particularly as they enter puberty and the small matter of plucking eyebrows, which causes no damage or threat to health or well-being, should definitely be considered. Many girls have started by age twelve anyway. And eyebrow plucking is not the sole domain of girls; many boys like to tidy up between their brows or remove stray or elongated hairs as well. This should most definitely be encouraged, if it makes your son feel better about himself and it's always a good sign to see boys taking care of themselves and their appearance.

When can girls shave their legs?
Once again, there is no set time for this and you will be led by your daughter. If she has copious and/or very dark hairs on her legs, she may feel embarrassed in skirts or shorts. This is a personal decision. Some girls have very hairy legs at the age of nine or ten while others have little until their late teens and some have almost none at all. If she mentions she'd like to start, by all means allow it. Show her how to do it, making sure she uses nice even strokes to prevent cuts and grazes, and to use soap or an emollient to make it easier and gentler on her skin. You may want to supervise the first few times to be sure she's not doing herself damage!

Can I insist that he bathes or showers? And until what age?
Good hygiene is extremely important for many reasons and a good percentage of teenagers (particularly boys) have to be nudged and reminded to bathe regularly. A daily shower or bath should be a regular part of his hygiene programme, particularly when he starts to exhibit signs of body odour. The idea is to insist from an early age so that it becomes a daily habit and continue to encourage it until that is the reality. You'd obviously feel quite silly telling a strapping 17-year-old to shower every day, but if his hygiene is suspect, you may have to.

When should I encourage my child to change his or her own bedding?
Kids can change their own bedding from an early age (*see page 53*). Make it easy by putting a spare set of sheets in his or her room, or in a place easily accessible. Show your child how to work the washing machine and leave him to it. If your teen starts washing his or her sheets or does so periodically, there may be a reason and you don't need to know what it is! Anything from period stains to

nocturnal emissions can embarrass a child, so give him or her the wherewithal to deal with the matter privately.

Pocket money

How much pocket money should I give my child?

Tricky question. Many people have a set schedule of pocket money, for example, a pound a month for every year of age up to about eleven or twelve, and then a fixed figure that increases with age. You'll need to work out how much you can afford (there is no point in bankrupting yourself because your child demands an exorbitant sum) and also what he is expected to pay for with his pocket money, his genuine outgoings and how much his friends are given. The latter might not seem important and in no way am I suggesting that you match it, but if your child cannot do half of the things his friends do on weekends because he can't afford it, you may find that you are not giving him enough. Be realistic and ask him to spell out why he needs more if he requests a raise. I know some parents who give their 16-year-olds £20 per month, with the potential to earn more by doing extra jobs around the house or babysitting; others get a whopping £100 per month, but are expected to pay for their own clothing, fares, telephones and all social events. Work out a figure, be prepared to compromise to some extent, listen to your child's feelings and his perceived needs, and once you've set it, be prepared to review the sum every few months. Some parents move from pocket money to an 'allowance' (*see page 383*) once their children hit their early teens, which teaches them budgeting skills and money management.

Should my child earn her pocket money?

Some parents provide pocket money for nothing; others demand that they see a return for their 'investment'. I firmly believe that all children should have regular and routine jobs around the house that are their responsibility as part of a household. Paying children to do their bit does nothing to encourage responsibility or help them see that there are plenty of jobs in this world that must be undertaken without pay – looking after our houses, doing laundry and cooking, caring for pets or the garden, and even taking care of cars. All children do need to learn what these chores involve and understand that these will always need to be done as part of independent living. Some people argue that a certain basic amount should be given to a child simply because he or she is a valued member of the family, and that giving a little money shows appreciation and encourages independence. Bigger jobs and extra work around the house can be paid for on a pre-arranged scale (*see page 169*).

A British survey undertaken in 2006 by the Halifax Building Society found that six out of ten children have to earn their pocket money by doing jobs around the home such as tidying their bedroom, cleaning the house or doing the washing up. Linking pocket money to work also gives kids the right to opt out of the work and decline the money when jobs should be undertaken regardless, but it does provide a powerful tool for parents – in other words, no work, no money!

When should I stop giving pocket money?

Most parents stop giving pocket money when their children finish secondary school education; during further education, they rely on either a regular living allowance from family, grants or loans. Some parents stop as soon as their child has a regular income of his own

- from a part-time job, for example. As long as your child is earning enough to meet his basic needs and has some extra to show for his hard work, this seems reasonable. However, if your child has taken a part-time job to earn more money towards his education, a car or even just a more expensive lifestyle, it would be unfair to cut out pocket money completely, as it will rob him of the initiative to improve his lot and penalise him for making an effort to earn more money. Certainly you should not be paying pocket money to anyone in full-time employment or who has enough money from other sources (government maintenance grants, for example).

Do I have the right to control how pocket money is spent?

No. The idea of pocket money is that it is a child's money to spend as a child sees fit. Obviously, if your child is using his pocket money to download pornography or on illegal online gambling, you can threaten to withdraw funding unless some changes are made, but kids need to learn to balance money, to work within a budget, to make choices about purchases and, actually, to make some mistakes! You can *encourage* your child to save or donate some of his money; you can ask him to cover certain expenses such as fares or meals out when the sum is decided between you, but ultimately you must leave him to it.

Are all children entitled to pocket money?

It would be unfair not to give children some money or at least the opportunity to earn money. Even kids have financial needs – funding their social life, buying the odd treat or magazine, saving for larger purchases and having the wherewithal to join in with her peers. Think how powerless you would feel if you had no money in your pocket and no ability to keep up with your friends or make a purchase with your own money. Children feel no differently. Some parents expect their kids to fund their lifestyles from 'gift' money given by relatives and by taking a job. In some cases there may be a genuine inability to afford pocket money for kids, but for the most part this seems unfair and even cruel. As parents we do need to provide for our children's basic needs and having a normal social life is one of them. Unfortunately, this costs money!

What do I do if my child requests increasing amounts of money?

First of all, ask some questions. A child who is increasingly desperate for money might have a problem that requires constant funding - an addiction to gambling, drugs, alcohol or even shopping, for example. Your child might be the victim of extortion bullying, where he's paying over money to avoid being hurt or victimised in other ways. In all of these cases, you need to get to the bottom of the matter and work out why more money is required, and then address the root cause.

It may be that your child does not understand the value of money and is trying to keep up with the lifestyle and purchasing power of more affluent peers. In this case, he'll need to learn that he must live within a budget and make choices. As long as he has enough to do what most of his friends are doing in their spare time, it should be sufficient. But open a dialogue and ask him to explain his growing needs. It can be helpful for your child to keep a log for a few weeks, outlining all expenditure. You can then see where he might be blowing money unnecessarily and make some practical suggestions for working within his budget. You may find that he's started paying for things that were once your domain, of his own volition. If he's suddenly buying most of his clothes, he might be justified in asking for more, as long as the expenditure doesn't wildly exceed what you would have expected to pay. You may also wish to change from pocket money to an allowance (*see page 383*), which will provide your child with more money, but also encourage him to make better choices. He'll soon find, for example, that if he increases his collection of CDs he has no money for new clothes or meals out with friends. Sometimes this experience is the most valuable – again, teaching the difference between needs and wants.

Pornography

I've discovered that my child is looking at and downloading pornographic material from the internet. What should I do?
It is normal for children (boys more than girls) to show an interest in pornography as part of their growing sexuality and as a tool for its exploration. Boys between the ages of twelve and seventeen are among the biggest consumers of pornography. Children today live in a highly sexualised world, and have access to more soft-core and graphic hard-core pornography because of its easy access and presence on the internet.

Pornography should not be encouraged. You may turn a blind eye to the odd naughty magazine while making clear your family's stance on the subject (*see below*). But if it becomes a driving force in your child's life and there are signs that he is viewing completely inappropriate hard-core material rather than looking at the odd naked body, you should be worried; pornography may seriously affect his sexual maturation.

Isn't it just naked bodies?
These days, what children are viewing is not just naked ladies or pictures of healthy, normal sex. They are seeing perversions in many cases, and you need to consider what this is teaching him

about sex, women and relationships. If you allow porn to be the principal sexual educator of your son, he will believe that girls and women (or men) want and enjoy being sexually abused, dominated and humiliated. Pornography is devoid of tenderness, caring or loving in its images.

Is there an ethical dimension?

There are also the ethical issues of the women and men involved in the porn industry who are exploited physically and emotionally, and harmed by their activities. As parents we have a responsibility to teach our children to consider others and societal issues, and pornography is one such issue.

Make it clear that you can install a filter to prevent him from viewing these sites, or you can trust your child by making it clear that under no circumstances will you allow pornography to be downloaded or viewed via the internet, TV or other options. Explain also that he could find himself in serious trouble if he unwittingly downloads or views child pornography, which is illegal and the centre of a highly orchestrated anti-pornography lobby and policing.

I'm worried that my child is becoming addicted to internet porn?

Unfortunately, internet pornography is the fast track to sex addiction. If your child has had regular access via the internet, you need to work out why his use hasn't been suitably policed and supervised.

Many kids who are addicted to sex are embarrassed and ashamed, so coming down like a ton of bricks is not likely to encourage your child to own up, and share the extent of his problem. Showing compassion and understanding of his situation, and his sexual needs and urges, is a much more positive way forward.

Most addicts, regardless of age and the type of addiction, will initially deny their problem. They may even shift the blame and become verbally aggressive. Your goal is to explain your family's values on this issue, and your concern for his emotional health and his approach to sex and relationships, without making him feel like a pervert. Tell him that you do not want pornography in your house in any shape or form. If he's unable to resist, you may need to consider counselling or even psychosexual therapy.

All addictions are dangerous because they take over our children's lives. Try to fill his time with healthy activities, and encourage normal opposite-sex friendships as much as you can. Put a filter on your computer and block porn through your TV with a password. Continue to reinforce your family values, and help him to understand why it is wrong, while showing understanding. The sooner you nip it in the bud, the better your child's chances of overcoming it successfully.

Privacy

At what age should I give my child more privacy?
Privacy is something that is very much child-led. Children do not begin to understand issues of privacy until they are five or six, although you will always find that there are times when your child wants to be alone at a younger age. Between the ages of ten and twelve, many kids begin to establish their independence – they close bedroom doors, seek privacy for telephone conversations, time with friends, and time alone. And because all children have a right to some privacy, you should avoid challenging this behaviour unless you have reason to suspect that your child is engaged in dangerous or destructive activities. However, you should continually establish clear rules about acceptable activities.

Does my child have the right to deny me access to her room?

A child's room is her private domain and represents a personal sanctuary where she can explore her growing independence and need for privacy. Obviously, you will need to enter to check that she is OK, and that she isn't engaging in dangerous or risky behaviours; you'll also have to ensure that her room is clean and safe. Many parents agree that the room will not be entered unless they knock first, or it needs to be cleaned (or clean bedding or clothing dropped off). On occasions when you do enter her room, try to avoid making judgements about her taste, messiness or personal belongings that she leaves laying about. Some kids deliberately leave clues when they are in trouble, so on some occasions you will have to balance biting your lip and leaving her to it with recognising the signs that your child is seeking attention.

If I'm worried about her, should I check her diary, phone or internet messages?

This represents a serious breach of privacy and trust, and should be avoided unless you have serious grounds for concern. And even then, you should only spot-check, rather than invading everything she holds private. The reality is that most children have some secrets from their parents, and a need to explore issues, feelings and thoughts surrounding their growing independence, burgeoning sexuality, friendships and relationships, and even belief systems. In a good relationship you will likely know much of what is going on in your child's head and life, but you will never know it all. Invading privacy because you feel you need complete control and knowledge will backfire, and you may end up making a fuss about something that your child really needs to deal with herself.

So, in a nutshell, unless you are very worried, give her freedom and trust.

If I find something unacceptable, should I admit to having broken privacy rules?

Probably not, because your child will never trust you again and rather than coming to you with problems or concerns, she will become more secretive. She may even become more rebellious because she feels that she is being watched, and is therefore powerless in her own environment. If you discover evidence of drug-taking, early sexual experimentation, friendships of which you do not particularly approve, smoking, alcohol or even lies she might have told you about her activities, it's best to use these as a platform for discussion without admitting your offence. If, however, you find something very serious to which your child will not admit, you can simply say that you have evidence, without giving the game away.

Should my daughter and her boyfriend be allowed to spend time behind closed doors? If so, from what age?

This is a difficult question, because it involves balancing your child's right to privacy, freedom and space, with her need for limits and boundaries. Unless they are planning to have sex in her bedroom, there is no real reason why she needs to be there alone with her boyfriend with the door closed. Not only is she unlikely to be old enough for this (unless she's in her late teens and in a secure, loving relationship), but it also puts forward the idea that you condone sex and sexual experimentation and are prepared to turn a blind eye. And although it may well be her request that she is allowed space behind closed doors, the fact is that she may find herself in a compromised position. Rules not only protect kids and give them boundaries, but also allow them to bow out of difficult situations by using them as excuses to friends.

A good compromise is to allow them to socialise in any room of your house, with the exception of her bedroom. Obviously, show some respect and don't go barrelling in when they are spending time together, regardless of the room, but keep an ear open in the event that your child needs or wants support. Sometimes it is necessary to use a bedroom – working on a computer, perhaps, or doing homework together – but it is a good idea to insist on an open-door policy. This rule is not based on your mistrust of her moral character, or a denial of her sexuality or need for privacy with her boyfriend. It's based upon the understanding that when she is in her room with her door closed, that's her way of telling you that she needs privacy for certain reasons.

It's tricky when your kids hit their older teens and may well be in a responsible sexual relationship of which you are aware. You'll need then to assess whether you are prepared to encourage or indeed allow your children to have sex under your roof (*see page 398*).

At what age can children be unsupervised in their own rooms or with friends?

There is nothing wrong with kids shutting the door because they want to be alone, or to have some privacy with a friend or group of friends. From the age of ten upwards this is a common adolescent desire and even need, and it should be respected – as long as your child is aware of the household rules and is committed to following them. You can employ trust from this age – checking regularly, of course, by knocking or calling out something like 'you OK in there?' or 'do you need anything?' – unless you have grounds to believe that your household rules have been flouted.

Puberty

When will my child enter puberty?

The hormonal changes of puberty begin as early as eight years old. But the physical changes aren't evident until several years later. In modern Western societies, puberty usually starts between eleven and twelve years old for girls, and between twelve and thirteen for boys. About 95 per cent of all girls will start somewhere between eight and a half and thirteen, and boys a year or more later, between nine and a half and fifteen.

What are the first signs of puberty

The first clear sign of puberty for girls is the beginnings of breast development, around the age of twelve. The first mark of puberty in boys is the start of testes growth around the age of thirteen, and penis growth around fourteen.

When will his voice change?

This process is different for all boys; however, most boys will notice their voices changing by the age of fifteen.

When will my child get pubic hair?

In boys, the growth of pubic hair over the penis and testicles is a normal part of puberty, and occurs over several years. Although all children are different, pubic hair usually begins to develop several months after the testicles begin to grow. The timing and amount of this hair growth is determined by genetic traits inherited from parents.

In girls, pubic hair develops about six months after breast development begins (*see below*) although in some girls, pubic hair is the first sign of puberty. Over the next few years, there will be a progressive increase in development of pubic hair and the external genitalia, leading to your daughter's first period, which usually occurs about two years after puberty begins and coincides with their fastest growth spurts.

My daughter is fifteen and hasn't exhibited any real signs of puberty. Is there a problem?

Puberty is considered late or delayed if it has not begun prior to the age of thirteen years for girls and fourteen years for boys. Recent studies have shown that puberty is occurring at an increasingly earlier age. It's possible that you've missed some of the early signs, such as her moods changing and her breasts beginning to grow. If there is genuinely nothing, it's worth paying a visit to your doctor.

When will my daughter's breasts start to develop?

The development of your daughter's breasts may be the first sign that you notice as she enters puberty. This begins with breast budding or the formation of small lumps or nodules under one or both nipples. These lumps may be tender and they may be different sizes at first. Over the next few years, breast size will continue to increase. At the end of puberty, your daughter's breasts will be adult size.

When does my son's penis reach adult size?

After your son's testicles begin to enlarge, and hair grows around them in the early stages of puberty, your son's penis will start to enlarge – first in length, and later in thickness. Although there is obviously variation between different individuals, your son's final penis size is reached four to six years after his testicles first started to enlarge – so roughly this length of time from the beginning of puberty. In many cases, it will be two years after your son has reached his adult height that his penis is fully sized.

The skin on my son's scrotum is becoming darker. Is this normal?

Yes, it is normal for skin over the scrotum to get darker as your son changes from boy to adult, and darkening of this skin is actually one of the first steps of puberty. It is noted to occur at the same time that skin over the testicles changes from a smooth appearance to a more rough appearance (called stippling). Also at this time, the testicles themselves will begin to enlarge.

At what age do boys get wet dreams?

Wet dreams (also called nocturnal emissions) normally begin about six months into puberty (so about six months after his testes have started to enlarge). The average age is fourteen.

Wet dreams are normal, and they are believed to occur when the body is not getting release from the hormonal build-up of the teen years or sudden 'dry spells' in sexually active individuals. Girls do get wet dreams, but they are far more common and much messier in boys! Your child may be embarrassed by wet dreams. You can keep a spare set of sheets in his room from the early teenaged years, and show him how to use the washing machine (*see page 279*) to help him to save face, but it's better to adopt a healthy approach, making sure that your child knows in advance that they are likely to occur, and that there is nothing abnormal or unhealthy. If you see the evidence, there is no need to say a word.

When will my child get hair under his arms?

Boys tend to get hair under their arms at the same time that they have their first ejaculations, their pubic hair is beginning to take on adult characteristics (becoming curlier, denser and coarser), and their facial hair is increasing on their chin and their upper lips. This can occur any time between the ages of eleven to seventeen, but on average, between fourteen and fifteen years old.

The average age that girls begin to get hair under their arms is twelve, but it can occur sooner or later than this. It normally coincides with a first period. Many girls wish to begin shaving their underarms at this point, and as long as she is given advice on undertaking this safely, it is acceptable.

See also Menstruation, *page 317.*

My daughter is showing signs of breast enlargement and pubic hair and she is only eight. Is this normal?

Sexual development before the age of eight in girls, and age of ten in boys is known as precocious puberty. Occasionally a child begins to develop sexually much earlier. This is more common in girls than boys.

Precocious puberty often begins before age eight in girls, triggering the development of breasts and hair under the arms and in the genital region. The onset of ovulation and menstruation also may occur. In boys, the condition triggers the development of a large penis and testicles, with spontaneous erections and the production of sperm. Hair grows on the face, under arms and in the pubic area, and acne may become a problem.

Are there problems with early puberty?

While the early onset of puberty may seem fairly benign, in fact it can cause problems when hormones trigger changes in the growth pattern, essentially halting growth before your child has reached normal adult height. Girls may never grow above 152 cm (5 ft) and boys often stop growing by about 157 cm (5 ft 2 in).

The abnormal growth patterns are not the only problem, however. Children with this condition look noticeably different from their peers, and may feel socially isolated and rejected by their friends. Adults may expect these children to act more maturely simply because they look so much older.

If your daughter is experiencing precocious puberty, it's worth seeing your doctor, who may be able to provide medication to slow down the process so that it is more in line with normal puberty, or alternatively, reassure you that the changes you are seeing are, in fact, normal.

Do all children get acne in puberty?

See Skin, *page 430.*

My placid daughter has turned into an irritable, emotional wreck since she started puberty. Is this normal?

Puberty does not only mark a period of intense physical growth and change; it also involves many, many emotional changes. Your child's mood will undoubtedly be affected; she may be tearful, irritable and moody as a result of the influence of the hormone oestrogen in her body; boys respond to the influx of the hormone testosterone. It is the abrupt and rapid release of these hormones that brings about extremes in emotion and mood. Fortunately, it's a temporary imbalance and will settle down, but it can be helpful to reassure your daughter that she is not going mad or losing control of her emotions, but that these swings are entirely normal.

Pubertal moodiness can occur up to a couple of years before the physical changes start, which can be worrying for parents (and kids), who don't realise what is happening.

Apart from this there are numerous other emotional changes. For example, your child will be pulling away from her family to some extent and relying more on peers in the process of becoming independent. Although this is normal and almost always child-led, it can be frightening and make some children feel slightly insecure, as they move outside the safety of the family unit for the first time.

It's worth noting that the physical changes of puberty – and dealing with the emotional aspects of growing into adulthood and independence – can cause your child to become extremely and suddenly tired. She may be on a high one moment, with boundless energy, and fast asleep on the sofa the next. This, too, is normal.

Relationships

When can my daughter start to have boyfriends?
Some girls are incredibly precocious on the relationship front, and form close relationships with boys in primary school. These attachments are as real and important to them as attachments will be later on in life, and it's important that you respect them and your daughter's feelings.

During the past several decades, the age at which young people start to date has dropped. Surveys show that girls are, on average, between fourteen and sixteen, and boys between fifteen and sixteen. In early adolescence, kids tend to date for fun and recreation; they may also see it as a way to upgrade their social standing. Young people at this stage of development are more self-involved when it comes to dating, rather than being interested in building a relationship with another person.

First love, however, is a different story. Normally based on attraction rather than self-interest, it tends to occur at different ages (depending on when your child starts mixing regularly with the other sex, and when her friends begin to form relationships within the group), but it is normal and usual for a first proper boyfriend to make himself evident between the ages of twelve and sixteen in girls.

The worrying thing for many parents is that apparent love and attraction suggest that sex is on the cards, and if you have a pre- or early adolescent in the throes of her first serious love affair, you are right to be worried. It is common for many children to have sex with their first real 'loves' – partly because they think it is expected, partly because they believe that the rush of emotions and attraction they feel are the signposts of a long-term relationship and partly because they are pressured to 'consummate' the relationship. It is, therefore, very important that you keep up a regular dialogue with your daughter and impress upon her that you realise the seriousness of her feelings, but that sex is something that must come with maturity. Although she'll hesitate to believe it when she's in love, you must explain that this boyfriend is one of many future boyfriends and she would put herself in a compromised position in terms of both physical and emotional health if she was to be involved sexually with all of them (*see* Sex, *page 414*).

Wise parents should support their kids through first (second and third) relationships with the fewest wounds and least hurt. The feelings of adolescents are as changeable as their moods. So first love usually goes very soon after it comes. The way you view your children's relationships is something they will hold on to throughout their lives, so if you want a good relationship well into adulthood, and want to have the ability to steer your child through difficulties as well as pleasures and joys, you will need to provide support and keep your opinions to yourself.

At what age should I allow my son or daughter to sleep with their boyfriend or girlfriend in our house?

The answer to this question must be based on your own morals, values and household rules, and before making any decisions, either way, you must consider them carefully. While times have certainly changed in terms of society's tolerance, views and approach to teenaged and pre-marital sex, this has coincided with a huge increase in sexually transmitted disease (*see page 424*), pregnancies (*see page 418*) and abortions (*see page 23*).

There is the issue of respect within the family home. Some parents might find it disrespectful for their children to openly flaunt sexual relationships. Alternatively, some parents believe that their children are being open about what's going on, and would prefer that sex took place under their own roof than in the backseat of a car or behind a bush in the park. Personally, I am not sure I see the difference. If you don't want to encourage early sexual encounters in your child, then don't make it easy. Part of the fun of being a highly sexed adolescent is, of course, the stolen moments, the healthy slipping around for a kiss and a grope – all a part of normal, healthy sexual development, which becomes more intense and goes further as your child gets older, and ready for the real thing. Remove the obstacles, and the natural progression and the fun that accompanies it are also removed. You may set your child up for something he is simply not ready for.

So leave the house off-limits, and explain very clearly why.

If I don't approve of the relationship, should I get involved?
There are many reasons why you should not get involved, and these are the same reasons why we should not forbid or discourage our children's friendships or friends (*see page 229*). Disapproval in a child's eyes is viewed as a personal attack, and it can have the effect of driving them into the clutches of someone who they may well realise is not right for them. Unless you have serious grounds to be concerned about your child's safety (perhaps she is being seriously

pressured to have sex or engage in drugs, and she is out of her depth, or she is being abused or treated very badly). In this case, you are right to intervene. Don't go in with all guns blazing against her partner; instead, try to get her talking about how women or men should be treated within a relationship; how they think a healthy relationship should manifest itself; and, how she thinks her current relationship makes her feel about herself. Kids with low self-esteem or an intense desire to have any relationship will put up with more than others, so it is your job to reassure them of their own worth and to make clear what a healthy relationship entails. Ultimately, you can only hope they will make the right decision; even if it means making a few mistakes along the way.

What happens if my daughter's boyfriend doesn't seem to treat her well?

Once again, take the time to talk to your child without appearing to criticise her boyfriend (see page 399), ensuring that she knows her own worth and has the strength to resist bad behaviour and to end things when they are not right for her. Only she can do this, though. If you become involved too heavily, you may well make them closer (nothing unites a couple more than a common adversary). She also needs to learn how to judge a poor relationship and its impact on her emotional health and her feelings; there is a process here called 'growing up' and although it's hard to witness, you can do little more than provide support, love and understanding, and to help your child find the emotional tools to stand up for herself and end things – without actually appearing to do so!

At what age can my daughter legally sleep with her boyfriend?

Your daughter must be sixteen and so must her boyfriend.

At what age can my daughter stay overnight with her boyfriend?

Your daughter may be invited by his family to stay after a celebration, or to go on holiday with them. You'll need to establish that his family has the same moral code as you do, and that they do not plan to encourage under-aged or teenaged sex by allowing them to sleep together. If separate rooms are on the cards, and they will be supervised, then there is no reason to decline, but make your views known to her boyfriend's family, and explain them to your daughter. Many young girls find themselves having sex before they are ready because they are pushed into situations that provide temptation or in which it is hard to decline. You may be aware that your child is already having sex with her boyfriend, but setting up or allowing situations to make it very easy is quite different to accepting the reality and providing all the guidance you can. Many young girls engage in sex with their first real love, not really understanding that this is often a short-lived prospect. They may feel ashamed and guilty when the relationship does end. It's important that we make it clear to our children that sex should be saved for as long as possible, and only once the relationship is serious and long-term. This also protects the self-respect of both partners. You want your child's first experience to be positive (*see page 414*), not forced.

Religion

Until what age do I have the right to ensure that my child is properly schooled in our religious beliefs?

In families where religion is important, formal and informal 'schooling' tends to take place from a very early age, and is very much a part of family life. There is no reason why this can't continue into adulthood. There may come a time when your child resists your religious beliefs, or eschews her own religion because it may be different to that of her friends; it may contradict things that she believes in; she may feel that it takes up too much of her time and be too great a commitment. She may suddenly become embarrassed by obvious signs of her religious leanings, such as wearing a burka, a cross or covering her head.

Adolescence is a time of great change and many religious parents are shocked to find that religion does not play such an important part of their children's lives, or that the schooling with which they have been brought up has been 'dumped' in favour of something (or perhaps nothing) else. First of all, don't panic. Many kids become rebellious at this age and say and do things simply to shock their parents. They also experiment with different beliefs, as a part of understanding themselves, their options and the reality of religious beliefs. Ultimately, the vast majority of children return to their parental code of behaviour and their beliefs once they've passed the experimental age (around seventeen or eighteen); parents may be disappointed that their children never embrace religion to the same extent as they do, but it's worth remembering that their faith will always be there and may grow stronger and be a more important part of their world when they move into adulthood.

At what age can my child decide her own religion?

If a young person is old enough and responsible enough to make decisions for themselves, then decisions about religion should be part of that responsibility. Parents decide what religion their child should be brought up with, but once the child reaches a certain age he or she is competent enough to decide what religion he or she wants to follow. This normally takes place at fifteen years old, but depends on the maturity and understanding of your child. This doesn't mean that you have to give up on your child; it may be a short-term commitment to another faith, and she may return to the fold at a later date; it may just be adolescent experimentation, perhaps because she wants to be more like her peers. She may, however, have found something that suits her beliefs and lifestyle more than the religion with which she was brought up, and this must be respected. The more respect you show for her choices, the more respect she will show for you.

At what age can my child decide to confirm her faith, regardless of my beliefs?
Most religions allow children to be confirmed in a particular faith at about thirteen or fourteen years of age, when they are old enough to understand all of the elements and beliefs, and are old enough to commit to the challenges of living accordingly. While most faiths encourage children from birth, most will not expect nor allow children to confirm their faith until they are old enough to do so. It is your child's personal decision, regardless of what you believe in. You can explain your reservations about committing to a particular religion, and you can expound your own beliefs, but you must respect her choice.

School

When is my child old enough to leave school?
At present in the UK, the school leaving age is sixteen; to be precise, all children of compulsory school age (aged five to sixteen), both those enrolled in school and those home-educated, must remain in education until the last Friday in June in the school year that they reach the age of sixteen.

What changes are afoot?

The government has confirmed that the school-leaving age will be raised to eighteen years, and that this will take effect in 2015. This means that children starting secondary school in September 2008 may be the first cohort who have a legal duty to stay in education until eighteen.

Pupils will not have to stay in the classroom or continue with academic lessons past sixteen but they will have to continue to receive government-approved training for at least one day a week, even if they choose to work. At present, the new leaving age only affects English schools; the Isle of Man has already said it will not follow suit, and Scotland, Wales and Northern Ireland have yet to confirm a similar increase.

Can I take my child out of school for holidays or family events during term time?

Under current regulations schools have discretion to grant leave of absence for purposes of family holidays in term time. They can approve up to a maximum of ten days in any one school year and, beyond that, can agree more than ten days if the circumstances are truly exceptional.

Parents are not entitled to remove children from school for holidays as a right. Leave of absence must be applied for and the decision to authorise absence for holidays rests with the school.

My son has been excluded from school for smoking. What are our rights?

Exclusion means excluding a child from a maintained (state) school on disciplinary grounds. Only the head teacher has the power to exclude a pupil from school.

There are two types of exclusion:

▷ Fixed period exclusion is for a short period and includes lunchtime exclusions. The pupil must return after the exclusion period has expired. In cases of more than a day's exclusion, work should be set and marked. The law allows head teachers to exclude a pupil for up to 45 school days in any school year.

▷ Permanent exclusion is also known as expulsion. The pupil cannot return to the school unless reinstated by the governing body or by an appeal panel. If a pupil is permanently excluded from school, his local authority (LA) has a duty to provide him with suitable education. This may be provided in another school, in a Pupil Referral Unit or by way of home tuition.

If your child is excluded you have the right to make representations to the school's governing body (an appeal). If the governing body upholds your child's permanent exclusion, you have the right to appeal to an Independent Appeal Panel.

Where can we get help?

For help, visit the Advisory Centre for Education (ACE), which provides an information pack about school exclusion and operates an Exclusions Helpline on 020 7704 9822.

Independent schools operate differently and your child can be excluded for breaching any of the school rules. Your child's school will be able to provide you with details of its code of practice and any appeal process available to you.

Can I educate my child at home instead of sending her to school?

The law allows parents to home-educate their children if they fulfil certain conditions. Bear in mind, however, that at school children are taught by trained professionals, and that it is important for children to learn how to interact with others. Parents will find the following guidelines useful when considering educating their children at home:

1. Parents must ensure that their child receives an efficient full-time education, suitable to his or her age, ability and aptitude and to any special educational needs the child may have, either by regular attendance at school or otherwise.

2. Although parents are not legally required to inform their Local Authority (LA) when they decide to home-educate their children, it is helpful to do so. But parents should formally notify the school where their child is registered that they intend to educate their child at home. It is also advisable that parents inform their LA of any significant changes in circumstance relevant to the effective education of their child, e.g. a change of address.

3. The LA will need to satisfy itself that a child is receiving suitable education at home, and will probably ask to visit the family home to talk to the parent and child, and to look at examples of work. The LA will need to be satisfied that the parent is willing and able to provide a suitable education. At the initial meeting the nature and frequency of future contact should be agreed.

4. LAs have no automatic right of access to the parents' home. Parents may wish to offer an alternative way of demonstrating that they are providing suitable education, for example through showing examples of work and meeting at another venue.

5. Where it appears to an LA that a child of compulsory school age is not receiving efficient or suitable full-time education, either by regular attendance at school or otherwise, the LA are under a duty to serve notice on the parent requiring them to satisfy the authority that their child is receiving suitable education 'otherwise than at school'. If the parents' reply is unsatisfactory, or if they fail to reply, the LA may issue a School Attendance Order (SAO).

6. The National Curriculum tests and assessment arrangements are developed and administered by the Qualifications and Curriculum Authority (QCA), on behalf of the Secretary of State. Information to support these arrangements is provided both electronically and in hard copy through the QCA's website at http://www.qca.org.uk and their publications on 01787 884 444.

Should my daughter be allowed to choose her next school when she moves on after primary school or into a sixth form college?

If your child genuinely has a choice (and not all children do, unfortunately), it is a good idea to allow her to have a say. You may have different criteria than your child; you will probably want a school that has a good discipline and anti-bullying record, good results at key stages, effective teaching, a good selection of subjects on offer, good pastoral care, proximity and a strong ethos of parental involvement. Your daughter, however, might be more interested in what sports or other activities are on offer and where her friends are going. The latter can be very important to many kids, and it's important to respect this. The transition between schools can be very difficult, and having a network (even small) of familiar faces can make this considerably easier. You may have found the best school around, but if she will know no-one and believes that she is not going to like it, you may be in for trouble. Try to shortlist a few schools that both of you like, and discuss the merits of each, so that she is feeling positive. If there ends up being little choice, at least she will have had a say at the outset and can see the good points.

How can I ensure that my child attends school and until what age am I legally responsible for making sure that my child attends?

You are legally responsible to ensure your child attends school until school-leaving age (presently sixteen, see above, increasing to eighteen shortly), and if she plays truant you can be fined or even face a prison term. In the UK, the government takes parental responsibility for children's school attendance very seriously.

Although there is no legal requirement for schools to notify parents of absence, you can certainly request this, and most good schools do, if they are not notified in advance of registration that a child will be absent. The legal threat of having a parent imprisoned should be enough motivation for children to attend. What's more, children do need to be brought up to understand the importance of education, whether they appear to value it or not. And it is illegal for your child to miss school, no matter what her feelings.

What are my rights with my child's school regarding behaviour?

When your child attends school you are effectively entering into a contract with that school with regard to codes of behaviour and rules, and in the marking and grading schemes it employs. If your child behaves badly, he will be penalised or punished according to a set procedure. You may be worried that other children in your child's class or year, or at the school in general, exhibit poor or disruptive behaviour, which affects the school climate and your child's ability to learn. In this case, you have every right to an explanation of its policy and methods of dealing with recalcitrant kids – speaking first to the school head and then the board of governors if necessary. You may find that a change of schools is the only option if you get nowhere.

What are my rights with my child's school regarding grades?

If your child's grades are not as you would have hoped, or overall the school's grades are poor, you should speak to your child's teacher/s to work out if there is a problem with your child's work or ability, and find out how this can best be addressed. You may discover that your child has a personality clash with a teacher. Taking his work to an independent teacher will help you to see if the marks are justified. The good news is that by year eleven in the UK, a good proportion of your child's work will be marked by an independent examining body. You may find your child needs some extra tuition in various subjects to lift his grades. If the school's grades are poor overall, you are entitled to ask questions of the teachers, head and board of governors, and should get a good overview of the system as part of a detailed response.

Can I be involved in helping my child to choose GCSE or A level courses?

All kids need guidance, particularly in this rather absurd system where the choices they make when they are fifteen or sixteen years old can actually affect their future career choices. GCSE courses are fairly standard, with a few opportunities for course selection. However, by AS and A level, most kids take only a handful of subjects and may find that the choices they have made will affect their choice of university, college or training/apprenticeship scheme. For this reason it is a good idea to speak to your child's individual subject teachers – and representatives from the place of learning or training that your child wishes to go on to, to ensure that all prerequisites are covered.

It is, however, one of the first chances your child has to make decisions towards his future. He should be given scope to make decisions based on what he enjoys and what he is good at, which will probably define the choices he makes later on in terms of a career. There is absolutely no point in pushing a child in a direction that will prove useless for his career plans, make him bored or unhappy, or cause him to struggle. You can offer suggestions – for example, keeping up English or a foreign language, which will be useful for most careers, or carrying on with something at which he excels but doesn't particularly love with a view that he may enjoy it much more when the course broadens at further education stage.

Either way, the choice must be his.

Can I insist that my child takes part in extracurricular activities at school?

You certainly can't insist that your child does anything at school, because once he's through those hallowed doors he probably has the right to do whatever he pleases. Some schools encourage kids to do at least one club or organised sport; some have very little on offer; others leave it entirely to the children. If you are struggling to get your child to be more physically active, or to do something more than hang around the streets with his friends, or sit in front of a computer, you can give a bit of an ultimatum, but with choices. For example you might say 'you really need to do at least eight hours of exercise a week. You can do some of this at school after hours, or we can sign up for the local gym or fitness programme. Which do you choose?' Let him choose from school activities, community service, local clubs or organisations. Kids will often choose school activities because they are usually free, and because their friends may be involved. Many schools now offer excellent programmes, such as the Duke of Edinburgh Award scheme, cadets, scouts, musical activities such as bands, orchestras, choirs, – all of which can round out your child's education, provide him with a few more interests and, of course, keep him off the street!

Self-harm

I've noticed little cuts on my daughter's wrists. She claims they are just scratches, but they seem quite deep. Could she be harming herself?

Self-harm is increasingly common in teenagers, with three harming themselves every *hour* in the UK. It's most common between the ages of thirteen and nineteen; and studies show that one in ten kids have harmed themselves by the age of sixteen. Apart from 'accidents', it's the second highest cause of hospital 'emergency' admissions. Four times as many girls as boys harm themselves.

Cutting is a very common form but, in fact, it can take many guises and include virtually anything that causes detriment or damage to health, such as cutting, burning, punching, head banging, hair pulling (trichotillomania), poisoning to cause discomfort or damage, insertion of foreign objects, excessive nail biting, scratching, bone breaking, gnawing at flesh, picking wounds, medication abuse, alcohol abuse, illegal drug use, starvation, binge-eating, vomiting. The problem is that many of these are considered to be socially acceptable, and therefore not diagnosed or viewed as anything more sinister than 'teenage fun'. For example, many kids will dabble with drugs and binge drink on occasion, but their motives are not necessarily to self-harm. Others do it repeatedly and push the boundaries in order to deliberately hurt themselves. A better term would, actually, be 'self-injury'.

Any unusual cuts on your daughter's body should be investigated; cutting is by far the most common form of self-harm in girls, and in many cases its obviousness is a cry for help.

Why do so many teenagers injure themselves through cutting? Is my child mentally ill?

Unfortunately, 'cutting' and other forms of self-injury are not only common but, in some quarters, viewed as being 'normal'. Certainly many teens admit they do it, and because it has been idealised and promoted to some extent in music, websites and films (even books), many kids are encouraged to try it. Like other 'risky' behaviour, it gives a buzz when endorphins kick in as a result of pain and the action of healing, and kids often become addicted. In some cases, kids actually compete to do the most 'damage' without being caught. In other cases, it is a solo activity.

Most people harm themselves as a method of relieving intense emotion, such as anger, low-self esteem (punishing themselves for being 'useless'), dissociation (distracting themselves from stress or something traumatic in their lives by drowning it out through pain), and control issues (it is one thing that a child feels she can control).

My son says he'll stop harming himself. Should I believe him or get help?

In most cases, when a teen has found a way of coping, he or she becomes dependent upon it – even if it did begin as a bit of a laugh, or as a 'trial' after seeing someone else do it. Once again, it is the adrenaline rush that accompanies pain that becomes addictive, as well as the huge release that follows.

Unfortunately, evidence suggests that kids who stop one form of self-injury resort to another in its place. These activities are often very secretive, and parents may be the last to know what's going on. It's important that you speak in confidence to your child's GP and ask for a referral to a specialist who can help him to deal with the problem.

Is it really dangerous or is there any likelihood that he will just outgrow it?

Self-harm of any description is potentially dangerous, simply because it is undertaken to damage the body in some way. Over time, this can have a dramatic impact. For example, when a child cuts over a long period of time, there is a danger of losing lots of blood, and depleting your child's system. The body's ability to clot blood may be reduced and his immune system can be weakened. What's more, there is a serious risk of infection, as implements used in cutting are not always very sterile. Scarring causing disfigurement can also affect self-esteem and emotional health both now and in later life. Most worryingly, however, a child who self-harms is 100 times more likely to commit suicide (accidental or not). There is always a risk of death when kids harm themselves because they may inadvertently cut an artery, for example, or cause serious infection, start a fire when burning, or suffer from liver damage/failure through overuse of drugs and/or alcohol.

Is there anything my daughter can do in place of self-harming? What can I suggest?

Some experts recommend switching to vigorous or even high-risk sporting activities (*see page 156*), which provide the adrenaline surge and buzz, and also allow them to feel that they are in control of their destiny. In the short term, it is suggested that instead of cutting/burning/pulling out hair, etc., that kids hold a handful of ice cubes and try to crush them manually, as it has the same pain/buzz effect without endangering health. Wearing an elastic band loosely on the wrist and snapping it can also be effective. Studies show that much harming is done on the spur of the moment, so encouraging your daughter to wait five minutes, do some relaxing breathing, go for a walk, take a shower, or have a cup of tea, might help keep her stable until the urge passes.

Sex

When do kids start to have sex?

The age varies tremendously. Research funded by the Economic
and Social Research Council shows British people – particularly
women – have changed their sexual behaviour over the past
50 years. The survey found that the age of first sexual experience is
getting younger.

By the end of the twentieth century 25 per cent of teenage girls
had experienced underage sex. A 2006 BBC Radio One poll found
that of the sixteen to twenty-four year-olds surveyed, 30 per cent
had lost their virginity before age of consent (sixteen), four per cent
before fourteen, while four per cent had not lost their virginity by
the age of twenty-five.

So your child may start thinking about having sex between the
ages of fourteen and sixteen and maybe even earlier.

When is the best time for my child to learn about the 'facts of life'?

The best way for parents to deal with their child's sex education is
to bring up the subject in a very basic way before the onset of
puberty (see page 392), or as soon as your child begins to ask
questions, if this is sooner. While the gory details do not need to be
discussed – particularly with an eight-year-old, for example – it's
important to be honest and to provide age-appropriate information
for your child. Make the conversation light-hearted and non-
judgmental, so that your child will feel that she can talk to you
about sexual matters. Some boys feel more comfortable talking to a
man – their dad, an uncle or even an older sibling to whom they are
close – and this is OK, too. From here, keep the subject rolling
rather than waiting to give your child one 'big talk', which can be

embarrassing for all and can make your child feel on the spot and uncomfortable enough never to broach the subject again!

Ask about how your children's friends view the subject, and try to get to grips with how much she has learned from her peers or in school – and how much of this information might be inaccurate or put forward the idea that sex is a commodity or a natural part of early adolescence rather than a part of a loving, serious relationship. And this is the most important part of any discussion you have about sex, with a child of any and every age. It needs to be made clear from the outset that sex is something that you mutually share (both partners are completely willing) with someone you love deeply, with whom you are in a serious relationship, and whom you trust. Sex is intimate and unearths a whole new set of emotions and feelings, all of which should be positive. Make it clear that if your child has any doubts or reservations, any guilt or distrust, or feels any pressure, she should decline.

What's more, she'll need to be aware about her growing sexuality and the feelings she may have. Many children mistake the lust of raging hormones for serious love during adolescence, and enter into a sexual relationship because they think it's the next logical step towards consummation or fulfilment of love. It's therefore very important that you discourage your child from getting carried away, and encourage her to wait as long as possible.

How do I make my feelings about sexual behaviour known to my child?

Don't hesitate to talk about your views in any situation but in a non-judgmental way. You can talk about STDs (*see page 424*) and point out how casual sex is leading to serious problems in teenagers. You can talk about how you feel about your partner/husband/wife, providing the understanding that having sex and then children in a

loving relationship is a natural progression because it is safe, secure
and you are very much in love. Be honest, too. You don't have to
overdo the suggestion that she ought to wait until she is in a serious
relationship, because you worry about the risk of pregnancy (even
with contraception), about the emotional impact when she is still
growing and maturing, about the legal situation (you must be
sixteen to have sex in the UK), and about the nature of sexual
feelings and urges and how they can be released in less extreme
ways (for example, kissing and petting does not always have to lead
to full sex). One 'talk' will probably frighten her or make her feel
cornered or like the law is being laid down, whereas a series of chats
over several years will cement your views naturally.

What level of sexual activity is appropriate at what age?
It is illegal to have sex under the age of sixteen in the UK, and it's
one law that parents can hang on to when they discuss the subject
with their children. If full sex is off the cards until that age, then it's
one less thing to worry about. That's not to say that it won't
happen, but if you make it clear that the law must be followed in
this instance, you are on safer ground. Kids begin to experiment
with sex from a young age. Some precocious pre-teens play spin
the bottle or even experiment with light petting with a boyfriend or
in a group situation where everyone is 'fooling around'. School-age
children may play sexual games with friends of their same sex,
touching each other's genitals and/or masturbating together. Most
sex play at this age happens because of curiosity, or as part of a
game – playing mummies and daddies, for example.

Preadolescent boys and girls do not usually have much sexual
experience, but they often have many questions. They usually have
heard about sexual intercourse, petting, oral sex and anal sex,
homosexuality, rape and incest, and they want to know more about

all these things. The idea of actually having sexual intercourse, however, is unpleasant to most preadolescent boys and girls.

Same-gender sexual behaviour is common at this age. Boys and girls tend to play with friends of the same gender and are likely to explore sexuality with them. This type of same-gender sexual behaviour is unrelated to a child's sexual orientation.

Some group-dating occurs at this age. Preadolescents may attend parties that have guests of both genders, and they may dance and play kissing games. By twelve or thirteen some young adolescents may pair off and begin dating and/or 'making out'. It is unusual for children to go beyond light petting at this age, but not unheard of.

Once kids have reached puberty and beyond, they experience increased interest in romantic and sexual relationships and in 'real sex'. As they mature, they experience strong emotional attachments to romantic partners and find it natural to express their feelings within sexual relationships. There is no way to predict how a particular teenager will act sexually, but most kids have petted heavily by mid-adolescence, and many kids have had sexual intercourse by the age of sixteen. The basic message is that there is no defined list of what is appropriate at various ages, as kids all experiment at different times, and the age of their partners can also make a difference. What is clear, however, is that too much too soon is unhealthy to growing bodies and minds, so keep an eye on what your child is doing and if he seems uncomfortable about anything at all, encourage him to talk – and in a gentle way, to slow down.

If I think my daughter is giving in to sex for the wrong reasons, how do I approach her about this?

This is tricky, as many girls will rebuff your interest or concerns because it is a private matter, perhaps because she already secretly has concerns and doesn't want to air them just yet, or perhaps because she perceives your disapproval to be an aspersion on her boyfriend. So go in lightly. Talk in general terms about the intimacy and love involved with full sex, and the importance of it being mutual.

If you get nowhere and you are very concerned about your child, you could just ask gently, in a quiet, warm moment, whether she's OK and whether she's feeling a bit pressured about the intensity of her relationship. You can't make her talk, but you can be there and you can offer as much advice and guidance as she is prepared to take.

(*See also* Relationships, *page 397.*)

Pregnancy

From what age can my daughter get pregnant?

Theoretically your daughter can become pregnant from the time she begins ovulating, which coincides with her first period. Most girls begin ovulating a little while after their first periods, but it is not established on a monthly basis for several months or even years after her period begins. Some girls start their periods very early, which means that they could, therefore, also become pregnant much earlier than others. On average, however, most girls begin their periods around age twelve and are ovulating regularly by fourteen or fifteen. Once your child has started her period, however, do not take any chances! She will require contraception if she plans to engage in sex.

Is my fourteen-year-old daughter physically able to have baby?

Having babies at such a young age comes with a number of possible physical problems. Younger mothers have, on average, more babies with a low birth weight, which can cause health complications for the child. Younger women also experience higher rates of infant death than women who have children at a later age. Many of these problems stem from the fact that a teen's body is still developing, and the stress of pregnancy can cause complications. A teenager's pelvis is not fully grown, and delivery can be painful and cause trauma to mother and baby. Finally, the shock of being pregnant, or not having support, can increase the likelihood of post-natal depression, which can be serious. With good nutrition, antenatal care and full support, many young teenagers can have a healthy pregnancy and baby, but there are always risks.

My son's girlfriend is pregnant unexpectedly. Should we support him or insist that he stays away?

Your son is undoubtedly as shocked as you are, and will have very mixed feelings about the whole situation. He might feel guilty that he is not pleased; he might feel that he wants to run away from the whole situation; he might be unsure about a decision to have an abortion or to have a child of his adopted; he might question his feelings for his girlfriend (there's nothing like the prospect of having to stay together for the baby's sake to dim romance); he might be worried that he is not involved in the decision; he might fear having to take on responsibilities at a young age and give up his hopes and dreams for the future. The feelings your son could be experiencing are limitless and for an immature adolescent, probably overwhelming. He unquestioningly needs your support.

Everyone makes a mistake. If a pregnancy has occurred, you must stand by him, no matter how disappointed or angry you may be. This will be one of the hardest lessons of 'cause and effect/actions and consequences' that your child may ever face, and you will need to guide him through his feelings, the options, and his responsibilities. Whatever happens, he must shoulder the responsibility and make some decisions. It may be that your son's girlfriend wants to make her own decisions, with her parents or counsellor; she doesn't have to tell her parents and she doesn't even have to tell your son. The fact that she did is good news, because there is now scope for communication. Without frightening her, ask her to talk to you and your son and possibly her parents, to come up with the best course of action for everyone involved. Make it clear that you will respect any decision she makes, but that your son would like to be party to it because he takes his responsibilities seriously.

Whatever she decides, your son must support her and any child that is the product. Help as much as you can, of course, but don't take on the burden. Your son's mistake is his own, and he does have to deal with the consequences as maturely as he is able.

(*See also* Abortion, Birth control, Relationships, Sex)

Sexuality

When do kids decide their sexual orientation?

There is no set age for this. Some children feel from a very young age that they are attracted to the same sex, and never have any feelings thereafter for the opposite sex. They have a constant feeling that they are, therefore, homosexual, and nothing that transpires during adolescence and even early adulthood does anything to shift this perspective. Other kids are confused throughout early to middle adolescence; it is not unusual for older children and teenagers to have crushes on members of the same sex or even to experiment sexually with the same sex during this period. It does not mean anything in terms of their sexual identity. It's important to make this clear to kids when you discuss sex and sexual feelings; many kids are confused to find that they have a crush or feel love or attraction to someone of the same sex, and therefore decide or worry that they must be 'gay'. Most teens will not be sure of their sexual preferences and identity until late adolescence and even early adulthood. Some never come to terms with it.

Is my child old enough to ask questions and be given answers about homosexuality?

If your child is asking questions, she is most certainly old enough to be given answers, and her curiosity should be taken seriously and viewed as a good opportunity to discuss a sensitive subject. Give her as much information as she requests, suitable to her age. Whatever you do, present a calm, non-judgmental and factual explanation to your child. Some of the most important qualities we want to invest in our children are compassion and tolerance, whatever our beliefs, prejudices or fears. Explain clearly that some people are attracted to and find companionship with members of the same sex, and that it is likely a biological proclivity, not something 'wrong with them'. Be positive and factual. You can explain that it is very normal to have feelings for the same sex in childhood and adolescence (*see above*) and that this is no indication of sexual identity. There is absolutely nothing to suggest that talking about homosexuality encourages your child to become homosexual; instead, it creates a much mature and unprejudiced viewpoint and an understanding of others' differences.

How can I tell if my child is gay?

Don't decide that your son is gay because he has decided to wear make-up, pink shirts or earrings. Don't assume your daughter is gay because she's dressed like a truck driver and is not remotely feminine. Similarly, don't assume this if your children do not have serious or even short-term relationships with the opposite sex in their teens or even early adolescence – some kids are late bloomers, and haven't found someone with whom they've 'clicked'.

In fact, there may be no recognisable signs at all until you discover that your child has had a serious same-sex relationship, or she tells you that she is gay. She may be just like any other kid at school – eating burgers, gossiping, even dating. You may have a hunch, in which case, you might want to discuss it with your child. Don't go in with all guns blazing and question her or accuse her of anything. Perhaps begin with an informal chat in the car about friends you may have who are gay, and ask her if she knows anyone herself. Make it clear that you see nothing wrong with being gay, so that when she does pluck up the courage to talk to you about it, or come out of the closet, she will trust you to love her regardless.

What do I do if I find out my child is gay?

Parents should love their children unconditionally, even if they do not live up to expectations, or choose a lifestyle of which their parents disapprove. Many parents are terrified about their children being gay. Unfortunately, there are still a huge number of myths around homosexuality, and a great deal of prejudice. These ideas are based on the ignorance that surrounds homosexuality. In reality, a great many homosexual people find long-term partners, live perfectly happy lives with the normal responsibilities; they foster or adopt children; they are good people with decent jobs and responsible citizens. A responsible adolescent isn't going to turn into a sex maniac because he has come out of the closet. Show trust.

What you have a right to worry about is the prejudice. Many gays are targeted by ignorant individuals, and there is a culture of bullying. This is one reason why your child needs to feel confident about and supported in his choice. If he has high self-esteem and self-belief he will be better able to withstand the pressure, and to deal with the prejudice. Furthermore, many young homosexuals are terrified about feeling 'different', and a good number suffer from depression and some even commit suicide because they can't face the ignominy of being 'gay', letting down their parents, or putting up with the flack. Your support is, again, crucial to helping him feel happy and confident about his choice.

The bottom line is that your child is the same child he was before he told you, or you uncovered the truth. He is still worthy of your love and respect, and he deserves to make his own choices in life. No matter what you are feeling, it is your responsibility to provide guidance, love and support.

What can I do if I disapprove of his sexual orientation?

Frankly, your disapproval does not matter. It may go against your religious beliefs, your moral code and even your gut instinct, but you must offer support and love, regardless of all of these things. Children have a right to make their own decisions and choices, and as parents we have a clear obligation to show respect. Your child is not committing a crime by being homosexual, and there is nothing he can do to change his feelings. If you make him feel dirty or wrong, you will isolate him, which can have devastating results; if you exclude him from your family, you will damage him and any future relationship you may have. Nothing is worth that. You can certainly express your concerns, as you would with any child, such as your hopes that he will settle down into an established relationship and find someone special, that he will not be hurt or ostracised by ignorant people, that he will protect himself when he has sex – all normal worries that a parent might have. But most of all, make it clear that you want him to be happy, and that you will be there to support him, no matter what his decisions.

Sexually transmitted diseases (STDs)

Can my child get an STD?

British teenagers are the most sexually active in Europe, according to a report published in 2006. A study by the Institute for Public Policy Research (IPPR) found that 38 per cent of British fifteen-year-olds had had sex in the period from 2001 to 2002. That compared to just 15 per cent in Poland, 16 per cent in Spain and was also greater than the countries with the second highest proportion – Sweden, Finland and Germany. Given that another poll found that 38 per cent of kids admitted to not using a condom for sex with a new partner (often because they were drunk), the chances of becoming infected with an STD (or STI – sexually transmitted illness) is high and increasing.

According to the BMA, 60 per cent of young people in the UK (aged sixteen to twenty-four) say they have unprotected sex (without the use of a condom), and 40 per cent use condoms incorrectly. Rates of sexually transmitted diseases are soaring among this age group. Genitourinary medicine clinics in England in 2005 reported 2,221 cases of STDs in patients aged thirteen to fifteen years, which included thirteen underage girls being diagnosed with syphilis.

So yes, some experts are calling it a problem of epidemic proportions.

What are the most common STDs and their effects?

Sexually Transmitted Diseases (STDs) are diseases that can be transmitted through body contact during sex. They are caused by viruses, bacteria and parasites. They can also be known as Sexually Transmitted Infections (STIs) or by their old name venereal diseases (VD). There are at least 25 different sexually transmitted diseases. What they all have in common is that they can be spread by sexual contact, including vaginal, anal and oral sex.

What is chlamydia?

Chlamydia is the most common treatable bacterial STD. It can cause serious problems later in life if it is not treated, including pelvic inflammatory disease, infertility and ectopic pregnancy. Appendicitis often occurs. Chlamydia infects the cervix in women. The urethra, rectum and eyes can be infected in both sexes (and can remain itchy and painful until treated). Symptoms of infection may show up at anytime, often between one to three weeks after exposure. However, symptoms may not emerge until a long way down the line.

What are crabs or pubic lice?

Crabs or pubic lice are small, crab-shaped parasites that live on hair and draw blood. They live predominantly on pubic hair, but can also be found in hair in the armpits, on the body and even in facial hair such as eyebrows. They can live away from the body too, and therefore can be found in clothes, bedding and towels. You can have crabs and not know about it, but after two to three weeks, you would expect to experience some itching. Crabs are mainly passed on through body contact during sex, but they can also be passed on through sharing clothes, towels or bedding with someone who has them. There is no effective way to prevent yourself becoming infected, though you can prevent others becoming infected by washing clothes and bedding on a hot wash. Lotions can be bought from pharmacies and applied to the body to kill off the parasites. Shaving off pubic hair will not necessarily get rid of crabs.

What is genital herpes?

Genital herpes is caused by the herpes simplex virus. The virus can affect the mouth, the genital area, the skin around the anus and the fingers. Once the first outbreak of herpes is over, the virus hides away in the nerve fibres, where it remains totally undetected and causes no symptoms. Symptoms of the first infection usually appear one to twenty-six days after exposure and last two to three weeks. Both men and women may have one or more symptoms, including an itching or tingling sensation in the genital or anal area, small fluid-filled blisters that can burst and leave small sores which can be very painful, pain when passing urine, if it passes over any of the open sores and a flu-like illness, backache, headache, swollen glands or fever.

What is gonorrhoea?

Gonorrhoea is a bacterial infection. It is sexually transmitted and can infect the cervix, urethra, rectum, anus and throat. Symptoms of infection may show up at anytime between one and fourteen days after exposure. It is possible to be infected with gonorrhoea and have no symptoms. Men are far more likely to notice symptoms than women. If left untreated gonorrhoea can lead to pelvic inflammatory disease (PID). This is an inflammation of the fallopian tubes which can cause fever, lower abdominal pain and backache. Sex may be uncomfortable. PID can cause a woman to become infertile or have an ectopic pregnancy. Gonorrhoea can cause inflammation of the testicles and the prostate gland, which causes pain. Without treatment a narrowing of the urethra or abscesses can develop.

What is hepatitis?

Hepatitis causes the liver to become inflamed, which can cause a host of problems in later life. There are various different types of hepatitis, the most common being hepatitis A, B and C. Each of these viruses acts differently. Hepatitis can be caused by alcohol and some drugs, but usually it is the result of a viral infection.

What is syphilis?

Syphilis is a bacterial infection. It is usually sexually transmitted, but may also be passed from an infected mother to her unborn child. The signs and symptoms of syphilis are the same in both men and women. They can be difficult to recognise and may take up to three months to show after having sexual contact with an infected person. Syphilis has several stages. The primary and secondary stages are very infectious. Latent syphilis refers to the presence of untreated syphilis. You can have no symptoms or signs of the infection, which is diagnosed by a positive blood test. If left untreated, you may develop symptomatic late syphilis. This would usually develop after more than ten years. It is then that syphilis can affect the heart, and possibly the nervous system. If treatment for syphilis is given during the latent stage the infection can be cured. However, if there has been heart or nervous-system damage before treatment is started this may be irreversible.

Your child should visit her doctor or a sexual health clinic (called a GUM clinic) if she has any reason to suspect an STD.

How can my daughter tell if she has one?

Anyone who is sexually active can be at risk from STDs. Some STDs can have symptoms, such as genital discharge, pain when urinating, genital swelling and inflammation. Many STDs, such as chlamydia, can frequently be symptomless. This is why it is advisable to have a sexual health check-up, to screen for STDs, if you think your child has been at risk. Symptoms of STDs can present themselves months after infection, and she can pass on infection during this time.

Is early treatment important?
Yes, very. Many STDs are very infectious and can cause long-term or permanent damage, including infertility if left untreated. Many STDs can be easily passed on to sexual partners, and some STDs can be passed from a mother to her unborn child. STDs can also aid the transmission of HIV.

Shoes

When can my daughter start wearing high heels?
According to the American Orthopaedic Foot and Ankle Society, girls should not wear heels until they are at least nine or ten, and after that, it should be no more than 2.5 cm (1 in) in height until early adolescence. Your daughter's feet are still growing and their shape developing; high heels not only affect the way her foot develops (throwing her weight forward on to the balls of her feet and toes), but also affecting her posture. The redistribution of weight and the inherent posture and foot problems associated with high heels affect a child's ability to perform everyday activities. With their feet squeezed and compressed into fashionable shoes, children are unable to walk long distances or for extended periods of time without experiencing discomfort.

While the odd night out in stilettos or wedges will not cause anything more than sore feet and toes, and perhaps the odd twisted ankle, day-to-day shoes (for school, for example), should be no more than an inch in height, and should be regularly alternated with well-supporting flat shoes to ensure that your daughter's arches, tendons and bones grow properly. In other words, shoes of varying heights should be worn no more often than flat, comfortable shoes or sandals, and preferably professionally fitted.

When can children start to clean and polish their own shoes?

This is a job that can be undertaken from about aged ten or eleven onwards. Earlier than that and you'll probably find polish smeared from hand to elbow, with little on the shoes themselves. When children get new shoes, even from a young age, it's a good idea to teach them about caring for them.

How many pairs of shoes does a child need?

Without meaning to sound sexist, girls tend to need more shoes than boys! Obviously you may have a budget that extends to innumerable pairs of shoes; however, in reality, most boys need the following: a pair of good-quality, well-fitting (professionally fitted, if possible) school shoes that are hard wearing, a pair of 'leisure' shoes, such as trainers or loafers (dare I say it, but these might need to be 'trendy'; the cost of which you can agree with your child, *see page 99*), and sports shoes, such as trainers or football/rugby boots as required.

Girls, however, tend to have a different approach to shoes and view them as an essential accessory rather than something functional. They will, therefore, require all of the above, as well as a few extra pairs – for evenings out, perhaps, or a pair to go with trousers, and another to go with dresses or skirts, and one for formal occasions. Your budget – and preferably hers – will dictate how many pairs of shoes she has, but it's worth noting that cheaper shoes worn only a few times might seem a waste of money, but they are unlikely to cause long-term damage to her feet if her regular shoes are well-fitting, and they can be disposed of when fashions or her wardrobe change. I'd draw the line at shoe madness, but a straw poll tells me that the average sixteen-year-old girl owns at least six pairs, including school shoes, sandals and those required for sport.

The good news is that your child's feet grow first in the pubertal growth spurt, and will have reached adult size well before it's over – in some teens as young as fourteen or fifteen. This means that shoes will obviously have a longer life and their regular replacement based on them wearing out rather than need.

Skin

My daughter's skin is very spotty since she began puberty, but her friends are fine. Is this normal?
It's unfortunate that changes to a child's skin coincide with their increased self-awareness and self-consciousness. Many teens are at their most unattractive, with spotty skin, gangly limbs and clumsiness, just when they need to feel good about themselves. There are a variety of different theories as to why skin is so affected during puberty. For one thing, it appears to be hereditary. If you or your partner were prone to acne or spots during adolescence, your child is more likely to as well.

During puberty the hair follicle produces lots of oil (called sebum). This oil (mixed with keratin) traps dirt and bacteria. When the pore is completely closed off a 'white head' will form. When the pore is only partially closed, blackheads appear. Washing the skin won't make a bit of difference at this stage, as excessive washing actually irritates the skin and prompts the glands to produce even more sebum and keratin. Another problem is allergies. Food allergies are responsible for many cases of adolescent acne and spots, so it's worth talking to your doctor about the possibility. Some experts also believe that stress can be at the cause.

The best thing you can do is to encourage regular washing (two times a day) with a gentle soap or cleanser, and using appropriate spot treatments (*see below*) on individual ruptures. It may help for your child to drink plenty of water, which encourages waste products in her body to be removed more effectively. Discourage her from squeezing as this can make things significantly worse, and if the spots are round, hard and don't appear to have a head, see your doctor, who can refer you to a dermatologist. Acne isn't a dangerous condition, but without proper treatment it can cause scarring.

Is it safe for my child to use spot creams?

Most spot/pimple creams contain a chemical called benzoyl peroxide, which breaks down and removes the dead cells on the skin surface. It also kills bacteria on the skin. The removal of cells from the top layer of skin unblocks the sebaceous glands (glands which secrete sebum), which become blocked in acne. This reduces inflammation of the gland as the sebum can then escape. Bacteria on the skin feed on sebum and produce waste products which further inflame the sebaceous glands, causing acne. Benzoyl peroxide reduces their numbers by reducing their food source (sebum) and by directly killing them.

There are no major side-effects, other than it makes your child's skin more sensitive to the sun (which means using a decent sunscreen), although some children can be allergic to it. If your child's skin becomes reddened, raised or itchy after use, you should discontinue.

Having said that, our children are subject to contact with many,

many chemicals, and alternating their usual spot creams with more natural products (or using the latter exclusively), such as those containing tea tree oil can help to reduce any toxic build-up.

How often should my child be cleaning her face and how?
Your child should be cleaning her face with a mild soap or cleanser and warm water, twice a day. Some teens use toners following washing, using a cotton ball or pad to remove excess dirt and sebum, and this is good practice as it removes the bits that soap doesn't reach. If your child washes more than this she could actually encourage the production of more sebum and irritate her skin, which leads to more spots.

Are antibiotics and other treatments appropriate for normal spots?
This is a decision your doctor or dermatologist will have to make. Antibiotics are not normally prescribed unless your child is suffering from severe acne – the goal being to reduce bacteria and avoid scarring. Antibiotics can, however, have many side-effects, so they should only be considered in extreme situations. And if your child is prescribed them, purchase some probiotics (healthy bacteria), which will help restore the healthy bacterial balance in her body.

What is the difference between usual teenage spots and acne?
Normal spots have white or black 'heads', although they may be raised and red before they rupture. They tend to be localised rather than covering the face, chest or back, and resolve themselves easily with regular washing and (if you wish) spot creams.

Acne is something slightly different. Acne is a very common skin disorder that most young people get in early puberty. It is caused by inflammation of the small oil glands (sebaceous glands) that surround the fine hairs on the face and chest. The severity of acne increases and, typically, reaches its peak around the ages of seventeen to nineteen. For most people, acne tends to go away by the time they reach their mid-twenties; however, very sensitive people may continue to have the disorder until they reach their forties.

During puberty, the production of male sex hormones (androgens) increases in both girls and boys, which can stimulate the sebaceous glands to produce more sebum. In some people, the sebaceous glands are extremely sensitive to androgens. These people, mostly men, get acne so severely that they need medical treatment.

The increased production of sebum makes the openings of the sebaceous glands narrower, which prevents the sebum from getting out. Meanwhile, the sebum production continues regardless.

The first symptoms are small, tender, red spots that later turn into pimples containing degraded fatty acids. The inflammation disappears over a few days or weeks, depending on the severity.

Severe acne can cause scars which will never disappear. Acne can also cause psychological stress and be socially disabling. An early effective treatment is therefore imperative.

When should we see a dermatologist?
If your child has spots that continually flare up across her face, chest and back, and do not respond to regular washing or over-the-counter creams; if her spots are painful and any 'spent' spots have left a scar or residual mark, it is a good idea to see your doctor, who can refer you to a dermatologist.

When should I encourage my daughter to start using moisturiser?
Most girls do not have a problem with dry skin, unless they are using products that dry or irritate their skin. It is not always the case, but the majority of adolescent girls suffer from oily skin rather

than dry skin. There is nothing wrong with applying a very light moisturiser after cleansing, which will even out skin tone and prevent areas from becoming chapped and dry; however, it is not strictly necessary unless your daughter has obviously dry skin; in other words, skin that looks powdery or scaly. In some cases, diet will make a difference. For example, a deficiency of EFAs (*see page 250*) can make the skin dry and itchy. Increasing these nutrients can often sort it out. You may suggest that your daughter rubs a little olive oil into her skin, which will nourish and protect without irritating, or otherwise to use a very light moisturiser or emollient. All girls (and boys) should wear sunscreen when they are outside, to protect from sun damage. From the age of sixteen or seventeen, a light regular moisturiser (preferably designed for young adults) is recommended. You don't have to spend a lot of money on this; aqueous cream, available over the counter, is a good choice. Otherwise, choose something non-oily, to prevent the pores from being clogged.

How often does my daughter need to shower or bathe?
Every day, for hygiene reasons (*see page 381*).

Smoking

When is it legal to smoke?
It is not actually illegal in the UK, to smoke at any age; however, it is illegal to purchase cigarettes before the age of eighteen (although, as I write, the UK government is considering lowering this to seventeen) in England and Wales and Scotland. No changes have yet been confirmed by the Isle of Man or Northern Ireland.

How old does my child have to be to buy cigarettes?

Eighteen, although if the wishy-washy government has its way, this may change to seventeen.

If I know my child is smoking, what can I do to try and stop her?

It's worth pointing out that children who begin smoking at the age of fifteen are three times more likely to die of smoking-related illnesses, such as lung cancer, heart disease and other cancers. Some 90 per cent of adult smokers began when they were children. Many long-term smokers acquire emphysema which prohibits them from breathing normally. A little visit to your local smoking clinic or a friend or family member who suffers from this debilitating disease should be a deterrent if nothing else, although we all know that children have a rather inflated view of their own mortality and omnipotence. Try to stop them as soon as possible. You will obviously have no control over what they do out of your house, but if you employ a smoking ban within your house, it's a beginning. There are a few other things you could do:

▷ Bring up the subject sensitively, so that your child doesn't fear punishment or judgement.

▷ Encourage your child to get involved in activities that actively discourage or prohibit smoking, such as sports.

▷ Begin talking to your child about tobacco early on, so that the message sinks in.

▷ Ask your child what she finds appealing or unappealing about smoking, and talk about it. Some kids smoke because it's 'cool' or because they like the 'buzz'.

▷ Discuss ways to respond to peer pressure to smoke. Your child may feel confident simply saying 'no', but many adolescents don't.

▷ Talk about money. Cigarettes are very expensive.

Until what age can I insist that my child does not smoke?

You can't force your child to quit, but you can discourage it (*see above*) until he is legally old enough. You can, however, forbid smoking in your house as part of your household rules. If you make it easy, it's more likely to persist. Show your displeasure, as it is a real deterrent to good health.

How can I make sure that my child is not smoking in my house?

For one thing, make it a household rule that no one (without exception) smokes in the house – which will also mean dragging your habit outside. Show your displeasure on health grounds, which should discourage your child from smoking in your presence (or even admitting to it). This is one case where the idea is not to profess knowledge, but to find every opportunity for it not to happen! With rules come penalties for breaking them; be tough and ensure that your children understand the reasons why you are taking the tough line. If you smell smoke, or see the evidence, then the penalties come into play.

Sunbeds

At what age can children use a sunbed?

Sunbeds are a real danger to your child's health and one of the leading causes of skin cancer (*see below*). Realistically, you want to discourage your children from using them at all. Obviously, one session before a holiday abroad is not going to cause serious problems, but kids (like adults) can become addicted to their use, and that's when problems start. The Sunbed Association, which governs about 25 per cent of sunbeds in the UK, prohibits their use by under-sixteens, and for good reason (*see below*); however, not all sunbed organisations are so honourable. Under-sixteens should be discouraged or even forbidden by you on health grounds; over that age, you can only pass on details of the dangers and express your concern.

What are the dangers and how can I discourage my child from using them?

According to a joint statement from Cancer Research UK and the Sunbed Society, everyone under sixteen should be banned from using a sunbed, because it substantially increases the risk of skin cancer. Malignant melanoma – a common skin cancer – increased by 24 per cent during the 1995–2000 period, and most importantly, it is the third most common cancer among the fifteen to thirty-nine year age group. About 7,000 cases are diagnosed in the UK each year, of whom nearly a third die. There are also more than 62,000 cases of non-melanoma skin cancer each year in the UK.

Sunbeds emit UVA and UVB radiation. In general, sunbeds predominantly emit UVA radiation, which is thought to be the least damaging of the UV radiation spectrum. However, in recent years, sunbeds have been manufactured that produce higher levels of UVB to mimic the solar spectrum and speed the tanning process.

Overexposure to UV radiation from the sun and artificial sources is of considerable public health concern. UV radiation plays an important role in the development of skin cancer, cataracts and other eye conditions, and suppresses the immune system. Cumulative UV radiation also results in premature skin ageing.

If vanity is the motivation for using sunbeds, you might point out that in a few years' time the wrinkles and sun damage (including discolouration and broken veins) may well not be worth the short-term gain. There are plenty of self-tan products available that do not cause cancer and do not damage the skin. Many of these are natural. Point your child in that direction.

Surgery

When does my child need my consent to have an operation?
Like all medical procedures, your child does not need your
permission to have surgery if he is deemed to be of sound mind
and believed to understand the procedures involved, as well as any
potential complications or side-effects. In fact, even if you say no,
his consent is of primary importance. If you believe he is
endangering his health, you can challenge this by court order (*see
page 258*). If your child requires an operation when he is in no fit
state to decide (after an accident or under the influence of drugs or
alcohol) he will normally require parental permission until the age
of sixteen (in some cases eighteen), and after that next-of-kin. In
emergency situations where there is no parent present, treatment
will be administered according to the child's best interests.

Can she consent to her own operation and at what age?
Your daughter can consent to her own operation at any age, as long
as she is deemed competent to make such a decision (*see page 256*)
and it is in her best interests. You can attempt to overrule her
decision, but unless doctors or surgeons believe that you are acting
in your child's best interests, she is still entitled to make the
decision. If you and your child's doctors disagree, you must apply
to the courts. After the age of sixteen, she has full right to decide
her own treatment.

**How old does my daughter need to be for cosmetic surgery
and does she need my permission?**
Your daughter can have plastic surgery at any age, provided you
give your consent under the age of sixteen. However, the NHS will

not pay for surgery unless she has been referred by a psychologist, who must prove that the surgery is necessary for emotional health. For example, a growing number of girls are getting their noses 'fixed', their breasts reduced or augmented, and boys are having ears pinned back because they are suffering from bullying that has affected their lives significantly.

Should I pay for cosmetic surgery if my child needs it?

This question can only be answered by you. If you can afford it, if you think it is necessary to protect your child's health and/or well-being, and if you genuinely believe that altering your child's body in some way is responsible, acceptable and/or ethical, then it may be something you want to consider. For example, if your child has a birthmark in an obvious place that embarrasses her, or if your son has 'bat ears', you may want to consider having them altered. But act with caution.

Adam Searle, president of the British Association of Aesthetic Plastic Surgeons, warns against carrying out cosmetic operations on children when they are too young. He says that in many cases characteristics such as small or asymmetric breasts will become less noticeable as the youngsters' bodies develop.

In reality, it is the little imperfections that make our children individual. From an early age they should be made to feel good about themselves, positive in their bodies, confident that there is more to a person than looks, skin or breasts, for example, and that not everyone must meet the Hollywood/pop star ideal of beauty, which fades just like everyone else's.

Swearing

Should I overlook swearing?

Younger children swear to try out new words and to gauge the
response they get, even if they are unaware of what the words
mean. If a child gets a great deal of attention for using
inappropriate words, he'll carry on doing so. The best response in
this case is a firm 'those are not words we use in this house or
anywhere', without over-reacting. Children often swear because
they think it's 'cool'. Unfortunately, foul language is increasingly
common in films, various media, magazines and it's used by people
our children look up to as role models, such as sports stars,
musicians and actors. Your child may use words that he genuinely
doesn't realise are wrong because everyone is using them. Raise an
eyebrow, perhaps ask him if the knows what it means and then
ignore it. It's likely that it will not be used again if the expected
reaction is not given. This doesn't mean overlooking swearing,
which can become a habit if it's not nipped in the bud; it simply
means reacting calmly and making your displeasure and offence
clear without causing a fuss.

Can I ban my children from swearing?

What your child does when she is out of the house is largely out of
your control, but you can make it clear that using offensive
language does just that – it offends. Children learn to express
themselves in ways that do not hurt or upset other people, and to
show respect. Make it clear that calling names is a form of bullying
and that it is hurtful and harmful.

You can ban swearing in your house (*see below*), by actively
discouraging the process and making it a household rule that no
offensive language is used under any circumstances, no matter how

angry or upset you may be. There can, on this basis, be penalties when the rule is broken, such as a withdrawal of privileges, a 'fine' on pocket money, a black mark on a star chart that halts progress towards a much sought-after reward – whatever works best for your child in terms of motivation.

How can I discourage my children from swearing?

Explain, early on, in your child's life that swearing is offensive, rude and disrespectful. Make it clear that it will not be tolerated in your house, and that if they choose to use it elsewhere, they must be aware that they are hurting and insulting people by doing it. Try not to swear yourself. Double standards never go over well with kids.

For younger children who pick up the words, be firm. Explain that you are surprised to hear them using those words because they are very rude. Tell them that they are not allowed in your house, no matter what. Don't ignore the behaviour in young children; they may genuinely not know what they are saying and they will require guidance.

Some families use a system of fining members who swear. Everyone is obliged to put a coin in a jar if they are caught. And this hits kids with limited resources, right where it hurts most. It'll also keep older family members on the straight and narrow.

Swimming

When can my child swim in a public swimming pool unsupervised?

According to the Royal Society for the Prevention of Accidents (RoSPA), constant supervision of children is essential. Although drownings in pools are extremely rare, evidence suggests that children under the age of eleven years are most at risk and toddlers are the most vulnerable. It is not sufficient to rely solely on the supervision of the lifeguard at the pool-side. Some pools allow children to swim alone from the age of eight or nine; however, unless your child is a very accomplished swimmer, it is important to have an adult there to keep tabs.

Ensure that you are familiar with the pool environment, recognise particular hazards, like changes in depth and check out where the points of help are and the location of rescue equipment. Be particularly vigilant in 'leisure pools' where there may be a number of features within the pool, like flumes, fountains and waves.

If you are supervising more than one child, do not leave one child in the pool while taking the other into the changing rooms, unless you are confident of the child's swimming ability and maturity. Whether you need to be in the pool with the child/ren you are supervising will depend on their age and swimming ability. Generally it is better to support non-swimmers by being in the pool. Younger children who are out of their depth in all, or most of, the pool will need physical support.

Should I allow my child to have a swimming party at our local river, pond or home swimming pool?

On hot days, it goes without saying that a swim is a great way to cool down, and a nice way to entertain friends. If you have a swimming pool, it seems absurd not to use it socially. However, it is extremely important to be aware of the risks.

Drowning is the third most common cause of accidental death among the under-sixteens. Young people who drown are often victims of their own misjudgement. Although learning to swim may help children who find themselves in difficulties in water, it does not follow that swimming ability makes children safe. Indeed, figures show that more than half of those who drowned could, in fact, swim.

You are ultimately responsible for children in your care, so any swimming party must be supervised by one or more adults who can swim, and who have basic lifesaving skills. Kids often become silly when their peers are around, and want to show off – a potential recipe for disaster.

Put all kids on a rota, where there is always at least one child sitting by the pool or pond watching the others. This does not mean placing responsibility for other children's lives on to the shoulders of a child, it simply means teaching children the importance of supervision and vigilance. This does not replace adult supervision either. Make sure there is no alcohol. Alcohol is one of the leading causes of drowning (implicated in over half of all drownings) because it impairs balance, coordination and judgement. Discourage running and prohibit diving when there are groups of kids, as unfamiliarity with depth can lead to serious accidents.

At what age can my child train to be a lifeguard?
There are several different programmes and qualifications available in the UK. If your child wishes to be a pool lifeguard, he will train to receive a National Pool Lifeguard Qualification (NPLQ), and must be sixteen years old before commencing training. The NPLQ is the most widely recognised lifeguard qualification in the UK and Ireland, with over 33,000 qualifying every year.

The Royal Life Saving Society UK's National Beach Lifeguard qualification is a nationally recognised award designed to establish competence for beach lifeguards, who are responsible for the safety of anyone using open water for recreation. Once again, your child must be sixteen before commencing the course.

For details of courses, visit Lifesavers IQL UK, at www.rlss.org.uk.

Should I insist that my child learns to swim?

Learning to swim is vital – drowning most often occurs when the victim is NOT planning on swimming or being in water. Knowing how to swim well is an important tool for many leisure activities, from boating, fishing, sailing, waterskiing, jet skiing to simply swimming itself. It's also good exercise and a great stress reducer, which can be helpful for busy kids.

Tattoos

At what age can my child get a tattoo without my permission?

Your child must be eighteen to get a tattoo without your permission. Even with parental permission, most tattoo artists will refuse to tattoo your child if she's younger than eighteen. If your daughter does find someone who will give her a tattoo without your permission, she could be in danger of serious infection (*see below*); if a tattoo artist is prepared to break stringent government regulations and guidelines, there is cause to doubt the cleanliness of the practice.

What are the risks of tattoos?

Quite apart from the fact that they are permanent, and therefore very much a lifelong 'skin accessory' which can prove embarrassing and unsightly as your child grows up, there is also a serious risk of hepatitis, septicemia and HIV if needles are not properly sterilised. A tattoo artist must use a new, clean, sterile needle for every tattoo he or she does. There is also a risk of bacterial infection at the site if it is not cleaned and cared for properly after being done; this can cause scarring, and lead to further, more serious infection.

There is also the embarrassment factor (*see below*). Tattoos are undoubtedly a current trend in popular culture, and many teen idols (from sportsmen and musicians to models and actors) have them. It's not surprising that kids want to take part; however, it is a good idea to ask your child to experiment with a temporary tattoo, such as henna, which lasts several days, before embarking on the real thing.

Can I insist that a tattoo be removed and, if so, how is this done?

If your child has had a tattoo done without your permission and she is under the age of eighteen, you are probably within your rights to insist on its removal. However, if it is in an unobtrusive spot and is not offensive, you may be better advised to leave things alone. Studies show that most kids regret getting a tattoo within two years of having had it done. Many kids get one in a rebellious moment, while under the influence of alcohol, or in a spur of the moment decision to express love to a partner or solidarity with a clique, gang or group. Your daughter will feel pretty silly having 'John' tattooed on her hip when John is long gone and Harry or Luke takes his place.

Removing tattoos is possible, with varying degree of success, depending on how it was done originally, where it is, what size it is and the type of pigment used. Tattoos aren't usually removed on the NHS but there are exceptions in some areas. Your doctor will be able to advise you and, if necessary, refer you to a reputable private surgeon. Private treatment can be very expensive, but it is essential that it is undertaken by a trained professional. A very small tattoo in an inconspicuous area can be removed by simply cutting it out and leaving a fine scar. Larger, colourful tattoos are usually removed using one of the following techniques:

▷ **Dermabrasion:** The top layers of the skin containing the pigment are rubbed away using mechanical means, after being treated with a combination of chemicals to break up the tissues. Scarring can be a problem.

▷ **Vaporisation:** The tattoo is removed from the skin by using a carbon dioxide laser. Again, scarring may be a problem.

▷ **Laser treatment:** Pulses of laser light are directed into the tattoo. The light passes harmlessly through the top layer of the skin, but is absorbed by the pigment particles in the tattoo. The particles heat up and are shattered into smaller pieces which can be removed by the body's immune system. Laser treatment is simple, low-risk and effective, although some scarring or pigmentation of the skin may result. Very rarely some of the pigments react with the laser to leave an even darker colour in the skin. The treatment only takes a few minutes but may need to be repeated several times, and it can be uncomfortable. A newer type of laser, used in YAG laser treatment, is particularly good at removing red, blue and black tattoo pigments. Some colours, such as fluorescent yellow, are very difficult to remove in this way.

Tattoo removal is usually done as a day case under a combination of local anaesthetic and sedation. Often, especially with laser treatments, several treatments are needed to effectively lighten the colours of the tattoo. And, unless the tattoo is cut out, a faint residual image remains even after many treatments.

Teeth

When can my child chew gum?
Although unsightly in some cases, chewing gum does have some benefits for your child's oral health. Chewing gum stimulates salivation, which helps neutralise the acid produced by bacteria.

Gum-chewing has been shown to stimulate and restore bowel function after abdominal surgery; the idea is that it represents sham feeding, which in turn activates a reflex (the cephalic-vagus reflex) that encourages gastrointestinal motility.

On the downside, too much chewing wears the enamel on the teeth and can cause problems with the jaw. The sweeteners, flavourings and preservatives in gum can cause diarrhoea, abdominal pain and flatulence (sorbital in sugarless gums); cinnamon flavouring has been linked to mouth ulcers, and liquorice flavouring (glycyrrhiza) can cause high blood pressure. Kids who chew a great deal of gum with sugar in it can suffer from more dental cavities (caries), suffer damage to their teeth (erosion) and previous dental treatment such as fillings or orthodontic braces (*see page 361*), and mercury levels are higher in excessive gum chewers because of the release of mercury from dental amalgam.

Kids can chew gum as soon as they are able to do so without swallowing (after the age of seven or eight) but its use should be limited, to prevent damage.

When do a child's last adult teeth come through?
Permanent teeth begin appearing around age six, starting with the first molars and lower central incisors. All permanent teeth should be in place by the age of thirteen, except the wisdom teeth (third molars). These may erupt any time between eighteen and twenty-five years of age. Adults have 28 permanent teeth, or up to 32 including the wisdom teeth.

When are wisdom teeth removed?
For one thing, they must all be in place before removal is considered, which could be well into your child's twenties. An operation to remove wisdom teeth involves making a small cut

in the gum, separating the tooth from the jawbone and removing it. The teeth might be taken out whole or in small pieces.

Sometimes, wisdom teeth don't come through the gum properly. This usually happens when there isn't enough space, or when the teeth are growing in the wrong direction. If they don't come through properly, they're called impacted wisdom teeth.

Taking out wisdom teeth is one of the most common operations in the UK; however, recent guidance suggests that most people do not need them removed, even if they are impacted. The National Institute for Health and Clinical Excellence (NICE), the government body that advises about treatments, suggests that an impacted wisdom tooth should only be taken out if it's causing problems, such as:

▷ An infection around the tooth.
▷ Damage to a neighbouring tooth.
▷ Decay (a cavity) in the tooth that your dentist can't treat.
▷ A cyst (a sac filled with fluid) in your jaw.

As we grow older, our jaws become smaller, often causing the teeth to 'crowd'. This can cause protrusions, make it difficult to clean teeth properly and be painful. For this reason, many dentists recommend removing wisdom teeth well before this process begins, to allow space for the natural movement of teeth. Your child's dentist will be able to provide advice.

When should my child be brushing her own teeth?

It is important to supervise your child's brushing until they are at least seven. Ideally, toothbrushing will be an intrinsic part of your child's daily hygiene routine, undertaken without question or murmur in the morning and before bed. It is no longer recommended that teeth are brushed immediately after meals, as this can wear away tooth enamel because of the high levels of acid in saliva after eating. Many kids are lazy and skip toothbrushing, so you may have to spot-check toothbrushes (particularly in adolescent boys) to ensure that it's happening. It's important to teach kids that brushing their teeth is essential, for fresh breath, strong healthy teeth, healthy gums, tongue and mouth. Reiterate the fact that failing to brush can lead to painful extractions, fillings and/or dentures, which are necessary even in young children with poor oral hygiene.

How often does a child's toothbrush need to be replaced?
For the best results, you should replace a toothbrush at least every three months, or when the bristles begin to show wear. It should always be replaced after an illness, such as colds or flu. It's worth remembering that toothbrushes are often worn enough to be replaced before they look worn. Bristles break down and lose their effectiveness, and worn and fractured bristles are a breeding ground for germs, fungus and bacteria. Worn toothbrushes can also damage gum tissue. Kids' toothbrushes require special attention and monitoring – bristle wear occurs quickly because children often brush with uneven strokes, and sometimes chew or bite on their toothbrush bristles.

Kids who wear braces should change their toothbrushes frequently because braces break down and fracture bristles and the toothbrushes lose their effectiveness. A new toothbrush is 30 per cent more effective at removing plaque.

Do children need to floss?
Once any two of your child's teeth touch each other, it's time to start flossing. Flossing helps prevent cavities by removing plaque and food particles caught between teeth. It should be an important

part of your child's dental routine. Your child should be able to floss his own teeth by the time he is nine years old.

(*See also* Orthodontics, *page 361.*)

Testicles

My son is embarrassed by having his testicles touched during visits to the doctor. What's the reason for this?

The main reason to touch your son's testicles is to check for any abnormality with them. It is important to be sure both balls are of approximate size, and that there is no unusual lump or bump on them. Cancer of the testicle can occur in teen males and it is discovered by the doctor (or even your son) checking the testicles. If this cancer is diagnosed early, most sufferers can have the testicle removed and have a good prognosis. Finding the cancer early is the key to the best outcome.

How often should my son check his own testicles?

Once a month is a good bet. Encourage your son to do it regularly in the shower, so he becomes accustomed to how they normally feel and will be more likely to identify a new lump or bump. Similarly, if your son feels any pain in or around the testicles, he should report this to his doctor. A lump does not always mean cancer; it may, for example, be a collection of veins called a varicocele, which are occasionally removed surgically.

Travel

When can my child be responsible for packing his own suitcase?

This is another 'the earlier the better' scenario. From young childhood, encourage your child to help with packing – sending him off with a list of items to collect, showing him how to fold or roll clothing to minimise wrinkling and maximise space, how to wrap bottles or breakables first in plastic bags, and then padded with clothing in the middle of the suitcase, and use a list, showing him how to tick items off. In this way, he becomes used to packing, and also aware of what packing for a trip away entails.

From nine or ten, kids can usually work to a list, ticking off as they go, and packing bags themselves. You will probably need to check before the bag is sealed. From age twelve, most children are capable of making their own lists (although talk them through it.) Let them choose their own clothing and pack themselves (giving it a once-over before you go to ensure that essentials such as wash bag, swimming suit and pjs have actually made it into the bag). By mid-teens, packing should be your child's responsibility.

Tack the packing list to the inside of your child's suitcase, so he can ensure that everything he brought returns home again.

When should my child be responsible for getting himself to school?

This will depend on your child's maturity, school policy, the distance to school and the safety of the roads on the way there (*see page 286*).

How old must my child be to travel out of the country alone?

As long as your child has a valid passport, has had the trip 'authorised' by a parent or guardian and will be 'signed for' at the other end, he can travel alone by air and usually train or coach, from the age of five. Most children are considered 'unaccompanied minors' if they travel without someone over the age of eighteen, until they are at least fourteen themselves. Some coach services require children to be at least eight before travelling alone, and suggest that there are no transfers or changes en route. Most children who travel alone at such a young age are visiting family members or close friends, and it is essential that you make the appropriate arrangements for them to be met at the other end.

Otherwise, your child is probably old enough to travel out of the country with friends, for short trips to a job, a supervised destination or work experience from the age of sixteen.

Is my child old enough to travel on the train alone?

There are no official age restrictions on trains in Britain, although it is assumed that a child under the age of five will be accompanied. Some lines ask for children to be twelve before travelling alone, so you will need to check this with the train company in question. Generally, however, children are probably capable of short trips by train from the age of ten or eleven, such as travelling to school or to meet a friend. Earlier than this, it is unlikely that they will be mature enough to deal with emergencies, problems en route, changes to timetables or difficulties with other passengers. Your child should have some practice under supervision, and be familiar with the network (preferably carrying a map) before embarking.

Can he use public transport?

The UK government actively encourages children to use public transport, and buses and trams are at present free for any child

of school age (currently between five and sixteen years of age).
I would suggest that five is too young for a bus or tram ride alone,
no matter how short. Ten or eleven seems a more appropriate age
(*see above*).

Is my child too young to fly alone?

If your child's trip is authorised by a parent or guardian, and she is
over the age of five, she is old enough to fly alone and qualifies as
an unaccompanied minor. All airlines have different criteria that
must be met, so check before you book.

When do kids stop being considered unaccompanied minors?

Once again, this differs between airlines (and travel companies,
buses and rail networks). Many airlines consider a child an 'adult'
when they are eligible to pay adult fares (usually over the age of
twelve or fifteen); however, others insist that a child be considered
a minor until the age of eighteen.

TV

At what age should I allow my kids to watch TV programmes after the 'watershed'?

The idea of the watershed (usually nine o'clock in the UK) is to
provide a safe viewing environment for younger children. As children
get older, they are likely to be up beyond 9 pm (and to have
televisions in their rooms), so programming is adjusted accordingly.
Most little ones are asleep by nine; however, there is concern about
children aged between eight and twelve who are thought to be the
most impressionable and vulnerable to influence from television
content. Younger children's viewing is easier to control and parents
feel that more adult material is 'over their heads'. By the time a child

has reached the teens, parents feel that he or she is mature enough to cope with more adult content, and control shifts accordingly.

The watershed then becomes a useful indicator of the kind of programming that may take place. The kinds of material that cause parents most concern regarding their children's viewing are those with violence, sex and swearing. So,for example, ITC rules state that a certificate-15 film can be scheduled at 9 pm, but 10 pm is the earliest for a certificate-18 film.

Are my children old enough to have a TV in their room?

The potential dangers of watching too much television are evidenced by a great deal of research. For example, studies show that children who watch a lot of television and have a set in their bedroom do significantly worse at school than others and are less likely to reach university. A series of studies published in 2005 indicate the damage done by television to children's development and progress at school. One, by scientists in New Zealand, found that those who watched the most television were the least likely to leave school with qualifications and had a smaller chance of getting a university degree. In another independent project, conducted in the United States by researchers at Stanford and Johns Hopkins universities, children who had televisions in their rooms were found to be lower academic achievers. Those without a bedside TV but who had access to a computer at home, did significantly better at mathematics, reading and language tests than their peers.

Previous studies have also linked bedroom TVs to overweight and aggressive behaviour. A variety of studies have also demonstrated that children who are heavy viewers of television are more likely to be linguistically underdeveloped, although a direct causal relationship has not been established.

It goes without saying that if your child has a TV in her room, you can have no real control over or idea of what she is watching – whether she is watching all night, or watching violent or sexually explicit content. It's almost impossible to control the number of viewing hours with a TV in the bedroom, and if they are hooked up to games consoles, it can be difficult to monitor that, too.

Should I let them watch films or programmes with age restrictions above their actual age?

Some programmes are worse than others. *See page 453.*

How much is 'too much' TV?

Ideally, and according to the results of various studies (*see above*), kids should watch no more than one to two hours of TV per day. As kids become older and are awake for longer, this can be increased by an hour (to a maximum of three), but this figure must include 'screen time'. That is, you will agree to a maximum of three hours a day in front of a screen, including TVs, computers, games consoles or DVD machines, and only when homework is done, when your child has fulfilled any family chores or tasks, has spent time with family, and is getting a regular, decent night's sleep. Too often TV viewing eats into sleeping hours, which can have a significant effect (*see page 55*).

Can I set guidelines for family viewing?

Absolutely, and it is really important that you do so, particularly if you have children of various ages whose viewing habits need to be monitored differently. You can work on the premise that as a child gets older he can watch a little more TV (up to the maximum threshold of, say, two or three hours a day), and he can watch a wider variety of programmes, too. It's easiest to set guidelines if there is one main family TV, as everyone in the family will have to negotiate their 'turn'; however, this isn't the reality in most families. A good idea is to sit down with the TV guide at the beginning of the week and have a look together at what is coming up – what would be entertaining or informative, what might help with a school project, when your child's favourite soap or series is on, films, sports events and whatever.

Do I need to supervise my children's TV viewing?
Yes, you do, even if it takes the form of an occasional spot-check or discussion of what he has been watching.

Weight

How much weight should my child be gaining as she grows?
Throughout childhood, weight can fluctuate dramatically, all within normal bounds. In the winter months some children put on a little weight, which naturally disperses when they are more active during the summer. Periods of stress or emotional problems, illness or injuries, can also affect eating habits and activity levels, causing weight gain.

From babyhood through to about five or six years of age, children accumulate more fat on their extremities (arms and legs) than on their torsos. Then, proportionally more fat accumulates around the tummy and trunk until adolescence. And then all goes mad! During the adolescent growth spurt, boys gain more fat on their trunks, while fat on their arms and legs decreases. In contrast, girls gain pretty much equal amounts of weight on their trunks and arms and legs during this period.

So the sudden appearance of a tummy after the age of six is not a sign of obesity, nor is it so if your adolescent daughter suddenly develops more fat all over. In boys, the adolescent growth spurt means an obvious increase in weight – but this is principally bone tissue and skeletal muscle and, some fat. Girls, on the other hand, experience a slightly less intense spurt in height, a less obvious increase in skeletal muscle, but a continuous increase in fat mass. In girls this starts around the age of nine or ten; in boys between the ages of eleven and twelve, although this obviously differs between children.

On average, children gain about 2–3 kg (5–7 lb) between the ages of six and ten. As adolescence and puberty begin, growth rates increase, first in height, and then in weight, although it is very normal for children to put on weight in advance of a major growth spurt. They fill out and then shoot up. Girls tend to reach a peak growth period around twelve years of age, which then slows down until they are about sixteen or eighteen. In their peak growth period (between the ages of eleven and thirteen), girls will put on about 7 kg (15 lb). It may be much more than this. In boys, the major growth spurt begins around eleven or twelve, and reaches its maximum around fourteen. Their growth rate then slows, but growth continues until they are about eighteen to twenty. During their peak growth period (between the ages of thirteen and fifteen), boys gain an average of 14 kg (31 lb). Boys also tend to gain less fat than girls do during this period.

All in all, a child's body weight may double between the ages of ten and eighteen. In boys the extra weight is mainly muscle; in girls, the extra weight is muscle and also fat on hips and breasts, giving them a more rounded shape. It's important to distinguish womanly curves from fat – when your daughter enters adolescence, she will change shape, and there is no need for concern unless weight gain is obviously more than it should be.

When do children lose puppy fat?

Puppy fat is normally gone at around six or seven years of age, but then different types of padding appear (see above). By the end of your child's adolescent growth spurt, excess baggage should be a thing of the past. Throughout childhood, weight can fluctuate dramatically, all within normal bounds, in advance of puberty and other periods of growth.

How can I tell if my child is overweight?

Weight gain can be insidious and creep up without you having noticed. You may find that you suddenly have a problem on your hands. Some parents state that they first noticed that their child had put on too much weight when they saw him or her in a swimming costume next to other, slimmer children, or they suddenly realised that toddler puppy fat had expanded into something quite different. It doesn't make you a bad parent to have missed the signs. And if you've missed an unhealthy gain in weight, or don't have a realistic picture of your child's overall weight, you are not alone. Researchers from the Centers for Disease Control and Prevention (CDC) in the US recently found in a survey of 5,500 children that 32 per cent of mums classified their overweight children as being 'about the right weight'. Most often overlooked were at-risk boys and younger children. It's not easy to judge accurately someone we love, particularly when we see them every day and become accustomed to their appearance. There's also some truth to the idea that we close our eyes to things we don't want to see.

One of the best ways to keep an eye on your child's growth throughout the years, is to plot his development using his personal health record (you will have one given to you when your child is born). There is a chart for girls and one for boys, on which you plot their weight and height. Ideally, your child should stick to the same centile line throughout his life, varying only slightly. If he is in the top centile for weight and a much lower centile for height, he is likely to be overweight. If there is a sudden jump from 50th to 90th centile in weight, there may be a problem. Your doctor can provide more guidance on this.

If you haven't kept a record of your child's height and weight across the years, it's not too late to start, and it's a good way to monitor both growth and potential problems. If your child is already well above the 85th to 95th percentile in weight for his height, and you are concerned that he seems overweight, now is the time to take action.

Another option is to check your child's BMI (body mass index). The formula for BMI divides a person's weight in kilograms by height in metres squared. If you use pounds and inches, multiply the result by the conversion factor by 705.

For example, a child who is 110 cm tall and weighs 25 kg has a BMI of 20 (25 ÷ 110 x 110 = 20).

In adults, a BMI of less than 24 is considered to be healthy; 25–29 is overweight and 30 or over is obese.

But because of the way children grow, it's impossible to categorise them so easily. For example, BMI declines from infancy to about five or six years of age, and then increases with age through childhood and adolescence. Kids tend to stick fairly closely to the same line throughout their childhoods, and you will want to establish that this is the case with your child. You can get BMI charts for children from your doctor.

How else can I tell if my child is overweight?

Most parents can tell by looking at their children whether or not they are overweight, and a quick investigation into their eating habits and activity levels is probably all the evidence you need to confirm suspicions.

Beyond the age of two, no child should have rolls of fat anywhere on their body, and certainly not on their midriff. If you can see and count their ribs, there is no cause for alarm. Musculature should be evident in most healthy children as should some evidence of a skeleton! From the age of about six, weight begins to fall from arms and legs (the extremities) and settle around the trunk. So if your seven-year-old is carrying too much weight around his thighs or upper arms, chances are he is overweight. Above we look at normal weight gain in children, and where the fat stores tend to sit as their body shapes change. Anything that seems to be quite different to the norm – for example, a teenage boy who suddenly seems to acquire fat rather than muscular thighs – is worth investigating.

What happens when you buy clothes for your child? Do you always have to purchase things two or three age sizes bigger because the waist will never do up, or the sleeves are always too tight? The waist is a particularly good guide because tall but slim children may need bigger age sizes because of their height, but in their case the waist invariably needs taking in to fit properly. This isn't a perfect guide as some younger children are simply bigger than the average, and still have the normal 'tummy' appropriate to their age, but you get the idea ...

It's also worth asking a couple of friends for their opinion, but phrase the question so that it allows them to answer honestly.

Does being overweight affect my child's emotional health?
Overweight children face many issues, often on a day-to-day basis. These include:
▷ Being teased or bullied and suffering from loss of self-esteem and risk of depression.
▷ More anxiety and poorer social skills. Stress and anxiety also interfere with learning.

▷ Social isolation and low self esteem may create feelings of hopelessness and depression.

▷ Having smaller social networks. In a survey of more than 90,000 teens, researchers at the University of Michigan School of Public Health and the Robert Wood Johnson Medical School in New Jersey found that overweight students were 70 per cent less likely than their healthy-weight counterparts to be listed as friends of their peers.

▷ More likely to develop chronic diseases at an earlier age.

▷ Have impaired quality of life – a recent study, published in the *Journal of the American Medical Association*, found that obese kids were 5.5 times more likely to have an impaired quality of life than healthy kids, putting their life experience on par with that of kids undergoing chemotherapy treatment for cancer.

What can I do if my child is embarrassed about her weight?
First of all, establish if there really is a problem. Many, many young women and girls have a skewed body image, which makes them believe they are fat and unattractive, when they are actually a healthy weight. It's very important in these circumstances that you invest in your child a sense of self-belief, self-respect and self-liking, and doing that involves making her feel good about herself. This is also important even if your child is overweight, as her confidence will undoubtedly take a knock (*see above*).

Children also need to feel good in their own skins no matter what they look like. There is no point in overlooking an obvious weight problem that affects appearance. Children are not blind, and they will feel ashamed if you do not show a willingness to discuss their concerns. Be honest with your child – agree that losing a little weight around her waist might make her skirt look better, but point out that if you work together on a more healthy lifestyle, she'll soon grow into her weight and look a lot slimmer. Forget about the idea of losing weight as a goal, as it will only create unhealthy habits. Draw attention to the most attractive parts of her body, and help her to take pride in them. All children – and adults – have to accept their bodies at some point, and the happiest people are those who can see the good in themselves, without being overshadowed by perceived flaws. Teach her to make the most of her best assets – it's something that she can continue to do into adulthood. Show how you make your legs look longer by wearing a certain type of trousers, or minimise a slightly tubby waistline by wearing fitted t-shirts. Explain that a little tummy, curvy hips and breasts are part of becoming a woman, and that being womanly is much nicer than looking like an ironing board. Boys, too, need to know that they aren't born with a six-pack on their abdomens and that a little weight gain in puberty is very normal. Kids need to see that not all of us are designed perfectly, and that the best way to get on with things is to make the most of what we do have.

Try the following tips:

▷ Do not label a child as fat, chubby, plump or even 'big'. Children hold great store in what their parents tell them, and build their self-identities on what they hear about themselves. By labelling a child you can undermine her confidence and create a self-fulfilling prophecy.

▷ Encourage your child in what she does well, let her know that you love and value and approve of her.

▷ Make sure your child has attractive and fashionable clothes. Helping her to look good is one way to encourage her to feel good about herself.

▷ Be especially careful if your child is a pre-teen daughter. Our culture teaches young women to base their self-esteem on the

shape and size of their bodies. If your daughter thinks you
are criticising her appearance, she may believe that you
find her unacceptable too. She may deal with her crushed
feelings by becoming anorexic in an heroic effort to please you,
or she may rebel and become even fatter as an expression of
anger and defiance.

▷ Be realistic about your child's weight. Genes do make a difference.
If a child is chubby but eats healthy foods in reasonable amounts,
and if s/he is active and has self-control, s/he may be genetically
predisposed to be heavier than average. Research suggests that
this kind of extra weight is not as unhealthy.

▷ Although it sounds simplistic, focus on health, not appearance,
and on more activity not less food.

▷ Become alert to any stress your child might be experiencing at
school or with peers. Remember that any form of extreme
behaviour is unhealthy and may indicate anxiety. It is not
uncommon for kids to attempt to soothe anxiety and solve
problems through the use and abuse of food.

▷ Talk to your overweight child about whether he or she has ever
experienced teasing in the schoolyard and if so, discuss how he
or she felt about it, and what he or she did or might do in
response in the future. This can be crucial in promoting self-
esteem and teaching your child coping skills.

▷ To help your child, you need to understand what triggered her
overeating and weight. You need to pinpoint when it started.
Was there the death of someone she loved? The loss of a
familiar babysitter? A separation or divorce in the family?

▷ Encourage social involvement in community, church and school
activities, which build social skills and confidence.

Should I put my child on a diet?

The food you serve your children should be the food that the whole family eats – it should be tasty, nutritious and healthy, with as few as possible of the foods that we know cause obesity and overweight. The whole point of a healthy eating programme is to ensure that your children learn to eat good foods, and carry on doing so throughout their lives. If it's a short-term 'fix', 'diet' or solution, and you revert to your old habits, your children will learn nothing, and any weight lost will eventually be gained. A healthy diet does include treats, the occasional fast-food experience, and the odd packet of crisps or a chocolate bar. No one is immune to the temptations of unhealthy treats, but as long as they are eaten in the context of an overall healthy diet, and eaten occasionally, there is nothing wrong with including them from time to time. But most importantly, cravings for junk food and treats do tend to disappear – or at least be minimalised – when our children are full, have a balanced diet with all the nutrients they need, are well watered and understand the importance of eating well. If you put a child on a diet, he instantly feels different, under pressure and restricted, which will ultimately backfire. Make it clear that the changes to your family diet are for health reasons, and make sure everyone is involved.

The importance of exercise can't be underestimated in terms of overweight. There is no point in adopting a healthy diet if your child sits on the sofa all day and watches TV. Exercise must be plentiful, regular and a part of daily life.

Health is the first and most important object of changing your family diet. A family that eats well and takes regular exercise will, in the large majority of cases, simply not suffer from weight problems.

Children should not, under any circumstances, be placed on a weight-loss diet. The aim of changing eating habits is to maintain weight until your child grows into it. Some children do lose weight when their eating habits change, particularly if they were very poor eaters, heavy snackers, comfort eaters or simply constant grazers, but losing more than a pound or so a week is not recommended, and you will have to make sure that your child is eating enough to grow and develop properly.

The main difference between overweight adults and overweight children is the fact that children are still growing. Overweight adults do need to lose weight for health reasons and because they have stopped growing, their intake can be cut fairly dramatically without compromising their future health. That's not to say that dieting is recommended for any age group because, as we've seen already, diets don't work. Only broadscale changes to eating habits that are consistently maintained will have an effect. But it's very important that both you and your children understand that you are not changing your eating habits to see the figures on the scale go down. If you can keep weight stable as your child grows, you are doing exactly what is required. Your child will grow into his weight.

Kids need plenty of regular meals and healthy food to grow and develop properly, to maintain mood, body functions, concentration and overall health. Restricting food will not only have an emotional impact and lead to further, unhealthy eating habits, but it can also damage your child's health, both now and in the future.

Could my child have an eating disorder?

Eating disorders are responsible for the highest number of deaths from psychiatric illness. The Eating Disorders Association estimates that about 165,000 people in the UK have eating disorders with ten per cent dying as a result, but experts believe it could be higher. At one time, eating disorders were thought to affect primarily pre-teen and teen-age girls in upper socio-economic groups. But according to the latest statistics, eating disorders are increasingly appearing in younger children and boys, and have infiltrated all socio-economic groups. The most common eating disorders are anorexia, bulimia and compulsive over-eating. But other disorders exist. For example, some people severely restrict the range of food they eat and some children have a psychological fear of food.

What is anorexia nervosa?

Around five per cent of young girls in the UK are estimated to have anorexia nervosa. Boys are much less likely to be affected, although that situation is changing. The condition results in death in 20 per cent of cases after 20 years of onset of the illness. Only around 60 per cent of anorexics recover. The illness is also one of the most controversial areas in mental health. Psychiatrists have singled out several characteristics which they say are typical of anorexics. These include: a dominant, over-protective and critical mother and a passive or withdrawn father; a tendency to perfectionism; a strong desire for social approval and a need for order and control. However, many of these characteristics have been the subject of dispute, particularly those relating to parenting. Whatever the case, a poor self-image is almost always at the root of an eating disorder, and it is this that needs to be addressed before there can be any hope of a cure. The media and its emphasis on super-thin models is also blamed by some for influencing the way people, particularly girls, see themselves.

In the US, over 60 per cent of fourth grade girls (nine-year-olds) in an Iowa study reported a desire to be thinner. By age eighteen, nine out of ten teenage girls in a California survey were dieting to lose weight. This perception of fatness is common even among girls with little body fat. In one study, 58 per cent of girls ages nine to eighteen thought of themselves as fat, whereas only 15 per cent were overweight based on height and weight measures. Fear of fatness, restrained eating and binge eating were found to be common among girls by age ten.

What are its effects?

Anorexia nervosa is a form of intentional self-starvation. What may begin as a normal diet is carried to extremes, with many reducing their intake to an absolute minimum. It is also characterised by obsessive behaviour. The majority of anorexics deny they have a problem (*see* Warning signs, *page 468*). Lack of food deprives the body of protein and prevents the normal metabolism of fat. The effects of this can include:

▷ Irregular heart beat caused by a change in the heart muscle. This can lead to heart failure and death.

▷ Cessation of or failure to begin menstruation.

▷ Dehydration, kidney stones and kidney failure.

▷ Growth of fine downy body hair, called lanugo, on the face and arms.

▷ Wasting away of muscles, leading to weakness.

▷ Constipation or bowel irritation.

▷ Osteoporosis caused by lack of calcium.

What are the symptoms of anorexia?

Symptoms of anorexia range from extreme weight loss for no discernible medical reason; ritualistic food habits, such as excessive chewing; denying hunger and exercising excessively to choosing low-calorie food and hiding feelings. A person with anorexia may be excessively thin but still see themselves as overweight.

The average age for onset of the illness is thought to be sixteen, although the age range of anorexia is between ten and forty. Around 90 per cent of cases are female. Most have no history of being overweight.

What are the warning signs?

▷ Does your child seem obsessed by fat or calorie content of food?

▷ Has he put himself on a 'diet' for any reason, from which he cannot be swayed?

▷ Does your child exercise obsessively, carefully calculating the number of calories burned during physical activity?

▷ Is your child frequently 'not hungry' or 'too busy' at mealtimes?

▷ Does your child disappear into the lavatory after meals?

▷ Have you noticed mood changes, including angry outbursts, isolation from friends, withdrawn behaviour, chemical abuse or depression.

▷ Has your daughter failed to start her period at a normal time or has it stopped?

▷ Apart from weight loss, does your child suffer dry skin, hair loss, rashes and itching?

What is bulimia nervosa?

Bulimia is thought to be two to three times more common than anorexia, but is not generally as physically dangerous. However, excessive use of laxatives and self-induced vomiting can cause rupture of the oesophagus, damage to the teeth from stomach acids, mineral deficiency and dehydration, which can have serious effects on health.

Bulimia was only officially recognised in the 1970s and is characterised by a cycle of bingeing and starving. Many bulimics seem fine, but experts say that, under the surface, they often suffer from poor self-esteem and self-image. Bulimics may have irregular periods or stop having periods at all because of excessive use of laxatives and vomiting. Using laxatives can also cause kidney and bowel problems and stomach disorders. It can be more difficult to recognise this condition, because your child may stay around the same weight, or lose weight more slowly. He may, however, had a puffy face, swollen fingers, muscle weakness and stomach pains, which can be an indication that there are problems, when associated with an obsession with weight, obvious signs of bingeing and purging.

Excessive vomiting can cause tooth decay, bad breath, mouth ulcers, sore throats and stomach disorders and may have serious long-term health implications. Some experts believe bulimia is the result of an imbalance of chemicals to the brain, but others think the illness is more likely to be linked to a lack of self-worth. It is thought that up to half of anorexics also suffer from bulimia and some 40 per cent of bulimics are reported to have a history of anorexia.

How can we prevent eating disorders?

Children who are anorexic are much more likely to be a product of a family who is over-concerned about weight and diet (and, for example, fat content of food). Avoid talking about weight or diets, even if your child does have a weight problem. Parents send strong messages to their children when they constantly complain about their bodies, discuss diets and obsess over the fat, calorie and sugar content of food.

Make family meals a daily occurrence. Many parents are surprised to find a child is anorexic because they have not eaten with them or seen them eating, for many weeks or even months. A new UK study shows that in the majority of families, children no longer eat with their parents on a regular basis; in some cases, as infrequently as once a month or not at all. Children should NOT be made responsible for their own food choices. Apart from the fact that they can make unacceptable choices that can damage their health, parents need to model positive eating habits, which will go a long way towards instilling healthy attitudes to food.

Always provide a variety of fresh foods from all food groups at meals. Don't force a child to eat, and give small helpings, even when children are small. They can always ask for more.

Parents have a powerful influence on their children's self-esteem and body image. In one study, self-esteem scores of kids aged nine to eleven were lowered when they thought their parents were dissatisfied with their bodies. Encourage your child to feel good about himself, no matter what his weight. Even if he is fat, he needs high self-esteem. Make sure your child feels loved and accepted for what he is, not what he looks like. Children with high self-esteem naturally gravitate towards habits that are good for them – taking exercise, good hygiene habits, dressing well and taking pride in their appearance (flaws and all!).

Where can I get treatment for my child?

Over 25 per cent of anorexics are so weak that they require hospitalisation. This may involve force feeding as well as advice on healthy eating and counselling. Many doctors believe that once a person's bodyweight has fallen below a certain level, they are no longer capable of making rational decisions. Other forms of treatment range from group therapy, family counselling and psychotherapy to antidepressants. Around one third of patients recover fully; another third improve significantly and the last third do not recover. Bulimics have the same range of therapies, including behaviour modification in some cases.

If your child does suffer from an eating disorder, you will need to address emotional issues to uncover problems affecting self-image and self-esteem. The most important thing you can do is to support and love your child. Showing disgust when he is overly thin or fat will reinforce a poor self-image. Let your child know that you love him and care about him. You can certainly show concern about his health, but make sure he is aware that your love and concern are not judgmental.

Encourage hobbies and activities that will help your child to feel good about himself – choose something at which he is bound to succeed. Draw attention to successes and overlook failures of any kind. Get some help for yourself. Join a support group with other parents in the same situation. Try not to blame yourself. There is a great deal of finger-pointing going on about eating disorders and parents often take full brunt. Even secure children can suffer from self-esteem and emotional problems after an upset, or there may be problems at school that you know nothing about. The best advice is to get to the root of the problem, and to find ways of addressing it.

Index